KEEP YOUR HEAD TO THE SKY

Interpreting
African American
Home Ground

The Holy Trinity, by the Reverend George Kornegay,
central Alabama. (Photo: Grey Gundaker, December 1993)

KEEP YOUR HEAD TO THE SKY

Interpreting
African American
Home Ground

Edited by
Grey Gundaker
with the assistance of
Tynes Cowan

University Press of Virginia
Charlottesville and London

THE UNIVERSITY PRESS OF VIRGINIA
© 1998 by the Rector and Visitors of the University of Virginia
Chapter 9, "Symbolic Geographies and Psychic Landscapes: Decoding the
Hegemonic Discourse of Urban Renewal in the Case for Billy Weems v. the
City of College Park, Maryland," © 1998 by Joanne M. Braxton

First published 1998

∞

The paper used in this publication meets the minimum requirements of the
American National Standard for Information Sciences—Permanence of Paper
for Printed Library Materials,
ANSI Z39.48-1984.

Library of Congress Cataloging-in-Publication Data
Keep your head to the sky : interpreting African American home ground
 / edited by Grey Gundaker with the assistance of Tynes Cowan.
   p. cm.
  Includes bibliographical references and index.
  ISBN 0-8139-1807-3 (cloth : alk. paper).—ISBN 0-8139-1824-3
 (pbk. : alk. paper)
   1. Afro-Americans—Social life and customs. 2. Landscape—Social
 aspects—United States. 3. Afro-American aesthetics. I. Gundaker,
 Grey. II. Cowan, Tynes.
 E185.86.K43   1998
 305.896'073—DC21   98-19998
                                                                         CIP

CONTENTS

List of Illustrations   vii

PART 1

Cosmology, Moral Force, and Expression in
    African American Domestic Landscapes

1   3
Introduction: Home Ground
Grey Gundaker

2   25
Vibrational Affinities
John F. Szwed

3   37
Bighearted Power: Kongo Presence in the
    Landscape and Art of Black America
Robert Farris Thompson

4   65
Art, Healing, and Power in the Afro-Atlantic South
Judith McWillie

5   93
Sacred Places and Holy Ground:
    West African Spiritualism at Stagville Plantation
Alice Eley Jones

PART 2

Symbolic Geographies, Contestation, and Reclamation

6   113
South of the North, North of the South: Spatial Practice in
    David Bradley's *The Chaneysville Incident*
George L. Henderson

7   145
A Search for Place: William McNorton
    and His Garden of the Lord
Frances Jones-Sneed

8   155
Rivers Underground: Rebellious Young Men, Community Parks,
    and the Surfacing of Culture in Barbados
Elizabeth Barnum

9   177
Symbolic Geographies and Psychic Landscapes: Decoding the
    Hegemonic Discourse of Urban Renewal in the Case for
    Billy Weems v. the City of College Park, Maryland
Joanne M. Braxton

10   193
The Slave in the Swamp: Affects of
    Uncultivated Regions on Plantation Life
Tynes Cowan

PART 3
Defining Places in Community Life

11   211
Liberty and Economy in Lowcountry South Carolina:
    The Case of the Freedmen's Bank
Marland E. Buckner Jr.

12   227
The Praise House Tradition on St. Helena Island, South Carolina
Vanessa Thaxton

13   245
"Trash" Revisted: A Comparative Approach to Historical Descriptions
    and Archaeological Analyses of Slave Houses and Yards
Ywone D. Edwards

14   273
Race and the Politics of Public History in the United States
Patrick Hagopian

Notes   295
Contributors   335
Index   337

ILLUSTRATIONS

Frontispiece
The Holy Trinity, by the Reverend George Kornegay, central Alabama

following page 8
Henry Jackson in his yard, Memphis
The yard of Henry Jackson, Memphis, Tennessee
Gyp Packnett's guardian figure, southwestern Mississippi
Victor Melancon's remembrance area, Hammond, Louisiana
Mrs. Hamler's remembrance garden of antiques, southeast Tennessee

following page 27
Bennie Lusane in his yard, northeast Georgia
Detail of Bennie Lusane's yard
Detail of Bennie Lusane's yard construction
Bennie Lusane's car dashboard
Anthony Braxton's notation system

following page 45
Shell and red streamer mark a driveway on Virginia's Eastern Shore
Victor Melancon's tire crown and palmetto, Hammond, Louisiana
Automobile drive shaft and headstone near Sparta, Georgia
Griffin Manning's fence with wheels, New Haven, Connecticut
Henry Williams's white trees with glass insulators, southeast Virginia
Door flanked by a snail and a white porcelain commode, Memphis, Tennessee
Broken and inverted vessels on a grave near Sparta, Georgia
Nkisi Nkandu, also known as *nkisi malabiri*, antitheft tree medicine made by
    Mayolo Pandi Maurice of Ndingui village, near Mouyondzi, Bouentza re-
    gion, R. P. du Congo
Telephone pole painted purple by Rachel Presha, Suffolk, Virginia
Cornelius Lee's bottle tree, begun in the 1970s, tidewater Virginia
Cornelius Lee's twisted vine section, painted red and white, at the fork
    of the branches of his bottle tree

following page 74
Marcel Duchamp, bottle rack, 1961
Ivan Tomkins's photograph of Bowens family graves, Sunbury, Georgia, 1930s
Eddie Williamson, Memphis, Tennessee

Detail of Lonnie Holley's yard, Birmingham, Alabama
The grave of Cyrus Bowens, Sunbury
Yard, Gros Islet, St. Lucia, W.I.
Bessie Harvey, Alcoa, Tennessee
Annie Sturghill in her "Yard of Colors," Athens, Georgia
Dilmus Hall, Athens
Dilmus Hall's "The Shoe That Road the Howling Tornado,
    May 31–1973, in Athens"

following page 96
Medicine stick discovered wedged in a wall of the Bennehan/Cameron
    House, Stagville Preservation Center, Durham, North Carolina
Alice Eley Jones pouring a libation at Horton Grove Quarters at Stagville
Professor Victor Maafeo, a native of Ghana, conducting a libation
    ceremony at Horton Grove Quarters at Stagville
Divining rod discovered in the wall of Horton Grove slave
    cabin at Stagville
Cowrie shell discovered in the wall of Stagville slave cabin

following page 122
Implications of the border for geopolitics of the text
Unmarked stones in a remote burial ground outside Chaneysville,
    Pennsylvania
Mount Ross Cemetery, Bedford, Pennsylvania

following page 159
A small park connected with a standpipe, Asbury, St. George
Asbury, St. George, standpipe without a trace of its former "styles"
Pride of Wilson Hill, Jackson, St. Michael
Planters beside the gate to "The Pride of Checker Hall," St. Lucy
Hugh Rock's sculptures, St. Lucy
Detail of Hugh Rock's sculptures, St. Lucy
Cow skull, tire, and root arrangement, Avis Town, St. Lucy
Pride of Checker Hall, St. Lucy
Detail of entrance to "The Pride of Checker Hall"
Crab Hill, St. Lucy
Detail of the Pride of Checker Hall, St. Lucy

following page 179
Proposed road system for Lakeland
Cub Scouts from Pack 1025 and members of Embry A.M.E. Church
James Alfred "Billy" Weems (1934–1980)
Wall bisecting the Lakeland of yesteryear
Lakeland citizens leaving Embry A.M.E. Church sometime in the 1960s
Lakeland homes destroyed by fire

PART 1

Cosmology, Moral Force, and
Expression in African American
Domestic Landscapes

1 INTRODUCTION

Home Ground

Grey Gundaker

FEW HISTORICAL DESCRIPTIONS EXIST of African American landscapes in the southern United States or the West Indies where residents worked their own will. Mainly, we are left to follow scholars like Dell Upton and Mechal Sobel in imagining how peoples of African and European descent sometimes differed and sometimes joined forces as they brought meaning to the same land.[1] But what about the spaces that were occupied primarily or solely by African Americans? Contemporary description of slave quarter and tenant life rarely stooped to the level of fine detail—the favorite hen pecking in the yard, a prized china pitcher kept free of field dust, the broom behind the door—that would reveal in any self-evident fashion how eighteenth- and nineteenth-century black Americans, owners of more self-possession than possessions, organized their surroundings.

As the twentieth century turned, those African Americans who had managed to acquire their own lands and homes struggled to hold onto them in the face of old age, back taxes, Jim Crow, and the depression. As Joanne Braxton shows in her chapter in this volume, midcentury brought yet more challenges couched in the deceptive rhetorics of technological progress and urban renewal. Interstate highways and so-called slum clearance wiped out whole neighborhoods. Yet African American home ground endures in the American landscape, from elite suburbs and tower apartments to the old homeplaces of the countryside, to the small table of family photos beside the bed of a housebound elder. Scale varies, but the claim, I am here, stays the same.

The chapters in this collection are about some of the ways that African Americans have invested actual and symbolic landscapes with significance, gained means to acquire property, and prompted rethinking of certain conventions in the interpretation of contemporary, historical, and archaeological sites. This introduction opens with several accounts in which a landscape serves emblematic purposes, instantiating the essential qualities of a larger frame of reference—a sense of rootedness, a moral orientation, a distinctive persona—for the authors who wrote about them.

In a sense, accounts like these, dating mainly from the early twentieth century, provide common ground for the book because they coincide with a recurring theme that emerges from many of the chapters, a preoccupation with the homeplaces and belongings of kin and of the generations immediately preceding our own. These parents and grandparents, people who seem knowable through recollection, have now, after their deaths, also become bridges to more distant pasts and larger historical currents. Whether in fiction, like Moses Washington of David Bradley's *The Chaneysville Incident*, explored from a geographer's perspective by George Henderson, or a living person like the praise house leader who helped Vanessa Thaxton appreciate these Sea Island centers for worship, elders direct the eyes of the young to places that are part of their history and thus also part of the shaping of their future.

HOME GROUND AS FRAME OF REFERENCE

Not surprisingly, the residents themselves usually provide the most evocative accounts of home ground. James Weldon Johnson set the stage for his autobiography with this memory:

> I have only faint recollection of the place of my birth. At times I can close my eyes and call up in a dreamlike way things that seem to have happened ages ago in some other world. I can see in this half vision a little house—I am quite sure it was not a large one—I can remember that flowers grew in the front yard, and that around each bed was a hedge of varicoloured glass bottles stuck in the ground neck down. I remember that once, while playing in the sand, I became curious to know whether or not the bottles grew as the flowers did, and I proceeded to dig them up to find out; the investigation brought me a terrific spanking, which indelibly fixed the incident in my mind.[2]

Johnson draws our attention to the instructive potentials of landscapes, their power as reminders of how and how not to behave.[3] His words show how landscapes become replete with moral force and a range of emotional temperatures. Imagine the loving indignation that Johnson's elders brought to bear on his bottom, but also imagine sheer affront at intrusion into the zone of "home" or the possibility for a well-lived life that a beautiful yard promises to passersby as well as to a tired resident who must leave home for work in a sometimes hostile world.[4]

Zora Neale Hurston also wrote of such a place, the site of her story "The Gilded Six Bits":

It was a Negro yard around a Negro house in a Negro settlement that looked to the payroll of G and G Fertilizer works for its support.

But there was something happy about the place. The front yard was parted in the middle by a sidewalk from gate to door-step, a sidewalk edged on either side by quart bottles driven neck down into the ground on a slant. A mess of homey flowers planted without a plan but blooming cheerily from their helter-skelter places. The fence and house were whitewashed. The steps . . . scrubbed white.

The front door stood open to the sunshine so that the floor of the front room could finish drying after its weekly scouring. It was Saturday. Everything clean from the front gate to the privy house. Yard raked so that the strokes of the rake would make a pattern. Fresh newspaper cut in a fancy edge on the kitchen shelves.[5]

Hurston leads her readers like guests through the gate, down the walk, and in the front door of the house where her main characters live. Along the way she notes ordinary objects—bottles, newspapers—and their modes of transformation—driving down, cutting up—to make the fancy edges for the sidewalk and the kitchen shelves that signal the house is a cared-for home. Moreover, Hurston sketches a style, a way of distributing formal reiteration and improvisation throughout the space of the yard and the temporal cycle of her characters' lives: white house, white steps, white fence; Saturday sweeping; and a mess of flowers blooming helter-skelter in season.

These two passages by noted African American authors both treat the yard as more than a landscape backdrop to human activity; it provides a frame of reference that ties a story to its moorings and directs interpretations of the story down certain paths, and not others.

Outsiders also recognized the importance of African American yards in channeling interpretations of people and places. Writing at about the same time, Minnie Hite Moody, a white local-color writer, opened her novel *Death Is a Little Man*:

Even on Judith Street the women try to make the door yards pretty, carrying water from the branch to revive the few cherished geraniums and begonias that in summer droop in the noon-heat of a blistering day. Eenie Weaver has the fanciest dooryard, with a fine hydrangea in a tub at one end of the slanting porch, and love-entangled trailing from old cooking pots suspended from the ceiling. Her yard is swept clean and bare; the walking-path is set off from the yard by a double row of broken tiles salvaged from the dump and outside the tiles is a thin spiky file of gladioli.[6]

Other passages from novels and autobiographies written between the 1920s and 1960s range in texture from "thick description" to sparse authenticating touches like a sieve over the door or a crossmark against witches grafted onto stereotyped scenes of poverty and gloom. However favorably inclined or negatively biased they may be, the authors of these works sought to give their narratives the particularity of inhabited place and sometimes provided useful documentation in the process.

During the same era Euro-American southerners' accounts of "their" residential and agricultural landscapes indicated they had adopted as their own practices and aesthetics with African and Caribbean parallels and probable precedents. For example, Ben Robertson wrote of his family farm in northeastern South Carolina:

> All of our houses stood in groves of original trees, and all of them had bare sanded yards surrounded by gardens of flowers. We did not care for green grass in our yards, as our country was a Southern country, and white sand to us was more restful and quieter-looking than grass. Besides, there was greenness all about us; the groves were green and so were the cotton fields and the valleys themselves. The white of the sand, shaded by the thick trees, formed an oasis, a solemn thing of contrast. Every Saturday morning with corn-shuck brooms, we carefully swept the yard.[7]

(One might reasonably ask who exactly is "we" in the last sentence, for African American "yardmen" were, and in some neighborhoods still are, the mainstays of garden care.) The swept yard of Robertson's memory is a site constituted in largely unacknowledged exchange and appropriated labor. This yard, like the yards of African Americans in the South and elsewhere in the diaspora, embodies an ethic of *landkeeping*, of reciprocity between persons and their location, as distinct from "landscaping," the craft of staging and maintaining vistas. Places like the Robinson farm or Eenie Weaver's yard are "cultural" in the sense that they involve recurring practices and values. But they are by no means "pure" cultural products. They do not take shape on virgin ground with new materials. Indeed, they take root in a given place as often by default as by choice. In a novel by William Mahoney, Dr. Jacob Blue walks through a black section of Matchez, Mississippi, near the river:

> Jacob passed a ragged-haired man in a gigantic overcoat who begged a quarter and then backed away from him bowing. Sitting on porches covered with green potted plants old men called how-do to him. Sticking up from the little clay and dust yards were porcelain

images of ducks, the white Virgin, black boot blacks, black dogs, white Jesus and other assorted colorful characters. These were the houses of the mill, waterfront and factory laborers, who were constantly in search of a home with grass and trees around it but who were limited to houses used by other races who left their mark; a crucifix left on the wall by an Italian Catholic railroad family, a dusty trunk left by a Swedish logger.[8]

Ornaments, like houses and lots, pass down histories and change identities.

Arguably, it is not so much distinctive features that give places a special character as how people in a place designate and make sense of differences and distinctions. Consider this passage from V. S. Naipaul's travel memoir *A Turn in the South*:

> We walked past Mr. Alexander's house. He was an old black man, formally dressed for Sunday, with a jacket and tie and hat; and he was in the bare patch of ground at the side of his house, practicing putts, or at any rate holding a golf club. The area in front of his small house was choked with ornamental garden statuary and anything that could be put in a yard as an ornament. He said his grandfather had started the collection; and then, with his own quicksilver sense of time, he said, "Two hundred years." Some of the pieces came from Jamaica in the West Indies; Mr. Alexander pronounced it "Jee-maica."
>
> Howard said, as we walked on, "You can tell he's an oddball. Not only because of the golf club. But because he's not in church."[9]

While Hurston described an African American yard whose exuberance remained within socially acceptable limits, Mr. Alexander and his yard are somehow over the edge, beyond the pale, and "not only because of the golf club." True, Naipaul, a Trinidadian of East Indian descent who grew up more geographically in than of the African diaspora, is well known for ambivalence, wherever his travels take him. But he also brought an alert transnational ear with him to the southern United States, an area reputedly at least as insular in its outlook as any island. Two-hundred-year-old garden statuary from Jamaica? Naipaul has heard borders leaking that far exceed in importance a particular neighborhood's guidelines for exterior decoration.

Readers should be alert to resonances with Mr. Alexander's words when, later in this essay, a homeowner says she has decorated her yard with "junk" and "antiques" (in the form of a porcelain toilet and her mother's sewing machine), or when another woman seems to date the hubcaps hanging beside her gate to "slave-time." Even without the literal-mindedness that interprets such remarks as erroneous dating, it is easy to assume the intent is self-deprecation or evasion. But several chapters in this volume show that objects in these yards bear witness to quite different criteria for inclusion, and that makers often use seemingly straightforward terms that hearers who lack the proper orientation simply cannot grasp.

CONTEXTS OF YARD WORK(S)

Yards like Mr. Alexander's (or what one might imagine it to be) are not common in African American neighborhoods. But they are not uncommon either. My anecdotal conclusion after eighty thousand miles of driving and a decade of fieldwork in eleven eastern states is that yards that surpass a certain threshold of visibility—yard shows, the subject of several chapters here, following Robert Farris Thompson's lead—are made by one or two expressive specialists per medium-sized town. Some locales have more, some fewer; but certainly many more people become makers of yard shows than become anthropologists or art historians. Nor is home ground always as limited in scale as the word *yard* may suggest. Frances Jones-Sneed's chapter introduces us to William McNorton, a southerner who migrated west and after an arduous search founded an expansive mountain sanctuary, his "garden of the Lord."

Ironically, just as some scholars are beginning to recognize that sites like this are blips on the timeline of a persisting mode of cultural production in African America, other scholars are insisting that "yard decoration" or "yard art" results largely from working- and middle-class interests which transcend ethnic or regional particularities. In this view, low-visibility decorative works evince quasi peasant and bourgeois industriousness (depending on the neighborhood), while high-visibility works called "folk art environments" and the like are labeled idiosyncratic ventures, spurred by individual creativity and visionary impulses that lie outside culture in the recesses of the psyche.

These interpretations conform comfortably with a representational convention of probable European and Euro-American derivation which distinguishes "art" from "daily life" and treats "creativity" as a universal quality (the flamboyant sibling of "intelligence"), which is distributed in varying degrees throughout the population. Always extreme in relation to the norm of occasional insights and expressive novelties, in the discourse of "creativity" large-scale efforts are "eccentric" or "great art" or somewhere in between depending upon their reception by the public. Recent art market interest in the work of "insane" and "compulsive" painters and landscape artists has helped to stabilize a category called "outsider art" for such works. A supposedly less pejorative label currently in use is "self-taught." Whereas works marketed under the rubric "folk art" tend to fit the visual contours of a high modernism with claws removed, works marketed as "outsider art" often involve more intense subject matter and visual features such as found

Henry Jackson in his yard, Memphis.
(Photo: Grey Gundaker, April 1989)

The yard of Henry Jackson, Memphis, Tennessee.
(Photo: Grey Gundaker, April 1989)

Gyp Packnett's guardian figure, southwestern Mississippi.
(Photo: Grey Gundaker, November 1991)

*Victor Melancon's remembrance area, Hammond, Louisiana.
(Photo: Grey Gundaker, April 1990)*

Mrs. Hamler's remembrance garden of antiques, southeast Tennessee.
(Photo: Grey Gundaker, December 1988)

object assemblage or high-affect imagery or highly compressed details. These features align more closely to the disjunctive/composite and parodic aesthetics marketed as postmodern than they do to the paradigmatic modern, although label application is of course at the center of much scholarly jockeying. What matters is that these art world rubrics and many others help to recruit yard works into processes of commodification, a highly mixed blessing which has brought useful cash to some artists but far more to dealers, collectors, and institutions.

Thus accounts of yard work and yard shows predicated on notions of the individual producer, distanced from his or her world, are predictable by-products of attempts to re-create or reconstruct the social and aesthetic background of those few collectible objects that pass from a yard through the market into a private or public collection. But focusing on isolated people and separate portable objects distorts the contexts of much African American visual and material culture. More accurately, dressing sites with objects—and also making miniaturized "landscapes" indoors—should be seen along with other grounding, landscaping, and landkeeping practices as part of processes that involve multiple expressive modes and communicative channels, and not as a discrete genre of material production comparable to, say, crafting handmade objects of clay or metal—although such skills, as well as topiary, masonry, horticulture, and painting, often figure in the process.

Making and keeping home ground encompasses widely varied activities and end products, from routine maintenance, planting, and tending; to hiding medications under porches and shrubs; to dusting property boundaries with nearly invisible trails of lime and pebbles; to stacking pyramids of stones and arranging glistening, flashing arrays of chrome, glass, and flags that are visible to passersby blocks away; to merely seeing the site in a particular way. Works vary in scope and complexity from compact assemblages to full-blown yard shows; from a private sanctuary tucked away behind the house to public displays of statuary, fencing, and flowers.

Yet despite this wide-ranging variation it is already clear, as the chapters in this book show, that home ground takes shape through conjunction among personal concerns, historical and economic processes, and a fluid pool of resources on hand. Broadly, at least four themes recur: protection and safekeeping, personal virtuosity, community improvement, and honor to family and ancestors. These all seem, in ways that defy precise definition, integral to the transformation of place into home. Often instantiations of these themes promote a moral stance through "orientation," positionings of the body in space, relations among people and things. Even when articulated verbally the orienting injunction is usually indirect; thus the title of this book: keep your head to the sky, a phrase that echoes from gravestone epitaphs to song lyrics to the towering sentinel that Gyp Packnett fashioned from a tree and a broken fan at the boundary of his yard in Mississippi.

GROUNDING HOME GROUND

The most important goal in the making of African American home ground is control over the surroundings in which one lives. In American cultural ideology the favored route to achieving and maintaining control is to own legal title to the property. Mutual aid organizations and institutions dating back to the Reconstruction era such as the Freedmen's Bank, which Marland Buckner discusses in part III, work toward this goal. But ownership is not always possible, and even when it is, a clear title is not enough. Thieves can still break in, false accusations can lead to land loss, and lack of say in law and politics can leave the small landowner virtually defenseless. But the crucial investment that makes a place home ground is not investment of money but of connections, of roots; thus land becomes the place of happenings: births, deaths, labor, friendships, disputes, and goings and comings of the generations. Indeed, the places where these connections exist, as in much of the former plantation South, African Americans have called "home" whether they own the land or not. These are the places where parents, siblings, and ancestors are buried, or should be buried if the world actually conformed to proper moral order, and the places of refuge that others have sought but not attained, like the multiple routes to the burial ground in *The Chaneysville Incident*, mapped by George Henderson's chapter, and the transformation of former plantation slave quarters into commemorative landscapes, as Patrick Hagopian and Alice Eley Jones show.

Some of the rights of the living in a place, therefore, derive from proximity to the family dead. Although huge numbers of African Americans moved to northern cities during the Great Migration, for most, connections with small southern towns and the relatives who stayed behind remained intact, and to these places many migrants returned home for burial. Thus it should not be surprising that the most stable repository of resources for making assertions of belonging and for warning away intruders from homes and yards is the burial mound.[10]

Relatively few domestic landscapes contain specific allusions to burial, but (as is also true for many Euro-Americans) the decorative elements of burials—flowers, fences, borders, vessels—also serve as decorations in yards. The network that links the home to the graveyard is complex and open-ended; probably it will continue to evolve as people move from place to place and as new technologies like power mowers alter landscaping practices and aesthetics. Some commemorative practices in or near the home date at least from the era of enslavement, but others are almost certainly transatlantic in scope.

However, their precise provenience may often remain unknown because similar ancestral altars and burial offerings occur in many areas of Africa and the Americas. Along with scholars' long overdue recognition that comparable objects and sites exist throughout the so-called New World comes new credence for the claim that some aspects of performance and material culture are so widespread as to be virtually pan-African. For example, although the community parks in Barbados which Elizabeth Barnum describes in her chapter address local concerns and point up the respectability of the youth who make them, the materials arranged in the parks also resemble those found in graveyards throughout the diaspora. As an ethnographic case study outside U.S. borders, Barnum's research not only reveals parallels and disjunctions between the United States and the Caribbean but serves as a reminder of the Caribbean ancestry of a significant percentage of people of African descent who have come to the States since the late nineteenth century.

Strengthened material links between homes and burials may also have resulted from the restrictions on religious and expressive activities that some African Americans experienced before the Civil War and even afterward, while living as tenants. Planters placed limitations on worship services, burial practices, and funerals. These ceremonies were important social and spiritual occasions for both Africans and African Americans. Adding to the hardship of slavery itself were the possibility that one's body might not be properly buried and the realization that properly buried or not, one's bones would rest far from ancestors and kin at the other extremity of the Middle Passage. For peoples whose social universe often pivoted on relationships between the ancestors and the living and whose sense of well-being entailed serving ancestors and spirits associated with specific places, communities, and descent groups, forced departure from the homeland assaulted the very foundations of family and personhood.[11] In the long run African Americans as a group have proved more than equal to the challenges these obstacles posed. Yet the fact remains that slaveholders retained immediate control over the material resources and time needed for proper burials and funerals.

Although some planters suppressed all forms of ceremony for the dead, on other plantations it was customary and practical to bury the dead quickly and then to hold the funeral at a later date. Writing in 1898, Susan Showers mentioned that sometimes the funeral was preached up to a year after the burial. According to the Afro-Americanist Melville Herskovits, allowing time to elapse between the burial and the funeral accords with widespread West African practices.[12]

When African Americans in the South began to honor their dead under the less restrictive conditions that followed emancipation, wakes, funerals, processions and orations, burial societies, and grave offerings assumed larger proportions. Indeed, their elaborateness struck some whites as excessive.[13] In an oft-cited passage Ernest Ingersoll described African American grave decoration in the late nineteenth century near Columbia, South Carolina:

> When a negro dies, some article or utensil, or more than one, is thrown upon his grave; moreover it is broken. . . . nearly every grave has bordering or thrown upon it a few bleached seashells. . . Mingled with these is a most curious collection of broken crockery and glassware. On the large graves are laid broken pitchers, soap dishes, lamp chimneys, tureens, coffee cups, sirup jugs, all sorts of ornamental vases, . . . teapots, . . . plaster images. . . . glass lamps and tumblers in great number. . . . Chief of all of these, however, are large water pitchers; very few graves lack them. . . . The negroes themselves hardly know how to account for this custom. They say it is an "old fashion."[14]

Within the last twenty years resemblances between African American grave decoration and African practices have been discussed in some detail, but awareness of these resemblances is hardly new.[15] For example, another observer in Columbia, South Carolina, contemporary with Ingersoll, compared broken china on black American graves with E. J. Glave's description of the grave of a Congo chief: "The natives mark the final resting-places of their friends by ornamenting their graves with crockery, empty bottles, old cooking-pots, etc., all of which articles are rendered useless by being cracked, or perforated with holes."[16] Today the motif of breakage also appears in commercially produced items like "broken wheels" made of Styrofoam that sometimes accompany sprays of real or artificial flowers at the funeral and on the grave.[17] Although breakage may be less prevalent in grave decoration than it was a decade or two ago, offerings of flowers, cards, and objects remain important. Families went, and still go, to great lengths to comply with the wishes of the dying; when they could not or would not comply, according to folktales the dead continued to make their wishes known. For example, N. N. Puckett wrote that Ben Rice of Columbus, Mississippi, "tells me of a man who asked to be buried in his own back yard. Two, four, then six horses were hitched to the hearse but they couldn't budge it toward the cemetery. Then two horses were hitched to the rear and easily pulled it to the backyard where the man was buried."[18] This story tells of an actual burial in a yard. Although such burials were rare, stories of this kind emerge from a very real concern about the reluctance of the dead to leave home and an appreciation of the importance of the dead in the continuing life of the family.

Furthermore, just as there was latitude temporally to distance interment of the body from the commemorative funeral service, so there was room spatially to distance the place of burial from the material commemoration of the lives of individuals and ancestors. Thus although the body rests in the graveyard, personal items like dishes and pitchers may be arranged in a special area of the yard or the house.

Allusions to burials outside the graveyard may commemorate particular individuals, or they may refer to ancestors and the dead in general. The important point is that when African American yard work goes beyond acceptable limits of decoration (as Mr. Alexander's did), it often contributes in some way to the extended network of activities that honor the dead, serve the ancestors, and locate the living in place. Arrangements of objects and plants in yards today draw upon African and European resources with the dual aims of healing the ruptures of captivity, migration, and urbanization and affirming roots for future generations. Furthermore, connections between the graveyard as threshold to the ancestral past and the homeplace as threshold to the unborn future inform recurring elements in the content and organization of sites across great spatial and temporal distances.

Although they have long recognized the importance of burial practices, scholars are only beginning to appreciate the integral relationship between burial practices and certain African American yards. The first, and still best, indications of the extent and complexity of this relationship is Robert Farris Thompson's *The Four Moments of the Sun*, written for an exhibition at the National Gallery of Art in Washington in 1981, and his more recent *Face of the Gods* of 1993. Thompson's essay in this volume summarizes his research on yard shows and their antecedents.

Historical accounts and ethnographic interviews support Thompson's assertion that links between the yard and graveyard reach back to the pre-emancipation period and across the Atlantic. For example, several magical spells which Harry Middleton Hyatt recorded in the 1930s link the yard and graveyard. One spell involved burying a frog in a grave in the yard, marked with boards at the head and foot. This procedure would make intruders "follow the frog," that is, die. Another spell involving yards that Hyatt recorded invoked a spirit named "Crawford" or "Crowfoot": "Now. The woods that you get . . . place them just as a-like there's a grave in it. You have to have a yard or either a house—it could be just that big, but long as you put one of 'em as a headboard on the grave that he lies in. Now, he's a hard spirit—that's why people call him Hoodoo. . . . you'll get him . . . by using the black cat bone. And when you get that black cat bone, he gotta come and appear."[19] Spells like this are certainly not everyday or acceptable practice. But they do point to a wider conceptual framework in which power has a double face. The replica grave localizes the spirit in the yard and opens a conduit between worlds which, depending on the circumstances, can help or harm.

The most detailed written account of a yard with clear references to burial practices and ancestors that I have found was published in 1912 by Effie Graham, a local-color writer whose works came to my attention through John Szwed and Roger Abrahams's essential annotated bibliography *Afro-American Folk Culture*.[20] Graham's purportedly fictional account describes the yard of "Aunt June," a woman who had been born into slavery on a plantation in Tennessee and later moved to Kansas. Although Graham's tone was condescending, her powers of observation were acute. Yet she obviously did not grasp the significance of what she saw.

> The first impression on viewing [the yard] was that of a half-pleasing, half-offending jumble of greenery and gleaming color; of bush and vine; of vegetable and blooming flower; of kitchen ware, crockery, and defunct household furniture. A marvelous mixture it was, of African jungle, city park, and town dump. . . . One noted . . . the unique receptacles for growing plants. Modern florists trust their treasures to the tender bosom of Mother Earth; not so Aunt June. She elevated her darlings in every conceivable manner. Marigolds bloomed in butter kits, and geraniums in punctured "deeshpans." Easter lilies were upheld by insolent punch-bowls, and johnny jumpups were ensconced in baby buggies. . . .
>
> "Seem lak dem lil jum'-pups suah do enjoy demselves crowdin' each other roun' in dat ole baby carriage," Aunt June would say. "Dem blue-eyed flowers make me reco-mem-ber Mis' Judge Cartwright's chillun I use to push roun' in dat ole baby buggy. . . .
>
> "Whose dat other baby carriage dar wif de white flowers hangin' over de sides? Dat's ole Mis' Preachah Newton's onliest lill gal's, what's daid. . . . I plant dem white posies in it. Just budded good when Mis' Newton come heah, Memorial Day. She lookin' hawd at dem lill buds an' she say, 'Don't pull dem po' things yet, Aunt June. Dey would be scairt out'en de cemetery, all alone. Keep 'em twell dey bloom out full.' . . . Lan' sake! dat nex' onliest kid o' hern, dat Ralph Newton. . . . Brekin' in heah an' tearin' up Jack, trompin' down flowers, only"—dropping her voice—"he—nevah—teched—dat—littles' baby buggy—where dem white flowers is."[21]

The littlest of the two baby buggies in the yard commemorates the life of a deceased child. The flowers in the buggy are white, a significant detail because white and the silvery iridescence of mirrors, glass, and water in African American and Central African iconography are reminders of the river/forest boundary that divides mortal and spirit worlds (see chapter 2). Graham goes on to describe another configuration of objects, one which refers more broadly to the ancestral dead and their protective powers.

> Easily the most conspicuous thing in the yard, and one highly prized by Aunt June, was a mound near the gate. Here, on a rounded pile of earth, was displayed such a collection of broken chinaware and glittering, bright colored glass as has not greeted your eyes since you looked last on your old playhouse. . . .
>
> On this mound were crippled cream pitchers, hotel gravy boats, lamp chimneys, whisky bottles, bar-room fixtures, bits of gay glass from a memorial window, crowned by the shattered remains of an old stovepipe, straight, upright, ready for action.[22]

Recall the emphasis on breaking and perforating the objects in grave decoration. Similarly, the objects in the gravelike mound in this yard were broken.

To outsiders like Graham, broken china and pottery in a yard suggest abandonment, trash, in other words, *junk*. Indeed, some observers have written off just such materials in African American yards, attributing them to the exigencies of poverty; to a "childlike" fascination with glitter and bright colors (hence Effie Graham's reference to a "playhouse"); or to imperfect imitation of whites—though it is rarely clear what white practice is supposedly being imitated.

Still, the first impression, junk, is not entirely misleading, and if objects themselves are reused and recontextualized, so too are seemingly transparent words. Some practitioners of yard work also use the word *junk* themselves, though in a specialized sense. For example, Mrs. A. J. Hamler of Hamilton County, Tennessee, called the objects in a corner of her side yard "my antiques" and "my old junk." Yet these objects, all painted white and most associated with family members, were clearly not ordinary castoffs. Mrs. Hamler surrounded a foot-pedal sewing machine and pots that had belonged to her mother with a fence made from the head- and footboards of old iron beds. In the spring white irises filled this part of the yard, and in the early morning throughout the year sunlight reflected like flashing strobes from the silver backing of spotlight bulbs mounted in a crape myrtle bush. Gradually, I began to recognize areas like this as yard-graveyards or places of remembrance. There are also historical precedents for such places; as Wyatt MacGaffey has written, "throughout West and Central Africa the rubbish heap is a metaphor for the grave, a point of contact with the world of the dead."[23] By extension, then, a "rubbish heap" of broken china in the yard acknowledges and makes room for the dead, as do whiteness, shells, cosmographic wheels that roll around the cycle of life and death, reflective materials, certain kinds of figures, piles of stones, special trees, and pipes.

Such objects, of course, also cue other, more commonplace associations, which is how the objects' links to deeper knowledge can mask in plain sight along busy streets and highways. However, the notion that yards like "Aunt June's" or Mrs. Hamler's are organized to communicate on multiple levels and thus demand multilayered historical, cultural, and personal interpretations contrasts with views like some of those expressed in a recent study of African American landscapes. For example, in his study *African-American Gardens and Yards in the Rural South*, Richard Westmacott has written:

> I found little obvious evidence of African beliefs among black gardeners. In many African religions, the earth and soil are sacred. . . . There was clearly a respect for the soil among gardeners in this study, but there was nothing sacred about it. Nor was there any indication of spiritual importance attached to any landscape feature. For some tribes in Nigeria, for instance, features such as streams or prominent rock outcrops were important spiritual symbols. . . . Some gardeners attached special meanings to certain plants, but in most cases these were very personal associations. Nor was any imagery found in garden design that was clearly rooted in African metaphysics. Because most of the gardeners were devout Christians, we did not expect to find recurring images that reflected animistic beliefs. For instance, the diamond shape, "a cosmogram that has become the signatory emblem of black traditional culture" was not observed in any garden. If it did occur, I did not see it.[24]

Westmacott's comments are disarmingly honest. Yet a diamond crossmark suggestive of marks against intrusion found throughout the diaspora appears on the cover of his own book. One wonders: do the yards and other landscapes discussed in this volume differ markedly from those that Westmacott visited? If Westmacott's photos are any indication, the similarities are in many cases striking. Further, the contents of several yards and the explanations provided by Westmacott's consultants are also similar. Consider the following account of the yard of Mrs. Susie T. Evans of Perry County, Alabama. Her nuanced use of the word *junk* seems almost identical to Mrs. Hamler's association of junk with the ancestral past: "Susie Evans had a delightful, shaded swept yard. The gateposts at the entrance to the yard were festooned with hubcaps. . . . Susie patrolled a mile in both directions along the paved road in front of her house.

She . . . picked up hubcaps when she found them. She told me: 'When I moved here I didn't have the money to buy things like I wanted. I wanted big white posts on the side of my gate. I get out there and when a wheel [hubcap] run off I stick it beside the gate. I call them "old slave-time junk.""'[25] What do we need to know in order for Mrs. Evans's words to make sense? Under Westmacott's heading, "yard art," they make very little. "Yard art" gives no hint of the connections between the yard and the graveyard that render hubcaps on a gate a viable substitute for "big white posts." And what have hubcaps to do with "slave-time"? Not much, unless they are, precisely as Mrs. Evans says, wheels: silvery, cosmographic wheels that rally the strength of the dead to protect the property and serve with mirrorlike implacability as their faces.

At stake in these different approaches is not only plausibility but the frame of reference for interpreting both specific places and the interplay of historical and emergent practices in sites as a group; in other words, the basic assumptions that researchers of African American visual and material culture bring to their work.

Either/or approaches like Westmacott's rule out multileveled interpretation. Instead, practices are either African or American, meanings are either sociocultural or personal, landscape features are either sacred or secular, and beliefs are either Christian or "animistic"—a term of dubious descriptive utility at best. Such approaches cannot accommodate consultants' explanations which use indigenous terms like junk and follow conventions of indirection in speech that avoid making explicit what should not be spoken of; nor can they convey the complexity and ambiguity built into the landscape through plants and objects with multiple associations like statuary and hubcaps.

The chapters in this volume aim to suggest alternatives. This collection took shape as a partial answer to the anthropological question: What would we need to know in order to understand . . . ? In this case, the coherence in African American yard works I encountered in the States and the Caribbean. It soon became clear that particular yards were only the tip of an iceberg. "Understanding," even of a very limited kind, would require learning about people and things that might at first seem quite remote from my starting point. This collection of chapters came together as my question intersected the diverse expertise and insights of teachers, friends, and colleagues from many fields relating to issues of home, landscape, and material culture. Contributors include visual artists, poets, geographers, historians, anthropologists, and museum curators.

The first part of the book contains chapters that describe African American domestic landscapes and relate them to moral and cosmological issues, to historical events, and to problems of interpretation. Chapters in part II explore intersections between the investment of significance in a particular place and the place as "contested terrain." Part III concerns institutions that anchor community life (the bank, the praise house, the historic site) and the interpretation of sites for, by, and about community members. Together the chapters sketch the diversity of possible approaches and, of necessity, suggest gaps in understanding beyond what we can discuss here. We hope this collection will motivate others to expand this work.

2 VIBRATIONAL AFFINITIES

John F. Szwed

THIS MEDITATION IS OCCASIONED by my encounter with the richly reticulated yard, house, and car assemblages of Georgia artist Bennie Lusane. Since the artist has chosen to remain virtually silent about the inspiration, sources, and meaning of his work, the full weight of interpretation falls on the observer (although the artist's wife, Elizabeth Lusane, willingly reads these works autobiographically, locating the components within different phases of family and individual history—her time as an Avon saleswoman; their ownership of a juke, a roadhouse dance club; Bennie Lusane's work in construction and roadwork; his taxi service, etc.) At first glance these works suggest the piecemeal accumulation and recycling of refuse and discarded household objects over a long period. But longer and more comparative viewing points to a larger configuration of works which Robert Farris Thompson has identified as Kongo-inspired Afro-American art. All of the recognized elements of this pattern are found in Lusane's work: *motion* (records, wheels, tires, phone and radio dials, clockfaces without hands); *containment* (bottles and jars, rock and pipe markers and boundaries); *figuration* (dolls, toys, animals); *medicine* (potted and free-grown plants); and *flash* (lightbulbs, mirrors, tinfoil, silver pans, flashlights). To these one might add—following Thompson's lead and recent research by Grey Gundaker—*enthronement* (chairs, benches, toilet seats).

In attempting to come to terms with Lusane's specific works and bring some order and discipline into my viewing of his art, I set myself the task of describing these assemblages. I assumed that words could suffice for adequate description, and perhaps they could for someone else. But I soon encountered difficulties in deciding where to begin the description, how to demarcate the parts, how to locate them and express their interrelationship. It occurred to me that even the simplest description presupposes some kind of theory of meaning and interpretation. The "established" arts presumably have a language of description developed to fit their own objects, one approved and validated by an interpretative community of institutions, critics, and academies. But such a description is unlikely to encompass works such as Bennie Lusane's; worse, their use might introduce unintentional irony by a mismatching of aims and form, as when—to choose an opposite example—anthropologists attempt ethnographic descriptions of their own cultures using methods developed for radically different ways of life.

Consider my notes on one of Lusane's assemblages:

> It is built up from a base of a six-drawer cabinet, with only two drawers in place. The other openings closed by two gray oven drip pans and a turquoise panel. A found, red plastic container lid is centered near the top of the cabinet, and a white plastic bucket raised on a white disc sits on the ground to the left of center. On each end of the cabinet is a single auto wheel cover, each cover of a different alloy. A central wooden post climbs from the cabinet's top, having two of its sides covered by flattened-out boxes which once contained bottles of Avon Black Suede cologne; three rearview mirrors face out from three different sides, and a pair of sunglasses is fastened to the fourth, along with a three-way socket with bulbs in place, and a mirror in a spotlight holder. But despite its size and centrality, this post is not weightbearing. At its highest point another, smaller post connects to it and continues to rise up to support the bulk of the work. Fastened to this second post is another rearview mirror, an opened, blue egg carton, an address-and-phone-number book with a telephone-dial cover, some white plastic lattice, a yellow Joy bottle, a yellow measuring tape which grows from the ground to the top, a large black plastic "N" mounted backwards with a red plastic hair comb above it, a white plastic skirt hanger, a green gift-wrap bow, and assorted colored bottle caps. Adjacent to these two posts at cabinet-top level are a partially filled half-gallon plastic bottle standing in a metal pan, a covered white plastic bowl, a silver ashtray, an uncovered white plastic container, and a table lamp with a yellow auto-wax can on top of its shade. Two turquoise plastic bottles are virtually hidden by a white cover.
>
> The uppermost part of this assemblage is based on several pieces of white foam packing material. On what might be the "front" a large yellow and orange plastic goose rests with small figurines of the Three Bears in front of it. Two wooden shelf brackets edged in chrome spread out winglike on either side, with bottles at their tips. Behind the goose sits a smoky plastic box with an alarm clock stopped at 9:23. Several cosmetic bottles sit near the top. From the

"back" side the goose is barely visible, and a disco record ("Ice T Is On the Way" and "It Takes a Real Man") is dominant, though partially obscured by a large white plastic pan. Two wooden panels with owls cut into them are positioned below at the same height as the shelf brackets on the other side. Various wires and cables lead out from this side toward trees and the house. Small silver light fixtures in the shape of hearts, clubs, diamonds, spades, stars, and hatchets are studded over the whole work, with Christmas tree lights mounted in them, though none appear to be electrically wired.

This description—as painstaking as I have tried to make it—is inadequate and painful to read. Some of the named objects are only approximately identified, and it is arguable whether or not they should be described by their original functions, even if I know them, which is not always certain. Every re-viewing of this work revealed something missing from my description. The fact is that these works are difficult to see. They resist single viewing and straightforward description and in fact seem to derive their form from a shifting interaction of shape, relationship, original and secondary function of parts, and position of the observer.[1] At one point the works may appear to be organized by categories of animals, at another by modes of travel. At the moment, at least, it seems to me that musical elements, motifs, and references abound in Lusane's art. There is a guitar on one assemblage, a record on another, a verse from an old rhythm-'n'-blues song taped to the driver's door of the Cadillac, figurines of Elvis Presley and a hound dog indoors, and taped to the center of the dashboard, this emblematic verse:

Hey Girls—Stick out your "can"
Here comes the
Decorating "Man"

This verse would appear to be a transformation of the only words that appear on the 1927 Luis Russell record "The New Call of the Freaks," although in that original the last line was "Here comes the garbage man."[2] A small plastic garbage can hanging from the rearview mirror (and thus over the sign) perhaps witnesses the link.

Faced with the difficulties of interpretation these works pose, and with Lusane's silence, I shamelessly fasten on to these implied musical parallels, even while knowing that on another day I may well see them differently. But right or wrong, the presence of musical elements would not be surprising here. Musical cross-references and influences are basic to Afro-American arts. In John O'Brien's *Interviews with Black Writers*, for instance, nine out of the sixteen major writers interviewed mention the importance of musical

Bennie Lusane in his yard, northeast Georgia.
(Photo: Grey Gundaker, May 1991)

Detail of Bennie Lusane's yard. (Photo: Grey Gundaker, May 1991)

Details of Bennie Lusane's yard construction: cookie cutters, Suede cologne label, dark glasses. (Photo: Grey Gundaker, May 1991)

Bennie Lusane's car dashboard. (Photo: Grey Gundaker, May 1991)

From Anthony Braxton's notation system, sketched by Grey Gundaker

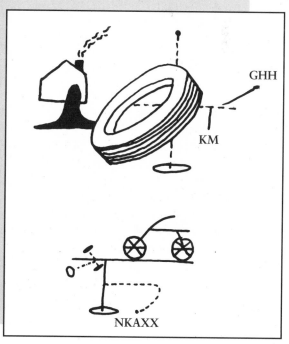

forms to their prose and poetry, while two others refer to the musical inspirations of yet four other writers.[3] The widely acknowledged accomplishments of black musicians are only part of the story here, but a very important part. Recently, Greg Tate suggested in the *Village Voice* that

> the reason black music cops a privileged and authoritative position in black aesthetic discourse is because it seems to croon and cry out to us from a post-liberated world of unrepressed black pleasure and self-determination. Black music, like black basketball, represents an actualization of those black ideologies that articulate themselves as antithetical to Eurocentrism. Music and 'ball both do this in ways that are counterhegemonic, if not countersupremacist—rooting black achievement in ancient black cultural practices. In the face of the attempt to erase the African contribution to the world knowledge, and the diminution of black intelligence that came with it, the very fact of black talents without precedent or peers in the white community demolishes racist precepts instantaneously.[4]

What seems most striking about the achievements of black musicians is that they cannot be easily understood as either simply a result of the direct continuity of African tradition or a variation on European tradition, but only as the unique product of the cultural process of creolization. And music, along with language, is the example par excellence of the process of creolization in operation.

Creole is a word common to all parts of the New World and even some of the Old, but one about which there is little agreement. Sometimes applied to a style of cuisine, a mode of behavior, or a person of a certain "color" or social status, it always seems to refer to a means of creating vernacular culture and as a way, a style, of doing things. Creole languages are sometimes referred to as "broken" or bastardized versions of standard languages. If regarded as words on a list, as discrete objects, written in a European writing system, they do look strangely—even comically—European. But linguists tell us that when put into use as speech, their grammar shows principles of organization that owe little to European language history. Rather than seeing them as dialects of European languages, creoles might be better understood as converged and reassembled languages, products of the joining together of two or more historically distinct languages under very pressurized circumstances such as colonization or slavery.

What makes this kind of language situation even more complicated is the coexistence of creoles with standard languages. In virtually every area where a creole is spoken, a standard language related to it is also spoken.

For instance, standard French is considered by the government and the schools to be the local standard language in Martinique. By no means is *créole* spoken or understood by everyone, yet everyone knows it to some degree and recognizes that its use is different from that of the standard language. (*Créole*, in addition to being the language of the underclass, is the language of pop songs, jokes, and the emotions.)

Generalizing from the creation of creole languages to creolization of cultural creations in other domains, we come face-to-face with this paradox: while it may be possible to identify the sources of individual components, when they are put into use, new combinations and totalities come into being which have no apparent specific relationship to their historical sources. In the case of language this means that while particular sounds and words can be traced to particular languages, the total speech that results is a new and emergent product. The same is true of music. Even if one can trace the sources of particular instruments, ensembles, and rhythms, when we hear them combined in performance, their sources are moot at best.

The process of creolization is often understood as being the result of raw necessity, as a make-do phenomenon, or as a function of secrecy. But expediency and privacy seem secondary to the process of interpretation, not only a result of adjusting to divergent cultural forms but also an act of mediation between different systems of values and meanings. When one system of interpretation is dominant, the minority system is sometimes forcibly translated into dominant terms, particularly where the parallels are few.

This is all the more complicated by the fact that in the twentieth century much black art has entered the broader public realm by having been adopted by commercially cultivated audiences of white youth. When musics originally created by black musicians for their own people were spread to a more specialized audience, the primary meanings were often lost or distorted. Describing the way in which late 1960s black soul music entered the world of the white teenager, for example, British writer Ian Hoare argues that what had for Afro-Americans been a broad-based shared aesthetic became for whites an alien art used in order to reject and contradict their own tradition. "This often means that black music is appropriated by way of a series of crude (and false) antitheses. Toughness is espoused because it is preferable to sentimentality; repression is opposed by license rather than liberation, bodiliness by brainlessness, a highly denied musical technique by an almost calculated technical incompetence."[5]

Cultural misunderstandings such as these sometimes produce bizarre new and creative twists. English acid house music of the 1980s was born from a misreading that allowed young dance club promoters to mix their

perceptions of black teen music with nostalgia for the recreational and exper-
imental drug scene of the 1960s. House music (a highly remixed, sparsely
vocalized disco-derived dance music developed in black southside Chicago
dance halls) found its way to English clubs thus:

> England's Acid House phenomenon is partly the result of a mis-
> take. . . . "We brought a lot of house records back to England with us
> when we were in Chicago," explains deejay P. Orrige. . . . "They all
> said 'Acid' on them so we thought that meant LSD, but it actually
> meant sampling. We didn't know that; we just thought "ooh, LSD."
> The misnomer results from Chicago slang for stealing someone
> else's sounds, "acid burn." The English acid house results from the
> marriage of Chicago beats . . . with "what we do on top, all our idio-
> syncratic bits of TV programs and all."[6]

It was by means of such misunderstandings that the spirituals came to be
seen reductively as sorrowful, Dixieland as good-time music, the blues as self-
pitying, etc. Such narrow aesthetic readings have had the effect of constraining Afro-American performers and artists, of holding them to social roles that
are at best stereotypically benign. Afro-American music is typically seen by
whites as exclusively social in function, albeit within a very restricted sense,
because it is a music which is developed in interaction, through performance,
rather than through solitary composition. Yet it is this very process of aesthetic-
through-performance that makes the music not just a style but an ethic. Many
musicians have struggled against these narrowed perspectives, sometimes by
demanding the same respect given to classical music; sometimes by broaden-
ing the terms to include dimensions such as spirituality, soul, and metaphysics
and by reaching for deeper historical and cross-cultural ties (in Egypt and
other parts of Africa, for example); sometimes simply by denying the existence of the imposed categories (so, in the early 1970s, jazz began to become
a marked term, sometimes enclosed by quotes, sometimes prefixed with the
same verbal flag of alert used by the Nation of Islam: "so-called").

One Afro-American composer and performer, Anthony Braxton, began
a rigorous campaign in the early 1970s to relocate black music, first by intro-
ducing a metalanguage to short-circuit facile interpretations ("vibrational
alignment," "affinity dynamics," "pulse track structures") and second by
extending its sources, functions, and meanings beyond the usual limits of
"Africa," "slavery," "segregation," and the like to world history, anthropology, and (with other new jazz composers of the '60s and '70s like Sun Ra,
Leo Smith, and John Coltrane) even to the solar system and the cosmos.
Braxton ceased to give titles for his compositions and performances per the
European practice and instead offered miniature drawings, perhaps not coin-

cidentally filled with many of the same elements as yard art—wheels, lights, images of motion, small figures, containers, and shapes, elaborately wired together. Thus, if critics were to write about a Braxton performance, they were obliged to reproduce the pictorial titles or undertake the difficult description of these title/pictures.[7]

This comparison of the new black music of the '60s and '70s to Bennie Lusane's work is not capricious, because during this period a basic reexamination of musical resources was under way. Performances occurred in which the accepted principles of tonality were questioned; a rebalancing of the relations of melody, harmony, and rhythm was undertaken; and the functions and even the proper venues of the music were heatedly discussed. For those who did not follow this new consciousness, much of the music of the period seemed unprincipled and without focus. Since it was no longer an "entertainment" music for drinking and dancing, it was not clear to how one should listen to it or what it was for.

It would be tempting to suggest recklessly that Bennie Lusane's and Anthony Braxton's arts are "about" the same thing, that they derive from common sources and have benefited from the same experiences so as to converge on common grounds from circuitous routes. But, more cautiously, all I want to say is that what they share, and what we can most effectively learn from them together, is that they both have come to employ creole ways of doing things and making meaning. These ways have resulted in producing a kind of art that Umberto Eco called the "open work": a creation susceptible "to countless different interpretations which do not impinge upon its unadulterable specificity," a work which offers an unusually high degree of possibilities in the amount of information provided and in the form of ambiguity entailed, and one which makes every reception of it "both an *interpretation* of it and a *performance* of it, because in every reception the work takes on a fresh perspective for itself."[8] Part of their message then, what they are about, is that these works must be approached in their own terms and in terms that are culturally relevant to them. What they teach us is how to look and hear again.

3 BIGHEARTED POWER

Kongo Presence in the Landscape and Art of Black America

Robert Farris Thompson

> If you go there and stand in the place where it was,
> it will happen again; it will be there for you, waiting.
> — *Toni Morrison,* Beloved

> His eye is always on the line of the diaspora,
> from Africa, across . . . the deep rural South and on into
> the Northern cities. And he weights and scales his perceptions
> so that the older strata of culture and experience are always
> the heavier. His South, like Toomer's, is dense African.
> His North is African still, following the presence of Black folks.
> — *Clyde Taylor, "Henry Dumas,"* Black World, *September 1975*

INTRODUCTION

DECORATED CLAY TOBACCO PIPES, excavated in Virginia and Maryland on the site of seventeenth-century plantations, constitute the earliest known art made by persons of African descent in North America.[1] "Fashioned in European form but decorated in a West African art style," these finds mark the beginning of an alternative visual tradition in what would become the United States.[2]

By the late eighteenth century, African-influenced dance was impressing even outsiders. One young white Virginian, Tom Sutherland, was pulled into its distinctive orbit; he danced a vigorous "Congo minuet" to banjo accompaniment in the late 1770s.[3] Mention of the well-known colonial dance in connection with Kongo was a sign of the influence of that distinguished, ancient kingdom on this nation. Such influence, culturally mediated from black parents to children, reflected the fact that a third, or perhaps a fourth, of all slave imports into North America came from the coast of Kongo and Angola.[4]

We encounter in Kongo a complex visual tradition. It was characterized, in part, by the writing of cosmograms, ideographic renderings of the universe and the place of man and woman within it.[5] The Kongo focus on traditional writing decisively lies within the dimension of gestures which inscribe concepts and ideals in stylized poses of the human body.[6] Also an idiom of Kongo art were myriad charms (*minkisi*, sing. *nkisi*). Powerful minkisi called *mbumba* or *lusoli* guarded fruit trees from thieves and prevented housebreaking and theft in general.[7] Related to these visual stratagems of spirit-embedding house protection were "medicated" yards or gardens. These were identified by the planting of special herbs or other visual additions which guarded, variously, against lightning or the entrance of evil forces.[8] Not only the yards or approaches to a house might be so guarded but also the main roads of a village and the four corners of a house. It was believed that through these places evil persons specially penetrated to spy on children.[9]

The tombs of the Bakongo culminated in a material writing system. Medicated graves included planted trees as "signs of the spirit on the way to the ancestors"; pipes or other signs of water passage to the other world; seashells, suggesting the same watery mediation but also signifying immortality by a pun linking *zinga* (spiral-form shell) with *zinga* ("live long"); and the last-used objects of the dead. The latter, often inverted basins or vessels, inscribe mystically "the last strength of a dead person." They were also pierced, or broken, to send them on their way with the spirit of their former owners.[10]

Aspects of this visual tradition, fixed in material writing, filtered into North America. Kongo tradition is therefore not limited in importance to the ancient situations in which initially it unfolded. It is also significant for its influence on the culture of black traditionalists in North America. In the towns and villages of the South it was reinscribed in novel social contexts, transcending slavery and later oppression.

Black American traditional burials, for instance, reveal telling regularities, like the importance of depositing on the tomb the last-used objects of the dead, plus seashells, pipes, pierced vessels, and planted trees. Cosmograms, charms, the association of twisted roots and branches with the presence of the spirit, and the guarding of houses with medicated yards and trees also passed into the lexicon of the vernacular art of numerous black North Americans.[11]

THE VOICE IN THE WHEEL:
RING SHOUTS AND WHEEL, TIRE, AND HUBCAP ART

The yodel, a chest/head, high/low snap across an octave, is one of the hallmarks of the singing of rainforest Pygmies in Central Africa. Dispersed across vast spaces, from Gabon and the southern Central African Republic to Haut-

Zaire, the importance of yodeling remains consistent in every Pygmy hunting band.[12] Some Pygmies use the yodel as vocal signature. This they do to combat loneliness in the forest and also to signal location when they are lost. The textlessness of their yodeling, unshackling sound from words, unlocks extraordinary freedom in the voice.

Ecstatic Pygmy yodeling influenced Kongo music. And then, via Kongo impact on North American black culture, yodel-influenced street cries turned up in Charleston, South Carolina; yodel-like "field hollers" emerged in the Mississippi Delta blues. Moreover, the late Bessie Jones, noted performer and interpreter of black folklore, told me in a conversation in 1975 that if a Sea Island Georgia black fisherman wandered into a strange creek and lost his way, he had only to shout out his special bluesy, yodel-like cry. Then, from afar, his family would hear the sound and say, "Jet lost! Let's go find him."

Earlier, in 1855, a train stopped in South Carolina in the night. Black workers shouted field cries by the railroad tracks, and Frederick Law Olmsted, then a writer for the New York *Daily Times*, heard them and was impressed. He called the cry "Negro jodling" and "the Carolina yell."[13] The Carolina yell continued the freedom of the Central African yodel in America. It made the presence of the black person known. It vocalized his deepest feelings. It traveled the railroads with the workers.

At some point, noting a similarity between the haunting wails of the locomotive whistle and the soulful oscillations of the field cry, blacks combined both sounds in certain blues. By the 1940s, if your ear was culturally prepared, you could hear a lonesome train whistle in the night and immediately think of black people on the move. From Memphis to Mobile. Goin' to Chicago, sorry that I can't take you. Albert Murray, the novelist, put these sounds, with all their originating forest/swamp implications, right into the pages of *Train Whistle Guitar*: "Mama always used to say he was whooping and hollering like somebody back on the old plantations and back in the turpentine woods, and one time Papa said maybe so but it was more like one of them old Luzana swamp hollers the Cajuns did in the shrimp bayous. But I myself always thought of it as being something else that was like a train, a bad express train saying look out this me and here I come."[14] These were the sounds that named the land for African Americans. The poet Daniel G. Hoffman has called the train whistle a quintessential symbol of black yearning.[15]

That fundamental voice has its visual dimensions. If African Americans appropriated the locomotive wail and made it theirs, then they also intuited freedom and the beauty of travel and transcendence in revolving, shining hubcaps, in the darker turning of a rubber tire, and even, sometimes, in the hard and resistant curving of a 55-gallon oil drum. Blacks in Trinidad during World

War II had transformed these same objects into percussion instruments, capable of playing notes.[16] They call it "pan"; we call it "steel band music." In the process oil drums, associated with car fuel, became the fuel of dance.

Similar qualities of visual propulsion informed the instrument of a black musician I saw sauntering down the streets of Port-au-Prince, capital of Haiti, in the spring of 1978. He was walking with his homemade banjo, made from a hubcap. A decade later, in 1988, Charlie Lucas, African American sculptor extraordinaire of Alabama, stood several metal human figures within the rims of wheels abstracted from automobiles and explained, "I'm trying to roll them." Automobile roll and automotive flash become visual equivalents to the train whistle in the blues. Train holler. Chrome circling. Black quest. Chrome seizes the reflective power of the sun, and modern vehicles suggest its motion. God's own moving point of illumination, the sweetest of chariots.

Some of these basic themes, particularly hubcaps and tires, roll space and time across the front yards and graveyards of traditional Black America, deepening ancient constants like the circular sign of the immortal journey of the soul. Note the importance of "soul" as an emblem of the black United States.[17] The spiral emphasis of the Kongo cosmogram moves through the ring shout and tire sculpture and hubcap sculpture across the country. In the process divisions of folk and high, vernacular and academic, secular and visionary, insider and out are exploded by a richer and collective understanding. *Zíbula makutu wa mambu*: with open ears hear matters of the spirit.

The late J. B. Murray of southeastern Georgia painted private moral messages around his front door and across a television tube. He sent them mystically racing through time and space. Such works distantly recall the glossolaliac writing-in-the-spirit of Solomon Lumuka Kundu, of Matadi, who lives among the Bakongo of Bas-Zaire. A vision of the universe as a reciprocating mirror of the living and the dead, and the relation of women and men to that cosmos under God, has indelibly influenced Black America. J. B. Murray was returned to that tradition when he was buried in a black cemetery bristling with graves decorated with lamps, vessels turned upside down, pipes, and a driveshaft traveling to glory with the spirit.[18]

Kongo priests mapped the journey of the soul within an ancient series of geometric cosmograms.[19] Circles or diamonds or spiral-form designs were used to encode a central message of the classical religion: woman as such or man as such are second suns, born in the east, flourishing in the north, fading in the west, and spiritually reborn as ancestors in the south. Compare Fu-Kiau: "A priest initiating his charge would use the sun in order to expound his teaching about the earth and the life of man, following the sun through its course about the earth and thus pointing out the four stages that make up the cycle of man's life: (1) rising, beginning, birth, or regrowth; (2)

ascendancy, maturity, responsibility; (3) setting, handing on, death, transformation; (4) midnight, existence in the other world, eventual rebirth."[20]
Extending a chain of mystical inspiration from tomb to nkisi to cosmogram,
Kongo ritual experts might chalk one circle (*dikongo*) on the earth and
another near the eye: "When the novice bends down to look at the ground,
he will have a vision of his entire departed *kanda* [clan], adults as well as
children, because the circle has turned into a mirror."[21]

Thus Kongo time is circular and the cosmogram, *dikenga*, marks a turning point—the crossroads, the tomb, the parting of the ways—where the pure
power of the dead brings its radiance to the present. When drawn, the vertical axis of the dikenga is the "power line" connecting God above with the
dead below. The horizontal axis, the "*kalunga* line," marks the water boundary between the living and the dead. The dikenga charts the soul's timeless
voyage. The soul cycles as a star in heaven. Thus the soul moves in time's
circle as an indelible point of light and certainty. This is why the Kongo moral
precept "From humiliation stems honor" (*mu diavwezwa mweti mena
dian'zítusu*) has such depth and resonance.[22] For according to this vision as
we die the "petty deaths" of accident and humiliation, the superior dimension to our consciousness has already distanced itself from the pain to plan
the appropriate counterattack, the appropriate return to full assertion. And
so we come back, stronger for the testing, more impressive for the return.

Kongo signs of cosmos[23] underwent a sea change in Black America. When
they were traced on paper and placed on the ground, invoking mystic mediation of a wish, the design remained fairly stable. There are two cosmograms
in Hyatt's monumental volumes on traditional medicine among the blacks of
North America, from Memphis, Tennessee, and Waycross, Georgia.[24]

Part of the series of American black expressions influenced by the Kongo
cosmogram are ciphers of the increasing presence of *mayomberos* (priests of
the Cuban-Kongo religion) among Latino migrants from Cuba in Miami and
the industrial Northeast of the United States. Mayomberos have brought
another creole form of the Kongo cosmogram to the United States, mystic
signs of spiritual protection (*bidimbu kia kandíkila*).[25] Botánica San Antonio,
for example, located in 1984 at 1630 Park Avenue in Manhattan, had
Kongo-influenced protective signs clearly chalked on the front door.[26] One
of them, a circle crossed by two downward-pointing arrows, with balanced
small crosses and small circles within the four quadrants, is very much like
a symbol which in northern Kongo protects a house by mystically fighting,
with arrows, against all evil. (The circles were interpreted as "eyes" and the
small crosses as "forces that balance the powers within the community.")[27]

Any crossroads in Kongo could serve as a kind of "found-cosmogram,"
a place to make contact with the other world through prayer and libation.

Similarly, a North Carolina black sacrificed a chicken at the fork of the road, asking salvation from an epidemic which had killed off the animals of his farm. The crossroads as an altar for special supplication turns up in the blues:

> I went down to the crossroads, fell down on my knees
> I went down to the crossroads, fell down on my knees
> Ask the Lord above for mercy, say boy, if you please.[28]

Sterling Stuckey, a leading historian of Afro-American culture, indicates that the Kongo ritual circle "was so powerful in its elaboration of a religious vision that it contributed disproportionately to the centrality of the . . . counterclockwise dance ceremony . . . called the ring shout in North America."[29] In the body of circling dancers was an unbroken social unity, a momentary realization of the path of the sun and its perfect wholeness.

Persons stepping within this circle of everlastingness sometimes, under the pressure of the handclapping, stamping, cries, and chanting, attained ecstatic contact with the other world: "The dancers form a circle. . . . Then they begin to shuffle in a counter-clockwise direction around and around. . . . A fantastic rhythm is built up by the rest of the group standing back to the walls, who clap their hands and stomp on the floor. . . . Suddenly sisters and brothers scream and spin, possessed by religious hysteria, like corn starting to pop over a hot fire." And out of this danced cosmogram came a power linking later musics, like jazz and rock, to the classical music of West and Central Africa. "The continued existence of the ring shout is of critical importance to jazz, because it means that an assortment of West African musical characteristics are preserved . . . in the United States—rhythms, and blue tonality,—through the falsetto break and the call-and-response patterning to the songs of allusion and even the motions of African dance."[30]

Wheel, tire, and hubcap ornaments in the yards of certain African Americans visually reflect, I think, this circling emphasis. These found circles of symbolized motion, I suggest, mirror the world-disclosing potential of the ring shout. They sanctify the soil, like a visual ring shout. I also think they mystically "wheel" antisocial spirits off the premises. I say this also on the basis of protective usages of wagon wheels and other motion emblems on black properties in Alabama and tidewater Virginia.

Thus the sculptor Charlie Lucas of central Alabama nailed a wagon wheel under his children's window as a fire escape. In tidewater Virginia, Cornelius Lee protects his premises not only with bottle trees[31] but also with the blades of a propeller, painted fire-engine red to match glass fixtures which he caused to emerge from car tires painted white. The crimson glass, of course, is of the type cyclists use to warn motorists to stop or slow down. Lee's sister, a mile or so away, protects her property with a pile of stones and seashells at roadside. From this deliberate pile emerge two red reflectors, like the gestures of an invisible officer, stopping traffic.

A car tire surrounding a century plant (also called yucca and Spanish bayonet) graces numerous black yards across the country. Fu-Kiau interpreted the decoration in Kongo terms: "The tire is a circle of an accomplished life. It is an *nkata* [circle, lap, symbol of competence] that holds the life of the plant, a symbol of the care that should be given to life in all its manifestations. It is really an encircling lap, like the crossed legs of a most important mother."[32] Compare the testimony of two black women, Ester Criss and Louise Williams, who made tire-encircling garden art in Leland, in the Mississippi Delta in the 1970s: "Our idea was we wanted to put the flowers in tires so the grass wouldn't grow around the flowers and ruin them. So we could keep the flowers clean. And we filled them full of dirt and put flowers in them."[33]

Skeptics might dismiss this action as simply a gardener's practical trick. But the Leland reference is but a tiny fragment from a massive black tradition, extending across the South from Memphis, to the Savannah River in Georgia, to the coast and beyond. In Alabama, for instance, the maternal grandmother of Charlie Lucas placed tires "all around the house, some standing up, some placed flat against the earth, with flowers growing in them."[34] She had positively built a motion barricade about her house. It is almost certain that Dilmus Hall, of Athens, Georgia, similarly used an alternate phrasing of the cosmogram, the sign of the diamond, to protect his windows and a corner of his house facing the street.

The life-giving wholeness and vitality rendered in the ring shout and wheel and tire decorations is paralleled by the importance of the hubcap in black material culture. Kongo symbols are double-edged. What attracts can also repel or wheel away. And so, as the old ring shout, also known in black Alabama as the "jubilee dance" (in the latter form the descent of the spirit causes people to get into a circle), comes in time to brim with texts, spirituals, and gospels, so the wheels, circles, tires, and hubcaps of African American vernacular art begin to fill with potent visual voices. When Rosetta Burke of Detroit, Michigan, encased her house in tires and oil drums and painted the legend "VOICES" on the treads of a tire placed upon her altar, she set in motion the chanting of a private vision.[35] She had composed a one-word spiritual to wheel round and round in God's own time.

Tyree Guyton, of East Detroit, received national recognition in the summer of 1988 for chasing crack cocaine dealers out of abandoned houses in his neighborhood.[36] This he did by activating the derelict structures with aspects of the motion parlance we have witnessed. He nailed tires and hubcaps to the walls of one house, explaining, "Curved space *spins*; I put some-

thing round on a square, on a house, and make it go."[37] And make the criminals hiding in it go as well. Indeed, the more tires and other objects he nailed
to the house, the more it became conspicuous. Passersby came in increasing
numbers, children especially, admiring and wondering at the decorations.
The resident drug dealers actually were forced to take their undercover operation elsewhere. It was a visual stratagem, and it worked, even as Joe Light,
an artist from Memphis, dealt with young men invading his backyard. Light
painted two arms-akimbo figures in spectral white upon his chimney "and
never saw them again."[38]

The black vernacular disposition to work with tires, cathode tubes, oil
drums, hubcaps, wheels, and other circular objects represents more than the
random utilization of industrial discard. Phrased another way, found icons
on black lawns or yards are not passive registers of the impact of automobiles and modern telecommunication on the black imagination. As more and
more evidence pours in from Black America, it becomes clear that an intel-
lectually selective process is at work. Tires, wheels, hubcaps and oil drums
are choices. They relate to the ancient circles of the spirit,[39] and as Tyree
Guyton put it, they make you "think of the big round ball we're on, in space,
constantly turning, round and round."[40]

These patterns, to repeat, suggest more than chance. Consider performers of early jazz "spasm bands" who played on hubcaps and shining metal
containers,[41] a taste extending to the chrome disks suspended in the air upon
which Marion Brown played modern jazz or the "steelphone" of Leo Smith's
black creative music in the 1970s.[42] The point can be made where we might
least expect to find it, in the phenomenon of the "prepared piano" in recent
Western concert music. Note the cultural differences distinguishing the "prepared piano" of Cecil Taylor from the transformation of the same instrument by, say, Stockhausen. "The implements he uses to play on the inside of
the piano are nothing like the ones that [John Cage, Christian Wolff,
Stockhausen, or Kagel] use. For instance, he uses bed springs, steel mesh
cloth, things that he lives around. And like those [European-oriented musi-
cians] are using rubber erasers, corks, and felt mallets. Cecil's is a much more
metallic sound, but the Western cats soften the piano down."[43] Like mobile
cymbals and hubcaps, Taylor's music projects metallic flash. But there is
more to the tradition than circles, flash, and a strong sense of motion.

YARD SHOWS AND BOTTLE TREES:
ARTS OF DEFENSE AND AFFIRMATION

A black family in tidewater Virginia, breaking up space between their house
and the road with found icons and other emblems, calls the design a "yard

show." Under this rubric and other appellations (black yard art, black yard design) has emerged an independent African American aesthetic of immense consequence and influence. Like all minkisi, yard shows in Black America carry a double edge: power to give and to take back, to greet and to defend.

Yard shows assimilate the artistic and philosophic values of classical Kongo culture. These are manifest in the recurrency and assuredness of the major themes: (1) rock boundaries; (2) mirrors on the porch, "to keep certain forces at a distance";[44] (3) jars or vessels, placed by the main door to the porch, "to send evil to its sources";[45] (4) motion emblems, like wheels, tires, hubcaps, hoops, pinwheels; (5) cosmograms, sometimes rendered as a diamond, sometimes as a circle; (6) flowers or herbs planted within the protective circle of a tire, sometimes whitewashed, sometimes turned inside out and decorated with knife-cut sawtooth edges, creating what is called in Alabama a "crown";[46] (7) root sculptures, found images, dolls, plaster sculptures of persons or animals, and, occasionally, stuffed animals; (8) trees hung with shiny bottles, or lightbulbs, or tinfoil, or shiny metal disks, and sometimes the bones of animals; (9) swept-earth yards with every blade of grass removed; (10) overlaps with graveyard decoration, including shells, pipes, rock piles, and sometimes even head markers; (11) plantings of protective herbs.

To repeat, the makers of yard-show art in North America work from formal principles of selectivity and emphasis recalling rationales of classical Kongo bearing. In fact the discourse of the yard show makes of house and property virtually one vast nkisi charm, especially where there is a mirror on the porch, like the mirror in the belly of *nkisi nkondi*. The nkisi tradition, brought to the United States from Kongo and Angola by Gullah Jack and other legendary healers, was a matter of embedding spirit in earths, keeping the spirit in a container to concentrate its power, and including with these earths material signs which told the spirit what to do. The gist of those expressions are seemingly regained in a creole art wherein the house guards the spirit of the owner and the icons in the yard guard or enhance that spirit with gestures of protection and enrichment.

There is a logic to the main visual principles of the yard show: *motion* (wheels, tires, hubcaps, pinwheels); *containment* (jars, jugs, flasks, bottles, especially on trees and porches); *figuration* (plaster icons, dolls, root sculptures, metal images); and *medicine* (special plantings of healing herbs by the door or along the sides of the house). These "decorations" may seem casual to persons passing by. But the sheer repetition of themes, coast to coast in Black America, hints strongly of conscious principles of connection.

The indelibility of the spirit coded in the dikenga lies implicit in the resonance linking yard shows to the graveyard in terms of carefully selected

Shell and red streamer mark a driveway on Virginia's Eastern Shore. (Photo: Grey Gundaker, June 1991)

*Victor Melacon's tire crown and palmetto, Hammond,
Louisiana. (Photo: Grey Gundaker, June 1991)*

Automobile drive shaft and headstone near Sparta, Georgia.
(Photo: Grey Gundaker, June 1991)

Griffin Manning's fence with wheels, New Haven, Connecticut.
(Photo: Grey Gundaker, September 1989)

Henry William's white trees with glass insulators, southeast Virginia.
(Photo: Grey Gundaker, November 1996)

Door flanked by a snail and a white porcelain commode, Memphis, Tennessee. (Photo: Grey Gundaker, February 1988)

Broken and inverted vessels on a grave near Sparta, Georgia. (Photo: Grey Gundaker, June 1991)

Nkisi nkandu, *also known as* nkisi malabiri, *antitheft tree medicine made by Mayolo Pandi Maurice of Ndingui village, near Mouyondzi, Bouentza region, R.P. du Congo. (Photo: Robert Farris Thompson, July 10, 1987)*

Telephone pole painted purple by Rachel Presha, Suffolk, Virginia. (Photo: Grey Gundaker, May 1990)

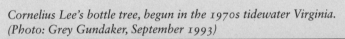

Cornelius Lee's bottle tree, begun in the 1970s tidewater Virginia.
(Photo: Grey Gundaker, September 1993)

Cornelius Lee's twisted vine section, painted red and white, at the fork of the branches of his bottle tree, tidewater Virginia. At the lower right is a television picture tube suspended from the tree. (Photo: Grey Gundaker, September 1993)

emblems of perdurance—rock piles, shells, pipes. Henry Dorsey had a mock grave on his lawn in Brownsboro, Kentucky.[47] Saul Hill, who moved to Los Angeles from Louisiana in 1920, so intensely decorated his yard with a cross (with diamond motif) and hypnotically repeated arrangements of pipes and tiles and tomblike slabs that it strongly resembles a traditional African American graveyard.[48]

Icons in the yard show may variously command the spirit to move, come in, be kept at bay, be entertained with a richness of images or be baffled with their density, to savor sunlight flashing in a colored bottle or be arrested within its contours, and, above all, to be healed or entertained by the order and beauty inherent in the improvised arrangements of icon and object. Although varying covert messages can be coded in such objects, we must not lose sight of the fact that for many of the makers of yard shows the main purpose is to give visual pleasure to their communities.

Yard shows, as I have indicated, are seemingly everywhere in the black United States, not just the South. They are in Detroit, Louisville, New Haven, Kansas City, Dallas, and Los Angeles. Accounts from the seventeenth and nineteenth centuries document possible sources in the classical religion of Kongo for these African American artworks.

Let us review the sources. First, we know from Dapper's text of 1670 that mystically protective objects guarded houses in the northern Kongo city of Loango in the seventeenth century:

> *Boessi-Batta* was another *nkisi* of major importance focussed on bringing into one's homestead objects acquired in long-distance trade, thus especially pertinent to merchants. It consisted of several parts: a large lion-skin sack filled with all sorts of shells, iron bits, herbs, tree bark, feathers, ore resin, roots, seeds, rags, fishbones, claws, horns, teeth, hair and nails of albinos . . . to this satchel were added two calabashes, covered with shells and topped with a bush of feathers. The whole set of objects, satchel and [the two] calabashes was placed atop a table-like construction outside the door of the house.[49]

Naturally yard shows in the South and in Los Angeles do not exactly duplicate this Kongo house-charm complex, for they are creole paraphrases that combine such traditions with contemporary American materials. Still and all, we note themes persisting today, shells, roots, rags, and, above all, the placement of two containers by the door.

The case for Kongo influence in the United States is strengthened by another description, this one by John H. Weeks in a book on Kongo life published in 1914: "Anxious mothers, after the birth of a child send for [a rit-

ual expert, an *nganga*] who brings with him a number of small conical basket traps. These he carefully places all round the doors of the house to catch
any evil spirits that might try to get into the house."[50]

The mysterious guarding of the house could be visually phrased by additions of certain kinds of cloths as well; "a pad of old native cloth is twisted
and placed on the article to be guarded, and the thief who takes anything
thus protected will suffer."[51] In Kongo colored rags hoist on a tree symbolized a problem within the community. Thus to deck a house in rag emblems
called on God to mend a broken situation, sending an invading felon to his
doom. Trees with bones tied to their branches or their trunks warned view-
ers that should they rob the premises, they soon would become skeletons.[52]

Trees are frequent media of moral intimidation in Kongo vernacular
symbolism. From Weeks's 1914 text: "An old basket hung in a fruit tree, or
against a door, will give backache to a thief, or cause him or her to become
sterile. A stone hung in a little palm-basket with some creepers twisted round
it and suspended from [an African plum tree] will give the person who steals
from it, or even attempts to climb the tree, a severe form of hernia."[53] Within
the contours of this tradition appear also hoops or circular constructions
which Bakongo translated, when placed before a house, as "an empty
world," "a dead world," meaning a kind of empty window through which
an aggressing thief mystically would fall down to his death.[54]

Broken pottery also was a sign of death, an emblem of the graveyard.
Proyart, writing in 1776 of the Vili areas around Loango, North Kongo,
made it clear that this dread sign of the end of life was suspended not only
from fruit-bearing trees but before the houses of persons who for one reason or another had to absent themselves for a long time, "for the most determined thief would not dare to cross the threshold when he saw it protected
by these mysterious signs."[55] This was the beginning of mixing the visual languages of tomb and home.

But all was not a matter of spiritual defense in these classical expressions.
We also perceive emphasized qualities of healing and affirmation. For
instance, making a ritual circle round a tree before a house in Kongo specially protected the plant and helped it grow. And this led to larger dimensions of positive herbalism, healers surrounding their houses with herbs, like
an emerald aura. Consider the house of the traditional healer Nzoamambu
of Manselele in northern Kongo. His residence is surrounded by some seventy-
seven specially planted trees and herbs. Most provide medicine. Some, however, protect the boundary or ward off lightning.[56] Dotting the perimeter of
a house with plants for healing is not unlike nailing blades of iron into nkisi
nkondi to signal the healing of problems of social discord and displeasure.

Now, Kongo medicated yards and doorways may seem impossibly distant from the modern United States, relics of a bygone pastoral level of simplicity, utterly without relevance for our times. But classical traditions often start at deceptive levels of outward simplicity and plainness. Odysseus, after all, surprised Princess Nausicaa doing her laundry in a stream. The infant Moses was concealed in bulrushes, not babywear from Christian Dior or Nieman Marcus. Christ was born in a manger, not the Holiday Inn. Yet Moses and Christ arose to redirect the course of Western consciousness. And when the best of the teachings of Moses and Jesus fused with the best of the classical religion of Kongo in North America, the result was The Old Time Religion. All three religions are one in hailing God as the ultimate moral arbiter. This is the rationale that illuminates the protective medication of the Kongo house and yard, for it is written that "[God] gave rise to all the minkisi in order to help the people."[57]

In the summer of 1987 I witnessed in northern Kongo an nkisi which one Mayolo Pandi had fashioned around the trunk of a tree to protect his orchard from thieves. The charm consisted of a miniature double-ended spear on the prongs of which were impaled a palm nut and an eggplant. Pandi suspended an nkisi sachet, a *futu*, on a string beneath the fruits, themselves material signs of punishment and retribution. The generic name of such a charm is *nkandu*. This means prohibition. This means law. This makes it criminal in God's name to steal from this tree. Bakongo see futu as a package wrapped by God. God calls upon the soul in the sachet to follow the thief and destroy him with disease or death.

Massive numbers of captives came from Kongo to New Orleans and Charleston and the Caribbean, and they brought their memories of the medicines of God as an irreducible fundament of their culture and their way of life. In spite of slavery and other problems, they managed to reinstate the material commandments of God. In 1791, on the island of Dominica, between Guadeloupe and Martinique, it was reported that "the blacks have confidence in . . . sticks, stones, and earth from graves hung in bottles in their gardens."[58]

This is one of our earliest attestations of New World Kongo house-protecting charms. It is significant that it mixes the world of the dead, the cemetery, and the world of the living, the household garden, to achieve its proper intimidating pitch. We can read the ideography of this New World nkisi fluently: earth embedded an ancestral spirit, commanded to use sticks as mystic arrows, and stones as mystic bullets, against all thieves or enemies. The sachets had changed from cloth to glass. The bottle tree had emerged in the Americas.

A later attestation, from Trinidad, builds another bridge from Kongo, via the black Caribbean, to North America: "More to prevent the pilfering of small boys than the ravaging of animals and birds [the black owner of a small farm] had scattered her plot with a miscellany of broken bottles, old tin pans, dirty colored rags, animal bones, barrel hoops and various constructions of the sign of the cross. The next day she placed a rusty barrel hoop around the [mango] tree, satisfying a belief that it would thrive better." The range of Kongo discourse is amazing. From Trinidad it simultaneously points toward the reinstatement of many of these themes in U.S. yard shows, like protecting flowers within a rubber circle.[59] The same rational also went to Cuba where Esteban Montejo reports that teams of Kongo magic-men used to compete, planting a plantain tree in the middle of a circle drawn on the ground and casting spells on that tree to make it bear fruit.[60]

New Orleans was a point of entry for such beliefs, direct from Kongo and indirectly from creole Caribbean sources like Cuba and Haiti. Thus the folklore of Louisiana now includes the following belief: "If a tree bears wormy fruit, chop a piece from the trunk and tie a bottle of water somewhere around the tree. Next year you will have solid fruit." Louisiana, furthermore, is no stranger to the concept of the medicated house, protected cosmographically: "Hide [roots and herbs] in the four corners of your house to keep things in your favor"; "plant gourd vines around the house to keep snakes away."[61] Winslow Homer may have unwittingly documented this last-mentioned creole pattern in his painting *Near Andersonville*, dated 1865–66.[62] In this work we see a black woman in apron and vivid head tie standing in a doorway. To the left of the door are gourd vines, perhaps house-protective, and to the right of the door is a basket, recalling protective baskets placed by doors in Kongo.

In tidewater Virginia today one is astonished to pass black house after black house and note two containers—jars or pots or jugs—guarding the door on either side. The custom also extends through Georgia and North and South Carolina. The noted artist John Biggers was taught this tradition in Gastonia, North Carolina, and given the rationale: mystic traps or baffles, coded as pottery decorations, palisade the house, causing "evil to go back where it came from." Added Biggers: "I remember the jars on the porch, they often contained objects in them considered to have power. It was a very individualistic form of phrasing, these medicines, actual or implied within the jars; knowledge of them was not necessarily shared. In any event, you don't mess with it." And he further commented that this practice is not limited to a Kongo heritage because on a trip to Ghana he noted an Akan person leaving jars around his house before leaving town on business, and "of course we knew exactly what he was saying."

The classical qualities of the medicines of God are perceived in the work of the remarkable Rachel Presha—known to some as the "Purple Lady" of Suffolk, Virginia—as described by Tom and Meredith Crocket: "There is a quarter mile stretch of Route 17 in Suffolk, Virginia, near the Portsmouth

County line where the telephone poles are all painted purple. There is a sense of joy and purpose in her activity. There are purple trees, purple shoes, purple chairs, purple brooms, purple wash drums, and a purple baby carriage."[63] These works recognizably fall under the yard-show rubrics of motion and containment but uniquely are unified by a single color. The most arresting approach to the style of Kongo material writing in this yard is a bundle of sticks bound tightly in purple cloth and tied to the crook of a tree. This amazing assemblage seemingly announces that intruders of malintent will be mystically "swept" or forced to deal with a unified army of spirits, bound in wood and ready to be released. This Afro-Virginian composition recalls, as well, black Cuba where Kongo men played a game of the same origin, *quimbundia*, in which they "got handfuls of magic sticks from the forest and tied them into bundles of five, to give each man strength."[64] Whatever Rachel Presha had in mind, her work bears powerful witness to the theme of the medicated tree in African American yards.

As to Mississippi and Alabama developments of this mode, the famous writers Eudora Welty and Truman Capote did not have to study Picasso in order to appreciate African influence on the modern world. Such power was right beside them in the form of Africanizing bottle trees. The aunt of Truman Capote recalls bottle trees made in the 1930s by Corrie Wolf, a black woman of Monroeville, Alabama, who worked for the family of Truman Capote. She would take a blooming crape myrtle and insert the ends of its branches into brightly colored bottles, explaining that evil was "attracted to bright colors and the first thing you know they are trapped inside the bottles and can't get outside."[65] The same rationale, based on the ancient Kongo metaphysical equation that flash equals spirit and spirit equals flash, informed the Kongo tradition of inserting in visionary sculpture bits of metallically gleaming beetles, to startle evil away. When the tradition reemerged in Sumter County in the far west of the state of Alabama, the idiom changed.[66] There the ancient forms of spiritual glitter were replaced by the hanging of tinfoil, lightbulbs, and other icons of light and brilliance in trees and the placement of mirrors on the porch, arresting or distracting evil with their flash.

In a marvelous personal variant on this tradition, the grandmother of Willie Collins of Los Angeles strung lightbulbs on a line within her yard. She believed that what is incomplete in the living world is complete in the world of the dead. Hence bulbs now empty of light would light up from the other world. But only the mystically prepared could see them.[67] James Seay's poem "The Bluebottle Tree" documents another style of arboreal nkisi frequently seen in Mississippi and other parts of the South: "Your bluebottle tree, a hard-won / Stay against confusion."[68]

Yard shows act upon black artists like an invisible academy, reminding them who they are and where they are coming from, an alternative classical tradition. The bottle tree or nkisi element no longer functions by itself but becomes incorporated in a larger moral fabric. One of the Alabama artist Thornton Dial's most intense compositions "signified" against men who waste nature, who fish in a river when they aren't even hungry. In this sculpture strong black and red slashes of paint cover discarded bottles that Dial rammed onto twisted driftwood. In his own words, Dial shows "the river sending its stuff against the spoilers, scaring them so much they jump into a ketchup bottle."[69] He thus criticizes waste with a humorous citation of one of the tenets of the bottle-tree tradition, the coaxing of evil into a container.

When John Biggers was a child growing up in North Carolina, he was taught two things about the bottle tree: (1) the myriad bottles would keep birds from the fruit, for "the wind striking the bottles would make a wonderful noise"; and (2) "if you put pots on the trees at the right time of the moon [i.e., when the moon was full] the bottle-tree would bring rain." Bakongo believe that when the moon is full, "things are fully happening." This is the propitious hour for certain rituals. When the rain falls, Bakongo children are told to dance, to please the rain. In return they receive the rain's blessing.[70] Compare this with what Biggers was taught in North Carolina, to get in the first rain of spring—"you'll never catch a cold, if you catch the first rain."

Biggers's cultural education also included learning how to place protective medicine: "Our tricks were put under the step to protect the house and they were called *inkabera*. To make an inkabera you took a piece of string and put it in a jar with water and put it under the step. The string would turn into a serpent if someone came to do you in." Biggers also saw mirrors on porches in Bessemer City, North Carolina, near Gastonia, and he watched medicinal herbs being planted around the edges of houses.

Cornelius Lee, an African American who lives in tidewater Virginia, responds to this classical tradition in an innovative way. Acting on a kind of inspiration—"a mind tell me"—around 1959 he tied two soda bottles together on a single strand of cord and hurled them up on a branch of a tree. They stayed on the branch. "I kept on doin' that til I filled the tree out." Lee says he makes bottle trees primarily for aesthetic reasons. He savors the randomness of the patterns formed by the hurled double bottles: "When you throw them up, they fall where they may, that's the beauty of it."

The glitter of the bottle tree rhymes conceptually with the flash of the mirror by the house. They are the obverse and reverse of the coin of Central African influence. Bottle trees are believed, variously, to bring rain, to make

trees bloom, bring luck, and ensnare all evil. It is premature to draw firm conclusions, but I have the impression that what distinguishes the North American
bottle tree from the more Kongo-looking bottle trees of Surinam, Trinidad,
and Eleuthera in the Bahamas[71] is a conflation of the tradition of placing vessels or baskets by doors to catch spirits and the tradition of hanging antitheft
devices from the branches of a tree. This would explain the different emphasis on trapping beings in bright glass. In addition, the custom of hanging bright
baubles on Christmas trees may well have stimulated the decking out of trees
with multiple bottles, sometimes leading to outright mimesis.

Yet even as they were changing, the tree nkisi were constantly interre-
lated in the black imagination with the decoration of the yard. Yard and tree
as unit created a joint exuberance that danced the icons from door to street.
That interrelationship is emphasized by William Eiland who witnessed bottle trees in Sprott, Alabama, northwest of Selma: "The practice [of making
bottle trees] went hand-in-hand with having a grass-free yard (except where
it was bounded quite carefully with old tires or bricks). The devil could hide
himself in the blades of grass; if the yard was gravel or dirt, there was no
place to hide. Likewise, a mirror on the front porch would frighten the devil
out of the front yard, since his reflection is even horrifying . . . to himself."[72]

But on close inspection the term *bottle tree* may be a verbalism that jams
the frequency of a fuller message. Eudora Welty's famous 1931 photograph of
a half-dozen bottle-laden trees in Mississippi's Simpson County includes,
between the trees to the left, a "bottle shelf" supporting a vertical flask and
another object. There was a comparable "image shelf" in the Kongo city of
Mbanza Ngungu in 1909–10, showing a Toby jug suspended on a plate.
Behind this was a china doll surmounting a gnarled and knobby trunk. And
there are image shelves outside many doors and along the front windowsills
in the black Americas, from the house of Gyp Packnett in southwestern
Mississippi to the Woodford section of Port of Spain, Trinidad.[73]

In short, bottle trees are part of a larger perspective involving not only
yards, houses, and gardens but images set up on shelves or other elevations.
In this way traditionalist African American homes are mystically "dressed"
with signs of simultaneous aesthetic welcome and arrest. Attempting to grasp
the yard-show complex in full caparison, we cannot isolate here a tree, there
a "face jug" (vessel or cup made into a Toby-like face through the addition
of white clay). African American yard art emerges from an array of traditions in creative collision with the West.

ROOT SPIRIT ART

Bakongo mystics also prized remarkable objects taken directly from nature,
like strangely twisted lianas,[74] roots, and branches.[75] Respect for forms

received direct from nature countered the geometric precision of the cosmo-gram. Wyatt MacGaffey, one of America's leading Kongoists, points out that "minkisi such as Funza . . . are believed to embody local spirits (basimbi, bankita) which are associated with strange twisted roots and oddly shaped stones." "Besides being the patron of twins and the originator of all charms, Funza 'owned' all twisted, stunted, or abnormal objects, themselves often regarded as incarnations of bisimbi . . . [which are] twisted, like certain roots and trees."[76]

Parts of this lore persist in the verbal and visual arts of Georgia and South Carolina. At Pooshee plantation, in Berkeley County, South Carolina, north of Charleston, in the second decade of this century, a black woman named Clara Milligan admonished white children playing beside a pool: "Got to be *really careful* if you go in that water," she said, "*simbi*'ll get you."[77] Something in her voice made these words indelible. In 1987 Nina Langley of Charleston, who was one of those children, could remember the warning clearly at the age of seventy-eight.[78]

Clara Milligan and her ancestors had extended the lore of the Kongo simbi into South Carolina. In Kongo important persons were believed to hide their souls in simbi pools. The pool was like a liquid nkisi in which one immersed and kept one's spiritual essence. Bisimbi, like attack medicines inside the water, guarded the soul by harassing or drowning all intruders. Hence a simbi pool could be considered "extremely dangerous, neither man nor beast can jump over it."[79]

There is a special fascination in American black vernacular art with simbi-like unusual natural wood formations, perhaps mediated in Black America by the mothers of twins. In Kongo culture the fertility of women was held to be under the charge of simbi spirits. Indeed, twins were bisimbi.[80] But, lacking a concrete study, this remains surmise. What is true, however, is that in South Carolina not only was the concept, simbi, recorded but also the notion, *mfinda*,[81] the forest boundary between worlds. Forest and water are in fact seen as one in the traditional Kongo imagination. (It is almost as if Aimé Césaire divined this fact when he wrote, "I have become a Congo, resounding with forests and rivers.") This belief leads logically to the image of bisimbi inhabiting not only bizarre wood from the forest but driftwood from the water.

Logs shaped by the action of water of Poplar Root Stream in Burke County, Georgia, became sculptures in the hands of Ralph Griffin, whose yard was filled with figures made from roots and gnarled wood.[82] "I go to the stream. I read the roots in the water, laying in clear water. There's a mir-acle in that water, running across them logs since the flood of Noah. Them logs, they been there since Noah's time, when the Flood got out all that water.

This is the water from that time. And the logs look like Old Experience Ages." The artist elaborated further on his process of creation. "I take the root from the water and have a thought about it, what it looks like, then I paint it red, black, and white, to put a bit of vision on the root."

In Cuba, found forked branches, held to be remarkable counters of the presence of the spirit, are such a strong element of the Kongo religion that the faith has come to be termed *palo* (stick, twig, branch, from the forest). In Cuba, Kongo worshipers take *lungówa*, ritual forked forest branches, and strike them against the floor or ground to vibrate the earth, to capture the attention of the spirits.[83]

There are other ways of activating twisted roots or branches. Things turned upside-down, from the vantage point of the living to the vantage point of the other world, express their own hermeneutics, their own concealed power. Said another way, the land of the dead simply inverts that of the living. Cyrus Bowens, working in a Sunbury, Georgia, cemetery where the grave mounds in the 1930s were covered with inverted plates or containers, made his famous "serpent" grave marker from wood found in the forest and caused it to stand upon an inverted branch.[84]

Similarly, in Memphis, Tennessee, the blind black artist Hawkins Bolden told me in 1988, while describing one of his arresting works, "I like to take a forked limb, turn it bottom side up, and put a face on the middle part." Bolden tended a small garden of okra and other vegetables in his backyard. Around 1965, he recalled, he began to protect his garden with a series of "scarecrow" images meant to keep away the birds. As his eldest sister, Elizabeth Williams, explained, "when people began to see them tree limbs and branches rising, with faces on them, they thought it was a voodoo garden but they were scarecrows.[85]

When he made this scarecrow, Bolden dressed the tree limbs with shoes and inverted a metal basin to read as a head. He punctured the container with hammer and ice pick to give it eyes, a gesture reminiscent of the ritual piercing and inverting of the possessions of the dead placed on graves.[86] The fact that Hawkins Bolden is blind does not prevent him from seeing with his hands. "I be writing mouths and tongues with pieces torn out of old carpets," he said, by way of characterizing the tessellated tongues which adorn many of his works.

His works are "seen" through their textures. They pass through his fingers as he works in his garden or underneath his house. They are seen as well through their daring abbreviations and elisions. He embellishes and protects a garden of visual distillations, where uplifted vessels of the bottle-tree tradition, inverted pierced vessels, inverted limbs and branches, and many other sources flow marvelously together.

MENDING MATERIALISM AND ASSERTING MORAL FORCE

Why the pull toward transcendence in yard shows? Toward spiritual, private symbols? Because of The Old Time Religion. Henry Dumas was right. North is dense African. California too. Wherever blacks transmute modern media with their lyric voices you sense the stress of the spirit. You hail a vision, flowing from Kongo and Angola, to Charleston and Congo Square in New Orleans. That bighearted power that Stanley Crouch traces from back-home blues to the jazz of Albert Ayler, the consciousness he tells us filtered through the Delta to Black America at large, parallels the rise of transcendence and spirit possession as vital elements in African American art.

Yard shows not only express spiritual concerns, they are conversations with the surround of neighbors and strangers. Thus a black woman in Austin, Texas, surrounds her house with plastic bottles filled with colored water, protecting her premises, she says, from roaming dogs.[87] She keys the color of the water to major American holidays—green and red at Christmas, red, white, and blue on the Fourth of July. Similarly, just as Mother's Day cards on tombs are a tradition of the black cemetery, so yard shows may formulate conversations with the ancestors. The same woman in Austin keeps on her porch an iron pot her mother cooked hominy in, as well as a stone her late husband collected on a trip: "We used to argue and now it's all I have of him." She explains the bottles on her lawn and in a tree—"They make noise against evil in the wind"—as "obstacles." People come, she says, people look around, and suddenly they feel that someone is watching over things. Glossing further this idiom of spiritual deterrence, she adds that pinwheels in her yard "keep those birds away; they see the colors and try to light on them and then it moves and frightens them away . . . my tire planters protect my flowers from outside dirt and water. Paint them white. Paint them all colors. Cut them in two and place them like arches all around the lawn."

The yard show wheels a people's soul across our nation. Some have supposed it mere idiosyncrasy, unrooted in larger social facts or value systems; but the voluble, endless parlance of the tradition, from coast to coast, confronts our world with a lexicon of memory and purpose. No piece of this intricate mosaic—bottle trees, face jugs, memory jars, rock piles in the yard—bears alone the burden of proof of heritage or meaning. It is the combination of all the elements together, in full and proper context, that announces this new art history, vernacular and American.

The confidence and fluency of the tradition have led to arresting works of art. Of a pair of house-protective "dolls" in southwestern Mississippi, for example, one has ribbons for legs, as if part of her body were crimson smoke; the other surmounts the head of an animal, is long of leg and commanding of gesture, and wears a pistol as a necklace. The mixture of charm and militancy is in perfect balance, exquisite evocation. These are dolls that preach.

Yard shows constitute a declaration of architectural independence. Not only do they free us from imagining that the landscape design of America stems from a single (read: European) heritage, but their mixture of toughness, memory, and camaraderie liberates us from the assorted nihilisms and apocalypticisms of so-called postmodernism and from other movements that have lost their way. Spirit does not date. Neither does it fear the garish world of commerce and technology.

African Americans are justly famous for what they say and do in blues and spirituals, gospel and rap. But they have also preached visually. Soul art turns, soul art wheels. In the process, the yards, the houses, and sometimes the cars, too, of visionary black and black-influenced women and men adhere to ancestral truths. Theirs is a force and a work that drives us all toward possibility and return.

4 ART, HEALING, AND POWER IN THE AFRO-ATLANTIC SOUTH

Judith McWillie

BENEATH THE SURFACES of what we call "culture" lie generative values and attitudes that are capable of sustaining themselves regardless of the boundaries that contain them. This belief sustains my life as an artist which, in an "official" sense, began almost thirty years ago in Memphis, Tennessee, in a class at a local state university. The instructor, who was a painter at the time, told about how, at the turn of the century, Marcel Duchamp and other European Dadaists had exhibited "readymades," everyday objects such as bottle racks and porcelain urinals, in fashionable galleries in order to confound a public who expected art to be made from precious materials such as bronze and marble. These displacements were intended to jolt aesthetes out of their narcissism and spiritual complacency, he said. But neither inscrutables like Duchamp nor the countless European and American artists who followed him were able to sustain a long-standing, communally based ideography in their work. They envisioned themselves as letting go of the past in order to make room for a more promising future. In 1946 Duchamp had said of Dada, "It was a sort of nihilism to which I am still very sympathetic. It was a way to get out of a state of mind—to avoid being influenced by one's immediate environment, or by the past: to get away from cliches—to get free."[1]

These strategies survived as analogues of the modern condition and, more recently, as emblems of a postcolonial world in which "syncretism and parodic invention are becoming the rule rather than the exception."[2] Still, the fact that we were studying Duchamp's "readymades" generations after they were created seemed proof enough of their mysterious efficacy.

Meanwhile, on a strip of land alongside the railroad tracks that bordered the university, forty-six-year-old Eddie Williamson was creating an elaborate rambling construction made of bottles, hubcaps, packing crates, carpet samples, and other discarded materials. Students and neighborhood shopkeepers called it "Parking Lot Eddie's Bottle Garden." The "bottle garden," which also served as Williamson's home (it was said that claustrophobia prevented him from living indoors), generated an ecstatic incongruity that asserted itself like a force of nature—human nature—boiling up out of a severely conflicted southern culture that had a history of denying its visionaries even as it succumbed to the truths they exposed. Eddie Williamson consciously and convincingly demonstrated the contrast between his own particular witness and the more orthodox enterprises of those of us who visited him. It seemed to me at the time that the "bottle garden" invited participation in ways yet to be discovered whereas Duchamp's works felt like "points in stellar solitudes."[3]

Twenty years later, shortly before his death in 1990, Eddie Williamson revealed that he was not unaware of the art world. He had studied photography for a year at the Chicago Art Institute on the GI Bill and had spent long hours in the museum there coming to terms with "art for art's sake." As he explained to me,

> There's a difference between camera art and what they call the "fine arts." The camera wasn't considered too much a part of the fine arts. It was a distinctive commercial venture. We were advised to use cameras as much as possible. It gave a commercial slant that an art student or a sculptor wouldn't even think about. The life of an artist or a writer in the fine arts—these artists—they're too poor! They have to live off of too little! And they can't relax and be civilized human beings and exercise enough intelligence to take care of themselves and be secure, so I would have preferred doing it commercially.

"Did you ever think of writing?" I asked. He answered:

> When it came to writing, there are just too many poor writers. It takes them so long! It's just like being a painter. You've got to be chosen by the environment that you paint in unless you finance yourself. And very few are able to finance themselves. The study of art gives you such an accentuation on individuality that you're likely to [he hesitated cautiously]—you wouldn't be able to give the public an accurate description of what you're talking about as a personality. You would always just show yourself. Take art you've probably studied, Vincent Van Gogh and people like that. What did he do? Cut his ear off? All that kind of crap? One eyed, one eared, living, trying to paint common people over in Holland or wherever his home was?

Walking through the surviving remnants of the "bottle garden" (it had been bulldozed the year before), Williamson returned to the theme of his work.

"This requires a lot of mental work through the functioning of your senses and rationality. Sense, reason, and decide! You do it for a given period of time. Not many people can do this at any time. For example, take a sightseeing tour to a place you've never been; you'll find that your senses are fully occupied. You'll find that God has his fingers in your hair from a long time ago!"

Williamson was educating me to the possibility that the "bottle garden" was part of something more vast and comprehensive. Still more elaborately constructed displays identified other Memphis neighborhoods such as "Orange Mound," "Boxtown," "North Thomas," and "Hollywood." Each seemed connected to others of like kind although their makers had never met each other. Many were constructed from the same types of cast-off objects: bottles, wheels, chrome-plated appliances, dolls, sewing machines, lightbulbs, sea-shells, pottery shards, cisterns, clocks, mirrors, and pipes or other types of hollow rods. At first, these yards seemed driven by the same transubstantive energies that compelled Duchamp to exhibit his bottle racks and urinals. But the social and psychological resonances of yard shows were more vivid and complex. These were works that would never exist as things apart. They contributed to a pattern seemingly paralleled in the deeper order of things. They existed "at the maximal intersection of all those energy flows which establish a work's complicated power nexus."[4] They might even reconcile divergent languages, idioms, and values.

Eventually I moved to Athens, Georgia, to take a job as a painter and professor while continuing to seek out the makers of yard shows. Subsequent travels across Georgia, Mississippi, Alabama, Louisiana, South Carolina, North Carolina, Virginia, Maryland, and up the east coast confirmed that by the middle 1980s many if not most communities along the way hosted at least one individual who celebrated the yard-show idiom, even in locations as remote as New York City. Within eyeshot of the Hudson River, in Manhattan's West Fifties, Ray Crabtree dressed his porch with a chained mannequin and set an inverted commode by the sidewalk. In Harlem a spectacular work by "Bob G" filled a vacant lot near an Ethiopian synagogue. A Cape Verdean community in New Bedford, Massachusetts, offered still another link. The creolizing tendencies of American popular culture were proving to be more vivid and syncretic than Duchamp and the Dadaists could ever have imagined.

I soon learned, through the works of Robert Farris Thompson and others, that in the South, if economic and psychological repressions were substituted for the geographic containment of Old World societies, racism, a pernicious parody of this containment, failed to achieve its separatist goals. In terms of provenance, the region's culture was shaped as much by African perspectives as by those of Western Europe. For over a century, and probably longer, African Americans such as Eddie Williamson had been gracing the southern landscape with a network of sustaining sites that linked the United States with other African-informed societies on both sides of the Atlantic. Meanwhile, the coming of age of their art in the last decades of the twentieth century signaled "an overarching transformation" in cultural priorities.[5]

By the early 1980s some of America's most distinguished arts institutions, including the National Museum of American Art of the Smithsonian, began expanding their curatorial activities to include the discovery and documentation of African American vernacular artists. Writers, collectors, poets, academics, journalists, and critics traveled throughout the United States to observe firsthand the triumph of vision over circumstance. In this climate the convergence of a grassroots idiom such as the yard show with the American "fine arts" establishment was only a matter of time.

A NEW SEED

"I'm cultivating the roots of a new seed from an old source," said the Alabama visionary Lonnie Holley at his home in Birmingham in 1986. Then, as now, Holley's yard was a densely packed cornucopia of items retrieved from local dumpsters and junkyards. The sculptures he generated from the objects he collected, along with his sandstone carvings, eventually placed him among the South's most prominent "self-taught" artists, reviving classic American imperatives of "affirmation in the face of adversity and improvisation in situations of disruption and discontinuity."[6] "I dig through what other people have thrown away to get the gold of it," Holley said, "to know that grandmother had that skillet and stood over that heat preparing that meal, so when I come home with that skillet, I've got grandmother, 'Grand,' someone who has authority and is capable."

Holley's perspective on what Marcel Duchamp called "readymades" and what art historians called "found objects" was distinctly spiritual, dedicated to the continuities of life in time. "To deal with me as an artist," he explained, "and see all of my art as art and not just as garbage or junk, is to see that I went to the depths of where no one else even would go to speak for life. . . . I'm sure that everything that has happened, all the ancestors that has had to pass away in order for the earth to be as it is, they was playing a part, like I'm playing a part in life today, just living and creating. Then I'll fade away and kind of fertilize the soil around my children. Then they'll live and they'll get children and they'll die to fertilize the soil around theirs."

For "the body needs energy to survive," said the late anthropologist Robert Plant Armstrong, "and it holds its quota of energy only so long as it is capable of doing so, for power is abrasive; it wears its vessel away; when the vessel is no longer sufficient to its energy, it dies, the energy itself to seek out new and more adequate forms."[7] In the cadences of science, Armstrong recalled the unidirectional orders of power associated with consumption, while Lonnie Holley speaks to cycles of return. The objects in Holley's yard are "experienced," not "used up"; "recovered," not just "found." So much the better if they were "cast-off." That they are "used" becomes central to their purpose. In shunning notions of obsolescence Holley and other African American vernacular artists discovered a means of releasing the moral force embedded in invisible histories, while employing art as an agent of spiritual transformation. "God said, 'I made enough in your yard that I could show my people how to change,'" says Holley, "and I have to work it all right back out of me so I can come back and handle another one. And that's what keeps me from going insane; and I think that's the way it is with every artist."

AN OLD SOURCE

In the cemetery of the Sunbury Missionary Baptist Church, in the Georgia tidewater region between Savannah and Brunswick, a mirror flashes from the palm of an impressed handprint on an upright concrete slab. An automobile headlight defines another marker with shells scattered at its base. Ivan Tomkins's photographs from the 1930s reveal the same monument when it was new along with another marked by a porcelain commode.[8] A metal pipe resembling a tree serves as an armature for bottles attached to extended "limbs." These works, including three large-scale wooden figures reportedly stolen sometime in the 1950s, were created by the "Reverend" Cyrus Bowens, distinguishing the Sunbury site as one of the most celebrated examples of African American vernacular art in North America.

In 1987, at the age of ninety-eight, Eddie Bowens, the artist's nephew, recalled how Cyrus and his wife, Rachel, had left their home on the Parker plantation to settle in Sunbury. "Rachel was from Colonels Island and he married her there. And consequently, they was living there and they built on it. Everybody had a home. But the island was not to be sold. It was the Parker place. Consequently Parker died and the son ordered them to leave—to carry what was on their backs; they couldn't carry a plant or nothing else, though."

After moving to Sunbury, Bowens became a renowned spiritual father of the Missionary Baptist Church. Later he experienced a call from God that instructed him to make images in honor of the family dead. He immediately began work on the family grave enclosure and stationed a hand-lettered wooden sign at the entrance, listing the names of both ancestors and progeny. He made the hand-print marker for Rachel, who was not yet deceased, and others for the rest of the family, including his father, Alec. Later, Bowens's children would mark his own grave by placing a dolphin skull on a cross and painting it silver, blue, or white at various times.

Few of the Bowens monuments remain intact today, but in the late 1980s when the cemetery was renovated, their surviving remnants were transferred to a local history museum. The photographic record and the living members of the Sunbury community therefore remain the only primary sources of information about Bowens's life and art. The lost wooden sculptures, photographed by Malcolm and Muriel Bell in 1939 and by Orrin Sage Wightman for his book *Early Days of Coastal Georgia*, were made from found wood selected for its resemblances to birds and serpents. When shown a copy of the Bell photograph in 1987, Eddie Bowens remembered: "This is absolutely a tree that was bended in the time of the big freeze. All them came out of the woods and he hewed them out. . . . And he put these rods all around [metal pipes in the ground]. They used to go out on the beach at Catherines Island. They was out at an old wrecked ship. That was where he got that rod. He put that rod in the cemetery to dress it. He liked to make an image of different things and put them in the cemetery. People would come by and they loved to see." The porcelain commode, the mirrors, shells, and rods, the anthropomorphic wood, the inspired ciphers, all had their origins in what Eddie Bowens described as "the old way that's not in the Bible."

In 1987 Eva Mae Bowens remembered that her father "did all them things." "The little man he had with a pipe in his mouth—he made all of them. Some of them before I was born. He always said, 'You don't be a preacher till God send you to preach.' He got up to go to preach at Riceboro Crossroads and at the praise house and right up to Sunbury. He was preaching, you know, 'God is up there. God is a big-eyed God. He sits in one place but he can see all over the world.' Sometimes the people would start laughing, but one of his nieces would get up and say, 'One of these days he's gonna preach your funeral!'"

THE MIGRATIONS OF MEANING

Cyrus Bowens's contributions to American art, like those of Eddie Williamson and Lonnie Holley, involve much more than a clever use of cast-off materials. "African traditional conceptions of being," says Gabriel Setiloane, a contemporary Anglican theologian of Sotho-Tswana ancestry, "show a belief in a potency locked up in objects and beings, or an Energy, a Force which is imminent in all things. It is everywhere; it flows through all things but it draws itself to a node or focus in conspicuous objects."[9] As Grey Gundaker has said, the significance of this belief stems from the reversal it enacts, "turning the power of expanded sight back on the world, saturating the everyday with personal and spiritual significance."[10] Bowens, Williamson, and Holley, along with the other artists introduced in this chapter, not only give us a new experience of what art can be, they reveal something more fundamental—that works of art maintain their efficacy regardless of the ways they are "appropriated." Arthur C. Danto, the postmodernist philosopher and critic, states this same idea in epistemological language. "Whatever they may mean, and however they may be perceived and responded to by their contemporaries, works of art are dense with latent properties that will be revealed and appreciated only later, through modes of consciousness contemporaries cannot have imagined. Because of the limits of historical and cultural imagination whole arrays of artistic qualities may be invisible until released."[11]

It thus remains curious that Cyrus Bowens was dressing the Sunbury cemetery at roughly the same time when Marcel Duchamp was mounting his assaults on Western cultural complacency, and with strikingly similar objects, a porcelain commode and a metal bottle "tree." Synapses of this kind may seem gratuitous, but they are the result of syncretisms reinforced by potent conjunctions in time. They spin their own "complicated power nexus," neutralizing distances by engaging more dynamic powers of synchronization. The contrasts between Bowens and Duchamp are, of course, a matter of genealogy and possibly (although not certainly) of intention. However, both men were keenly aware that art is "dedicated to the management of energies in the world," that it is metaphysically functional as well as aesthetic, that it is sometimes "in presence" and sometimes not. "The work-in-invocation tends to exist in an ambient of time," says Armstrong, "what has happened to it in the past is portion of its being. . . . This is due to the fact that the invoked work exists only in performance." Like Duchamp's bottle rack, "a powerful secret society mask in West Africa may very well have no reality of presence as it lies wrapped in cloth among the rafters of a house, but it becomes translated into glory when it is invoked in rite."[12]

THE POWERS OF INVOCATION

In the 1930s Harry Middleton Hyatt, a priest of the Episcopal Church who was also a folklorist, recorded "beliefs accepted by many negroes and white persons" in the South including those associated with specially configured objects. Transcribed from Ediphone cylinders, Hyatt's conversations were later published in five volumes under the title *Hoodoo—Conjuration— Witchcraft—Rootwork: Beliefs Accepted by Many Negroes and White Persons, These Being Orally Recorded among Blacks and Whites.*

In his first encounter with an African American spiritual doctor, "Doctor Lindsay" of Richmond, Virginia, Hyatt was shown a "shiel" made of roots and flora, including Jerusalem bean, devil's shoestring, High John the Conqueror root, bloodroot, Samson's snakeroot, devil's bit, and a bulb from a plant called life everlasting. Dr. Lindsay explained that these ingredients normally were suspended in water or perfume and kept in a bottle, but because the bottle had been broken, they were tied in his handkerchief and regularly "fed" (moistened). When an unwelcome visitor entered his house, said Lindsay, "he'll find his eyes is scattered . . . because I keep my red pepper burning and my sulfur and my old shoe's soles; I keep my head all perfumed and my house decorated . . . I dress my track—my shoes is dressed . . . I keep my shoes full of good red pepper and salt and sulfur." Dr. Lindsay was a practicing healer, as precise in his art as warranted by the needs of those who consulted him. "I'm coming round here to bathe your feet," he told one client, "and dress this house. And when I dress this house . . . you will have no more trouble." "To catch a spirit, or to protect your spirit against the catching, or to release your caught spirit—this is the complete theory and practice of hoodoo," wrote Hyatt.[13]

In a global context, however, Robert Farris Thompson has shown that hoodoo in the South retains elements of West and Central African classical religion, the "perdurance and importance" of which are "defined in terms of the richness of the associative values clustering about its most appropriate expressions."[14] Lindsay may have been perceived as "superstitious" by neighbors insensitive to the strategies of cultural resistance, but his grounding in the transactional skills of the religion situated him within the ranks of other spiritual doctors on both sides of the Atlantic who knew how to "comfort the impulses" in another's way of thinking.[15]

The following account from Grenada, West Indies, illustrates how restrictions on traditional practice were less severe in the Caribbean than in the American South. In 1893 an "Obeah Man" named Mokombo told Hesketh J. Bell, "I'll tell you that 'dressing a garden' means setting Obeah for the thieves."

> From out of his basket, he produced a number of small and large medicine bottles, each filled with some mysterious liquid; then taking up a position in front of a plantain, he tied one of the vials onto a bunch of fruit and then began muttering a sort of incantation. . . . He would then pass on to another row of trees and perform the same ceremony. Having hung up all of his stock of bottles, Mokombo next produced from his basket a tiny little black wooden coffin, apparently empty. This he placed with much ceremony in the branches of a cocoa tree and on the top of it put a saucer containing a little water and a common hen's egg floating in it.[16]

Still another example of a medicated garden from the West Indies, photographed in Gros Islet, St. Lucia, by the artist Paula Temple in 1986, confirms the longevity of these strategies. In the same year, near the community of Wadley, Georgia, a local resident told the artist William Paul that merely tying chicken bones in a fruit tree would render the same protective effects.[17]

In a conversation at her home in 1987, the artist Bessie Harvey of Alcoa, Tennessee, told about how she returned to her birthplace, Dallas, Georgia, in order to get "roots under the ground that are all little people." These became the source of her art which flourished in the last decades of her life and was eventually exhibited in the 1995 Biennial of the Whitney Museum of American Art. She warned:

> Some think it's evil. People accused me of voodoo. They say you're "sorcery" or "witchcraft," or you work evil powers. I don't know why they believe this to be. I think that's backwards. I think the world's been taught backwards. My mother said, "Keep that thing because one of these days you're gonna find out what goes with it." And I really believe she knew what was to follow. All through life I have thought that the trees was praising God. I talk to the trees. All the roots are little people. . . . I'm giving all praise and thanks unto God. I'm able, through God, to see the faces and bring them out where the world can see them. That should say something! We've all got to be together to bring out Him—to make it the Whole. They call it art, but what is art? That's a big question and I'd really like to hear it answered. Where the world got the name for art, I can't say. But, yesterday touched me in today and made me well.

THE POWERS OF PRESENCE

"A 'work of art' in the Western sense," says Robert Plant Armstrong, "is an object or event caused to be 'a work of art' because . . . of the excellence of its conception and execution." Yet there are cultures, for example those in black Africa, where the work is caused to be what it is—to own its power— precisely because of its "who-ness" or "what-ness," because of its "powers of invocation."[18] Suspicious of the art world's emphasis on rarity and connoisseurship, which he viewed as alienating and exclusionary, Armstrong suggested the phrase "affecting presence" as a more accessible means of describing the way value is attached to particular objects. "The universe of the affecting presence is not one of apartness and special nature, nor of irrelevance as we in the Western world have permitted our philosophers to make it appear to be. . . . Within the affecting presence lies energy, of which form is the visible dimension. . . . To imagine a conceptualized and discrete category of speculation about the affecting universe as an order of reality that is special and different from all others is probably unwarranted: a tyranny of ethnocentrism."[19]

By 1961 even Marcel Duchamp seems to have been considering the same ironies. He carefully explained:

> A point I want very much to establish is that the choice of these "readymades" was never dictated by any aesthetic delectation. This choice was based on a reaction of visual indifference with, at the same time, a total absence of good or bad taste. . . . I realized very soon the danger of repeating indiscriminately this form of expression and decided to limit production of "readymades" to a small number yearly. I was aware at the time, that for the spectator, even more than for the artist, art is a habit forming drug and I wanted to protect my "readymades" against such contamination.[20]

Duchamp's statement, however facetious, may seem naive or disingenuous by today's standards, but it suggests that he had discovered, intuitively at least, the degree to which his own "readymades" depended on "the powers of invocation." "Through the change from inert matter into a work of art," Duchamp said, "an actual transubstantiation has taken place, and the role of the spectator is to determine the weight of the work on the esthetic scale."[21] By limiting the production of "readymades" to "a small number yearly," Duchamp capitulated to the art market's demand for rarity while, at the same time, subverting its taxonomies. The old taxonomies have continued to operate, however, in various forms, in the fields of anthropology and art criticism. Robert Plant Armstrong, for example, distinguished between "works-in-invocation" (those identified with spirits or personifications, requiring "the validation of investment by external power") from "works-in-virtuosity" whose aesthetic autonomy, he said, "is neither augmented nor diminished" by the conditions in which they are displayed.[22]

For most of the twentieth century, however, these sorts of distinctions have become gradually more tenuous. Today, even Westerners have begun to admit that the primeval needs gratified in "the powers of invocation" are no less crucial to them than to spiritual doctors and obeah men such as Dr. Lindsay or Mokombo. It is only that Dr. Lindsay and Mokombo never ignored them in the first place. In the meantime, Duchamp and other modern artists subverted prevailing tastes to such an extent that, aesthetically, many actually prefer the directness of vernacular art to the cultivated mannerisms of "fine art." I believe that Duchamp's legendary status in the United States (a status unparalleled in Europe even now) is due in no small measure to the fact that he opened doors to the kinds of convergences being explored here. His obscure references to "the fourth dimension" were a means of encouraging the probability of such convergences without trivializing their

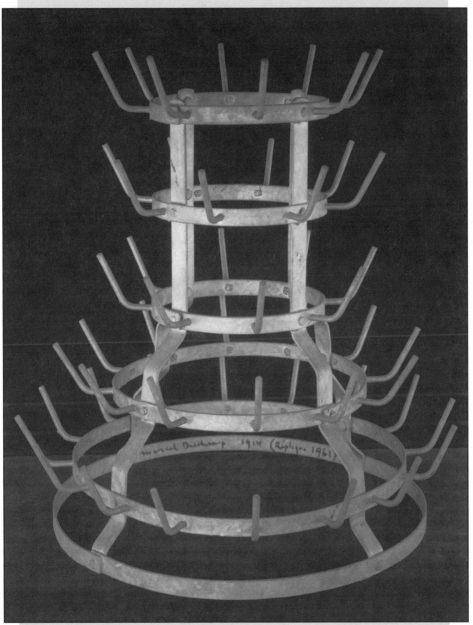

Marcel Duchamp, bottle rack, 1961. Estate of Marcel Duchamp, on loan. (Courtesy of the Philadelphia Museum of Art)

Ivan Tomkins's photograph Bowens family graves, Sunbury, Georgia, 1930s. (Courtesy of the Cate Collection, Fort Frederica National Monument, National Park Service, U.S. Department of the Interior, housed at the Georgia Historical Society, Savannah)

Eddie Williamson, Memphis, Tennessee. (Photo: Judith McWillie, 1989)

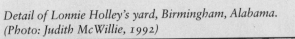
Detail of Lonnie Holley's yard, Birmingham, Alabama.
(Photo: Judith McWillie, 1992)

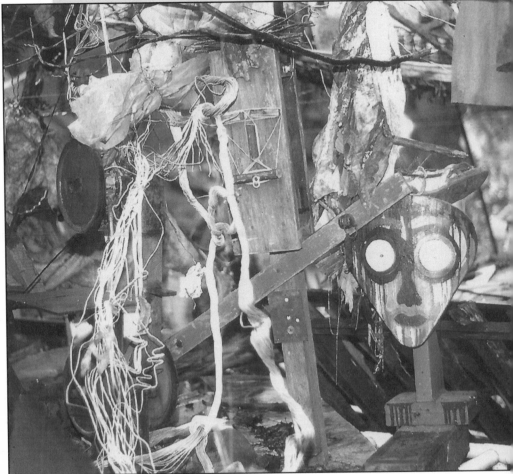

The grave of Cyrus Bowens, Sunbury, Georgia. (Photo: Judith McWillie, 1984)

Yard, Gros Islet, St. Lucia, W.I. (Photo: Paula Temple, 1986)

Bessie Harvey, Alcoa, Tennessee. (Photo: Judith McWillie, 1987)

Annie Sturghill in her "Yard of Colors," Athens, Georgia.
(Photo: Judith McWillie, 1988)

*Dilmus Hall,
Athens, Georgia.
(Photo: Judith
McWillie, 1986)*

*Dilmus Hall's "The
Shoe That Road the
Howling Tornado,
May 31—1973, in
Athens."
(Photo: Judith
McWillie, 1976)*

mystery. According to William Rubin, former director of the Museum of Modern Art, Duchamp stated that "if a shadow is a two dimensional projection of a three-dimensional form, then a three dimensional object must be the projection of a four-dimensional form. Thus the simplest object holds the possibility of a revelation."[23]

AN AFFECTING PRESENCE

In 1987, in Clarke County, Georgia, Elijah Davenport stacks chrome hubcaps next to his mailbox and ties others to a fence, "to keep the birds out of the garden." He hangs plastic bags full of human hair in trees, "to keep the deer away." In a flower bed next to his front door, he inverts a white porcelain wash basin and attaches a plastic milk jug on top. Later he adds a circular metal trivet to the configuration. Throughout the yard more images of rotation, illumination, and motion are sustained. At the entrance of the driveway, terra-cotta cisterns painted white hold carefully sorted bundles of objects including the stainless steel bodies of worn-out kitchen appliances along with lightbulbs, translucent reflectors, and an effigy of the cartoon character Snoopy. In Dr. Lindsay's world the cisterns would have been used to collect rainwater, "water from the sky," which, in addition to performing its powers of bodily refreshment, was the only water considered pure enough for "spiritual work."[24] But according to Davenport they merely support a great fence decorated with woven strands of printed cloth, electrical cord, blue flagging tape, foil chewing gum wrappers, and spark plugs. Behind the house a chair made from scraps of wood and metal stands next to a "scarecrow."

In Memphis, Clarence Burse nails a mirror to a tree in his yard and surrounds it with toy dolls, rotating fan blades, aluminum lamp poles, and brightly colored plastic bowling pins. The mirror is camouflaged behind a fence made of bedsprings. For Burse, a retired factory worker, it is a means of observing neighborhood street life from the safety of his home without having to leave his favorite chair.

In the yard of Fox and Juanita Flemming of Oglethorpe County, Georgia, a silver-painted automobile wheel casing borders a flower bed in a presentation sequence that also includes a sewing machine and a wagon wheel. The Flemmings' "arrangement" animates both linear and cyclical time, tracing multiple stages in the evolution of an invention that continues to undergo adjustments at the end of the twentieth century. The sewing machine, itself driven by a wheel, converts a visual pun into a prayer, "May these flowers, sewn in the revolving cycles of God's time, forever renew themselves."

To these yards add George Walker's on Sapelo Island, Georgia, with its revolving fan blade and washing machine drum; Victor Melancon's in Hammond, Louisiana, with its boundaries marked by "spirit writing" on aluminum; Bennie Lusane's clock and guitar towers in Royston, Georgia; Robert D. "Lightnin" Watson's antenna sculptures in Palmer's Crossing, Mississippi; Charlie Greer's painted concrete millstones with cast suns and moons in King's Mountain, North Carolina; Ruby Gilmore's masked facade and monumental fence in Hattiesburg, Mississippi; West and Sue Lathern's backyard extravaganza in Oakman, Alabama; George Kornegay's "sacred mountains" in Brent, Alabama; Henry Jackson's chrome-emblazoned fence in Memphis; Hawkins Bolden's "scarecrows," also in Memphis; Tyree Guyton's Heidelberg project in Detroit; Bob Harper's yard in Houston, Texas; the ones Lizzetta LeFalle-Collins documented in Los Angeles; and those recorded by Robert Farris Thompson and Grey Gundaker in Kentucky, Mississippi, Virginia, Alabama, New York, and Connecticut.

A few miles from Elijah Davenport's homestead, Annie Sturghill dressed her yard in Athens, Georgia, with aluminum foil flags and pie pans, terra-cotta pipes, chrome fender fragments, blue bottle grids, rocks painted white, glass figurines, red plastic cups, white bleach bottles, a quilt wrapped around an upright ironing board, and a copiously expanding array of plastic flowers. "It's my Yard of Colors," she explains. "I look at God's sunshine hitting all this metal and I enjoy it. I don't care if anybody likes what I've got going on here, I enjoy looking at it."

To suggest that the significance of Annie Sturghill's yard is only in the eyes of its beholders is to ignore its place within the continuum of other dressed yards. Its iconography and utility resonate with still more transfinite works whose "energy syndetically derives from host sources external to the work, as such." In this case, "linear, evolutionary growth tends less to dominate than ardent proliferation," while "physical and metaphysical repletion" exposes the dynamics of tradition, not coincidence.[25] The forces of recognition and response that drive these dynamics emerge even more convincingly as specific sites change over time. When one of Sturghill's relatives urged her to do away with the "trash" in front of her house, a neighbor was commissioned to bulldoze the site. But the partial demolition of the "Yard of Colors" only served to expose its deeper secrets. The classic vocabulary of African American yard dressing—ceramic pipes at the corners of the property, stones carried from one's birthplace and painted, a chrome hubcap leaning on a foundation block, a fan blade by the mailbox, a blue bottle grid rotated to form a pristine diamond shape—these elements remained inviolate.

At the same time Sturghill's yard was less a means of protective insulation, like Clarence Burse's or Elijah Davenport's, than it was a "show," a spirited expression of exuberance and virtuosity on her part. If tradition was its "bone," Sturghill's personal aesthetic was its flesh and blood. "I go across the street and I come back and I feel and shape what I want and I go back and shape it again. Whatever I do today and don't like I will do it different tomorrow," she said. The yard was distinctly personal in its feverishly layered compositions that exposed its maker's delight in visual puns and humorous analogies. Less than a week after the yard was destroyed, she redressed it, indulging her passion more insistently than ever. A planter filled with "sprouting" red plastic spoons, upended and stuck in dirt, was "watered" by a stretched sock "pouring" out of a plastic cup dangling from a rosebush. A photograph of marching guards at Buckingham Palace became the backdrop for a collection of chalkware ducks. A turquoise wine bottle embossed with a scalelike pattern became a spectral peacock when Sturghill crowned it with a delicate blue feather. Fragments of figurines were reassembled into witty conjunctions of human and animal parts. The quilt wrapped around the ironing board supplanted the more traditional scarecrow.

Sturghill's chief means of employment was as a housekeeper, and one of her clients had been the Georgia painter Lamar Dodd, whose work she displayed in her living room. She was familiar with the provisions of artists' studios, including the still life assemblages they used to study the interplay of form and light. The iconography of her yard, however, and her fidelity to the tradition of object encoding layered her work with crosscurrents of meaning and intention that extended beyond her personal aesthetic preferences. From her point of view, the license to make art was impossible to separate from religious witness. She might never be called "Reverend" (the honorific version of the title rarely extends to women), but she more than made up for this in the hymns and recitations she performed for the strangers who visited her yard.

To a preacher life's a sermon. To a joker, life's a jest.
To a miser life is money. To a loafer life is rest.
To a soldier life's a battle. To a teacher life's a school.

Life's a great thing to a thinker, but a failure to a fool.
Life is just a long vacation to the man that loves his work.
But it's constantly dodging duties to an everlasting shirk.
To the honest faithful worker life's oh so ever new.
Life is what you make it. Friends, what is life to you?

—*Recited by Annie Sturghill, August 30, 1988*

STOMPIN THE BLUES

Like Annie Sturghill, Dilmus Hall, also of Athens, Georgia, used art to breach the web of containment that threatened to make him invisible. He had held a variety of jobs including a stint as a fabricator of cinder blocks when, sometime in the 1950s, a house fire and a financial setback tested him to the limit. "I went into the side yard with a shotgun and put it to my head. I don't know what happened next except that God had other plans. The gun went off by itself and I had a blackout. When I woke up I saw that I had fallen into a pool of water. I came to and from that time on I didn't drink. And it was a month before I had hearing in my right ear."

After the fire Hall built a new house of cinder blocks and decorated it with bright blue and yellow diamond shapes and concrete bas-reliefs of suns and moons. The porch's roof was bordered with slats whittled into points, rendering the effect of an inverted picket fence. A wooden crucifixion scene was nailed to the top of a support post. The crucifixion shared its station with a set of truncated wooden constructions trimmed with the same blue paint as the house. In one, a spiraling wisteria vine bisected a bentwood arc, like a bow and arrow. The ubiquitous grave-inspired objects associated with African American yard dressing were discreetly scattered about, but they were eventually eclipsed by Hall's more elaborate wood and concrete sculptures. One of these, a life-sized concrete tableau, *The Devil and the Drunk Man*, stood in the side yard facing the street where it served as an occasion for Hall to recite parables such as this one recorded in 1984:

> God asked the devil did he consider his servant, Job. The devil said, "Yes," he'd considered him. But he said if He would take that hedge that He'd built around Job that was his power of protection, he'd cuss you to your face. God said, "OK, he is in your hands. I'll give his body over to you, but his life is my own." Job was afflicted with boils because those boils was of the devil. No quicker than Job saw that his faith could make him whole, then God healed him. Because the devil was of war. He was not of peace. He was of war. The devil was testing him with the war of the flesh. That was the devil's power. Then God took care of Job and healed him.

Hall's honorary title, "Reverend," confirmed his community's active association of art with religious sensibility, but he left no doubt about the way he personally interpreted his role. "I have been an artist all my life," he said, "but the older I got the more I understood about it. Listen, you cannot push your way beyond nature. You can't do that. You got to do what you're gonna do on this side of the state that nature has set for you. I was cut out to be just what I turned out to be, see?"

Hall's most public work, a neighborhood landmark, consisted of a black shoe suspended in a handmade glass box that hung from a metal pipe that was planted by the street curb. A hand-lettered sign identified it as "The Shoe That

Road the Howling Tornado, May 31–1973, in Athens." The storm had wiped out fashionable neighborhoods in Athens, disrupting community life and business for months. When it blew the shoe into Hall's yard, his neighbors warned of ominous consequences. "I'll concentrate on it and I'll know what to do," he responded. Within days, an article appeared in the local newspaper with a photograph of Hall confidently standing next to his new shoe shrine along with a commemorative poem he'd composed for the occasion.

> I am a lonely shoe
> Without a mate. What will I do?
> Over and over as I roll
> Oh tornado you are taking your toll
> If someone would be brave
> To me and my mate he might save
> Sometimes I pass over a limb
> Then I say my chance is slim
> And swinging so high above
> the many demolished buildings
> someone dearly loved
> Over a limb and through a tree
> I say, oh what mercy can be
> I look for a second or so
> At some tall trees that had to go
> Then I look quickly around
> There are dangerous wires all over the ground
> Let all of us pray
> That the next tornado will go another way
> That it will cease to strike here again
> The home of the free and many brave men.

> You may see this shoe at my home, hanging from a glass box, 1001
> Dearing Street. Come and see for yourself. It is free for all to see.
> —*Dilmus Hall.*

In a series of crucifixes from the mid-1980s, Hall transcended the cleverness and charm stereotypically associated with folk art. These are works of stark and searing empathy in which Christ, the two thieves, and "the soldier that pierced his side" confront one another. In one completed shortly before his death in 1987, the head of Christ is made from a wooden ball punctured with an arc of nails and mounted on top of a flat plank. Hall undercoated the figure with silver-colored paint and then poured red and black enamel over it, establishing the image of an open wound that splits the length of the figure. The wire arms, painted black, are inverted from their normal outstretched position. In Hall's version they are bent downwards, resting on either side of the "hips." The lance-bearing soldier is diminutive— nothing more than a black stick with a red top. Except for a toothpick threaded horizontally through the mouth of Christ, this sculpture bears little resemblance to the more overtly representational ones Hall created before the mid-1980s. He explained the toothpick with a story of the Good Thief.

> At that time, people were fearful of the Romans because they were a mean race of people and they was the ones that crucified Christ. When Christ was on the cross, this old Roman king sat on his seat and looked. And the Scripture says it got so dark that you could feel the dark going through your fingers. And he called someone, and they answered him. And he asked the question, "Can you see me?" And they said, "No". Well, that darkness represented the agony that Christ on the cross was going through. So he said, "I can hear you, but I can't see you." And he confessed this way: "Surely the man they had on the cross was the son of God!"
>
> I say I believe that devil was saved because he confessed. Now, there was crucified two other people—one on the right; one on the left. The one on the left criticized Jesus up there on the cross; said, "If thou be the son of God, save yourself and come down off that cross. If you come down, we will believe you. First save *yourself* and then save others!" And the other was in agony. He begged mercy. Said, "Father, if thou go into the kingdom that I've heard you talk about, save me, a sinner." The Bible says Christ quit dying. He quit dying and spoke to that fellow on the right and blessed him for pleading like he did, and he said to him, "This day thou shall be with me in paradise."
>
> See, we had to put that toothpick in his mouth to represent the stain of death. We've got to fix these things so that an onlooker will understand. You see, an artist is a particular instrument.

Dilmus Hall acted on his beliefs with works that were modestly accomplished yet profoundly receptive to "the powers of invocation." Thus the local focus of his life did not lessen the powerful resonances of his art. Hall's statement that the artist is "a particular instrument" is telling in that he consciously translated the powers of myth into his own contingent circumstances, converting the spiritual range of his experiences from intimate to epic scale. "The choice between good and evil is preceded by an even more fundamental choice," says Adin Steinsaltz, a leading scholar of religion, "whether to give spiritual or moral expression to the contradiction inherent in one's humanness or to try to ignore that contradiction." Indeed, "the question should not be how to escape the perpetual struggle but rather what form to give it, at what level to wage it."[26]

THE SHAPES OF TIME

Robert Plant Armstrong's comment that the work-in-invocation tends to exist in "an ambient of time" takes on new meaning in light of Steinsaltz's statement, for it is only in time that the "spiritual or moral" dimensions of art begin to be released. As Annie Sturghill indicated, the passage of time compresses experience into a core of perception that characterizes one's life and work. Art is a material sign of this process and, as such, operates in a dimension that is often described as "transcendental." This can be difficult to grasp, Armstrong continues, because "our explicit Western preoccupation with 'pure form' tends to assert our determination to endow time with the shapes of space rather than the other way around."[27]

Yet another artist from Georgia, Zebedee "Z. B." Armstrong, of McDuffie County, explicitly pursued these tensions. The objects he collected were almost always round: electric fan blades, stereo turntables, jar and paint can lids, automobile wheel casings. These he enshrined in wooden armatures, painting them white and "taping" (as in "binding" or "wrapping") them with a grid of black and red lines. He carefully labeled the orientation of each: "top," "bottom," "sides," "back," "inside," "outside." He supplemented the grid with sequences of numbers—usually from one to a hundred—and lists of hours, days, months, and years. This incantatory practice reminded him, he said, of "the sun, the moon, and the stars" and of "the final days when time have been, but it won't be no more." "I praise God in everything I do," he said.

In Z. B. Armstrong's universe the dichotomy between "time's arrow and time's cycle," between the "intelligibility of distinct and irreversible events" and "the intelligibility of timeless order and lawlike structure,"[28] is resolved in the godly nature of man and woman which endows them with powers of discernment appropriate to their inherited responsibilities. There are other instances, however, in which discernment of this sort required a more circumspect approach as well as the ability to recover and integrate fragments of lost histories. In 1937 Dr. Lindsay told Harry Middleton Hyatt:

> You got leading stars. You have a star in the East, a star in the West, a star in the North, and a star in the South. We have a star in the East that represents our first queen, Elizabeth. It is a prodigal star of Gathrun. Why, it was the leader when Christ was born. It was the first bright star that shinin' brighter than the lilies of the valley the night the Newborn Child was born.

The star in the West follows the Gerath of the Canaan. It is the evening star; it is the main star. . . . Gerath of the Canaan was a great man, just like a king. The star of the North, well, it is a star showin' it is a bright star, but it is small. It is a quivering star. It is a star [that] represents the heading of the whole world. The fallen star which that leads in the South represents the bodies of water of the European countries of Africa. . . . This is why it is a fallen star. The star that's in the East, it rises between two and three o'clock in the morning. The star in the North, it rises when the sea tide rises. It is a star that works with the wind. It shows to be more attached at the wheel of the earth that the world do go around. . . .

When the great kings was prophesidin, one went north, one went south, and the one whom that was in the North, he soon came, you see, by being a high man—he soon came to a rath of sea level. The one that was in the South, he had to go seven decks down. See, this old world we're on, here, it's seven decks down; and the South is seven decks below sea level, you see. And, on that occasion, that's why this star is a fallen star.[29]

Dr. Lindsay's mastery of converging mythologies serves a dual purpose here. The parable of the Leading Stars is designed to brace the listener aesthetically while exhorting him to take account of moral discrepancies. Lindsay's practice as a healer addressed these discrepancies on a daily basis as he synthesized elements from an African religious heritage with the demands of living in the depression-era South.

"The mythic is the pregnant radiance suffusing a work," says Robert Plant Armstrong, "the synchronic is its faceted brilliance. . . . It is a stone cast into the waters of time, the rings of its impact ever more broadly encompassing."[30] This notion of time cycling and encompassing is manifest in "the four moments of the Sun" and inscribed on grave markers and homes across the country, including Dilmus Hall's.[31] Says Lonnie Holley:

The Spirit have gave it to me like this. A sunshine for each time period, to show the difference in them. . . . It seems like one big cycle from within, like a spring. You start at the innermost part of the spring and you move outward as you grow. And as you grow, this materialistic body, which is flesh, takes its place, acts, then it falls back to the beginning to re-create itself. Man was supposed to know all about all the things that had been created on earth from one time period all the way to another. God has blessed us, man and woman; she's the continuation of mankind. The children turn into the world itself.

Wyatt MacGaffey states that the Kikongo term for this sign can also mean "star" and that such ideograms are "integrated" signs in European terms, perceived as stable essences, whereas in Africa they are a "statement of relationships."[32] This distinction is crucial because it points to the means by which material and intellectual exchange drives the powers of syndesis (the connective and conjunctive powers that relate one form of expression to another) and accounts, in no small measure, for the way time activates the moral dimensions of art. "The syndetic work is unconfined," says Armstrong. "Its power is, in marked measure, the power of time itself, not only the time in which it is enacted, but time absolute—utter continuity."[33] In coming to terms with the irreversible events of the past in relationship to life's ever-repeating cycles of renewal, the individual stands a chance of maintaining this continuity.

Lonnie Holley expressed this discovery by deliberately invoking the ecstatic. "You can see time as it develops itself. It develops itself with power. Time is standing still if one is not moving in it, and if one is moving in it, time moves so fast that we cannot keep up with it. We can speed through time, and then we can be in time and not move at all. Man could stay still, and time won't even matter. But if man is moving in time and trying to keep up with time itself, then he'll somehow or another be like time, outrun himself. Because there is no distance; there is no limit; no space hidden."

"The expression, 'the child is the father of the man,'" says Wole Soyinka, the contemporary Nigerian dramatist and Nobel laureate, "becomes, within the context of this time structure, not merely a metaphor of development, one that is rooted in a system of individuation, but a proverb of human continuity which is not unidirectional." "If we may put the same thing in fleshed-out cognitions, life, present life, contains within it manifestations of the ancestral, the living, and the unborn. All are vitally within the intimations and affectiveness of life, beyond mere abstract conceptualism."[34] "No philosophy nor ontological fanaticism can take that away. It is also an affective social principle which intertwines multiple existences."[35]

CULTURAL PRIORITIES

Artists are acutely aware of these "multiple existences," but translating them into "affective social principles" is a transgenerational process over which they have limited control. Duchamp spoke often of this. "In the creative act," he said, "the artist goes from intention to realization through a chain of totally subjective reactions. His struggle towards realization is a series of efforts, pains, satisfactions, refusals, decisions, which also cannot and must not be fully self-conscious, at least on the esthetic plane. The result of this struggle is a difference between the intention and its realization, a difference which the artist is not aware of. . . . The creative act takes on another aspect when the spectator experiences the phenomenon of transmutation."[36]

Gianfranco Baruchello, Duchamp's friend and protégé, must have been thinking of this statement when he described his mentor as a "time machine," and he might also have been thinking of twentieth-century America when he tried to imagine what happens inside a "cultural cocktail shaker." Do all of the elements manage

> to coalesce into a sarcasm and some new form for a "modest pro-
> posal," do they shape themselves into nodes that explode into polar-
> ities where all sorts of contradictions are yoked together, do they
> excite extremely complex thoughts that create philosophical syn-
> thesis, illuminations, moments of awareness, and little epiphanies
> that last only for a second, do they constitute a mechanism for cre-
> ating complications, and miming the dream as though to make par-
> allel dreams exist contemporaneously while exciting the absurd on
> the one hand and the paralogical on the other?[37]

These issues are not confined to the past. Nor are they merely the famil-iar fixtures of postmodernist speculation. However ironic and contradictory they may at first appear to be, they awaken a deeper impulse toward the rec-onciliation of once-divergent realities. Embedded in the works discussed in this chapter, and articulated by those who created them, are distinct possi-bilities that inform the lives of twentieth- and twenty-first-century Americans in ways yet to be fully estimated.

The issue here is not whether the banality of the familiar depreciates the mythic and the spiritual, but whether the mythic and the spiritual can act on this banality and transform its meaning. If so, then the "ritual formality" of Duchamp's bicycle wheel and the "ceremonial dignity"[38] of Dilmus Hall's "Shoe That Road the Howling Tornado" are landmarks along the same con-tinuum, while the convergence of African American vernacular art and the emerging aspirations of a new generation offers at least a hint of the ways in which image and effect might once again be reconciled.

5 SACRED PLACES AND HOLY GROUND

West African Spiritualism at Stagville Plantation

Alice Eley Jones

INTRODUCTION

T HE CREATION OF SACRED PLACES AND HOLY GROUND was vital for the connection to community, nature, and God. The material symbols of that connection and the powers contained within are ever present and everlasting. Traditional healers teach and guide initiates so that they might teach others to be reborn spiritually. Spiritual birth is necessary for the melding of family and community to the dead, the living, and the yet unborn. The cowrie shell, medicine stick, and divining rods represent man's need to be connected to the powers of the universe. Spiritual symbols, sacred places, and holy ground strike a cosmic balance. One does not function without the other. They become the pillars which support human spirituality.

THE DEAD, THE LIVING, AND THE YET UNBORN

Ten years have passed since my first summer at Stagville Preservation Center in Durham, North Carolina. I arrived at Stagville that long-ago summer as a graduate student majoring in history at North Carolina Central University. I had been awarded the Stagville Fellowship which afforded me six weeks of study and research at the site of the former plantation.

I was most anxious to create a new way to interpret the African presence beyond genealogy and slave labor. I wanted to speak to their humanity, their spirit, and to their connection to other groups who had also settled in the North Carolina piedmont.

On my very first day at the center I was shown a wooden stick which had been resting in a corner of my office. Something within me knew the walking stick was important, but I had nothing concrete with which to work. Only the feeling that the stick was speaking to me. Perhaps unraveling the language of the stick would help me to better interpret the person who created it.

I remembered having seen walking sticks in John W. Blassingame's *The Slave Community—Plantation Life in the Antebellum South*. I checked my worn copy and found the sticks on page 38. I reread chapter 1 in its entirety and decided that my research would focus on West African spiritual survivals at Stagville.

The following week I invited a friend, Dr. Faheem C. Ashanti, to tour Stagville Center and asked for his assistance. Dr. Ashanti is a counseling psychologist and a traditional healer and priest. We toured the site, but he informed me that several tours would be necessary in private. He also would require the freshly shed skins of blacksnakes. I was instructed never to touch the skins but to lift them using a wooden stick or tree branch into a holding bag. I was never to accept a skin from anyone else. I alone could retrieve the skin and place it in the bag. The staff at Stagville was very cooperative and never failed to inform me of a skin's location. Stagville Preservation Center does not want for the presence of blacksnakes, and Dr. Ashanti was most grateful for this bounty.

That summer was a summer of studying Zora Neale Hurston's *Tell My Horse* as I unlocked the mystery of the walking stick's preparation. I began to understand the uneasy feelings I had whenever I entered the slave cabins. I studied books on African religion and spiritualism. I learned how to pour libation as a sign of respect to the ancestors.

Before I poured my first libation, I had become troubled by nightmares about snakes. I had become fearful of my work with Dr. Ashanti and had declined his offer of training as a traditional healer.

One day I drove to the site of the slave cabins alone and poured libations. I raised the cup of wine high over my head and asked a blessing for the dead, the living, and the yet unborn. While I still declined Dr. Ashanti's invitation to become a traditional healer, my sense of dread and nightmares were replaced with self-confidence and a sense of historical purpose.

I have come to view the dead, the living, and the yet unborn as the West African Trinity. Through the years I have traveled to many plantations searching for evidence of West African spiritualism, and I have always found symbols and signs and retention in their descendants. Generally descendants do not know that they are carrying on African traditions; they only know it feels right and their parents did the same thing before them.

To understand the African, one has to understand the spiritual nature of the African, for the African, the European, and the Native American all held cultural concepts of magic and religion which they melded together in the North Carolina piedmont. In its landscape, vegetation, and weather the piedmont looked more like Africa to the Africans than Europe to the Europeans. West African spiritualism thrived because wherever the African went the spirits accompanied him. He was a total spiritual being. The African, European, and the Native American were connected to one another by the magic of their religions.

WEST AFRICAN SPIRITUALISM

The dead, the living, and the yet unborn: this was the singular path every traditional African walked. The journey was preordained and began before birth. It was a matter of fate. Life was to be lived in the here and now. There was no hope for a future or a better life. Heaven is not hoped for nor hell feared in the hereafter. The African was the center of his religion, with the power to bless, curse, and honor the ancestors.[1]

In traditional religions there were no creeds to be recited; instead, the creeds were written in the heart of the individual, and each African was himself a living creed of his own religion. Where the individual was, there was his religion, for he was a religious being. His journey began before birth and continued after death.[2]

Traditional religions had no missionaries to propagate them, and one individual did not preach his religion to another. There was no conversion from one traditional religion to another. Each society had its own religious system, and the propagation of such a complete system would involve propagating the entire life of the people concerned.[3]

What Africans did was motivated by what they believed, and what they believed sprang from what they did and experienced. Belief and action in African traditional society could not be separated: they belonged to a single whole.[4]

Children were born both physically and religiously. The rites of birth and childhood introduced the child to the corporate community, but this was only an introduction. The child was considered a passive being and still had a long way to go before being confirmed as an adult. He grew out of childhood and entered into adulthood physically, socially, and spiritually. This was also a change from passive to active membership in the community. Most African people had rites and ceremonies to mark this great change, but a few did not observe initiation and puberty rites. The initiation of the young was one of the key moments in the rhythm of individual life, which is also the rhythm of the corporate group in which what happened to the single youth happened corporately to the parents, the relatives, the neighbors, and the living-dead.[5]

Initiation rites have many symbolic meanings, in addition to the physical drama and impact. The youth are ritually introduced to the art of communal living. This happens when they withdraw from other people to live alone in the forest or in specifically prepared dwellings away from the villages. They go through a period of withdrawal from society, absence from home, during which time they receive secret instruction before they are allowed to rejoin their relatives at home. This is a symbolic experience of the process of dying, living in the spirit world, and being reborn (resurrected). The rebirth, that is, the act of rejoining their families, emphasizes and dramatizes that the young people are now new, they have new personalities, they have lost their childhood, and in some societies they even receive completely new names.[6]

Another great significance of the rites is to introduce the candidates to adult life: they are now allowed to share in the full privileges and duties of the community. They enter into the state of responsibility: they inherit new rights, and new obligations are expected of them by society. This incorporation into adult life also introduces them to the life of the living-dead as well as the life of those yet to be born. The initiation rites prepare young people in matters of sexual life, marriage, procreation, and family responsibilities. They are henceforth allowed to shed their blood for their country and to plant their biological seeds so that the next generation can begin to arrive.[7]

Initiation rites have a great educational purpose. The occasion often marks the beginning of acquiring knowledge which is not otherwise accessible to those who have not been initiated. It is a period of awakening to many things, a period of dawn for the young. They learn to endure hardships, they learn to live with one another, they learn to obey, they learn the secrets and mysteries of the man-woman relationship, and in some areas, especially West Africa, they join secret societies each of which has its own secrets, activities, and language.[8]

It became increasingly evident to me that the very nature of the slave trade ensured the retention of West African spiritualism in the New World. Chattel slavery was a labor-intensive enterprise which depended upon youthful and strong African boys and men between the ages of fifteen and thirty-five. The same could be said for the female captives as well, although females generally did not fill the holds of slave ships as did the vast numbers of male captives. However, slave ships did transport huge numbers of initiated men and women to the New World, men and women who understood the spiritual dangers of being separated from the living-dead and the yet unborn. Their separation from their ancestral land was therefore a separation of the physical as well as the spiritual. The collective memories of creating sacred places and holy ground was simply transported to the New World. It was and is a religion of secrets, symbols, and ceremonies.

The adult African who was enslaved without benefit of rites of passage was forever a child and unworthy of any rights of adulthood. Even if he escaped he would have to be initiated as in the case of West African Malidoma Patrice Somé who wrote:

> When I was four years old, my childhood and my parents were taken
> from me when I was literally kidnapped from my home by a French

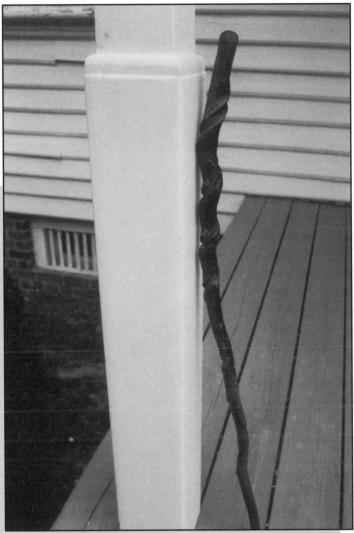

Medicine stick discovered wedged in a wall of the Bennehan/Cameron house, Stagville Preservation Center, Durham, North Carolina. (Courtesy of Historic Stagville of the North Carolina Department of Cultural Resources; photo: Kenneth McFarland)

Alice Eley Jones pouring a libation at Horton Grove quarters at Stagville. (Courtesy of Historic Stagville of the North Carolina Department of Cultural Resources)

Professor Victor Maafeo, a native of Ghana, conducting a libation ceremony at Horton Grove quarters at Stagville. (Courtesy of Historic Stagville of the North Carolina Department of Cultural Resources; photo: Kenneth McFarland)

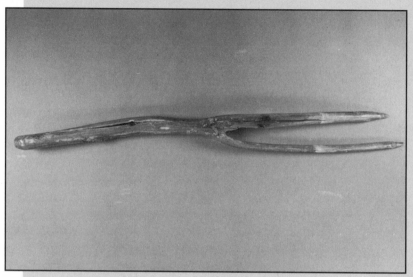

Divining rod discovered in the wall of Horton Grove slave cabin at Stagville. (Courtesy of Historic Stagville of the North Carolina Department of Cultural Resources; photo: Kenneth McFarland)

Cowrie shell discovered in the wall of Stagville slave cabin. (Courtesy of Historic Stagville of the North Carolina Department of Cultural Resources; photo: Kenneth McFarland)

Jesuit missionary who had befriended my father. For the next fifteen years I was in a boarding school, far away from my family, and forced to learn about the white man's reality, which included lessons in history, geography, anatomy, mathematics, and literature. All of these topics were presented with a good dose of Christianity and its temperamental god who forced everyone to live in constant fear of his wrath.

At the age of twenty I escaped and went back to my people, but found that I no longer fit into the tribal community. I risked my life to undergo the Dagara initiation and thereby return to my people. During that month long ritual, I was integrated back into my own reality as well as I could be.

For me, initiation had eliminated my confusion, helplessness, and pain and opened the door to a powerful understanding of the link between my own life purpose and the will of my ancestors. I had come to understand the sacred relationship between children and old people, between fathers and their adolescent sons, between mothers and daughter. I knew especially why my people have such a deep respect for old age, and why a strong, functioning community is essential for the maintenance of an individual's sense of identity, meaning, and purpose.[9]

The millions of enslaved Africans who eventually came to live in the New World were equipped to re-create the secret holy ceremonies and practices of their homeland. The old men and women moved freely among the black and white plantation inhabitants. The blacks usually understood and were able to interpret the secret symbols, while for the most part they were hidden in plain view of whites.

To non-Africans, sculpture may well seem the greatest of the African traditional arts—because that is the art they most often see. But to Africans, the most important art is dancing. Dance fuses the two central concerns of African life: religion and community relationships. It is sometimes ritual, in observance of birth and death, puberty and marriage; sometimes festive, honoring the special days of the gods and spirits who guard the village. Sometimes it is just recreational. Except for esoteric events, dancing usually involves the whole village. Men, women, and even little children—bobbing on the fringes of the adult dancers like corks on a swelling tide—move in response to complex and compelling rhythms. The source of the rhythm is almost invariably drums, for drumming is the music of Africa. The most astonishing element in African drumming is not sound, however, but rhythm.[10]

When the law silenced the drums, Africans transferred and preserved the rhythm of their drums using their hands, feet, and voices, as is evidenced by the number of work songs, river chants, railroad songs, and field songs witnessed by whites through the years and generally misunderstood. In time their meaning and purpose also faded from the collective memories of blacks as well. However, the African could not escape the rhythm of his speech pattern, his walking gait, his body language.

For most enslaved West Africans, escape and eventual return to family and community were a very remote possibility. Within the New World, the American South, and Stagville plantation there arose a system of education for Africans to be initiated into secret societies which addressed their spiritual needs beyond Christianity.

The education of Voodoo priests and root doctors in the United States and the Western world occurs within a different environmental setting than that of Africa. Instead of formal schools and large groups, the training takes place in small private voodoo temples; most often, in the private homes of the voodoo priests and root doctors. This instruction is nearly always on a one-to-one basis, and the ancient tradition of secrecy is maintained and required.[11]

If you ask a Voodoo priest or root doctor where he obtained his knowledge, he will tell you he received it from his father or grandfather, for it is handed down from father to son like any other valuable; or he will tell you that one of his older friends taught him due to close friendship, or that knowledge of root work is known by most people.[12]

Dr. Ashanti described the Voodoo priest or root doctor initiation process as an example of the nine-day ceremony. Note the importance of the snakeskin:

> Upon the completion of the basic education program, the aspiring Voodoo priests and root doctors must undergo a rigorous initiation process into the profession. The initiate generally enters a week of seclusion in which he or she eats only a special diet of herbs, roots, and fruit, in addition to performing secret activities of physical and mental ordeals. This initiation process if often supervised by several Voodoo priests and root doctors. At the end of the initiation the individual is given a spiritual name and is ready to begin his or her internship.
>
> The following account is an example of nine-day initiation ceremony of a Voodoo priest. The most important act of a Voodoo priest is to approach the altar of God. This cannot be accomplished without the crown of power, which is earned through initiation. In this case the crown of power was a blessed snake skin. The education of a Voodoo priest without the crown of power is like receiving a college diploma without the four years of classroom instruction. It is useless.
>
> For six days and nights, the initiate had to avoid sexual inter-

course, normal meals, evil thoughts, alcoholic drinks, and tobacco. This ceremony took place in the home of a Voodoo priest. The initiate was required to wear a new pair of underwear every five hours of the day. At the end of the sixth day, he was crowned and dressed with three blessed snake skins. He was moved, blindfolded, to another location for the next three days. He was undressed and make to lie for three days on a special bed surrounded with nine lighted candles. No regular food was given to him during this time. It was here that he was introduced to the master Voodoo priest and a most frightening large live snake crawling freely about the room.

The three snake skins he received during the first six days were made into special garments for him to wear, and this is all he wore for the next three days. One skin was coiled into a crown for his head, one wrapped for his shoulders, and one made into a girdle for his hips and thighs. All the places of the body have a special importance. These special garments were then placed upon the altar of the great God, the throne of the snake. The snake crawled upon the special garments to give them his power.

He lay upon the bed without speaking or eating for three days waiting to be accepted or rejected by the great God. His spirit left his body and went on the long search for spiritual knowledge and food. He had many psychic experiences. On the ninth day he was awakened from his visions and given a sacred bath and a powerful holy name. The master priest painted secret symbols of the Gods upon his body in the colors of red, black, and yellow. Then he was dressed in the robe of a Voodoo priest and seated in a chair. Other Voodoo priests came into the room and performed secret rituals, but none talked to him, nor was he allowed to speak to them.

The index finger of his left hand was cut to draw blood which was put in a small cup. The blood was mixed with holy wine. The other priests also took blood from their fingers and did likewise with a cup. He drank the mixture from their cup and they drank from his cup. This ritual was followed by a splendid meal of all types of food. There was much joy and laughter during this midday celebration. However, the final ceremony was to take place in a rural area, deep in the woods at midnight. At the appointed time, the initiate and the other Voodoo priests all traveled by car to the final location.

Deep in the woods was a clearing with four lighted candles, representing the four corners of the world and the four winds. The initiate was taught the secret chant, in an African language, of the Gods. On nine separate sheets of blessed paper, his name and petition was written nine times. A black goat was led to the center of the circle of priests, and its throat was slit. The blood of the goat was swept vigorously back and forth around the body of the goat. The nine sheets of paper were then presented to the great God of all creation and the eight lesser Gods by the master Voodoo priest. The earth God and mother of all mankind was appeased. A white candle was set upon the grave of the goat and the initiate was accepted by God as a new Voodoo priest.[13]

The African slave trade, traditionally viewed in terms of the physical removal of African bodies from the physical aspects of African geography, forced the strong sense of African spiritualism which survived, underground. There was no holy book or sacred churchyard left behind in Africa. All that the traditional African needed for the creation of holy ground and sacred places he found on the plantations and in the cities of the South. Initiated Africans who landed in the New World were thus fully equipped to continue time-honored traditions which connected them to the dead, the living, and the yet unborn. Hidden in plain view of non-Africans who had little knowledge of West African spiritualism and its connections to dance, rhythmic body clapping, singing, architecture, and artisan crafts.

In comparing the shotgun house with Voodoo temples I found remarkable structural designs which are very similar. The front porch may also play a spiritual role rather than an architectural one in African building practices. Dr. Ashanti addressed the architectural design of Voodoo temples:

> In comparing the basic architectural design and inner appearance of modern Voodoo temples, especially in Haiti, we find a remarkable similarity to the temples of the African Egyptian Mystery system. The basic architectural shape of a Voodoo temple is either oblong or rectangular. In Haiti, there are four main temple sections, (1) the hounfour, the temple itself, including material structure; (2) the peristyle, the roofed area with a single centerpost, where most ceremonies occur; (3) the doors in the wall that lead to the bagi, the inner sanctuary of the temple, and the room containing the altar for the Gods; (4) the private room of the priests. Although the structure is of crude materials, wood, tin, mud bricks, and thatched roofs, the entrances, doors, walls, and ceilings are decorated with symbols of the Gods in the colors of red and black. The symbols of heavenly elements, the stars, moon, sun, and planets, are displayed on the ceiling of the bagi, or inner sanctuary.[14]

The ability to create holy places and sacred ground forced the enslaved African to become creative in his desire to have spiritual protection and spiritual connection. Evidenced by three discoveries at Stagville Preservation Center, some of the practices continued well into the 1850s.

WEST AFRICAN BUILDING TRADITIONS
AT STAGVILLE PLANTATION

The enslaved West Africans who helped to construct the Bennehan-Cameron house, slave quarters, and outbuildings at Stagville came from cultures which possessed very old building traditions. Like most Old World building traditions, certain precautions had to be taken to ensure protection from the many harmful spirits which could possibly be found living in one's home.

In symbolism a house is expressed as an enclosed space and also as a receptacle which, like the chest and the womb, is a female in character. As a secret enclosure it also symbolizes the repository of all wisdom. Within the home, fire symbolizes the soul of the family and the sense of domestic continuity. The threshold or doorway serves as the boundary between the foreign and domestic worlds. The walls also symbolize protection from the forces outside the home. The orientation of a building with the sun was of immense symbolic importance.[15] The structures with entrances which faced east or west were in most demand.

Although a house may be protected by magical and religious rites from the assaults of external spirit forces, the house is also, paradoxically, the abode of domestic elementals who have one common feature: they are capricious, troublesome, hard to please, and even spiteful. But it is in matters connected with death that the magic of the house is most apparent. When one of the family is due to pass over, according to tradition, the family ghosts discreetly return and await the reunion.[16]

Little else of the potent magic of the building trade has survived in the modern world. The African over the years adopted and maintained the building magic of Europeans. New homes are still blessed by priests and ministers, and public buildings and bridges are still ritually opened, and the first sod of a new site turned with a new spade.[17]

In my 1986 graduate thesis I documented three spiritual symbols discovered in various buildings at the former Stagville plantation. I wrote:

> In 1799 Richard Bennehan added the present two story section onto his house at Stagville. In the dark of the night a slave wedged a crooked walking stick between the two sections. The stick was placed to bring evil spirits to the Bennehan family.
>
> The walking stick was not discovered until February 1977 when workmen discovered it still wedged between the two sections of the house. Curiously, a large black snake was resting beside the stick when it was rediscovered.

The hickory stick has a spiral indention from its tip to its crown. It is three feet in length, and the exterior is smooth to the touch. The smooth texture was obtained by roasting the tree limb in hot coals until the bark slipped off. The spiral represented a snake, the symbol of Damballah, a West African god whose signature is the snake.[18]

The walking stick was wedged between the two sections of the Bennehan house which face east in one direction and west in the opposite direction. This secret method of laying a curse permitted the diviner the luxury of calling forth the spirits without being in their vicinity.

The disappearance of livestock was almost always attributed to the slave's appetite for fresh meat. In retrospect, however, animal sacrifice was a practice associated with divining spirits. Animals may have been ceremoniously slaughtered and sacrificed to summon any number of spirits the diviner deemed appropriate. The body would have been buried deep in the woods as to avoid detection.

Plantation slaves attended church at the Fairntosh Chapel, but attending a white church and listening to a white minister had little to do with slave religion. The religion of the slaves was based on complete spirit possession and that was not possible with the tame sermons heard in the white church. Spirit possession was the only way to please God, and this was the driving force behind the secret religious ceremonies where the slave could sing, dance, and shout in such a frenzy until the spirit entered his body.

In 1851 plantation slaves constructed four cabins and the Paul Cameron barn at the Horton Grove area at Stagville. In 1980 a divining rod was discovered nailed to the brick nogging behind the wooden planks of the exterior wall. The mortar gives evidence to the fact that the rod was placed in the house at the time of construction. West African tradition holds that family spirits have to be moved when villagers move from one place to another.

In 1977 a cowrie shell was discovered in the hearth at the site of one of the original slave cabins to the rear of the Bennehan house. The cowrie shell was used for money in Guinea, located on the West African coast.[19] In addition to monetary and artistic purposes, the cowrie shell is also used to ensure spiritual guidance over bodies of water.

CONCLUSION

Walking sticks, divining rods, and cowrie shells represent but a small harvest of the West African spiritualism which dots southern landscape. The South is a region built primarily by enslaved Africans who possessed an ancient building tradition. A working knowledge of these traditions, coupled with modern X-ray technology, may reveal more hidden symbols.

Traditional African people viewed nature and their role in the universe as one of harmony and balance. There were forces which disrupted this balance from time to time and threatened to disconnect the African from the dead, the living, and the yet unborn. But the African understood his connection to his Supreme Creator, the mother earth, the rivers, and the heavenly planets. To maintain constant protection, balance, harmony, and spiritual connection, he became the main repository of spiritual wisdom.

Removed from his ancestral home, he nevertheless spoke to his spirits in his ironwork, wood carving, weaving, and other artisan skills. In his architecture, secret societies, and the work of his hands he has made the southern landscape a holy and sacred place.

The Old World Africans chose to create sacred places and holy ground in the New World as symbols of spiritual power and control. Had the slaveholder been able to control the spiritual aspect of the African's life completely, the dominion over his human property would have made the African truly docile. When time and opportunity presented themselves, sacred symbols and signs became part of who Africans were in the New World. For the most part, their meanings are now faded from traditional history. African American homes and yards abound with African characteristics of expression which still speak to the power and the protection of the ancestors.

The nature of West African spiritualism is privacy and secrecy. One may enter only through initiation. A small number of symbols may become common knowledge, but the deeper connections are always held in trust. The root doctor and the Voodoo priest thus play the vital role of teacher and gatekeeper to the dead, the living, and the yet unborn. Those born outside the traditions rarely learn their secrets. Those who are initiated rarely reveal them.

The traditional carver creates very important religious pieces and usually, but not always, holds a very exalted place in a community, along with the blacksmith, who may also be a carver. Except for utilitarian pieces like mortars and pestles, their work was commissioned by customers rather than carved in advance for sale in the market.

The African wood-carver is not considered an artist by his community. He may be a farmer who carves or a smith who is endowed with magical powers. There exists between the wood-carver and the blacksmith a special spiritual connection. The iron ax, the adze, the chisel, and the knife are usually made by local blacksmiths. The tools of the wood-carver are considered as sacred objects and are not freely handled by community or family members.

The responsibility for understanding the operation of forces issuing from divine power, and of controlling them in a meaningful way, lies in the hands and power of his medicine stick. It is the priest who communicates the need for a certain form to the carver if it is to have some spiritual endowment.

Secret societies, supporting the spirit, maintain standards of behavior by special initiation tests, rituals for many occasions, and oaths of secrecy. They supervise morality, uphold traditions, and dispense justice. They set standards for art forms from birth through puberty, marriage, and death. Masks, sculptures in the form of ancestor figures, fetishes, dolls, medicine sticks, and ritual implements (rattles and drums) conform to these traditions.

African art gives form to the supernatural and invisible spirits. It is the African way of living in the physical world. The African makes no distinction between his art and his crafts; he lives with what he wears, uses, and creates. It exists because it came before him and is now given to him. In turn he will pass it on to the next generation. Here again, the dead, the living, and the yet unborn are an intimate part of everyday life in traditional Africa.

The wood-carver must be on intimate terms with the blacksmith and the spirits of his chosen tree. He must also understand the characteristics of wood, the use of the tools, and the stylistic language of his community. His carvings must express his automatic, spontaneous, and instinctive spiritual impressions.

Carved sticks are usually admired by the members of the community as symbols of power, taste, and social position. Some signify that their owners have undergone the process of initiation to become rulers or priests and therefore are entitled to the rights and privileges of spiritual leadership.

The various human and animal images carved on sticks are chosen for their natural traits or for connections they are believed to have with the spirit world. Crocodiles are known for their patience, dogs for their intelligence. Warthogs are believed to have a special relationship to spirits. Human heads may represent intelligence or a specific ancestor who can aid the priest. Birds represent the form of the witch.

In the United States medicine sticks carved with serpents are often called conjure sticks. The priest or root doctor is often called "Doc." The reptiles on a stick are associated with illness and are so powerful it is deemed safe only for the priest to touch. In the United States, as in Africa, only the initiated may possess such a stick. The medicine stick is the symbol of the power the priest has in connection with the dead, the living, and the yet unborn.

Eclectic Africans used charms less by category than by what they actually seemed to do. Some of the most common African charms and their uses are listed here.[22]

Twisted copper rings	Prevent snakebites
Palm-frond archways	Shield village from disease
Pieces of straw	Protect crops from harm
Bundles of feathers	Guard occupants of a room
Raffia brooms	Keep away burglars
Animal carvings	Ensure a good hunt
Animal teeth	Keep off wild animals
Iron bracelets	Promote fertility
Bundle of sticks	Guard the home
Divining rods	Seek protection from ancestors
Bamboo whistles	Defend against witchcraft
Goatskin pouches	Ward off illness
Chewing sticks	Prevent quarrels
Cowrie shell	Protection
Heavy anklets	Protect weak children
Staffs	Give power to owner

PART 2

Symbolic Geographies,
Contestation, and Reclamation

6 SOUTH OF THE NORTH NORTH OF THE SOUTH

Spatial Practice in David Bradley's *The Chaneyville Incident*

George L. Henderson

> I take space to be the central fact to man born in America,
> from Folsom cave to now. I spell it large because it
> comes large here. Large, and without mercy.
> —*Charles Olson*, Call Me Ishmael

> New York has become as Virginia.
> —*Frederick Douglass*, My Bondage and My Freedom

INTRODUCTION: SITUATED, SPATIAL PRACTICE

A THIRD OF THE WAY into David Bradley's "historical reconstruction" of rural Pennsylvania in *The Chaneysville Incident*, John Washington (first-person narrator, occasional protagonist, and a young black historian expatriated to Philadelphia) recollects something about his father, Moses Washington: "Once he had descended [from the attic] and grabbed me by the hand and dragged me down the stairs and out the back door and on a long and exhausting and silent tour of the Hill, hauling me by the hand up one street and down another, again and again, for two solid hours, without saying a single word, and when he was finished with whatever it was he was doing he had picked me up and kissed me wetly, and there had been tears in his eyes."[1]

This chapter is concerned with the "whatever it was" Moses Washington was doing on that march in their small south-central Pennsylvania town. It argues for a reading of the novel through activities that I call spatial, or situated, practice. Spatial practice, as the above example hints, is always double-edged. It indicates in this case that while Moses and all of the black characters in *Chaneysville* are exiled to the Hill, the Hill is nonetheless that worrisome site called home. These are characters who would understand, though in different and conflicting ways, that "we are born into relationships that are always based in a place," as Madan Sarup writes. And they would understand, though circumspectly, that if this is also a place of exile, then "exile can be deadening but it can also be very creative."[2]

The basic assumption driving my analysis is that people live their lives within social relations that are indeed made and embedded in space. This is simply to say that geography is social, that the social has a material expression in landscapes which in turn help make social relations stick. But the chapter also assumes that no form of power, no spatial constitution of power, is complete. This dialectic—that the very terrain of subjugation can also be won as a terrain of partial liberation, that our very bodies constrain us but are yet the site of our living—seems to me to be the riddle at the heart of that manic, circular father and son tour.[3] As an adult John Washington would himself comment on this way of seeing the world. Early in the novel he expounds upon modern mass transportation systems, wryly observing that because each mode—plane, train, and bus—marks and shapes class and race relations, together they give the lie to the very notion of the popular, the mass, the democratic. "Even the most efficient society loses control" of the democratic illusions it fosters, he says. It is in this very passage, however, that John takes one of those buses back to his rural, small-town beginnings; back to nurse Old Jack, his "Uncle," through a final, fatal illness. That is, the bus provides John with agency just as it marks his social self.[4] Once again then there is this heaping up of spatial meaning and practice in the course of everyday life: social spaces are concretions of given social relations and are appropriated as tools for personal projects. This is what is meant by spatial, situated practice.[5]

There are endless examples upon which to draw (and I also want to show in various instances that African American signifying practice can double as spatial practice).[6] Accordingly, many tantalizing ones must remain undeveloped. Instead, short of an exhaustive review of spatial practice, it should be emphasized that nothing happens in the novel without the border between North and South being the context, the sine qua non, within and against which the many spatial practices of *Chaneysville* occur. Spatial practices are often very much about the fact that there is no clean line between North and South, that the border is in reality a zone, a landscape in itself, with its own dangers and its own opportunities, too. This zone, the fictional "South County" just a stone's throw from the Maryland line, may be more accurately spoken of as a kind of inversion, in that it lies, in Du Bois's words, "south of the North, yet north of the South." Within this landscape there is no line that can be crossed easily into safety, no ground that can be tread

upon lightly, no past that can be demarcated irreducibly or returned to inno-
cently. Indeed these would be impossibilities anyway, for the border is also
a domain of punitive topography. Here the Appalachian slopes rise unfor-
givingly, as if to invite confusion, or at best repetition, until some way out
may at last be found.

Part and parcel of spatial practice on the border are stories. That is, spatial practice is not only what these characters do (and cannot avoid doing),
it is what they talk about and in talking implicitly "theorize" and signify
about the spatial practice they do. "You want a story, do you?" Old Jack
would often ask John, but usually not until they were hunkered down in
Jack's cabin, over the Hill in an even "blacker" part of town. A candle would
be lit and whiskey toddies poured. In other words, if talk is a kind of practice,
it is also a spatial practice, in this instance a storytelling that signifies on the
very haven outside of which stories would not be safely told.

Now, of the tales of hunting and tracking game, of tricking and
double-crossing whites, that comprise this multistoried novel, the pivotal one
concerns the legend, possibly true, of a group of runaway slaves trapped in
the border zone by a posse of southern slave catchers and opportunistic
locals. John learns that troubling questions surround this incident at
Chaneysville. Not the least of these is, What really happened? But there are
others: Who will speak for the dead fugitives (or even find out what they had
to say)? Who should listen? And why this place? Both John and Old Jack
know scarcely more than the existence of the legend, but like his father, John
wants the details—how the escape was prevented, where the bodies were
buried, and who buried them. And so he broaches a different kind of storytelling when, and precisely because, he brings the professional historian's craft
to bear upon his researches (not coincidentally, allowing Bradley to make
cause with the reader, who is entreated to reverse the usual suspension of dis-
belief). The result, over and against what John says at one point, that we
know a lot about the past, maybe too much, is that he drenches his narrative in references to real historical agents and place-names, in recountings of
the slave trade and 1850 Fugitive Slave Act, and in vibrant resonances with
African American folktales and tropes more generally. But it must ever be
recalled how this world-outside-the-text comes to us: it comes through John
and his notes and is rendered as a distinctive outcome of spatial practice. It
takes on meaning accordingly: for every historical fact brought to bear on
the narrative, the more sharply the irony is etched that the quest for historical certainty is the sign of John having left—socially, geographically—the
"traditional" (read rural, black, male) circuits of knowledge in the first place.
According to Old Jack, the price of having left is forfeiture of the black, and

especially black male, habitus. And for John to have come back is to have come back as an abstraction with decidedly urban questions and decidedly white perspectives. The whole of John's endeavors are placed in a signifying relationship to this social and geographical lack. Old Jack makes no secret of his views, his resentments, and as if to concede them, John obliges in the end by burning the notes that made possible his reconstruction of the slaves' fate. The note burning, like the tales that can be told only at Old Jack's cabin or in the surrounding forest commons, serves to instruct readers yet again of the primary theme, that stories are constructed within social geographies and addressed to them. If what cultural historian Gerald Early warns (with echoes of John in the background) is accurate, that "preserving too much may give just as distorted a view of our past as saving too little," then it must be decided what can be said, how much to say, when and where to say it, and what sort of trace to leave behind.[7]

John Washington is, then, not as culturally distant as Old Jack accuses him of being. Old Jack himself once advised, "Fire gives a man say." It confers the power to make a statement and to withdraw it leaving the barest of traces. If note burning reminds us that stories are situational, dependent on content and intent, then it is also not the rupture it seems to be. For John's activities are situational all along. John struggles with the very idea that Judith, his white lover, should be his most intimate audience (just the opposite of Old Jack having once struggled to make an audience of John). And when John burns his notes, it more punctuates than erases what Old Jack has taught him about the social space of storytelling. Old Jack would disagree, but John's hard-won self-acceptance of Judith as an audience is more like a fulfillment than a rejection of the place- and race-bound traditions to which Old Jack would hold John. When it comes to talk and to storytelling, these traditions, though transformed by racial border crossing, comprise what we might call a moral economy of information. (Whereas the economy of information merely refers to the amassing and transmission of information, the moral economy of information is geared to preventing surplus. Thus I mean something like the reverse of the material shortages that James Scott and others have seen as being regulated by the moral economies of peasant societies.)[8] The standards of the moral economy of information are hardly agreed upon, however. Rather, what constitutes too much to know or enough to know is what the main characters fight over. For example, whatever John finds out through his professional exertions is, for Old Jack, always already surplus and dangerous information; surplus because John needn't have left the "Town" to begin with and dangerous because it disturbs the boundary between black and white (in both senses). From Judith's viewpoint it is the opposite: John needn't rehearse the historical litany of racial hatred since it puts their already troubled relationship further at risk; the litany would be surplus because it would fail to disturb the racial divide. But when all is finally told and John burns the notes, this signifies his double and intertwined commitment both to Judith as a chosen audience (the story ends with her, and she helps end the story) and to, let's say, a Jack-centered place of telling, the border zone, in which a key part of John's and Judith's identities has been imbricated and presumably resolved. In the moral economy of information, then, storytelling is involved in a set of negotiations whereby storytellers are answerable in revisable ways to the conditions under which information is discovered and related.

This leaves ample opportunity for signifying as a situated, spatial practice. John signifies upon the supposed transgression of having left the "South County"—not to mention upon gaps and biases in the historical record of which he is alleged by Old Jack to be the sign—by exercising the extraordinary set of landscape reading skills taught by Old Jack himself. He uses these skills in order to piece together the final and most essential details of the fugitive slaves' demise, details that are themselves absent from official records. But one might also say that the landscape turn, which leads John to the slaves' burial ground, enables the continued search for historical certainty, a search which, if Old Jack is to be trusted, marks John's departure from the sedimented knowledges of rural black culture. Yet John more than draws upon both archival and landscape readings. The question about the fate of the escaped slaves yields an answer that neither Old Jack's brand of sedimented knowledge nor the archives would dream of: the fugitive slaves were buried (read: respected, worried over, grieved for) by a local white farmer, who put their graves adjacent to his own family plot. There is no dichotomy, then, between the supposed historical truth of the archives and the supposed cultural mythology of tradition: each is capable of generating falsehoods and truths. That Judith and John make this last discovery in the graveyard more or less together reinforces the utility of John having left, having widened his own spatial practice, years ago. It is an old, old landscape that John returns to read, but he reads it differently for having left. Foucault advises that histories told at different levels are different histories, but what Judith, John, and Old Jack know is that stories told in and from different places are different stories.

It is tempting to read *Chaneysville* as one of those sorts of works in which everything in the world-outside-the-text that is relevant to the text is already in the text. Its energies have that prodigious, relentlessly searching quality, hardly represented by Bradley's uncharacteristically chaste words, that *Chaneysville* is a "work of historical reconstruction." (The forepages tell us so.) But what I have been trying to establish and will explore in the remainder of the chapter is that we should focus less on what he reconstructed and more on how the work of reconstructing history is shown to us. I want to acknowledge first in what follows, however, that such work itself has a history: *Chaneysville* wants to explain a certain past, but it still remains to be conjectured what sort of past explains the novel, especially its combined sensibility toward spatial practice and the talk that is spatial practice (which I have called the moral economy of information). For this task it will be fruitful, I hope, to explore the historical geography of the wary storytelling protagonist.

STORIES TOLD FROM DIFFERENT PLACES: NORTH OF THE SOUTH

Chaneysville's historicity and its representation of African American spatial, signifying practice can be explored by placing the novel in the context of what have come to be called the slave narratives. Now, a possible objection to drawing this parallel is that slave narratives concern individuals who survived their escape, whereas the novel's escaped slaves represented in that last culminating tale do not. Instead they must "haunt" someone else into telling it for them.[9] (This makes it all the more possible to think of John as a surrogate escaping-escaped slave.) This objection only problematizes what is so centrally important to the slave narratives to begin with, namely, the conditions under which a full account of a slave's captivity and escape should be given, and to whom. In this regard the antebellum narrative of Frederick Douglass points the way, not coincidentally because of his objections to slave narratives. I want to suggest that one of the central problems identified and revivified in *Chaneysville* conforms to the ethical concerns raised in Douglass's metacommentary. Here is Douglass:

> While . . . it would afford me pleasure, and perhaps would materially add to the interest of my story, were I at liberty to gratify a curiosity which I know to exist in the minds of many, as to the manner of my escape, I must deprive myself of this pleasure, and the curious of the gratification, which such a statement of facts would afford. . . .
>
> The practice of publishing every new invention by which a slave is known to have escaped from slavery, has neither wisdom nor necessity to sustain it. Had not Henry Box Brown and his friends attracted slaveholding attention to the manner of his escape, we might have had a thousand Box Browns per annum. The singularly original plan

adopted by William and Ellen Crafts, perished with the first using, because every slaveholder in the land was apprised of it. . . .

I have never approved of the very public manner, in which some of our western friends have conducted what they call the "*Underground Railroad*," but which, I think, by their open declarations, has been made most emphatically, the "*Upper-ground Railroad.*" Its stations are far better known to the slaveholders than to the slaves. . . . In publishing such accounts, the anti-slavery man addresses the slaveholder, *not the slave.*[10]

Douglass rejects not only a (the?) culminating narrative moment in one of the few popular outlets available for African America to represent itself to a "dominant culture." He proclaims his willingness to deny himself the pleasure of what ought to have been a cathartic moment, because the antebellum slave narrative, though the product of the escapee, was still fully enmeshed in the social relations of slavery. The single slave may have escaped those social relations, but the mass-produced narrative had not: it could quite easily be shipped back across the border to do mischief and wreak havoc. Print kills—no less from the very turf of the American Renaissance.

But as Douglass continues his explanation for why he is writing what may then (from the perspective of the moral economy of information) be called the slave's antinarrative, it becomes plain that his denying himself pleasure is not what it at first seems:

Such is my detestation of slavery, that I would keep the merciless slaveholder profoundly ignorant of the means of flight adopted by the slave. He should be left to imagine himself surrounded by myriads of invisible tormentors, ever ready to snatch, from his infernal grasp, his trembling prey. In pursuing his victim, let him be left to feel his way in the dark; let shades of darkness, commensurate with his crime, shut every ray of light from his pathway; and let him be made to feel, that, at every step he takes, with the hellish purpose of reducing a brother man to slavery, he is running the frightful risk of having his hot brains dashed out by an invisible hand.[11]

So as to punish slaveholders, Douglass refuses to tell his story fully. There can be no doubt that this not only brings a certain pleasure; it is a continuation of the act of escaping, a form of spatial practice. It is signifying practice, too, in that it produces new information in the very act of restricting information. Douglass, in a sense (and perhaps only in a rhetorical sense), does not want a complete escape. He is the consummate "professional fugitive" who wants now to watch his quarry squirm. Identity and pride are at stake, too. That is, by recognizing the duty not to tell, Douglass reaffirms his own wits. If he had revealed his means of escape, he would have ultimately demonstrated only foolishness by endangering others. By not telling all about himself he reasserts himself and his trickery all the more strongly, while punishing the slaveholder and slave catcher. As such, what James Olney sees as Douglass's divergence from the conventions of the slave narrative—that the narratives revel in the escape episode—is actually a fuller, deeper expression of the narrative.[12]

There is possibly an added critique at work. Douglass knew that had he printed the details of his escape, he would have added to the "interest" of his story. For an obvious reason—the potential "interest" of the slaveholding reader—he had to make his story less interesting than it might have been. But if Douglass also took sympathetic readers into consideration, as other ex-slave narrators did, he might have wondered if the pleasure taken in the details of escape emotionally validated slavery for such readers. (He hints as much when he refers to withholding "gratification" from "curious" readers.) That is, when it comes to the experience of reading "stories," they have logics of their own: plot climaxes justify and are justified by the trials preceding them. From a narrative point of view the sympathetic reader's delight in the slave's trickery and ingenuity absolutely depends upon the horrors of slavery laid out previously in the narrative: what in the social arena is a genocidal horror too easily becomes in the aesthetic literary arena dangerously enthralling.[13]

If such an interpretation has merit, then for Douglass it was ethically incumbent upon him to reposition the slave narrative back into social relations and to keep it there. Yet, as I have hinted, it is really less accurate to claim that Douglass was suppressing his story than to recognize that he is simply (strategically) trying to tell another, the story of his wit and, importantly, of his righteousness. The telling of this other story is, then, the assertion of his situated practice north of the border, his sharp awareness that all practice is situated—and this is one way in which he signifies to his former masters and fellow fugitives. He does not stop there but turns his signifying upside down and aims it at himself. To wit: Douglass goes on to signify on the narrowness of situated practice in the first place. "I have never placed my opposition to slavery," he says, "on a basis so narrow as my own enslavement, but rather upon the indestructible and unchangeable laws of human nature, every one of which is perpetually and flagrantly violated by the slave system." In autobiography his aim is not to proclaim the "heroic achievements of a man"; it is to "vindicate a just and beneficient principle, in its application to the whole human family."[14]

Now it is difficult at best to imagine John Washington using such expressions as "whole human family." He is, for other historical and personal reasons, far less optimistic about "society." Still, Frederick Douglass in 1845 (and again in the 1855 version of his autobiography) is instructive for a reading of 1981's *Chaneysville*. The contradiction Douglass raises (that the missing detail in one kind of story is the sine qua non of another) suffuses Bradley's novel precisely because the history that binds both is not over (nor of course did it begin with Douglass). *Chaneysville*, too, concerns the ethical grounding for African American storytelling; it is as much a novel about the occasions for storytelling and about audience as it is anything else. Both of these texts ask, What conditions need to be met in order to know certain details? What are the proper conditions for the accumulation and communication of knowledge of any kind? What kind of story is being told when the details withheld in one story can finally be revealed in the new one? But let me be clear about my proposition: more than rhetorical similarities join these texts. Placed beside Douglass's close-to-the-vest account, John Washington's informed ruminations do not so much explain history, though they do aim for a good bit of that, as the Douglass mode of jeremiad explains them. This is an African American history in which knowledge should not be let loose to flap in the wind "with neither wisdom nor necessity to sustain it."

This sort of sensibility, the Douglassian mode, is present in Bradley's novel partly by the mere fact that the first, chronologically speaking, of the Chaneysville "incidents," the death of the fugitive slaves, is the most deeply buried and hardest to render. Though mentioned early, it is told last. (The other incidents, in chronological order, are Moses Washington's first appearance in town; the near lynching of Josh White, who fell in love with a white farmer's daughter; the suicide of Moses Washington at the burial grounds of the fugitive slaves; and John's own return to town and final reckoning with Judith.) The reason, it would appear, is so that the purpose in telling about the incident may be constructed along the way. Douglass, too, prepares his reader for the withdrawal of "interesting" details in that he begins the autobiography by telling us about the details of his own life that were withheld from him: his birth date, the identity of his alleged white father, knowledge of his mother, and so on, all of these things being considered by the slaveholder to be important to the hegemony of the slave system.

One may read most of *Chaneysville*, then, as one reads Douglass: as a constructed moral economy of information. I think we can locate the novel's concern with this by recognizing not only that the most important story comes last, but that what prompts John Washington to begin his story, or ensemble of stories, is quite different from what prompts him to finish it.

John's motivations shift, or even more precisely John acquires motivation. At first the only cause for storytelling is a tautology. The novel begins with John responding to the call of his dying "uncle," Old Jack. This is context without real motive. It is story for story's sake—this is after all a novel, and it must have a beginning. Old Jack occasions a beginning, obliging the reader by commencing to die. The real significance of his dying, the switch from its formal, literary role to its posing an epistemological threat to historical storytelling, is only later (but not too much later) drawn out and related explicitly to John's project:

> And then I began to think about what a man's dying really means: his story is lost. Bits and pieces of it remain, but they are all second-hand tales and hearsay, or cold official records that preserve the facts and spoil the truth; the sum is like a writer's complete works with crucial numbers missing. . . . But the gaps in the stories of the unknown are never filled, never can be filled, for they are larger than data, larger than deduction, larger than induction. Sometimes an attempt is made to fill them; some poor unimaginative fool, calling himself a historian but really only a frustrated novelist, comes along and tries to put it all together. And fails. . . . And so . . . he peppers his report with deceptive phrases—"it appears" and "it would seem" when he is fairly sure but has no evidence.[15]

Much is being said in this passage.[16] Encapsulated in it is an attitude not only toward Old Jack's impending death but toward all death, all loss of persons, of story, of ever really knowing the past. It is possible to speak of a moral economy of information precisely because full knowledge is not possible. John states the significance of this ironically and by innuendo. He says that the historian, always already a fool, is "really only a frustrated novelist." The historian fails, it seems clear, less because he can never get the facts than because he hasn't learned how to be like a novelist. The novelist, by turn, is not frustrated because he doesn't have access to historical facts but because he does not yet know how to make a story. And thus the real gambit is launched: that it doesn't so much matter whether one has the story. It matters that one has a story, which doubly means that what a story is about and what it is for are indivisible questions with mutually shaping answers. Stories are told on a need-to know-basis. They are always metatales. Old Jack does not tell John the story about Josh White and the white woman, for example, until he figures out that John has taken up with a white woman, too. With this story, which includes Josh's reincorporation into the black male habitus, Old Jack signifies on John having adopted a spatial practice that takes him too far afield. Or, stories are riddles. "Fact is," Old Jack reminds John about

```
┌─────────────────────────────────────────────────────────┐
│  ┌───────────────────────────────────────────────────┐  │
│  │        NORTHERN STATES=LOWER RISK                 │  │
│  └───────────────────────────────────────────────────┘  │
│        ↑   SLAVES MOVING NORTHWARD   ↑                   │
│  ┌───────────────────────────────────────────────────┐  │
│  │   UPPER TIER OF BORDER ZONE=HIGHER RISK           │  │
│  │     ↑                              ↑              │  │
│  │   Implications of the border for geopolitics of   │  │
│  │   the text: maximum opportunity to represent      │  │
│  │   acts of black resistance / thick description    │  │
│  │   of landscape and spatial practice               │  │
│  │     ↑                              ↑              │  │
│  │   LOWER TIER OF BORDER ZONE=LOWER RISK            │  │
│  └───────────────────────────────────────────────────┘  │
│        ↑   SLAVES MOVING NORTHWARD   ↑                   │
│  ┌───────────────────────────────────────────────────┐  │
│  │        SOUTHERN STATES=HIGHER RISK                │  │
│  └───────────────────────────────────────────────────┘  │
└─────────────────────────────────────────────────────────┘
```

Implications of the border for geopolitics of the text

Unmarked stones in a remote burial ground outside Chaneysville, Pennsylvania, possibly signifying the burial place of the runaway slaves memorialized in The Chaneysville Incident. *(Photo: George Henderson)*

Mount Ross Cemetery, Bedford, Pennsylvania. The empty area of lawn at the rear is a possible burial place of the runaway slaves as told in other versions of what became of them. (Photo: George Henderson)

his father, "you found out somethin' about Moses Washington, you knowed for sure either he wanted you to find it out jest 'xactly the way you done it, or it was a lie. An' most times, it was both."[17] Or, per Douglass, they are just plain admonishments which themselves are the stories. It remains for the reader to see what John's story will be.

This makes for some vexing, albeit interesting, reading, because it is not clear that John wishes to tell a story of his own at all. Moreover, the novel's central mystery is the question of whether or not he will have one. He does on the other hand retell a few of Old Jack's stories. But these have already been authorized by having been told once before to John as a boy. Once again we may look to Frederick Douglass for guidance. Douglass's wits and his paradoxical wish to deflect attention away from himself (paradoxical because he was after all writing autobiography and asserting his presence vis-à-vis the social relations of slavery) provide a needed explanation for the occasional frustrations of reading *Chaneysville*: John's white lover Judith nearly has to drag the story of the escaping slaves out of reluctant, ornery John, who is ornery for reasons similar to Douglass. In fact she has to drag out of him nearly everything he tells her. Their sparring regularly interrupts the narrative, seeming like an artificial intrusion to keep the novel's multiple time horizons going.[18] But the duel provides essential context. John's reluctance serves more than to tell us (again and again) about his pain, his grievances. Like Old Jack before him, he is now the caretaker of stories, and like John before Jack, Judith must prove herself worthy before John. These things fold into each other. John opposes racial oppression, not because of what he endures personally but on principle. The potential danger with Judith is, at best, that she will listen to him less on principle than out of love for him personally and, at worst, that she will resurrect the old white paternalism. He demands that she separate these impulses out. But there is a crucial difference between Old Jack's stories and the story of the escaping slaves that John eventually, conjecturally, pieces together. The latter story does not exist yet as a story until Judith could become an audience. Until she can become one, something which only happens when on her own initiative and against his wishes she follows him back to the border, John punishes her like Douglass punishes his former master. In sum, Judith is the liminal figure that the white race historically has been in America. Part abolitionist, part slaveholder, she challenges John with her being-as-audience.

STORIES TOLD FROM DIFFERENT PLACES: SOUTH OF THE NORTH

The work of historical reconstruction depends upon more than audience, however. It depends on a method by which reconstruction can take place. A central tension in the *Chaneysville* stories therefore emerges over the fact that the work of historical reconstruction at times sits side by side with preternatural, or near preternatural, insights. The argument I shall be working toward is that these two methods, as it were, are themselves roped into a moral economy of information. Here are two scenarios to consider.

One is Moses Washington's funeral. Here, John is just a boy, and Old Jack, following Moses' instructions, has come to assert his place as the boy's mentor:

> And then Old Jack came. It was as if a boulder dropped into a pool; the silence had that same hollow sound to it that water makes as it swallows a stone. He stepped into the middle of the room and looked around, swaying drunkenly, blinking like some weird sleepy reptile. There was a collective gasp throughout the room. Old Mrs. Turner, who was noted for seeing signs and omens in nearly everything—she claimed to have foreseen Moses Washington's death in the actions of a flock of birds—stood up and raised her hand above her head and began to wail, her voice rising from a low, barely audible whisper to a keening that was painful to the ear. I heard a rush of feet as my mother came in from the kitchen.
>
> Old Jack took another step forward, his eyes searching. They came to rest on me. "Mose tole me," he said. "Tole me to come for this here boy. An' I come." The statement must have stunned everybody, for no one moved when he advanced upon me. . . . Suddenly my limbs were free from paralysis, and I let go with what must have been my first accurate punch: a short, chopping overhand right that landed squarely on Old Jack's wart. He howled and jumped back, and with that the spell was broken.[19]

The second scenario comes from the novel's opening line: "Sometimes you can hear the wire, hear it reaching out across the miles; whining with its own weight, crying from the cold, panting at the distance, humming with the phantom sounds of someone else's conversation."[20]

Surely, the work of historical reconstruction—the assertion of veracity—must step lightly around a figure like Old Mrs. Turner, who is briefly introduced (and then promptly dismissed from the novel altogether) in passage one above. Our reading that she is known for seeing signs and omens in "nearly everything" invites a flip response. Would it be better if she saw them in only a few things? Probably not. Either way we are encouraged to read her as excessive, loud, and loony; drunk like Old Jack but given to harboring spirits of another kind. Not that she is to be disliked, or liked; she simply is Old Mrs. Turner who is rendered harmless by her excesses. She lives in an excessive reality of beliefs and practices that simply do not matter. She "claimed" to have foreseen Moses' death but, well, he died anyway. She can just go ahead and believe what she wants; for the moment she adds local color to this comedy of the parlor. Or at least this is the conceit of the moment, for rather than being merely a figment of John's memory, his representing her is integral to how he constructs himself (and the novel itself).

From the beginning, looking now at passage two, John "hears" the wire, "hears" phantom sounds. Anyone who has used a telephone knows what he is talking about: dim echoes, nearly intelligible voices, annoying clicks, and faint tappings. But there are orders and gradations of the invisible-audible that test the category of the "rational," and Old Jack and John come to represent the full range. We make no mistake, then; Old Mrs. Turner shines amid a whole constellation of preternatural images.

Paradigmatic of the invisible-audible are the sounds carried along with the wind as it wends its way along the hillslopes. Old Jack swears that they are the souls of dead Indians panting from the hunt. John swears that it is songs he hears, but he tires of these "folk" readings when he enters his teenage years. He is determined to hear them as nothing more than physics. "I had realized that the sound I called the singing of the wind was not singing at all, or panting, either; that it was just a sound, like a car honking. . . . It was something that you didn't have to believe in; it was something you could know."[21] Yet the sounds defy what he supposedly "knows," just as at the very beginning of the novel we are told that telephone wires are more than they seem to be. As he keeps listening to the wind, the sounds turn to singing again. "I had sat there, clutching my toddy, trying to perceive that sound as I had known I should, trying not to hear voices in it, trying not to hear words. But I had heard them anyway."[22]

A number of questions surface around the narrative's attitude toward Old Mrs. Turner and the way she is dispensed with, versus John and Old Jack who are given considerably more staying power. I want to argue that she is not written off quite for the reasons we might think she is and that when she is written off, it serves to boost John and Old Jack's cause. Even while her character is introduced and withdrawn in a heartbeat, what she represents means everything to the relations between historical reconstruction and preternatural vision. But, for a moment, let's read against this grain. One possible reading, if we are to take the accusation that Old Mrs. Turner is just plain crazy, is that John and Old Jack's beliefs are belittled accordingly. This is not likely, however, in light of the seriousness with which we are generally encouraged to take John and Old Jack. Another reading is that Bradley just doesn't know what to make of Old Mrs. Turner. She sees things of an order also seen by the other two characters, but there is simply an unresolved contradiction in how credence is distributed. But if she is really that extraneous, then someone else's dropped teacup ought to do just as well. Still another reading is that we are indeed meant to take metaphysics seriously. Our belief in Old Jack and in John thereby ought to spill over and make us believe in her, contrary to the advice of the narrator, the difference being that the "actions of a flock of birds" just weigh in less than the soulful sounds of the wind. This seems nearer an acceptable reading because contrapuntal sequencing as a form of signifying is a structural feature of the novel. The grounds for Mrs. Turner's dismissal, then, are that someone is about to do what she does better than she does it. The question of which epistemology is right or wrong, metaphysics or regular physics, is beside the point. The point is that Old Jack (and John) have been placed on the signifying stage with Old Mrs. Turner. She is indeed "out there," but Old Jack is even more so, so she wails when she sees him. (It takes one to know one: who better than Old Mrs. Turner to announce Old Jack's arrival, to know him as he is.) But then John whacks Old Jack, who howls and jumps back, repeating the movements of Mrs. Turner. One wails, the other howls, and the spell is just as dramatically broken, by a little boy no less, who upstages both the outsiders to become the center of attention. And that is exactly where he is supposed to be—because it circles the square: in the first instance, Old Jack was sent to collect John by Moses, the grandest signifier of all, who apparently stirs things up even after his death.

If the point then is not to get trapped by the truth or fiction of characters seeing things or hearing voices (given that this is "work of historical reconstruction") but to understand the signifying that goes on among the characters and to see Old Mrs. Turner as part of John and Old Jack's signifying world, then the point of all the signifying is simply that everyone within and outside the story should see signs and omens of some kind in everything. Moreover, if one misses that point, then one is cut off from certain kinds of pursuits and certain versions of stories.[23] Whether this is taken as a matter of the world of souls and spirits or in a strictly this-worldly sense is of little account, so long as the questioning of appearances continues. John knows this only too well. Everything means something more than it is and can be read as structured by the often unacknowledged rules of which it is a part (e.g., his planes, trains, and buses). So when John continually clobbers Judith with his rationalisms and bland statements of historical fact, which, more to the point, are often stormy effusions of fact, this is almost always to brandish what are for his specific purposes useless surpluses and to signify on where facts seem to be missing almost by design.

"You know," she [Judith] said, "you have to wonder. Here you are, hot-stuff historian, superscholar, able to leap to conclusions in a sin-

gle bound, and half the people who know you think you're brilliant
and the other half think you're crazy, but everybody agrees there's
something special about you, even if they don't understand what the
hell it is. You can make a bonfire by rubbing two dry facts together,
so long as you're talking about the Punic Wars and Saint Francis of
Assisi, or the Lost Chord and Jesus Christ. But let you come within
twenty miles of where you live and it all goes out the window.
Because you don't really want to know, John. You want to win. You
want to beat Moses Washington and whatever—"

"No," I said. "Not now. Not anymore. Now I just want to
know the truth."

"Then what's stopping you?"

"Facts," I said. "Don't you understand? There aren't any facts.
All that about the runaway slaves and Moses Washington, that's
extrapolation. It's not facts. I've used the facts."

"So get more facts."

"There *aren't* any more facts."

"Then forget the facts," she said.[24]

We know what's coming next: "And suddenly I heard his voice."[25] There
simply is no other place for the narrative to go but for John to begin hearing
things (again). This time we are left to wrangle over whether he is reminisc-
ing, daydreaming, or "really" hearing Old Jack's voice. (When he tells the
reader what he hears, it is not clear if he is also telling Judith. Indeed, what
he never comes right out and says is that if it is true that things mean more
than they appear to, that wind can really be singing, then it must also be true
that there never will be sufficient, empirical fact, for such facts will always
be appearances anyway.) What follows is the last, long culminating tale
where John divines the story of the fugitive slaves and relates it to Judith.
The connections between this new development and earlier intimations are
now clear and multifold. Point: John had once before abandoned the singing
of the wind, only for it to return to him more insistently. Point: the text had
abandoned Old Mrs. Turner, only for her modus operandi to be reasserted.
She serves after all to prefigure John's own ambivalence about whether to
believe or not to believe in signs. And point: only a combination of archival
research and a superbly nuanced landscape-sign reading allows John to make
his best effort at piecing together the slave legend and its connection to his
own family. Thus John surmises from where Moses' body was found that
Moses, too, had discovered the gravesites. The implication is that Moses had
taken his life in an attempt to follow C. K. Washington, his grandfather, into
the next world. Moses had surmised (so John himself surmises) that C. K.

was one of the buried black bodies in the graveyard who had taken his own life, as had the entire party of escaping slaves whom C. K. was trying to curry to freedom. The difference between Moses and John, however, is that Moses took that final, most unambiguous step and followed C. K. into the Twilight Zone, as Judith sarcastically puts it.

There is ambiguity, then, about what John believes with regard to the traffic between the quick and the dead, between this world and another. He is not unlike William Wells Brown, the escaped slave made famous through publication of his slave narrative. Brown relates having visited an elder, "Uncle Frank," on the eve of escape. "Uncle Frank" was revered by blacks and whites alike as a fortune-teller, a reputation which Brown does not fully go along with but as a matter of practicality respects.

> And it was generally believed that he could really penetrate into the mysteries of futurity. Whether true or not, he had the name, and that is about half of what one needs in this gullible age. . . . However, I paid the fee of twenty-five cents, and he commenced by looking into a gourd, filled the water. Whether the old man was a prophet, or the son of a prophet, I cannot say; but there is one thing certain, many of his predictions were verified. I am no believer in soothsaying; yet I am sometimes at a loss to know how Uncle Frank could tell so accurately what would occur in the future.[26]

Of the two dimensions to the "I" in this passage—an "I" complicit with the audience's skepticism and an ambivalent "I" who needs to say that if Uncle Frank was right, well, then, he was right—the latter, who thinks that maybe he can't afford not to be gullible, holds greater interest. At the very least, to be ambivalent is simply to keep one's eyes open. Putting a finer point on the matter, the ambivalence is essentially a restatement of the absurd terms of a racist world. ("This I know will sound strangely to the ears of people in foreign lands but it is nevertheless true," Brown remarks. "An American citizen was fleeing from a democratic, republican, Christian government, to receive protection under the monarchy of Great Britain.")[27] Another fugitive puts it succinctly. A dream, she advised, is "as good a sign in the south as ever was."[28] Dreams, regardless of whether one is a strict believer in signs and omens, are good signs because the South is already other-worldly. There is the necessity of subscribing and not subscribing at the same time. Such seems to be John's status.

Under Old Jack's training, John is open to revelations of all kinds and relies on these for his spatial practice. Especially vigilant regarding the ways in which the extraordinary may be immanent in the ordinary, he maintains a heightened sense of physical surroundings. This means having the keenest knowledge possible about the physical qualities of a place, the weather, the lay of the land, location of caves, directionality of ridges, and so on. It would not be enough, for example, to think that the wind suddenly sounds like singing. One wants to know if that sound is the wind or singing but can only know such a thing by having learned that what sounds like wind may not be wind. This also means understanding human beings' most minute ecologies and gestures, a lesson that begins several years after Moses' death when John first goes up to his father's attic. There he discovers Moses' files on C. K. (along with the account books for Moses' liquor trade which kept nearly every member of the white power structure under his thumb).

> Beside the lamp was a small box of matches. I looked at those things for a long time, trying to understand why the matches were there, in the open, not put away. For I knew the way in which those men's minds had worked: put things back when you are finished with them; put them in the same place every time, so that when you need them you won't have to guess or fumble or even think. And then I realized that I had made an incorrect assumption (although I did not think of it in those terms). I had assumed that I was stepping into the scene at the middle of a cycle, when in fact, I was stepping into the beginning of one. They were beside the lamp because that was where he would want them when he first came in—to light the lamp. *Then* he would put them somewhere out of the way. His last act before blowing out the lamp and leaving would have been to take them out again and place them where he could find them easily, in the dark.[29]

But because Moses, who was left-handed, had left the matches in a place where a right-handed person would leave them, John (at this point barely into his teenage years) figures out that his father wanted him to pick up where he had left off. Because his father wants John to turn into a reader of landscapes, he has turned the attic into a "landscape" to be read. He has, one might say, signified upon the ground. No word had been spoken between them about this intended transmission, a virtual repeat of the tour of the Hill. Moses trusted that once John discovered the sign of the matches' position in the attic landscape, John would already be capable of undertaking his duty: to have discovered the sign at all was to have begun to read signs. One might suggest that whether John was successful or not was, again, of no real account. The point—the story—was that John get on the road to questioning appearances.

However, once John again takes up that task, goaded by his return to the "South County," many years have gone by during which he has been living in Philadelphia. John's spatial practice has thereby widened. But if Old Jack could have the last word, he might say that space has practiced on John, too. This is indeed the point which Old Jack scornfully signifies to John. (This whole business of going back to the "South County" also thematizes the African American diaspora, for which, via John, Old Jack has nothing but contempt. To Jack, the massive urbanization and northward movement of blacks in the wake of Reconstruction amounted to little.)[30] When John insists on taking Old Jack to a hospital, Old Jack, a master of innuendo, snaps, "What I need don't travel."[31] Shortly thereafter Old Jack lets it fly:

> "I can see it in you, the way you move. You useta move strong an' easy. You still got the strength, I guess, but you ain't used it. You ain't kept up with it. That's what comes a city livin'. . . . Your blood's got thin from livin' inside a houses all the time, with no time in the woods. You walk funny; that's on accounta your feet is all flattened out from standin' around on cement all the time. You set in a chair like it's home. I don't know what's at the bottom of it. Maybe you ain't been eatin' enough fresh-kilt meat, or you been drinkin' watered whiskey, or you been messin' with the wrong kind of women."

Then: "That's it, ain't it," he said. "It's a woman." Later: "Johnny," he said. "You started trustin' white people, ain't you?" Finally: "This woman a yours. She's a white woman ain't she?"[32]

These devastating salvos are aimed at more than John. They are a wholesale indictment of the great northward rush of African Americans to the cities of the industrial heartland—conflated with Jack's critique of his two despised groups, white people and women. Beyond his own cabin Old Jack does not see that anything has changed or could; nor does anything change in the cabin except for the ever-aging Jack. American space for Old Jack might as well be like that described by Frederick Douglass after the 1850 Fugitive Slave Act: "By that act, Mason and Dixon's line has been obliterated; New York has become as Virginia; and the power to hold, hunt, and sell men, women, and children as slaves, remains no longer a mere state institution, but is now an institution of the whole United States."[33] As far as Old Jack is concerned, there is no point in leaving if there is no place to go.

Regardless of his love for Old Jack, however, the impasse of city-countryside-border marks the spot where Old Jack ceases to offer John any new insights. This is so not because Jack is wrong about stagnating race relations but because John has traveled in spite of them. Yet it is after all in the home landscape where John discovers that history is not entirely what he, or anyone else apparently, thought it was.

COMING INTO THE COUNTRY: THEORIZING LANDSCAPE IN CHANEYSVILLE

When John left the "South County," he did so primarily to escape. He was that figure which Bracha Lichtenberg-Ettinger calls the "inverted exile," the "traveller to an unknown, desired destination."[34] The problem now is how John can make future destinations a little more desired because they are a little more known. The "truth" about the slave legend presumably points to a solution, because John thereby comes to understand how much the slaves' fate set in motion a chain of events whose outcomes lead right to him. Crucial choices for John's life in the present are laid bare in the process. Yet any such opening is very much an unintended consequence of John's return, the sole purpose of which was to respond to Old Jack's deathbed call. This very contingency signifies on what is so important about the way things happen in *Chaneysville*: all other things being equal, they happen situationally. Landscape thus assumes what to some readers may seem like an almost precocious significance. (Think back to the matches in the attic.) Drawing on one popular meaning, one could say that events and actions are quite actually (and literally, of course) landscaped in *Chaneysville*.

But perhaps the most significant aspect of John's reading of landscape is that the chain of events begun by the slaves' death leads to him in more than one way. The "South County" is of fundamental importance to John because it is the scene of repeated, though incommensurable, histories; precedents, as it were, from among which John must choose. On the one hand, landscape reveals a history of suicide in the Washington family. The first of these is committed by C. K., when he and the escaping slaves end up trapped at the border and decide to take their own (and their children's) lives instead of granting victory to their would-be captors.[35] Moses' own obsession with C. K. then leads him to take his life, too. While not exactly in danger of suicide, John has obsessions strong enough to put him on the path to total alienation. On the other hand, John and Judith have themselves repeated a history that they did not even know existed. This is very much a history that also resides in localities, in bodies. This history—of racial divides being breached in small ways—does not undo or much change the grander narrative of oppression and violence, but it can be useful for specific selves in particular settings. We come to the graveyard, then:

> "Who buried them?" she [Judith] said. "Who buried them there like that? Pettis [the slave catcher]?"

"I don't think so," I said. "I don't know why he would."

"Who, then? Crawley and Graham [black agents of the Underground Railroad]?

"That's what Moses Washington thought," I said. . . .

"What do you think?" she said.

"They were buried next to a family graveyard. They died there, but they didn't have to be buried there. They were buried with the same spacing as the family stones . . ."

"You're saying the miller—what's his name? Iames?—you think he took the time to bury them like that, to figure out who loved who?"

"Yes," I said. "That's what I believe."

"But he was white," she said.

"I know," I said.

"Why would a white man . . . why would you think a white man . . . ?"

I heard the soft squeaking of the chair as her body stiffened, as she turned to try and see my face.[36]

John and Judith's discovery disrupts known (or presumed to be known) history in a locally useful way and points up the contradiction of John's education: John uses Moses' and Old Jack's spatial practice to theorize what they could not. Drawing upon a place-based knowledge, which marks what is in/out of place, John retraces every one of the slaves' and slave catchers' probable movements, every one of C. K.'s evasive maneuvers. Old Jack and Moses had taught John about knowing what the ordinary is so as to be open to the extraordinary, but this must now be read ironically in the case of the fugitives: they are out of place precisely because they are in a place. (Readers can turn this insight around to evaluate critically the novel's broader and unexamined terms of landscape. What is missing in the novel, for example, is the history of how Old Jack came to be left alone and let be in the landscape, or territory, he calls home. There is an implicit romanticization, reification even, of the rural, of the homestead. It is never posited that a time could come when Old Jack would be kicked off his land or at least denied the usufructuary rights he liberally enjoys over an extraordinarily broad swath of terrain. It is not that such access is unimaginable. It is that so little explanation for it is offered in a novel that aims to explain so much. There is an elaborate, enabling social geography, in other words, that is as pervasive as it is taken for granted in the novel.) With this knowledge of an unexpected history in hand, John, who has poured every ounce of his being into uncovering the past, has now himself been uncovered by that past. The breaching of the racial divide which John and Judith embody is not without some precedent, it turns out. It, too, has a history. None of these developments, of course, mean that Old Jack's methods have been renounced. If anything, landscape and spatial practice, as John rehearses it in the telling of the slave legend and the discovery of the burial site, reaffirm the old skills, just in an unforeseen way.

Renderings of landscape forcefully send the novel's two essential arguments home. First, through landscape, events are revealed to be always already contingent, just as signs of unaccounted-for possibilities are shown to be always already available. Second, while landscape and the particularities of place change the way events happen, understandings of place are themselves events which have a spatial basis. John does not know until he sets foot on it that the landscape of the burial ground tells a history of race relations different enough from the usual findings to be specifically useful to him. Through landscape, knowledge itself is shown to be always already partial (no one can be in all places at once). Yet landscape is a kind of actor, too. John can uncover the history of the escaped slaves by a superbly intricate reading of the local setting. He can discern the exact chasms that C. K. must have jumped over, the streams that he must have crossed, etc., precisely because the landscape has acted contingently on the characters that cross it in the act of their own spatial practice—for which landscape is a set of structuring possibilities in the first place. Landscape has to be understood not just as a visual arrangement, then, but as the set of conditions for practice and agency. Contingency outs, in the end. But contingency does not mean that just anything happens. Contingency is useful to think about because it allows an argument to be made against essentialist forms of determination while at the same time admitting a place to specific structuring geographies. From this point of view, the structuring geography of the borderland, south-central Pennsylvania, means a great deal.

SPATIAL PRACTICE AT THE BORDER

The border, defined by the states (and especially the counties) that lie just north and south of the Mason-Dixon Line, has historically been a hot zone of race relations and/as spatial practice of a particular kind. It was preeminently a place where the usually invoked differences between the North as a site of emancipation and the South as a site of enslavement broke down. For example, the white population of the southern portions of the northern border states tended to be sympathetic to the South. Conversely, the border was a zone of southern encroachment in that enslaved blacks fled from the southern border states—Maryland, Virginia, Kentucky, and Missouri—more than from anywhere else in the South.[37] The social-spatial significance of the border was the disruption and inversion it represented: even though its southern tier was the lowest risk region from which to flee, its northern tier was the most dangerous place toward which to flee.

The border was altogether a belt of hyper spatial practice which intensified with the passage of the Fugitive Slave Act of 1850. At the same time the law threatened the very notion of a border between North and South at all. The slave laws, as ignominious, terroristic creations legitimated by the Constitution's recognition of human bondage, had as their ideal the capture of runaways in so-called free territory. The hallmark of the 1850 law that made it different from the preceding fugitive slave laws was the federal apparatus it set up for captures.[38] That there was a federal apparatus had consequences of its own, however. For if the North did not want the South telling it what to do, it did not want the federal government dictating to it either. A kind of schism followed. Many northern states and localities, in fact, did little to cooperate with federal officials. Yet the border counties north of Mason-Dixon teemed with whites willing to land a hand, as many in the "South County" of *Chaneysville* do. Border practice was thus free to express itself.

Runaway slaves had the good fortune that the law was in many ways impractical, however. As Stanley Campbell has argued, "An adequate Fugitive Slave Law would have required the great majority of northern citizens to have been suspicious of every strange Negro whom they saw and to report his presence in the community to proper authorities. It would have provided machinery for the arrest and extradition of slaves upon the same basis as criminals."[39] The authors of the law failed to account for the many ways in which northerners did in fact object to it. In Harrisburg, Pennsylvania, for example, many whites turned against the law because they did not want to have to determine whether a black person was free or not; or because they objected to out and out kidnapping; or because they objected to law enforcers making private profits on the side; or because they rejected the harsh treatment and family separations that runaways met with.[40] These or similar objections were part of the motivation for local retaliatory legislation against the fugitive slave laws.

The fugitive slave laws in fact bred resistance of many kinds. Armed, forcible resistance, led by African Americans, erupted across the northern landscape. During one of these episodes a captured slave was ripped from the arms of a federal marshal in a Boston courthouse, and in Detroit federal troops were called to prevent freed blacks from stealing a captive. As in many other cases around the country, this person's freedom was ultimately purchased. In consequence of the Fugitive Slave Law's impracticalities and resistance to it, many more slaves escaped from the South than were returned.

Pointing out northern resistance to the law, however, says nothing about the fact that the law made fugitives run harder. Those who were already in the North ran farther north, and those who had not yet left the South or were on their way, and who had in mind the idea of freedom just over the Mason-Dixon, now stood corrected. Moreover, as Campbell is at pains to emphasize, when slave owners and slave catchers adhered to due process of the law, the law was enabling and effective.[41]

There was no getting around the spatial expression of the law's failures and successes, and I mean to imply the double meaning of those words when applied to this situation. Because of the expense of slave catching, very few slaves were returned from New England and the upper Midwest, just as most slaves who were captured were taken from northern states just above Mason-Dixon. Not only was it cheaper to retrieve fugitives from a place closer to home, but border whites, as I have said, were often less hostile to the idea and practice of capture.[42] Bedford County, then, where the town of Chaneysville is situated, is a case in point. William Hall, a Bedford County judge, devoted a special chapter of his 1890 reminiscences to the topic. "There was a time," he begins, "within the memory of men now living, when it was opprobrious to be called an abolitionist in southern Pennsylvania. No word of contempt was fuller of meaning or more odious." He continues:

> If slaves ran away from Maryland or Virginia and came through southern Pennsylvania, hand-bills offering a reward were circulated and posted up in public places. They were sent to postmasters and put up in the post-offices and taverns, often by the postmasters themselves, and there were men in Bedford county, as in other border counties, who were not only willing, but watchful and anxious, to capture runaways and get the reward. Hand-bills with regard to runaway slaves were received and treated with the same respect as those giving information of a stolen horse, and offering a reward for its capture and the arrest of the thief. The fugitives followed the mountains which run northwardly, and the slave-catchers lay in wait, both by day and night, at the crossing places of the roads, and arrests were made without any warrant or process of law. Negroes and mulattoes were captured, and bound and conducted back to their owners or to slave-catchers in Maryland, without any man daring to question the proceedings or to inquire by what authority doest thou these things, or who gave thee this authority? They were taken along the public roads and through the villages bound, and without any man caring or daring to question or even inquire into the authority of the captors. Nay, more than this, such was the terrorism of the time, such

the fear of being regarded as an abolitionist, that cruelty and actual death were inflicted upon fugitive blacks by slave-catchers, armed with no authority except a printed hand-bill with the alleged owner's name appended to it, upon more than one occasion in Bedford county, and no notice of the occurrence was taken by any official nor by the newspapers.

Yet attitudes were apparently divided along class lines. Hall notes that the "name of a slave-catcher was nearly as much a stigma as the name of abolitionist. The public sentiment of the better class of the community condemned both with an equal measure of contempt. The slave-catchers were, for the most part, a despicable set; they were men who drank whisky, chewed tobacco, played cards and loafed around village taverns."[43] There was nonetheless an apparent code of silence. In short, Pennsylvania was a place of brutal irony. This state, first to abolish slavery by legislation (and thus encourage the growth of a substantial community of free blacks in Philadelphia), arrested more fugitive slaves than any other northern state.

By nullifying the idea of a liberated North, the fugitive slave laws paved the way to the zones of resistance known as the Underground Railroad, whose "tracks" began at the border and extended north to Canada. Long vaunted in abolitionist accounts, the politics of this "institution" were in fact murky. Popular (white) perceptions of the railroad are largely traceable to postbellum abolitionist accounts which typically point up their own heroism and adventures as opposed to the slaves. It was these streams of books and articles in magazines and newspapers that helped to reinforce the mythology of a moral North and a heinous South: "Hundreds of such newspaper stories furnished readers with a picture of the underground railroad as an abolitionist institution, dotting the entire North with stations and giving fearless humanitarians an opportunity to strike a severe blow at the wicked slave system of the South."[44] The railroad, still romanticized, hardly constituted a resurrection of liberated space in the North. It was instead a site of recombinant racism. Fugitives were commonly kept at a distance by those who gave them safe harbor and prohibited from entering the homes that often served as the so-called stations. Fugitives typically did not eat with so-called agents and sometimes were shackled. For many years the role of Quakers was overemphasized at the expense of blacks who helped each other find a way out of slavery. Nor was the railroad a formal system. Rather it was contingent, flexible, and local. It was based more on individual wits than on set rules and precise routes. Most agents only knew of other agents one or two stations away.[45]

As I have suggested, most of the slaves who escaped into Pennsylvania came from neighboring states. The south-central portion of the state offered sites that were, once again, both enabling and constraining.[46] Like the port of Philadelphia into which many fugitives poured, the Appalachians with their long valleys were a natural conduit northward. By the same token, these narrow channels were flanked by long ridges which afforded multiple sites for surveillance. Moreover, valleys often ended abruptly at the bottom of a ridge that would seem to come from nowhere. Imagine a giant slingshot lying face down on the ground. One would enter the open space (a valley) between the two arms (ridges), only to face an abrupt closure where the arms join the handle (the beginning of another ridge). The landscape, so promising and so foreboding, virtually forced contingencies upon the runaways.

Far more important than the fixed stations of the Underground Railroad were the contingent, improvised sites. Virtually every landscape feature entered into the calculus of escape. Slaves hid out in caves, woods, and hollow trees; lay in wheat and corn fields; jumped fences that eluded horseriding slave catchers; used the nighttime or whole seasons as places of hiding; hunkered down in thickets, woodpiles, and caskets; disappeared into funeral processions; found wild onions and pine pitch to keep hounds off the scent; cross-dressed, blackfaced, and powdered; dressed like Quakers and passed as gentry. The world was what they had to run from, but it gave them a staggering array of resources with which to work.[47] Likewise, forms of communication along the railroad were contingent and "local in usage." Special knocks or raps, passwords, and metaphors were developed as the situation allowed or called for. Routes themselves resembled nothing like the clean lines shown on maps of the Underground Railroad. "The exigencies that determined in what direction an escaping slave should go during any particular part of his journey were, in the nature of the case, always local."[48]

Returning to Bradley, it is his attention to the history and geography of border contingencies and improvisations such as those just discussed which makes his work so forceful. What I mean by this is that sensitivity to the intensified contingency of the border offers the maximum opportunity for him to represent acts of black resistance in the persons of C. K., the escaping slaves, Moses, Jack, and, finally, John. Within an area that is quite small, he has managed to cram a world of spaces, which as a consequence of border historical geography are rather thickly described. The more there is the threat of being cut off at the pass, as it were—as happens during the several episodes where C. K. and the fugitives or Moses and Old Jack must get to a place first in order to avoid capture or a lynching—the more opportunity there is to display what is known about alternate routes, wind direction, or the way sound travels. And the more opportunity there is to signify at the oppressor. In short, the illustrative diagram shows the way in which the geography of risk encountered by escaping slaves—especially the difficult negotiations demanded at the border zone—translates into a textual strategy, that is, the

thick narrative descriptions of landscape and spatial practice in Chaneysville. It is disturbing news, to say the least, that C. K. and the fugitives, and
Moses two generations later, are stopped dead in their tracks. These events
seem like major contradictions until one recalls that it is not really the purpose of the novel to represent the terms of racism but to construct ever thicker
signifying relations. There may indeed be the legend of the escaping slaves
who take their own lives when they are quite literally cut off at the pass, but
what that legend is doing in the novel and what it means to John and Judith
is the question.

I want to return then to the "passing" of the slaves and to the burial
ground more generally to identify the density of its meaning to the various
parties involved. To the slaves, their passing both indicates the next world and
signifies to the slave catchers that their flight northward has been successful
after all. (They are no longer chattel.) The burial ground discovery gives John
the opportunity both to demonstrate to Judith that he is not a believer in
"ghosts" to the degree his father was and to signify to her that he nonetheless
has been steeped in a local knowledge and spatial practice separate from hers.
But the discovery, as Trudier Harris points out in *Exorcising Blackness*, also
gives Judith the opportunity to signify back at John. Judith poses the question
of who buried the slaves and the probability of white involvement. This is
important because as John sloughs off old, overdetermined selves, there is now
a historical grounding for the race-crossing self *he* has become. Yet the "story"
that James buried C. K. Washington and the slaves is just that, a story invented
by Judith and John in the process of circumnavigating the race relations they
are already in. Finally, the burial ground raises and posits an answer to the
metaquestion: Why write about escaping slaves who failed to escape successfully? The reason is not sentimental, it is eschatological: because no one
"escapes." In Douglassian terms this is the safest kind of story to tell, a story
which reminds one of the social relations through which one always must
work. In the end John doesn't "escape" the knot of race relations, although
he does proceed with them more productively, or so readers are led to believe.
The further point is this: John is ultimately not a character who exists in order
to tell stories; he, like Frederick Douglass, tells stories (completes the slave
narrative) in order to exist, to set his existence aright. The ultimate proof is
the legacy of fire (of having say) he leaves behind: he burns his own notebooks
and leaves behind Moses Washington's so that someone else may discover a
story for themselves.

CONCLUSION

I began this chapter with a side trip into the narrative of Frederick Douglass
and his powerful warning about the moral economy, the regulation, of infor-

mation. In a similar vein John Washington speaks: To know too much, as he sometimes feels is the case, is to forget what things should be known for. To know too much is precisely what happens when one thinks one knows enough. Moreover, as the signifying struggle among Old Jack, Old Mrs. Turner, John, and Moses indicates, it is best to retain a constructive ambivalence about what one "knows." What one seeks are places (both figuratively and geographically speaking) where active construction and reconstruction of knowledge, where vision and revision, can be carried on. It seems to me that landscape has been given this function as a sort of regulator of "doing" knowledge. It marks departures and arrivals of various kinds. John turns to landscape when the facts run out, in order to make it do what the facts would if they could. But to make the landscape speak its facts, he must turn to the divinations of tracking and trailing taught to him by Old Jack. A point of emphasis: I am speaking of more than just intuition here, for what enables John to read this landscape (the burial ground, which by now must be read synecdochically as definitive of all ground) are the rules of reading taught to him by Old Jack and shown him by Moses. Historians' (whites', according to Old Jack) methods of inquiry are not so much intended to merge with vernacular (black) methods as the two are called upon to signify to each other, to produce sparks. It is the sparks, perhaps, that we are after. Fire. Having say.

I want to close by suggesting that spatial practice in *Chaneysville* has a meaning other than the double terrain of subjugation and emancipatory transformation. Again Moses and John's crisscrossing of the Hill is pertinent. In an essay on literature, Sartre suggests that the more an "object" in a narrative exchanges hands, the more meaning accrues to it and to people.[49] When father and son trace and retrace the Hill, there is the proposal that it has not been done enough—that spatial practice also means bringing social space into being, maintaining it, and signifying, railing, against the possibility of nothingness. "If indeed every society produces a space, its own space," social theorist Henri Lefebvre writes, then "any 'social existence' aspiring or claiming to be 'real,' but failing to produce its own space, would be a strange entity, a very peculiar kind of abstraction unable to escape from the ideological or even the 'cultural' realm. It would fall to the level of folklore and sooner or later disappear altogether."[50] For the reason Lefebvre gives, buttressed by the note burning, I would argue that Bradley means to locate this novel as a representation of a history which is not yet over and yet which must be retold for new and changing reasons: history is a moral economy of information that must be discovered differently and anew.[51]

Yet it may legitimately be asked whether, at the end of the day, this is an argument that can be upheld by a novel which is after all also a mass-marketed commodity: readers are positioned ironically; they do not have to earn what

John and Judith do. Indeed, as fallacious as it might be in some forms of literary reckoning, it is difficult to imagine what a fully "earned" reading of the novel, that is, a reading earned on the novel's own terms, would look like anyway since John's notes, as it were, can only come to real-world readers by way of a commodity exchange that brooks no worries over such things as moral economies. However, short of any "earned" reading, the simple fact that *Chaneysville* is indivisibly a work of historical reconstruction and a novel means that real-world readers are bound to revisit in some form John Washington's dilemma over fact and fiction. Certain questions are thus likely to come up in readers' minds. Is there a real town called Chaneysville? Which town and county are the "Town" and "South County" of the novel? Is there a legend in the area having to do with ill-fated fugitives on the Underground Railroad? Did the Underground Railroad, such as it was, pass through there? As I have hinted at various points, the "Town" is Bedford, the "County" is Bedford County. These, along with Chaneysville in Southampton Township, Evitts and Tussey Mountains, Town Creek, Chambersburg, and Rainsburg, and just about every other place mentioned in Bradley's novel, may in fact be found on Pennsylvania maps. There are ways then of trying to verify what *Chaneysville* tells, although these would necessarily fall short of an earned reading, always impossible anyway. Perhaps it would be better then to turn the question around a bit and ask what sort of negotiated meanings the writing of *Chaneysville* entailed at its inception. If an earned reading is chimerical, the earning that the novel itself represents, that is, the moral economy of information that the novel is a part of, may be inquired after.

Recently I went to Bedford and in talking to several people there learned that more than one version of the legend exists. That, as in *Chaneysville*, one view is that the slaves are indeed buried in the Iames family cemetery, the slaves' unmarked memorial stones next to the family's marked ones. But another version is told that the bodies of the killed slaves were taken to Mount Ross, the cemetery for African Americans in Bedford, to be buried in unmarked graves which presently constitute the only "empty" area of the cemetery. This is a space at the back, left quadrant of Mount Ross which everyone knows to leave alone.

And then there is debate over whether the slaves took their own lives, were killed by someone upon their request, or actually were protected from their pursuers. Charles Blockson, in *The Underground Railroad in Pennsylvania*, cites David Bradley's mother as the source of this version:

> In the Chaneysville area the citizens swung into immediate action under the leadership of the Lester Imes [variant spelling of Iames] family to protect a group of fugitive slaves who had escaped over the

Cumberland Mountains with slave catchers closely pursuing them. The blacks stated to the Imes family and a few of their neighbors that they would rather die freemen than return to the inhumanness of slavery in the Cumberland, Maryland area near the Mason-Dixon Line. The friends of the escaping blacks concealed and protected them from their pursuers and prevented the return of the fleeing blacks to bondage.[52]

In the local, "official" history of Bedford County, *The Kernel of Greatness*, there is this version: "On the Lester Imes farm below Chaneysville one can still find the markers for twelve or thirteen graves of runaway slaves. Mr. Imes relates that when the slaves realized their pursuers were closing in on them, they begged to be killed rather than go back to the Southland and more servitude. Someone obliged."[53] One man I spoke with insisted that the slaves would never have given up without a fight.

In crude terms *Chaneysville* is a text within an ongoing Text whose mysteries could partly be solved (exhumed) but which no one seems particularly interested in solving. Instead the impulse seems to be to keep the sparks flying. One might speculate that the signifying relationships have changed with the publication of *Chaneysville*. If the novel began by inserting itself into already ongoing stories, a text within the Text, it now threatens an inversion. To restate the code, a text may now determine the Text. My conjecture is that the slave legends are more thought about with reference to Bradley's version and to the knowledge that his is the one version that has traveled farthest from the border. (Indeed, not everyone, including African Americans in Bedford, are comfortable with him as a spokesman.) It seems clear that it is precisely because the story has traveled well outside the border—the novel has recently been reissued with a glossy new cover and is available in bookstores all over the country—that Bradley's version, not just of the slave legend but of race relations in the "Town" generally, must be contested. No one needs to be told that space signifies.

7 A SEARCH FOR PLACE

William McNorton and His Garden of the Lord

Frances Jones-Sneed

> Before any choice there is this "place," where the foundations
> of earthly existence and human condition establish themselves.
> We can change locations, move, but this is still to look for a place;
> we need a base to set down our being and to realize
> our possibilities, a here from which to discover
> the world, a there to which we can return.
>
> —*Eric Dardel, L'homme et la terre: Nature de la réalité géographique*
> *(trans. Edward Relph, from his essay on*
> *"Geographical Experiences and Being-in-the-World:*
> *The Phenomenological Origins of Geography")*

A FRICAN AMERICANS MIGRATED to the West for the same reasons that European Americans did: for greater opportunities in employment and freedom from the restrictions of class. However, unlike their white counterparts they also wanted a place that was free of the restrictions of race as well. Black men, like white men, were fascinated with the idea of seeking a place in the West to find personal freedom, land, and riches. After emancipation African Americans were interested in becoming independent landowners. The idea of landownership made African Americans feel independent and in charge of their destinies; however, only a small percentage of ex-slaves acquired and held land after the Civil War.[1] Following emancipation, "most blacks became wage earners, sharecroppers, or tenant farmers, rather than independent, landowning farmers."[2] It took tremendous effort for African Americans to establish a place of their own and maintain an identity distinct from their master after slavery. Yet many managed to establish a place for themselves after their slave experience by wedding African and European traditions.

This chapter investigates the idea and meaning of place for William McNorton who migrated from Virginia to the Montana Territory in 1879. He established a place for himself in Montana that conformed to the environment and social customs of the local community rather than what place represented for him in Virginia. Montana in this early period offered single men the opportunity to make a small fortune if they had capital to invest or were willing to work hard. According to Eric Dardel, all humans "need a base to set down our being and realize our possibilities."[3] William McNorton desired a place to realize his potentials, and the Montana Territory seemed a good place to begin.

Place can be defined as an idea that can free or restrict an individual of any perceived barriers and empower them to achieve in ways not possible in their former homes. McNorton came to Montana as a free, young, single man willing to work hard to establish a place for himself—to invent himself anew without any of the history of a slave heritage. "Although place is closely related to space and landscape, its experiential dimension is qualitatively different from that of landscape or space . . . in geographical experience, a place is an origin; it is where one knows others and is known to others; it is where one comes from and it is one's own."[4] Virginia was McNorton's place of origin, but he sought another place to make his own—a place different from Virginia. One explanation of space in this context is that "human existence is spatial and its spatiality embraces closeness, separation, distance and direction as modes of existence."[5]

McNorton tried to adapt to the new space he entered by conforming to the environmental and social climate that was already present in northwestern Montana. However, after a number of failures to adapt to the social climate of Montana, he returned to a model that resembled his former home in Virginia. He constructed a place that made space a part of his everyday experience and then invited others to share it with him rather than venturing out to become a part of the larger community. McNorton's invented place was not only physical but was also spiritual. He called the place he constructed his "Garden of the Lord." He became Adam in a reconstructed Eden and invited others to enjoy the bounty of the place.

Most African Americans who left the South before World War II migrated to northern cities, but there were some who went west. African Americans migrated to the western territories long before the "exodusters" got Kansas fever, but 1879 marked the time when a flood of African Americans left the South to go west. There were about 10,000 blacks in the 1879 migration west, and before the end of the next decade almost 60,000 blacks journeyed west. Only about 35,000 migrated to the Far West from 1890 to 1900, but the population of African Americans in the West continued to escalate slowly over the next four decades. When African Americans migrated west they took with them the knowledge of land and how to cultivate it, as well as "deeply entrenched ideals regarding social order and well-being."[6] They believed that their lifework as farmers would prepare them to deal with this new place. The memory of what it was like to be a slave gave them the psychological strength to handle this new environment. Land they believed would be the liberating force that would define their freedom and worth, economic and personal. Moreover, they knew from their experience in slavery that owning land meant economic independence. Surely, in freedom, land was necessary to further shield them from a lifetime of servitude on someone else's land.

Kansas was the first western destination of the majority of African Americans in the nineteenth century, but others, mostly single men, went farther west to the Dakotas, Nebraska, Colorado, Montana, Washington, and the Oregon territories. They were often the only blacks in places largely populated by whites, and the only other blacks in the area were family members who migrated there after them. Although they went west for similar reasons to whites, blacks also desired an environment free from the race and class prejudice that they had faced in their former southern homes. Most of these men did not migrate directly from the South to the Far West but worked their way, often on boats and other conveyances, until they came to a place where they believed they could make a living.

African Americans, even during slavery, formulated their sense of place and created a mental, physical, and spiritual picture of the overall structure and character of a perfect place. When they found it in the West they sacrificed almost everything to keep it. These people found the land and freedom to create their dreams. William McNorton is one example, and his story points out certain historical truths about the western environment and the struggle of blacks to discover their place there.

Richard White writes that black migration to the West followed the pattern of the Kansas Exoduster migration of the 1880s when African Americans established small communities and encouraged others to come west. The seemingly individualistic efforts of McNorton and others may not be a divergence from this pattern. As an example, the number of black soldiers who served and decided to stay in the West also acted as recruiting agents for family members. McNorton's brother served in the Twenty-fourth Infantry unit and was stationed in Missoula, Montana.[7]

William McNorton created a place for himself in this western environment. His story tells us what it was like to be an African American on the mining frontier of the Montana Territory of the mid-nineteenth century. McNorton came to Montana to free himself of the race and class barriers that he found in his home state of Virginia, and he expected the same rewards others found in this new place. Whites and blacks in Virginia, the state where

Africans first landed in the new British colony, had a deep attachment to place. As one former slave said of the state: "I been here a long time, and I ain't tire of staying." Many ex-slaves moved around after the Civil War, but most stayed close to "the homeplace" because they had a deep attachment to it. "However, slaves in Virginia were outside the system of landownership. They were on the land, tilled the land, and were generally given private gardens to cultivate to supplement their own food, but the land did not 'belong' to them legally."[8] Nevertheless, blacks in Virginia had a strong spiritual attachment to land. After all, no man could own land; only God owned land, and man was only a temporary caretaker. Yet legal complications did not cloud blacks' sense of spiritual and physical attachment to the homeplace.

William McNorton was born in Virginia on August 22, 1866, a year after the abolition of slavery. His mother was a house slave on a large plantation in the tidewater area of Virginia. It was rumored that William and his two brothers were the offspring of his mother's master, who gave her enough money to educate them after slavery. A description of McNorton and his brothers confirms that they were nearly white.[9] McNorton came from Virginia to Montana in 1887 where he homesteaded first on the east side of the Clark Fork River between Belknap and Thompson Falls. Much later he moved to the Blue Slide area where he developed his well-known "Garden of the Lord." His garden became a showplace, filled with fruits, berries, and vegetables that he gave to anyone who wanted them at no charge. His name is well known in Sanders County even today, because William McNorton became a legend in this small northwestern county.

He came to Sanders County because of his brother's affiliation with the Twenty-fourth Infantry at Fort Missoula, and from all accounts McNorton loved Thompson Falls and the people in it.[10] There were also indications that many people in the community liked him as well. He was respected for his intelligence and the way that he made his fortune from mining and timber interests. McNorton learned early that he had to conform to the environment and social order of Thompson Falls to prosper there. In so doing, he became one of the richest men in Sanders County and did not endure the same kind of persecution that Native Americans, Chinese, and other blacks faced in some Montana communities.[11] African Americans made up a small percentage of the Montana population, and William McNorton engaged in employment where very few blacks worked—mining and timber. Blacks came to Montana as part of the gold rush after the Civil War. However, most of them "came as servants of white families, many more to work in the service economy or as day laborers, and a fraction of them as miners and entrepreneurs."[12] They comprised 2 percent of Helena's population in 1870 and built thriving communities in other major urban areas. Very few blacks settled in the northwestern part of Montana where William McNorton eventually settled, perhaps because it was so isolated and the urban areas offered a safer refuge, more community life with family or friends.[13] No matter what the reason, at least three other black men besides William McNorton came to this isolated mining and timber town.

McNorton fared better than the other men. One referred to in the written records only as "Nigger" George was beaten to death with an ax handle while defending his gold claim. Another, whose name is not recalled by the people in the community, left the area but is remembered as being a good cook in the mining camps. The third one, Tom Matthews, was an ex-prize-fighter who occasionally sparred in the local bars.[14] William McNorton had better luck and perhaps a different approach to life than the other blacks who lived in Thompson Falls. African Americans established social clubs and churches in cities such as Virginia City, Butte, and Helena during the early 1870s that became centers of community life.[15] McNorton did not have these outlets in Thompson Falls, but he did find social outlets like the other miners in drinking and gambling. He seemed to see no difference in himself and the other people in the town.

This seeming indifference to race on McNorton's part may have been the root of all his troubles and why his name is part of the recorded history of Sanders County. Of course, a large part of the problem deals with the complicated issue of race and McNorton's philosophy about it. He was a mulatto who had been educated with the help of his white father and accepted into this all-white setting in Thompson Falls. McNorton believed that in this new environment he was inviolate from the ravages of racism that were often found in post–Civil War Virginia. Although Thompson Falls was not without the virulence of the system of racism, it did provide for his lifetime a freer setting to build a place for himself than Virginia.

All that is left of the story of William McNorton is shrouded in local legend, but the facts are straightforward. He laid claim to land in Sanders County in 1889 and staked timber and mining claims on the Blue Slide,[16] selling the timber to the railroad and promoting mining ventures. He profited greatly from both ventures, and later he bought property in Thompson Falls and built a fine two-story white frame house with a wraparound porch. His house was one of the finest and most distinctive in the community. A neighbor remembers that he also sold a patent for rail joints to the railroad for $50,000. By the age of thirty-four he was a rich man with timber, mining, and patent interests. Yet after fourteen years alone in this isolated place, McNorton needed a wife and family to progress socially and politically in the community.[17] Single women were scarce in this part of the country, and McNorton turned to a method that many single men in the West used—the mail-order bride.

He corresponded with a widow, and she came to Thompson Falls on July 4, 1900, with her young child to marry him. A newspaper account of the wedding read: "The band interspersed sweet strains of music through the day. Dancing was indulged in, and at 12 o'clock, the music of a wedding march played by the band, William McNorton, one of Thompson's substantial citizens, marched to the hall accompanied by the lady of his choice and the couple were publicly married. The crowd formed arches with their hands through which the couple marched."[18]

The wedding was held at night with a torch as the only source of light. Because of his light skin color, Ella Skinner, McNorton's white bride, did not realize that he was black. According to one account, "In the dark of the evening 'Nigger' Bill's features were hardly discernible from those of a white man. The woman never knew that it was a huge joke or that she had married a Negro until afterwards."[19] She realized the truth the next morning.

The white population of Thompson Falls seemed amused by this mixed union. There were no laws in Montana restricting marriages between whites and blacks. Nonetheless, there were laws restricting blacks from attending schools with whites, testifying against whites in courts, and preventing them from voting.[20] Although there were no laws preventing such a marriage, the sympathy of the town went to the white bride. In their memories of her they make it clear that she only stayed in the marriage because she had no other options for herself or her young child. There was no physical violence leveled against McNorton. The marriage ended after six years in 1906. Skinner, provided with a tidy settlement from McNorton, stayed in Thompson Falls and remarried twice, to white men, before her death in 1948. In 1909 McNorton traveled to his home state of Virginia where he met and married fourteen-year-old India Penn, a mulatto woman. He brought his new bride, her grandmother, and her brother back to Thompson Falls, but his marriage to Penn was even more short-lived than his first to Skinner. Penn's grandmother eventually intervened, believing that her granddaughter was too young to sustain a marriage. More important, she believed that McNorton was an abusive spouse. A divorce was granted in 1910, and his property was seized for the settlement. Penn received a larger settlement sum than Skinner, and as a result McNorton mortgaged his property. Eventually, the bank foreclosed for nonpayment in 1920.[21]

After two disastrous marriages and the loss of his property and most of his other assets, William McNorton's life course changed. He tried to make a place for himself by adapting to the environment and social values of the

Thompson Falls community, but he failed. McNorton then took a different tack by constructing a physical space that resembled the Virginia environment more than the Montana landscape. He contracted with the Northern Pacific Railroad to acquire two sections of land on the Blue Slide. Although he was given a lifetime grant, the company would not allow him to do mining in the area. On these two sections of land McNorton finally found his place in the West. There he built a cabin and outbuildings, dug a fishpond, and cultivated his "Garden of the Lord." Also, at this time he began to have visions. Refusing to speak for seven years, McNorton began wearing a crown of thorns on his head and referring to himself as "King David."[22]

During the last eighteen years of McNorton's life, he cultivated the garden that contained grapes, pears, prunes, apples, and peaches. Amazingly, the garden thrived above the frost line through the late fall. He also maintained his pond well stocked with fish. However, he never sold anything, giving away his fruits and vegetables to anyone who wished to make the journey up the long, narrow, isolated road. McNorton explained that his garden was so plentiful because of God's blessing. He found a way to irrigate it by building a small dam at the mouth of two tunnels about 1,000 feet into the mountain, creating a narrow gorge that allowed the water to flow down to his terraced gardens.

McNorton turned to farming when he was fifty-four years of age, preferring before that time to work in mining and timber, supplying ties to the railroad. A friend remembered, "Bill contracted in the tie business, hiring men to cut the ties. He carried them from the yard to the sleigh and took them up to the railroad at Kildy. He made more money in this trade than ranching."[23] However, he found that the small house he built for himself on leased land gave him more pleasure than the two-story white frame house with the wraparound porch. He discovered that his garden was more pleasurable than any of his mining or timber ventures or his attempts at domestic bliss.

Unfortunately, after his conversion experience, many people became afraid of McNorton because of his impromptu sermons and predictions. Also, he allowed his nearly white hair and beard to grow long and wore overalls with a felt hat adorned by a crown of thorns. He believed that God provided him with this place on the Blue Slide because of his loss of everything that he worked so hard for all of his life. He also believed that it was God's beneficence that caused the productivity of his garden. When asked about the beauty of his garden, he always replied, "The Lord takes care of [it]."[24]

The community labeled him a religious fanatic, and on May 4, 1938, a complaint was filed against him for being "so disordered in the mind as to be dangerous to person and property." He was sent to the state asylum for the insane where he died two months later at the age of seventy-two. The town's leading newspapers carried the story of his death with headlines that read, "King David Dies" and "King David the Lord."[25] Although some of this was probably written in the same tone as the coverage of his marriage, William McNorton was remembered for the place he made for himself in Sanders County. He was a religious fanatic, eccentric, wealthy, a cultivator of a fine vineyard and orchard but not very successful in marriage. There is no greater testimony to one's sense of place than that others retain a memory of you when you are no longer a part of the place.

Quintard Taylor writes about three black men similar to McNorton who found places in nearly all white communities in the West. The first, Oscar Micheaux, known better as a pioneer black independent filmmaker, migrated from Illinois to South Dakota in 1904. There he "became the most famous black homesteader on the Northern Plains, in part because he left accounts of his activities in two fictionalized autobiographies, *The Conquest* and *The Homesteader.*" Micheaux "broke out" 120 acres of prairie when most of his homesteading neighbors cultivated only 40 acres.[26] Finally he went back to Illinois, married, and returned to South Dakota, persuading his new wife to homestead acreage in an adjoining county. Neither the marriage nor Micheaux's attachment to the land lasted long. Two years later he skipped town with borrowed money to make his fortune in the film industry, never to return to South Dakota's soil. Micheaux used his experience of place on the Plains to write two books and finance his film—in this vein, the place served his needs well.[27]

The two other examples, Robert Ball Anderson of Nebraska and James Edwards of Wyoming, make better comparisons to McNorton. Anderson, an ex-slave from Kentucky, moved to Nebraska after the Civil War in 1870. He settled first in southeastern Nebraska and when that failed moved to the Nebraska Panhandle where he succeeded in acquiring over 2,000 acres of land worth almost $100,000. His philosophy was simple: "I lived alone, saved, worked hard, lived cheaply as I could." His perseverance paid off because he became one of the richest farmers in the state, eventually marrying a woman fifty-eight years younger than he and hiring her two brothers to help manage the farm. He said: "I am . . . old now, and can't do much work. I have a good farm, well-stocked with plenty of horses, cows and farming machinery . . . fruit trees, grapes and berries, and have money in the bank to tide me over my old age when I am unable to earn more. . . . I am a rich man today, at least rich enough for my own needs."[28]

James Edwards migrated from Ohio and reached Wyoming in 1900, homesteading his first 90-acre plot in 1901. Eventually Edwards would own 10,000 acres of land in Wyoming in Niobrara County. He also married a younger woman once he had carved out a place for himself, and his wife made his two-room log cabin a showplace in the county. Edwards once said after being called "Nigger Jim": "Y'all call me Nigger Jim now, but someday you'll call me Mr. James Edwards." His reply is reminiscent of the respect that William McNorton, alias "Nigger Bill," wanted for himself. The following quote by a white neighbor was written about James Edwards. It could easily have been written about Anderson, Micheaux, or McNorton: "All in all . . . he was a good man, and was liked in the community. His feet, as all our feet, were made of clay, but my memories of him are good. I have a lot of respect for any black man who invades a white territory, makes a living for himself, and builds a home as elaborate as his was on the prairie."[29]

Black men, like white men, were respected and liked for their talents and success in the West. Yet, for black men, race became an important factor, and their chances for success were better in communities where they settled together rather than as individuals. These men were successful, for all intents, and Anderson and Edwards were more fortunate in their marriages, encouraging other relatives to join them. Also, their land was inherited by family members who continued to farm it.

Micheaux left the land early for other pursuits, but William McNorton isolated himself from the community and created a place for himself for the last half of his life that seemed to satisfy his spiritual and physical needs. Although he spent the final months of his life in an insane asylum, William McNorton was not a failure. He died as he lived: boldly and alone. The legend of this man remains not as a result of family memories but as a chapter in the history of the place where he chose to live the majority of his life. One writer believes that "the Natural world provides refuge."[30] McNorton found a refuge in the northeastern part of Montana and chose to live and die there. What he failed to find in relationships with humans he found in the natural world because "each of us harbors a homeland, a landscape we naturally comprehend. By understanding the dependability of place, we can anchor ourselves as trees."[31] William McNorton, although he was not born in Thompson Falls, chose to live and realize the possibilities of his lifetime there.

8 RIVERS UNDERGROUND

Rebellious Young Men, Community Parks and the Surfacing of Culture in Barbados

Elizabeth Barnum

BARBADIAN POET KAMAU BRATHWAITE compared the culture of Barbados to an underground river. Steeped in British tradition on the surface, Barbados also has its own variety of Afro-Caribbean culture that is not readily apparent to outsiders or openly discussed.[1] In other Caribbean locations, maroonages were established by escaped African slaves in remote areas. In Barbados, with a dense population and few unsettled interior portions, the only available maroonage for Barbadians was within their minds.[2] By being able to supply the appropriate "face" they were able to organize interior sensibilities, as Hilary Beckles noted, "by taking underground those elements which could survive without public display."[3] Barbados is considered the most "Anglicized" of Caribbean islands, and the hidden face of its maroonage often took more subtle forms of resistance.

This undercurrent is most eloquently articulated in Kamau Brathwaite's *Mother Poem* in which Barbados's African mother is compared to its underground rivers.[4] As a porous coral island, Barbados's water supply comes from an underground system of springs and rivers. You may see a glisten above ground, and then it disappears again as all the while the underground watercourses nourish the land. Likened to maroonages, the continuation of African forms such as "Africanization of Christianity" has been expressed in West Indian churches and that of other African forms in "marketing habits, family patterns, speech (dialect), magic-medicine (obeah), and religious practices: Po/kumania Vodun, Shango, etc."[5] These examples point toward possibilities for there to be sufficient material available for creole versions of these forms to appear elsewhere in their visual forms. Particular assemblages of materials found in community parks may be an example of an appearance of one of Barbados's underground cultural streams.

A manifestation of underground "religion and philosophic world view"[6] may have surfaced in the small landscaped plots called community parks. This chapter represents a preliminary consideration of Barbadian community parks.[7] It does not seek to outline these historical connections; rather it seeks to describe the phenomenon of community parks appearing between 1990 and 1995 and to raise the possibility of their connection to larger symbolic systems available throughout the diaspora. Further, this preliminary exploration asks for fuller historical and ethnographic study of both public and private spaces in the Caribbean. Fragments appearing in historical accounts and pictures from other locations suggest that the phenomenon of community parks is a continuity of, and bubbling up of, a strong undercurrent available in the underground rivers of Barbadian culture.

These parks, prominent in the late 1980s, were recognized by the local media and the government but have begun to disappear, perhaps to reappear in another form. Some have suggested that they are just a fad of youthful industry; however, the imagery and juxtaposition of symbols appear too potent to dismiss them simply as an accumulation of plants, paint, and objects arranged for purely decorative purposes. While this chapter does not seek to interpret the symbolic placement of objects, it is tempting to relate these arrangements to those occurring in other African diaspora contexts. The elements in the community parks, as much as they look like elements in dressed yards of the southern United States, could as easily have little or no connection with them. However, these symbols appear in diverse locations from Bahia to New Orleans and from New York City to Havana, wherever people have survived the Middle Passage and centuries of enslavement and cultural suppression. Shrines or altars were necessarily in a "code" that could exist unrecognized by slave masters. Thus trees, roots, pierced coins, and other seemingly innocuous items encoded powerful symbolism and medicine.[8]

However, one cannot overlook the fact that Barbadians watch CNN and read two daily local newspapers, and that many have traveled to the United States both on holiday and as agricultural workers in the American South.[9] Fashion and fad are much a part of the Barbadian social scene. When one woman sets up a coal pot[10] to sell roast corn on the highway, in "two Tuesdays" several dozen others sell the same product at the same price in similar locations. This trend has been repeated among the ubiquitous beach vendors' offerings as well as in the interest in name-brand clothing among Barbadian youth.[11] In short, an idea, a fashion, or a fad can become popular within a short space of time and can die out as quickly as it became popular.

Skeptics can easily discount the connections to African American yard shows by pointing out that tire gardens were promoted by the Barbadian agronomist Dr. Colin Hudson as an ecological alternative for small-scale kitchen gardens on thin rocky soil that also keeps discarded tires out of the landfill. Phrases used to describe the elements and color choices in the community gardens were along the lines of "the paint we had" or "the paint someone gave us." The other materials were most often described as "found" objects put to practical and aesthetic use. Wheels (from wagons, sugar machinery, etc.) are used at entrances to the driveways of great houses of white planters and perhaps were imitated by community garden makers.[12] As with obeah, Barbadians will tell an outsider that it does not exist in Barbados due to the sophistication and education of Barbadians, yet most Barbadians are aware of obeah's signs and symbols.[13]

Some on public land, some on private land, these parks contain found objects such as tires, bike and outboard motor parts, toy cars, painted rocks, and special plantings. For nearly two years, from 1991 through 1992, many communities in Barbados had at least one park, and the phenomenon received considerable media attention. By December 1993 many had become overgrown by bush and had disappeared without a trace, yet some continue to prosper.

The parks, constructed and maintained primarily by unemployed young men, were put forth in the news media as efforts by youth to improve vacant lots in their communities. In contrast to reports of rising gang activities, the media showed these parks as efforts at productivity. The *Sunday Sun* reported: "The main objective of their effort is to show that all unemployed youths are not involved in lawlessness, dishonesty or associated with gangs, but have certain skills which could be utilised, if given the opportunity."[14] In another report a resident of the Redman Village housing project said that "young men from the housing districts lime on the block, people say that they are gangs but that is not so since liming was from the time of creation."[15] "Lime" is defined by Barbadian author Frank Collymore as "to stand in a group on a side-walk or near some frequented spot, and indulge in chit-chat, sometimes passing remarks at passers-by, especially females; to loiter in groups."[16] What is considered to be acceptable, inevitable "liming" by some, is seen by others as dangerous activity, especially when groups of unemployed youth are engaged in it. Furthermore, neatly organized spaces are part of the Barbadian construct necessary for showing dignity and respectability to the outside. Therefore, to "lime" in a disorderly location shows lack of self-respect and invites others to treat you without respect.

The "institutionalization" of the parks culminated in a contest judged by the National Conservation Commission, the Youth and Community Development Department, the Barbados Youth Council, the Barbados Environmental Association, and the National Trust. "The parks were judged according to park design, cultural community activities, use of native Barbadian plants, methods of garbage disposal, ingenuity of rainwater collection, use of correct plant material for existing microclimate and park maintenance."[17]

PARK LAND AS DISTINGUISHED FROM PRIVATE LANDS

The idea of inside/outside pervades the Barbadian presentation of self in speech indirection, dress, and other aspects of life. Laborers, maids, and factory workers wash, spray deodorant and perfume, and change into skirts or suits before emerging from the workplace and entering public transport or private car to go home. Contrary to the New Yorker who will wear walking shoes in the street and change into dress shoes for the office, the Barbadian worker wears the dress shoes in the street and changes to the more comfortable shoes when not in the street. An individual's occupation is rarely betrayed by public dress, and one would suspect from watching people go to and from work that everyone works in air-conditioned offices rather than as carpenters, gardeners, day laborers, or maids.

Characteristic Barbadian chattel houses and neat yards dot the landscape. "Well-kept," "neat," and "tidy" are the adjectives frequently used in tourist brochures and publications to describe the Barbadian house and yard. Despite a concern for neatness and tidiness of house and yard, other parcels of "rab" land fall into bush and become heaps of rotting garbage, abandoned appliances, and old cars. These uncultivated lots stand in sharp contrast to their manicured neighbors. Although a householder may spend hours making his or her own yard tidy, some have no compunction about throwing refuse into empty neighborhood lots despite the government's regular garbage collection.

Barbadians take home ownership and its presentation very seriously. An estimated 80 percent of Barbadians own their own homes, but not necessarily the land upon which they stand.[18] While the front of a Barbadian home is painted, landscaped, and tidy, there is typically "paling," a high fence of galvanized sheet metal, around the backyard. This back area is an extension of the inside of a Barbadian home that is kept hidden from public view. Laundry, fish cleaning, and haircutting are tasks that are accomplished in the hidden parts of the yard not on display to the public.

The house site is clearly demarcated by a fence, a hedgerow, or ideally by a wall with a wrought iron gate. The fence or wall is the first layer separating the house from the outside. The front yard is usually planted decoratively with flowers, shrubs, crotons, or other plants. It has recently become fashionable to spell out words in small, low-to-the-ground bushes.

The second stage toward the inside is the veranda. The veranda always faces the road. Even though there may be a spectacular view to the back of the house, in many houses the only window facing the view is a small high window in the toilet. Family members may sit on the veranda and watch people pass on the road. Long conversations take place with family members on the veranda talking to those in the road without inviting the visitor onto the veranda or into the house. Acquaintances may be entertained on the veranda, and a single woman may entertain a man on the veranda, usually with her parents present. Once the man is allowed beyond the veranda, it is assumed that the couple has a sexual relationship. The veranda is usually painted a different color from the house walls, demarcating it as a separate outside room of the house. Inhabitants of houses without verandas can be seen sitting at the windows calling out to passersby or conversing with them for long periods of time, without inviting the person into the house. There may be a fabric curtain or curtain of beads between the veranda and the interior of the house so that the breeze can pass but people can't see in.

Traditional Barbadian homes, such as chattel houses, are built in stages as the family can afford them. The first stage built is a single peaked one-room house with a shed roof attached to the back. The farther one moves into the interior of the house, the more private the activities. As the family can afford them, additional houses are added, and the first stage becomes the parlor or sitting room and is referred to as the "front house." Despite its small size this room is typically decorated with as much heavy large furniture and decorations as it can hold. A settee and two matching chairs are the starting pieces with additional furniture suites being added as they can be afforded. A well-furnished 8-by-12-foot room may contain a couch and two large chairs, a settee and two matching chairs, and a variety of shelves and tables to hold numerous vases of plastic and silk flowers, ceramic ornaments, stuffed animals, and ornaments made from mahogany, clothespins, glue, and varnish. The walls also will be ornamented with brightly painted plaster plaques made from commercial molds and a clock, either an imported one as elaborate as possible or a locally made highly resin-coated mahogany clock with roman numerals or elaborate gold numbers. Religious pictures are as common as framed copies of oil paintings of the European countryside. Pictures of famous men such as Martin Luther King, former government leader Errol Barrow,[19] or John F. Kennedy have nearly replaced the pictures of H.R.H. Queen Elizabeth II.

The separation of public and private living spaces and the keeping up of appearances are both significant constructs in relation to community gardens and yards. Community parks were mostly constructed on rab land or someone's land that wasn't in use. In many cases the area had been used as a dumping ground, containing the flotsam of daily life that has no place either in the manicured front yard or even in the hidden backyard.

When these spaces were cleared and "dressed," they contained many of the recurring elements described by Robert Farris Thompson in yard shows

A small park connected with a standpipe, Asbury, St. George.
(Photo: Elizabeth Barnum, 1991)

Asbury, St. George, standpipe without a trace of its former "styles."
(Photo: Elizabeth Barnum, 1995)

Pride of Wilson Hill, Jackson, St. Michael. (Photo: Elizabeth Barnum, 1995)

Planters beside the gate to "The Pride of Checker Hall," St. Lucy.
(Photo: Elizabeth Burnam)

Hugh Rock's sculptures, St. Lucy. (Photo: Elizabeth Barnum)

Detail of Hugh Rock's sculptures, St. Lucy. (Photo: Elizabeth Barnum)

Cow skull, tire, and root arrangement, Avis Town, St. Lucy.
(Photo: Elizabeth Barnum, 1991)

Pride of Checker Hall, St. Lucy. (Photo: Elizabeth Barnum, 1995)

Detail of entrance to "The Pride of Checker Hall."
(Photo: Ken Corsbie)

Crab Hill, St. Lucy. (Photo: Elizabeth Barnum, 1991)

Detail of the Pride of Checker Hall, St. Lucy. (Photo: Ken Corsbie, 1991)

in the States, including painted rock boundaries, mirrors, containers, wheels, motion emblems, root sculptures, figures of humans and animals, materials with "flash," herbs, and gravelike decorations.[20]

Thompson describes these yard shows of the American South as "one vast nkisi charm" in which the main visual principles of the yard show include motion, containment, figuration, and medicine. Barbadian community gardens appear to contain many of these elements.

1. White rock borders appear in all of the community parks. They outline flower beds, mark the boundaries of the parks, and spell out words, typically the names of the parks.

2. Mirrors and shiny surfaces are seldom found; however, the whitewashed borders and tree trunks may be related to the "kaolin as spirit-repelling flash" found in Kongo contexts.[21]

3. Planters at the corners and entrance ways were features of several parks. Flowerpots were once at the entrance to "The Pride of Checker Hall" but were removed when the plants died.

4. Motion has been depicted by a toy car mounted on a boat motor in Avis Town, St. Lucy; a motorcycle at a minipark shrine-altar at Asbury St. George; white wagon wheels at Crab Hill, St. Lucy. There are white wheels with red centers at Wilson Hill, St. John, with a central large white wheel with red circle around a square in the center; a tractor tire mounted into the ground at Mango Park, Sergeant Street, St. John, and a propeller-like metal X nailed to a tree next to a coop of hundreds of pigeons. The cooing and flapping wings can be heard in and around the park.

5. Cosmograms: The Pride of Checker Hall has a square with a diamond that has been crossed drawn into the cement at the entrance to the park.[22] A wheel containing a circle within a square was found at Wilson Hill. Kites, traditionally made by men and boys, also display a cosmogram-like format.

6. Plantings of flowers or herbs growing within the "protective circle" of white rocks or tires were almost a standard in nearly all of the parks. Red and white flowering plants were found frequently.[23]

7. Root sculptures were found in Avis Town and in other locations, mostly as painted tree stumps. The sculpture garden of Hugh Rock in St. Lucy makes use of branches and roots in combination with other elements.

8. Bones: A cow skull, painted white with red dots, hangs above the entrance of Mango Park. Painted eyes with red center and light blue and black concentric circles stare out to the road attached to a wrought iron entranceway. When the park first opened, blue and yellow flags flew

from the gate. The wrought iron is painted alternately yellow and blue. In Avis Town a cow skull painted half green and half red hangs from roots and tree branches. A bicycle tire inner tube was draped over a nearby branch. (Behind this arrangement is the metal shell of an automobile, itself a kind of skeleton and an especially interesting element, given the parks' emphasis on neatness.) In the private garden of Hugh Rock, cow skulls and bones hang from a bare tree painted white. His sculptures in the garden are figures bearing potted plants in either hand.

9. Swept earth occurs in some of the parks, but pounded-earth areas are more likely to be found near liming areas and in and around shelters. Traditionally, the area around Barbadian homes was swept and sprinkled with white sand or marl, particularly as part of Christmas preparations. As it can be afforded, this practice is being supplanted by concrete paving. At Checker Hall broken tile has been inlaid into the walks.[24]

10. Graveyard-like decoration: At Mango Park in St. John stands a gravelike aquarium with conch shells at the two front corners. The structure is painted white and has shells embedded into the concrete, also painted white. A small manufactured plaque with a drawing of a cricketer and the inscription "25 not out" is mounted on the front of the aquarium. The "25 not out" refers to Barbados's twenty-fifth anniversary of independence in 1991.[25] The Pride of Checker Hall has a gravelike concrete structure. "Jesus Lives" is painted on the front end and a passage of Scripture on the side. An herb garden elevated to hold a plaque stands on top of the structure. A checkered lighthouse, approximately 2½ feet tall, stands in front of the structure.

In the center of the park, a tombstonelike monument was erected to display the awards plaque. Rain and sun began to destroy the plaque so it is now kept in the home of one of the park's founders.

11. Several parks had plantings of herbs, in white rock surrounded beds and/or inside of tires.

Several parks were also devoted to nationalistic themes and part of the twenty-fifth anniversary of independence celebration. The map of Barbados figures prominently in a number of parks. Drawn out in white stones, the shape of Barbados is surrounded by red plants. The white and red theme is further repeated in a half circle around the words "Pride of Wilson Hill" spelled out in white rocks with the large white wheel mounted in the visual center of the park. This central wheel surrounds a square inside of the circle.

In another park in Bayfield St. Philip, a "hedge in the shape of Barbados with 11 parishes was grown and a large rock was placed in the middle of the garden. Later in the year, the residents will get a picture of the late Prime

Minister Errol Barrow and put it in the rock so that all could remember the good he did for this island."[26]

The colors of the Barbadian flag are blue and yellow, and these national colors appear in virtually all of the parks in connection to national symbols, such as the flag, crest, or map of Barbados. The significance of the blue and yellow might also be related to its "traditional ancestral and protective overtones" as pointed out by Grey Gundaker and others in relation to the African American context.[27]

When asked about the choice of colors used in the parks, all the makers I interviewed indicated that they "used whatever paint we had or was given to us." Despite that, almost all parks have items painted in white and red, or green, white, and red, or the national colors, blue and yellow.

Although many parks fell quickly into decline, the top three prizewinning parks, Mango Park in St. John, Pride of Checker Hall in St. Lucy, and Pride of Wilson Hill, continued to be maintained when I visited them in 1995. These parks share some similar features that perhaps have led to their survival. All are located in rural villages; all have multigenerational participation; and all have a core group or individual leader who is identified as the person who keeps the park going. In the case of Mango Park, there is an official association with elected officers and a formal rental arrangement with the owner of the land, Codrington College.

Traditionally, the rum shop or village shop has been the gathering place, particularly for men in the community.[28] While women and children may enter the shop to buy groceries, "respectable" women typically do not "lime" with the men, although brief exchanges, banter, and joking often occur between women and the men liming there.

Men in the rum shop talk cricket and politics, play dominoes and warri, and drink. In many cases community parks almost seem to be extensions of the rum shop by proximity and by virtue of the activities taking place in both places. However, language used to describe the purpose and activity of the park more closely resembles that of respectable "yard" activities than the "crossroads" activities as discussed by Roger Abrahams in a Vincentian example.[29]

Indeed, house and yard tend to be the province of women in Barbados. And the parks, primarily initiated by young, unemployed men, represent "order, acting sensible, decorum, being behaved, stability, passivity, being enclosed, protected, circumspection, quiet, harmony, respectability, maintenance, truth, honesty, cooperation and loyalty."[30] Attempts at projecting these qualities over public perceptions of unemployed youth as unproductive, lawless gang members were what led several of the parks to come into existence.

Perhaps it was also necessary for the youth to "lime" somewhere other than in the local shop where they were likely not welcomed by an older generation of hardworking employed men. Generational differences and interests also account for these age-set separations. At the same time, these young men often are not welcome to spend the day liming in their mothers' houses and yards with their friends. The vice president of Perseverance Park in Lower Richmond, St. Michael, was quoted in the *Barbados Advocate* newspaper as saying: "We usually lime out here, and perhaps because the dump was nearby, people looked at us as if we were garbage. About a year ago we tried to clean it up, but people kept dumping garbage. We tried several times since then, but on Sunday morning of August 25, we decided we would definitely clean it and see it remain clean."[31]

In Avis Town some young men cleaned up the park while others messed it up, "so the fellows got tired and 'mash up' the park." These young men said that the items in the park had no particular meaning; they found them in the bush and used them. By April 1995 the park in Avis Town was overgrown and strewn with garbage; no evidence remained of its prior organization. A series of rough liming benches alongside what had been the park was built under a tree.

Certain parks no longer maintained as parks, such as the one in Avis Town, continue as a rough liming spot of benches under a tree. That particular park was purposely "mashed up," destroyed by the head of the park when he found that youth were using and abusing the park, throwing garbage in the park and then refusing to help with the park's maintenance. Breakdown of community or outside destructive elements can be responsible, as in the destruction of a park at Charles Rowe Bridge in St. George allegedly by Ellerton, St. George, youth.[32]

Another park at Crab Hill, St. Lucy, quickly became overgrown, perhaps due to the proximity of the village shop with its pool table and restaurant. Since this shop was larger than most, it was not necessary to maintain a separate liming spot. Without intergenerational involvement,[33] the less established youth grew older, got jobs, moved away from the district and/or acquired family responsibilities that kept them from spending time or having the inclination to maintain the community park space.

In Crab Hill, St. Lucy, the park fell out of fashion. The makers were teenagers at the time and have moved on to other responsibilities. By January 1995 there were only overgrown pieces remaining. A wheel was found in a bush, another one broken on the nearby track. The plantings seem to have been maintained to some degree since the trees and plants had matured.

The first-place winner in the 1991 park competition, Mango Park, is located on a steep hill facing the road directly across from a rum shop. The entrance of yellow and blue painted wrought iron had triangular yellow and blue flags hanging from it when the park was judged in the competition. A cow skull painted white, red, and green is affixed in the center of the wrought iron entrance arch; its eyes, painted in concentric circles, stare toward the road. Pathways and stairs chiseled into the terraced face of the hill allow for several of the park's decorations to be seen from the road. Large tractor tires painted white with red, yellow, and green treads are mounted upright. "Mango Park" is painted in red on the side of the tire. A now defunct shell-embedded aquarium stands about halfway up the hill. Above stand a large model of a cannon, a wishing well, a flagpole, and a rock painted with a face and the national colors. Another smaller rock is painted like the Barbados flag with a cutout trident attached to it. A homemade and nonfunctional basketball hoop is mounted on a pole below the cannon.

The park features a shady liming area with a pounded-earth floor, galvanized roof, and a series of benches on various levels for sitting, lying down, or playing cards or dominoes. A copy of the rental agreement is posted in the building. Because of the vegetation, the spot is fairly private and sheltered from the road. The park members maintain over one hundred pigeons in coops behind the liming structure. Cooing and the sounds of flapping wings are features of the park.

THE PRIDE OF CHECKER HALL

Located in a fishing village in the northern parish of St. Lucy, "The Pride of Checker Hall" won second prize in the 1991 competition. The smallest of the three prizewinners, the park is located on a corner lot and used with the permission of its owner. While several area youth help with the park, we were told that one man, David Door, is the main organizer and cohesive force behind the park. The concrete and stone entrance is flanked on either side by two places for plants. A square, a diamond, and an X are incised at the top of the red painted steps. A painting of the Barbados flag flying over palm trees is on the left side of the entrance while the Barbados crest is on the right. A small figure peeks above the inscription "The Pride of Checker Hall" on the archway.

A pathway leads from the central entrance archway to a central monument where park awards were once displayed and plants planted in a bed in front. To the right at the end of a pathway a white bench stands, and a white concrete ridge encircles a heart-shaped bed of earth, in the center of which is a white rock with a red patch inscribed "one love." The park is edged in a similar white concrete ridge with red, green, and yellow painted stones embedded in it.

On the opposite side of the path a walk leads left to a wishing well and a concreted area with embedded painted stones and flower beds. Farther up the path a checkered lighthouse stands before a monument marked "Jesus Saves" with planting of small flowers or herbs on the top in an angled bed.

PRIDE OF WILSON HILL

The third-place winner in the 1991 competition was the "Pride of Wilson Hill" in the parish of St. John.

This park, reached by passing through rich agricultural land, is located in St. John. When we arrived on the afternoon of the 1995 May Day bank holiday, men were preparing to cook. The first man we met was washing pig tails in the standpipe in the front of the park in preparation for making a community pot of food. As when we visited any of the parks, a local resident, usually one of the park's participants, appeared to answer questions and show us the park.[34]

The elements of the park are oriented in symmetrical fashion to the road. The perimeter corners are marked with wheels painted white with red centers. The painting of wheels in red and white was described as having been done with "paint we had." In the center of the park is the largest wheel, with a white square in the center and a red circle inside of the square. "Pride of Wilson Hill" is spelled out in separate sets of bushes on the left, on the right, and in the center. Three white statues to the right, center, and left face the road; the cherubic white figurines with containers on their heads are made from commercial molds and stand symmetrically in relation to the three rows of large cassurina trees (obviously planted long before the park's founding in 1991) running from the road to the back of the lot. A now defunct aquarium is centered near the front of the park. Logs mounted and painted green act as perimeter markers at the front of the park. In the center to the left of the shelter stands a rock with a plaque documenting the founding of the park.

In the back of the lot Mr. Wilfred Moore has cultivated a garden with vegetables and fruit trees. Pumpkin vines were in abundance along with nearly ripe bananas. As a retiree, Mr. Moore keeps up with the garden while the others are at work. Introduced by one of the younger men as the "father figure" of the park, he had resided in the district since 1945. The men we met at the Pride of Wilson Hill are men primarily between the ages of thirty and seventy. The land is part of the Klinch Place (Wakefield plantation), now owned by Clico, a large insurance company, and used with its permission.

To the left side of the park is an open shelter. A cable spool acts as a table in the center. An Earthenworks Pottery "National Trust Open House 1994" plate is displayed on an upright. The arch-shaped entrance to the shelter is knotted out of greenish-blue nylon fishnet rope. This "liming spot" has a gas stove, a bench, an upholstered easy chair, and other furnishings. A portable television tuned to the West Indies test match with Australia was placed on the central table. On this day the men were enjoying the cricket game, each other's company, and a few drinks, and we were treated like visitors to someone's home.

The success of the planting of the park was indicated by one of the fellows who stated, "If you look around at the houses, everyone has plants." Every home in the district has plants and a love of them. While the house and yard are under the supervision of the women, the community park is clearly a man's place. We were told that women come into the park to help with the cooking only on major workdays when all of the men are otherwise occupied clearing the land and landscaping.

CONCLUSION

Because of the underground nature of Barbadian Africanisms, it follows that the language that Barbadians use for description to outsiders will necessarily be phrased in acceptable surface terms and not in terms that describe what exists below the surface. Referring once again to Brathwaite's *Mother Poem*, a prayer meeting takes place where Brathwaite's uncle, a carpenter, once carved African deities in secret on Sundays.[35] "Tie-head" women in a trance state chant, "shang . . . sssssssssssssssssssssssshhhhhhhhh."[36] Even in a trance state the sacred word *shango* cannot be articulated aloud.

In my fieldwork in Barbados, several times when references were made to African religious symbolism, where an understanding was reached, a mutual understanding was recognized with a nod or a nonspecific phrase like "ya know ya know." For example, in an interview with a Barbadian painter, I had come to an understanding of the cosmology articulated in the painting space which the transcription of words from the audiotape does not reveal. This artist signs paintings that are spiritual or mystical in nature with one name while other paintings done for commercial purposes are painted under his Christian name. According to Brathwaite, these references are like "writing in water"[37] for they appear, are understood, and then evaporate.

On another occasion, I passed a community park in St. Phillip with a Rastafarian friend. I was interested in exploring the park, but my friend intimated that there is too much energy in those places and one has to be careful about entering them.

Community parks are men's spaces containing cosmologies and displays of community values. Outward appearances and maintenance of the neatness of living spaces relate to self-image in the community. Productivity and nationalism are expressed in the creation and maintenance of the park space. "Pride and industry" is the national motto inscribed and painted along with national symbols. While containing elements that are bubbling up from underground rivers, these parks are about maintenance of Barbadian community values.

9 SYMBOLIC GEOGRAPHIES AND PSYCHIC LANDSCAPES

Decoding the Hegemonic Discourse of Urban Renewal in the Case for Billy Weems v. the City of College Park, Maryland

Joanne M. Braxton

NOBODY TALKS ABOUT IT MUCH ANYMORE. I'm sitting at my comfortable dining room table in my beautifully landscaped upper-middle-class neighborhood at three o'clock in the morning in October 1995 reading a copy of the January 1969 issue of *Argus*, a magazine published by the journalism department of the University of Maryland at College Park. The article I'm reading is called "Just across the Street: Urban Renewal at Lakeland." Here's a sample of the narrative: "Inadequately maintained lots cluttered with junk and one even housing a goat beckon fair game for Lady Bird's beautification program. Non-existent public facilities and poor street layout make the area even more undesirable."[1] Visions of urban rose gardens dance in my head.[2]

A map titled "Possible Plan for New Roads" shows two bridges, neither ever built, crossing the B&O Railroad tracks; it carries the caption, "The proposed new road system would bring Lakeland into greater contact with the other sections of College Park."[3] Yet another note, one truer to the eventual outcome, suggests: "Another possibility (suggested by the Park and Planning Commission) is to rebuild Lakeland into an apartment community with University patronage definitely in mind."[4]

The photographs show smiling or laughing Negroes; the image is underscored with captions like, "Many of the residents of Lakeland do not understand that their houses will be torn down."[5] One photograph in particular catches my eye. It shows a slightly overweight black man in a plaid shirt laughing. The caption beneath the photograph reads: "Bill Williams, a lifelong resident of Lakeland, laughs scornfully at talk of Urban Renewal, although he lives with his three sons in one of the worst houses in the Lakeland area." And there's a quote from Mr. "Bill Williams": "Man, let's cut this jive about improving Lakeland. See, once you improve it, it's no longer Lakeland."[6]

Damn, I'm thinking, they didn't even bother to get his name right. And then I'm wondering if this student "journalist," Lynn Petzold, knew anything about Billy Weems, like maybe that he had a couple of years of college to his credit, or that the house she refers to was a historic structure, the first school for blacks in that area, founded by Billy Weems's grandfather, John C. Johnson, who used to take the streetcar to Upper Marlboro and get the cast-off books from white schools for his little school on the edge of the wilderness, this at the turn of the century??? That before this time, blacks from Lakeland who wanted to go to school had to walk ten miles to Bladensburg, that even then, the only option for high school was at Howard University,[7] just a little bit farther away? I'm wondering if she had any idea that this man, my brother, waged a one-man war against urban renewal in writing, if she had read anything that Billy had written, composed on a manual typewriter and distributed by hand, mailbox by mailbox, over a period of years?

I thought of the utter presumptuousness of it all and wondered if she had ever watched a town founded by her great-grandfather die? If, in fact, her great-grandfather and then perhaps her own father had ever had to stay awake at night with a rifle or a shotgun in his hand to protect the family and what they owned from people of a different skin shade who set real fires and shot real bullets from outside Lakeland into our poor homes? If she did not know, if she had not read, if no one ever sat her down before the fire and told her stories, if her mother and grandmother had never had to lie flat on their bellies to avoid the randomly fired bullet,[8] then what could the symbolic geography of Billy Weems's consciousness have meant to her? I wondered if she had gotten an A on her assignment?

Standing inside the circle looking out, I imagined a different set of questions from the ones she'd asked. Where are the voices of the people who were displaced from the homes they loved by urban renewal? How did their psychic landscapes differ from the ways in which they were imagined as "others" by those whose voices predominated the discourse of "urban planning" and "urban beautification"? What were the factors that contributed to the satisfaction of residents in areas viewed as "blighted slums" by outsiders? What role did kinship networks and neighbor relations play? Was the war on poverty just that, or was it some form of internal colonialism that merely drove poverty underground, making it less visible and therefore less offensive to the majority? Were the talents of artists and writers put to work in the advancement of urban renewal in the same way that the talents of landscape artists were put to use in the nineteenth century to advance the expansion of the railroads? How many times was urban renewal put to use to remove communities of former factory workers, maids, cooks, and janitors from land that had become increasingly valuable with improved public transportation? Was there a relationship between urban renewal, the development of public highways, and Cold War era civil defense policy? And again, where are the voices of the people who were displaced by urban renewal?

Sitting in my mother's living room at Lakeland today, I look out the window at a solid wall that bisects the Lakeland of yesteryear. I'm reflecting on the proposed plan for the two bridges never built (one would have been visible from here) and the improved roads that were supposed to bring Lakeland into greater contact with other sections of College Park, but I'm looking at the Berlin Wall and experiencing the Maginot Line.[9] I think of my great-aunt who lived next door, whose father had been a slave until he was five years old, and how much she loved the view of Lake Artemisia, where I had learned to ice-skate when there was still a road to the low ground on the other side of the tracks where I grew up. I think of how being deprived of the view of that beautiful lake that had been the heart of Lakeland had affected that old woman, and I know that this is more than a physical landscape to the people who have sown and reaped on this bit of land that was considered "deep country" before the beltway was built, the mere plan increasing the value of everything within its eventually circling arms. My Aunt Agnes's husband, George Gross, and their son, my cousin Elwood, had worked for the University of Maryland for many years, as had my father, who had been, among other things, chauffeur to the president of the university in an era well before blacks were admitted. When he drove H. C. "Curly" Byrd's limousine to Ocean City, he had to wear his chauffeur's hat to walk on the boardwalk. For even though Harry Braxton looked white, his employer knew his racial identity, and the etiquette of inequality must be upheld. Before flood control, before the beltway, the land hadn't been worth much, and my community serviced the university as clerks and janitors, maids and cooks, and childcare workers who must often leave their own children unattended to help feed their families. So what happened?

I wanted to learn the language of urban renewal, to give myself some chance of decoding its hegemonic discourse, and to better situate Lakeland and Billy Weems in relation to it. Thinking in terms of landscape and urban planning, I browsed deeply in publications from the 1930s through the 1970s devoted to those issues. I read and reread articles from the *Journal of the American Institute of Planning* and the *American Planning and Civic Annual,*

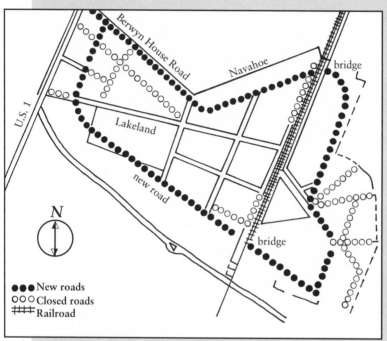

Proposed road system for Lakeland. The bridges across the tracks were never built, and the community has been completely cut off from the land on the other side of the tracks.

Cub Scouts from Pack 1025 and members of Embry A.M.E. Church. (Photo: Harry M. Braxton Sr., ca. 1960)

James Alfred "Billy" Weems (1934–1980). Weems died of a heart attack after a beautiful stand of old trees was bulldozed by urban renewal to build a shopping center at "the cut," a traditional gathering place of black men. Friends say that he died of a broken heart. (Photo: Harry M. Braxton Sr.)

*This wall bisects the Lakeland of yesteryear, separating the
"redeveloped area" from the lake that gave the town its name.
(Photo: Harry M. Braxton Sr.)*

*Lakeland citizens leaving Embry A.M.E. Church sometime in the
1960s. (Photo: Harry M. Braxton Sr.)*

Most Lakeland homes were, in fact, destroyed by fire, allowing neigh-boring fire departments the opportunity to test their firefighting skills. (Photo: Harry M. Braxton Sr.)

the journal of the American Planning and Civic Association, lingering over a listing of officers and board members that included names like General U. S. Grant III, Laurance S. Rockefeller, Frederick Law Olmsted, and Carl Feiss, a frequent contributor to APCA on the topic of urban renewal.[10] Gazing at a photo of General Grant (U.S. Army, ret.) from an issue of the journal, I saw the visage of his better-known namesake, the commander of Union forces in the Civil War.[11] Damn, I think. This was war. They needed the army for this. The army, money, a plan, a "master plan" if you will, and more money. Grant, Rockefeller, Olmsted, and Feiss, among others. Albert Bettman, of Cincinnati, Ohio, wrote an article for the APCA called "Urban Redevelopment Legislation." Here Bettman says that "the particular types of functional uses for which the existing buildings and land are used have ceased to be appropriate, socially and economically, in their present location; as, for instance, the continuation of crowded workers' homes after the workplaces have moved a long distance away."[12] In the case of Lakeland, I thought, the lack of appropriateness became apparent to monied interests after improved transportation brought service workers from farther away, after the beltway was planned and the land within it became more valuable.

This thinking jives neatly with a theory expounded by Morton J. Schussheim in the *Journal of the American Institute of Planning*. Schussheim states: "The original purposes of urban renewal were bold for their time, but now they are too limited. Renewal is still conceived as a means of dealing with pockets of residential blight and with other current problems of central city obsolescence. Now, a new concept is necessary. Incorporating a more powerful set of procedures, renewal must be reoriented to the positive exploitation of opportunities for economic development and to the positive accomplishment of physical development on a metropolitan-wide basis."[13] I thought of the notion, expressed in the *Argus*, that Lakeland should be rebuilt as an apartment community with university patronage definitely in mind, and how this had been partially accomplished.[14]

In an article in the same journal called "Needs of Our Growing Population: Space for Our Congested Cities," architect Carl Feiss, planning and urban renewal consultant to Washington, D.C.'s Parks and Open Spaces Program, suggested the development of the "space city" as an alternative to interplanetary travel as a means of addressing urban flight to the suburbs resulting from "a natural human desire to escape to light and air, to individual rather than group choices, to flexibility of movement, and to the amenities."[15] Again I thought of Lakeland with its rural landscape, the timeless stream behind my childhood home on Richmond Avenue filled with fish, the Lakeland Elementary and Junior High School, our three churches, the two black stores that served our everyday needs and formed part of the basis of our economy, the backyards filled with roses, peonies, and four-o'clocks, the large subsistence gardens which fed families year-round, and the numbers game, always illegal and subsequently usurped by the state lottery.

Before urban renewal, the people of Lakeland had choices. The town was not, in those days, an urban area; urbanizing Lakeland through urban renewal, bisecting it with the Berlin Wall, tearing down the old Victorian houses, many of which were not in bad shape and were very dear to us, building the section 8 and apartment housing that would be filled mostly with people not from Lakeland were, in part, a response to white flight from Washington, D.C. Due to our proximity to the university (less than one mile), space had to be made for the children of the white elite who needed apartments for the four years they would attend the University of Maryland. But if space had to be made for them, what would happen to us? True, we too would benefit from the new roadways and the beautifully planned and landscaped malls, plazas, and shopping centers that supported this regionwide development, but we did not gain in "light and air" and in "individual rather than group choices."

"My children and their peers, the jet propulsion physicists, are deeply concerned with space ships. I am interested in more terrestrial matters—*space cities*," wrote Carl Feiss.[16] Urban renewal, as a response to white flight from the cities then, was America's internal space program. It was also part of America's Cold War civil defense strategy in that the interstate highway system which supported it was designed, in part, to create good routes of evacuation in the event of nuclear war. And let's not forget Lady Bird's rose garden and that other war, the War on Poverty, with its goal of a hygienic, beautiful countryside. "Ugliness is bitterness," said Mrs. Johnson, in her welcome address to the White House Conference on Natural Beauty. "That is a great problem and a challenge. Most of the great cities and great works of beauty of the past were built by autocratic societies. . . . Can a great democratic society generate the concerted drive to plan, and having planned, to execute great projects of beauty?"[17] The question, then, might be: Was urban renewal in Lakeland, and in general, the result of a democratic process or an autocratic one? Much lip service was given to the notion of community participation, but how much community participation was there in the decision-making process, really, and who decided who would be heard? To be sure, there are different perspectives on these questions, based, in part, on the personal experience of the speaker, the community from which he or she comes, and his or her class, racial, and regional alliances.

The articles by Feiss, Schussheim, and others of like thinking tended to dominate the hegemonic discourse of urban renewal, but within that discourse, from which the persons most immediately affected by urban renewal were excluded, there was an undercurrent of critical thinking that ran against the main stream. For example, I preferred the thinking of John Dyckman in his article on "National Planning for Urban Renewal: The Paper Moon in the Cardboard Sky," Peter Marris's "The Social Implications of Urban Redevelopment," and Marc Fried and Peggy Gleigher's "Some Sources of Residential Satisfaction in an Urban Slum."[18]

Fried and Gleigher identified kinship networks and neighbor relations as sources of residential satisfaction and stability that contributed to resistance to urban renewal in New York City's West End. They argued that "the belief that poverty, delinquency, prostitution, and alcoholism magically inhere in the demolition of the slum has a curious persistence but can hardly provide adequate justification for the vast enterprise of renewal planning." Peter Marris acknowledged that "urban renewal, because it usually displaces the poorest of the city's population, raises issues of the underprivileged in contemporary America: the persistence of racial intolerance, the growing pressure on minorities to assimilate the values of the dominant culture; the failure of the world's richest nation to deploy its resources effectively against squalor and deprivation . . . the program cannot achieve its purposes so long as slum communities are merely displaced or scattered . . . measures are needed that raise the status of slum communities." This was thinking that had some appeal to me, but I noted that it supposed the survival of so-called slum communities as communities.[19]

And still, I thought the discourse entirely hegemonic, as the people most affected by renewal and redevelopment did not read, write, or respond to the articles read by the architects and city planners who read and wrote for the *Journal of the American Institute of Planning* or the *American Planning and Civic Annual* or the other journals that largely determined the philosophy if not the course of urban renewal. The articles composed by my brother on his manual typewriter, mimeographed by him, and distributed by hand, door to door, along with minutes of the Lakeland PAC meeting and the notes kept by my mother and others in the community, become, then, a valuable resource for examining the ways in which resistance emerged in one community that was eventually destabilized by the broken promises of urban renewal.

APPENDIX

Excerpts from the Billy Weems Papers

NOTE: James Alfred "Billy" Weems (1937–1980), a sanitation worker for the City of College Park until he lost his job, waged a one-man war against urban renewal, composing, printing, and distributing protest essays in his "spare time." In the following excerpts from Billy's papers, original spelling, grammar, and punctuation have been retained.

From "Better Get Something On Your Mind"

Lakeland was first inhabited by Blacks in 1901. Lakeland had previously been an exclusive all white town with a train depot, a post office and a community hall. Lakeland's town held Colored, living along the Paint Branch and Indian Creek without a school closer than Bladensburg. These people seeking an education had to walk to school or catch the train, the fare to be paid with the few pennies earned and saved.

The new inhabitants of Lakeland and the people surrounding Lakeland saved their pennies to build their first school in 1907, high land bought and paid for. They moved up from the jungles along the Paint and Indian, from Berwyn, from Berwyn Heights and College Park. For some reason or other, isolation or uniting, we were grouped together. There were people that had to drag their homes up from the swamps, many of the town homes had been destroyed by fire. This was a community building, building the Lakeland we have today and are *losing*.

Yes, we are losing Lakeland. There have been *petitions, proposals, different codes*, high taxes without any benefit from money spent, county or townwise. There was a time when you could cry UNCONSTITUTIONAL and changes that the constitution is no more, meaningless. *If I am wrong, show me.*

Billy Weems

From "Let Me Have Something, Mine" (n.d.)

Lakeland was once a beautiful all white place. The houses here were big, beautiful and roomy. A few still remain. There were some bigger, bigger ones that were burned by the retreating, I mean they were mysteriously destroyed by fire. The point I'm trying to make is that these are hand-me-downs. Everything is handed down to us.

When we (Blacks) came up from the jungle along Paint Branch we were coming out into the light. In those days a drizzle could keep you home. We were leaving the darkness, coming out to see. To see you have to *look*.

When this place is built we'll be asked to move away. Maybe College Park or Berwyn. I'm sure there are enough shacks in the area to take care of us. Then too, we might find a boat in our yard or maybe the former tenant might leave behind last year's car. (You know, a used car.) I would be proud to live in Berwyn or College Park. But I would not be happy. My face *would not* smile. This is progess?

Billy Weems

From "DO YOU KNOW THE FATE OF LAKELAND IS TO BE DECIDED NEXT WEEK?"

Once Lakeland High School became Lakeland Junior High, and then Lakeland Elementary. Today Lakeland High School is to become nothing in an attempt to take land from the people that own, actually stealing). The reason they say to integrate so our Black children can get an education can get an equal education. HA. What's really happening is that the heart of Lakeland has to be removed. (School transplant.)

Lakeland has *low enrollment*, (Ahem) qualified teachers, cafeteria-gym-auditorium combined, limited traffic and spacious playgrounds. It would be more sensible to lighten the load than create *more load* to the overloaded. It would be cheaper (tax wise) to bring 2 or 3 buses in than it would be 6 or 7 busses out. After all a parent shuld have something to say about the educating process of his child. There are enough *real* people around. But then, there's that word lunatic. Probably. . . . . . . I wonder what ole Abe Lincoln was thinking about?

Billy Weems

"HO HO HUM" (n.d.)

I smell a stink in the air. Really, its too peaceful to be so stinky. 'Alls well that ends well. I know the end is not in sight. We had better prepare ourselves. Because the forces are regrouping for another assualt. We have to be prepared for anything. The end is just another beginning.

We all agree that we love Lakeland and what it stands for. We agree that we need *our school* more now than ever before. The reason I say our school is because it is.

The Board of Education is the Board of Education. I guess they try to do the right things but they don't know (they just don't know) or they try to ignore the right. For instance, they know that if there is a meeting early in the moring (like 10 o'clock) we will miss a day's pay, (hunger). They know the meetings in Upper Marlboro cause parking problems (hunger and lost autos). They know that we'd be there, beware, the next meeting may be held in Salisbury, 7AM and on a Saturday. I guess they think they are helping us. I wonder what they really know.

Let us be reasonable. If we are weak, let us be weak to the strongest-not to the weakest.

I don't know anything about Urban Renewal. I do read and the sign reads, "Urban Renewal for the City of College Park". But this is all Lakeland. *Lakeland is Lakeland and not* College Park. If I wanted to live anywhere else in the *College Park Area*, I could but *not relaxed*. Dig. (Did I say my face would not smile.) I am happy living in Lakeland, but can I be happy. HUH.

DO RIGHT. Leave the school open and me alone.

Love
Billy Weems

From "The Giant Eraser Is Ready to Wipe Us Out" (n.d.)

A meeting was held in Upper Marlboro Tuesday, March 11, 1969 at 10AM to continue the discussion on whether Lakeland Elementary School schould be closed as a Public school or used for other purposes in which the community could benefit.

Many people were surprised at our turnout even though this particular time of day was picked foe so serious a matter. And there were enough people there in favor of keeping Lakeland open for the next two or three years it will take to build a new school conveniently located for the residents of Lakeland and Berwyn. I don't know how many of us will be around though. I hear through the grapevine that urban renewal will try a new approach with another name. (Could be that these are trying times) . . .

The way things are now the giant eraser is ready to wipe us out and it will be like we never were. I say *IT WILL BE*. Right now is the time to come out and be counted. It's not too late if we cat now.

Billy Weems

From "Our Next Flood Will Be Deep" (n.d.)

It seems as though *our* representatives have gone wandering they seem to forget they are the representatives of the people. *They are us* with our wants and needs to be taken of first. When blunders are made everyone suffers. But we

must rember that they too, are human and as a human suffer human traits
(gree, etc.) I hope sincerely that we can get better from them than what we
got. Until we do, our representatives need our guidance. We are the people.

Billy Weems

From "Truth or Deceit," April 8, 1969

Last evening a meeting was held in the First Baptist Church concerning nothing. I was late getting there but was there long enough to grasp what is really
happening.

Prior to this meeting a meeting was held over the school with our *so-called
leaders* using words like "tomorrow, next time and etc." It has been told me
that I became interested too late. The question I want answered is, *"Why is
it too late?"* One leader says "I could have sold you down the drain a long
time ago." *Did he?*

I used to think that there was hope for us. *"Keep the Faith"* simply means
BELIEVE. "We SHALL OVERCOME" means *we are looking you right in
the eye we can see Truth or Deceit."* Pray tell me waht you see when you look
into a mirror.

Billy Weems

From "I Want Our Community" (n.d.)

I want our school. I want our community. Maybe you will look at me and
say, "He doesn't have much", but I have you, and you are me, if I have to
go, so do you. I don't have much, I don't want much.

When I think of Urban Renewal and all the changes proposed. I think
first of traveling through space, landing on the moon and then coming back
to Lakeland.

Billy Weems

Progression
for my brother, Billy Weems

and we went down to "the cut"
(because of what they had done there
and because that was your "other home")
me and Kilroy and Laurie
and Ginny

to celebrate you home

we poured our libations
to celebrate you home

we got the mixture of white ort
and lemon juice just right

we shook it up like you used to do

we poured our libation
i held the bottle high
a stream of liquid vanished
into the scorched August earth

we passed the bottle around
we drank deeply
we passed the bottle again
before we broke it

and drove away
in Dad's old white Dodge

Joanne M. Braxton

"Progression" appeared in the *William and Mary Review* 23:1 (spring 1985).

Sometimes I Think of Maryland

big old houses have passed away
like summer's dust

green apples / poke salad / the A.M.E. Church
blue sky and Rev. Baddy's sermon

the safety of Grandma's rocker
a lullaby from her knee / her sweet voice

her hands so clean and praying / or scolding
she tends her mother's grave
her father was a slave

"go to sleepy little baby
go to sleepy little baby
when you wake patty patty cake
ride a big white pony"

a brown flood breaks the banks
down at the branch / where i wrote my first poem
flowers bloom in a vacant yard
where there was once a house / with a porch
and six low steps with carpet painted on

i place my head next to earth
and listen deep for voices
recognition / memory
song

close my hand over empty soil
where once grew corn collards
and tomatoes 2 lbs. big

close my eyes to see the patchwork quilt
of time and impossibility
that covers me like *kente* cloth

and i close my eyes to see
no longer growing up but older
a woman who bleeds with the moon
and waits for a child
to burden with this heritage

Joanne M. Braxton

"Sometimes I Think of Maryland," the title poem of Braxton's only collection
of poetry, originally appeared in the September 1972 issue of *Black World*.

10

THE SLAVE IN THE SWAMP

Affects of Uncultivated Regions on Plantation Life

Tynes Cowan

OR ANGLO COLONISTS IN NORTH AMERICA, the land of the New World was at once inviting and threatening: inviting to their sense of exploitation; threatening to their sense of order. Carving out of the land a new nature—along with a new nation—based on rules of classical symmetry, the southern planter especially faced a stubborn region that would not come under his rule: the swamp. William Byrd and George Washington exemplify this classical mind-set: Byrd mapping the Great Dismal Swamp, making boundary lines in the chaos; and Washington heading a canal project there to make the swamp useful and profitable. After the formation of the Republic and the growth of the romantic imagination, the swamp begins to signify much more than waste and annoyance. A region of death (as opposed to mere waste) which is simultaneously teaming with life, it becomes a liminal space, a meditative space. For both classical and romantic era Anglo Americans, the swamp served as a contrast to the cultivated and controlled plantation spaces. If the classical Anglo sees the swamp as a nuisance, the romantic sees it as alluring for the same reason: its chaotic, threatening nature.

Although the change among the gentry in perception of the swamp is largely attributable to this change in philosophical outlooks from one era to another, one particular image associated with the swamp, the runaway slave who seeks refuge there, must have considerably provoked this change in the white imagination. The use of swamps by runaways, of course, did not begin after the Revolutionary War. During his 1728 expedition through the Great Dismal, William Byrd "came upon a Family of Mulattoes, that call'd themselvs free, tho' by the Shyness of the Master of the House, who took care to keep least in Sight, their Freedom seem'd a little Doubtful."[1] Byrd calmly mentions the existence of numerous slaves in the region whose obscurity renders them safe from "their righteous Neighbours" on surrounding farms. By the end of the century, however, this same image would not be taken so casually. Fear of maroon camps and rebel gatherings, bands of runaways committing "depredations" on the community, fueled stricter slave codes and greater punishment for offenders. Along with other gothic notions of the region that replaced the classical utilitarian view, the swamp became a haven for the fugitive slave and, therefore, a place of danger in the white imagination. As the image of the slave in the swamp seared itself into the white mind (producing great anxiety even if mixed with a tinge of thrill), why couldn't the same image have promoted resistance, pride, and hope among the servile population? The purpose of this chapter is to explore the uses of swamps by Afro-Americans in the antebellum South. White reaction to that use is fairly well documented, but the possible effects of the nearby swamplands on the minds of the enslaved is unclear.

There are many references in slave testimony and white writing about slaves running off to the woods. In some cases "the woods" is simply a catchall phrase denoting any wild, uncultivated spot on or neighboring the plantation. In some cases, for my purposes, a distinction between swamp and wood is unnecessary, and in other cases it is crucial. When referring to the attitudes of those left behind on the plantation (white or black) toward those who have run off to the woods, a distinction is usually not necessary. Descriptions of some hiding places made in "the woods" could as easily refer to forest or swamp. But when the wilderness is seen as either a barrier to the slave's escape or a barrier to white pursuit, the distinct attributes of the swamp are important to discuss. In addition, specific iconography is important when considering the more spiritual meaning that might be read in the swamp—as with the romantic iconography of the funereal hanging moss and the lonely crane. Nevertheless, the examples drawn here of slaves escaping through a swamp or actually taking up residence within one are limited geographically. Much of the information available comes from eastern Virginia and North Carolina, because this region contains the Great Dismal Swamp which, like the extensive bayous of Louisiana and Florida, provided runaways with hundreds of square miles of wilderness in which to lose pursuers. The lowlands of Virginia and North Carolina also contain other numerous, if separate, swamps. Still, swamps are common throughout the South to the extent that David Miller, in his book on swamp imagery, calls the swamp "the landscape equivalent of the Cavalier myth."[2] It seems that any plantation would have a swamp of some size within walking distance, and such proximity to a region that is not under white control would likely spark the imagination of the enslaved.

The imposing nature of the swamp certainly presented a deterrent to any slave thinking of escape, so their concept of the region could be formed in balancing the dangers of the swamp against abuses on the plantation. In *Roll, Jordan, Roll*, Eugene D. Genovese asserts, "If most slaves feared to think about flight to the North, many feared even to think of short-term flight to the nearby woods or swamps." As evidence Genovese offers the observations of Thomas Wentworth Higginson and the words spoken to Fanny Kemble by an old Georgia slave woman. Both draw the conclusion that the snakes and alligators were the greatest slave catchers in that they would either dissuade running or serve to turn the runaways around. "Slaveholders . . . usually took a calm view of their runaways and expected an early return. After all, their slaves had a long way to go to get to the free states, hardly knew the way, faced trying conditions in the woods, and sooner or later—usually sooner—would come home."[3] Despite this assertion that the return rate was high, the fact remains that the dangers of the swamp were not a complete deterrent, since slaves still felt it worth the risk.

Harriet Jacobs illustrates the fear of the swamp that may have led to the assumption that the region acted primarily to keep slaves at "home." Those helping Jacobs to escape tell her at one point that she must return to the swamp where she had already spent one night. "I could scarcely summon the courage to rise. But even those large, venomous snakes were less dreadful to my imagination than the white men in that community called civilized."[4] Jacobs builds up her fear of the swamp to fit her literary persona, the woman of taste and refinement who, because of slavery, is not allowed to remain unsullied and completely virtuous as a white woman might. Being forced into the swamp is typical of her character constantly having to choose between one "evil" and another. Despite the sentiment and occasional melodrama with which Jacobs presents her story, this dilemma must reflect a common choice facing the slaves. Tom Wilson puts the rationale behind his choice to flee through the swamps more succinctly: "I felt safer among the alligators than among the white men."[5]

Nevertheless, stories such as that told by Jacob Branch would likely serve to increase fear of the wilderness among slaves. Branch relates the story of Charlie who runs off to the bayou to avoid punishment for not meeting the quota for grinding cornmeal. Exposure to the freezing waters up to his knees forces him to return to the plantation kitchen where he thaws before the fire and dies. Charlie's own body could serve to signify the dangers of the swamp as clearly as a public whipping victim might ingrain the price for running away in general (or for getting caught). But Charlie's was an unpremeditated plunge into the swamp, one that came from the necessity of the moment, not from careful planning. At another time of year, he could have found no better place to evade pursuers. Swamps surrounding a plantation could serve as more of an incentive to escape than discouragement, because "individual escapes were more likely to be made good where natural obstacles to pursuit were the most severe; in the United States, swamps always invited running away, permitting the slave a measure of protection from his pursuers that open country could never have afforded him."[6] This is the case for Dora Franks's Uncle Alf who, having been severely beaten after running away and put immediately back to work, decided to "work right hard till dey left. Den, when he got up to de end o' de row next to de swamp, he lit out again."[7] Apparently, Uncle Alf feels he just needs a little head start and time to get into the swamp to make good his escape this time.

As a physical boundary, a natural fence around the plantation, the swamp can be seen as the source of containment or the goal to reach and/or cross. The other side of this boundary is a more level playing field, so to speak, where, once inside, the runaway could use the terrain to his or her advantage. It serves this purpose for Jake Williams who is last seen walking toward the swamp, but Jake is pursued by an overseer with several dogs. He climbs a tree to get out of reach, so the overseer climbs up after him. He "kicked de oberseer raght in de mouf, an' dat white man went tumblin' to de groun'. When he hit de earth, dem houn's pounced on him." Jake heads north with the lead dog. "De res' of de pack come home."[8] It does not seem a far stretch to believe that the swamp might resonate with a particularly positive overtone in the minds of the slaves back on the plantation who see a slave go in and the dogs return along with the body of an overseer. This white body might resonate more loudly, signify more strongly the nature of the swamp than Charlie's cold, stiff corpse. At any rate, slaves did run away to the swamps in large numbers.

Besides offering the individual slave a defensive position in the moment of running away, it also served the purpose for maroon settlements. Working together, runaways could not just escape but could set up communities and protect each other. This point is dramatically demonstrated by Octave Johnson who ran off at the start of the Civil War and lived with some thirty other men and women about four miles from the plantation's big house. This was close enough to steal pigs, chickens, and beef cattle from the plantation, but "one day twenty hounds came after me; I called the party to my assistance and we killed eight of the bloodhounds, then we all jumped into the Bayou Fanfron; the dogs followed us and the alligators caught six of them, 'the alligators prefered dogs flesh to personal flesh.'"[9] While belying the notion that alligators prefer dark meat,[10] Johnson's story illustrates the sense of safety that could be provided by the swamp that might outweigh the dangers.

As a group of runaways might provide each other protection from slave catchers, they also helped to promote a sense of domesticity in their living arrangements. Although Johnson lived in this runaway community for a year and a half, his living arrangements, sleeping on logs and burning "cypress leaves to make a smoke and keep away mosquitoes,"[11] seem rather modest compared to other such communities. In his description of the Dismal Swamp made during his 1783–84 visit to the United States, German traveler Johann Schoepf notes a much more tranquil, domestic, and permanent lifestyle of the runaways within. "Small spots are to be found here and there which are always dry, and these have often been used as places of safety by runaway slaves. . . . So these negro fugitives lived in security and plenty, building themselves cabins, planting corn, raising hogs and fowls which they stole from their neighbors, and naturally the hunting was free where they were."[12] Such a serene and unconcerned description of maroon life seems out of step with the view white planters would have had toward the scene. In fact, referring to the farms neighboring the swamp as the fugitives' "neighbors" may well have insulted these planters. In contrast to Schoepf's lighthearted account, antebellum southern newspaper stories noted by Herbert Aptheker are punctuated with horror at the prospect of growing communities of Negroes within the swamp. For the most part, these news accounts focus on incidents of violence in encounters between whites and maroons, the deaths incurred among the white population, and the air of defiance among the maroons. The fear caused by such accounts can be read in a letter from concerned citizens to Governor Thomas Bragg of North Carolina that describes the depredations being committed by the fugitives and asks for assistance to bring them out of the swamps.[13]

The level of concern among the white citizenry also can be gauged by the level of reaction taken against the outlaws. Although sometimes local volunteers or bounty hunters would go into the swamps after maroons, often, as Ulrich B. Phillips notes, "other agencies" would have to do the job. "For example the maraudings of runaway slaves camped in Belle Isle swamp, a score of miles above Savannah, became so serious and lasting that their haven had to be several times destroyed by the Georgia militia. On one of these occasions, in 1786, a small force first employed was obliged to withdraw in the face of the blacks, and reinforcements merely succeeded in burning the huts and towing off the canoes, while the negroes themselves were safely in hiding."[14] The size, then, of this swamp seems its most striking characteristic—large enough to provide safety even from an invading force. The topography of other swamps likewise could determine the success or failure of a community as well as the type of depredations committed upon the neighboring farms.

In 1816, near Ashepoo, South Carolina, a large maroon community, formed by the consolidation of several bands of runaways, established itself in the swamps created by the intersection of the Combahee and Ashepoo Rivers. As a staging ground and hiding place, this site had seemed the natural choice for each of the bands. The difficulty in extricating them is noted by Governor David R. Williams. "The peculiar situation of the whole of that portion of our coast, rendered access to them difficult, while the numerous creeks and water courses through the marshes around the islands, furnished them easy opportunities to plunder, not only the planters in open day, but the inland coasting trade also without leaving a trace of their movements by which they could be pursued."[15] As time passed, however, swampy terrain would not be enough to keep a large band of runaways safe if they were too daring in their raids. If frightened and determined enough, the government could find the muscle to take them out.

In Newbern, Virginia, in 1830, for example, a group of sixty slaves were all surrounded in their swamp and killed by the military. During the summer of the following year, such news reports of rebellious slaves basing their operations in swamps must have been on the public's mind during Nat Turner's Rebellion in Southampton, Virginia. When the leader escaped after the uprising, "it was . . . strongly suspected that he had secreted himself among the thick brush of Dismal Swamp, but although the whole swamp has been thoroughly scoured even to its darkest and deepest recesses . . . and a great many runaway slaves found therein, no discovery could be made of 'Gen. Nat.'" From experience, the white public makes the automatic assumption that these rebels have hidden themselves in the swamp. From here, the connection is made between runaways in the swamp and other notorious rebels: "It is not improbable the Blacks might have supposed in case of a defeat, [it] might afford them as secure a retreat as did the almost inaccessible mountains of St. Domingo to their black brethren of that island."[16] This comment provides some insight into just how seriously the white population would have taken a camp of maroons hiding in a swamp. For years after the insurrections in Haiti and San Domingo, slave owners along the eastern seaboard of the United States held a tremendous fear of slaves from the West Indies. States enacted laws against them, such as one in North Carolina: "The General Assembly in 1795 passed a law forbidding any person coming into the state with the intent to settle to bring with him any negro . . . from any of the French, Dutch, Spanish, or English West Indies."[17] Although the fear of rebellion might wax and wane along with news of rebellions elsewhere, it seems likely that the image of a community of free blacks living in the wilderness would have been a constant source of anxiety.

One tactic for fighting future rebellions would be to make an example of a Turner-like leader. In at least one case, killing was not deemed enough. Squire, who had led a band of outlaws for three years in raids from the

Cypress Swamp outside New Orleans, was captured and killed in 1837. His body was put on display in the public square. The focus upon a group's leader, however, was not new. At times, a persona was created around the group's leader such as "the General of the Swamps" around Wilmington, North Carolina, in 1795.[18] A military title applied to a fugitive slave would tend to mobilize the gentry for fear of armed rebellion, but it did little to add an air of "civilization" to the leader's public image. In a letter to his father, George Blow wrote in 1816 that a "General Sampson" was leading a rebellion of slaves. While impressing upon the Blows the seriousness of the military threat, the title "General" was seen as a clownish "aping" of proper military decorum.[19] What stands out, then, in such a title as "General of the Swamps" is the swamp with its wild and dangerous associations. Some accounts show that it was the "wild" ones, the recently enslaved Africans, who gained a reputation for running to the swamps, but wild or not when they entered the swamp, it is likely that their appearance would be altered enough by life in the swamp to add to a wild (thus threatening) public image. In the case of Dora Franks's Uncle Alf, when he finally returned from years in the swamp, "he look like a hairy ape, without no clothes on and hair growin' all over his body."[20]

Despite the enormous anxiety produced in whites by these images related to the swamp, the actual use to which the region was put by runaways is a different story. According to R. H. Taylor, the main concern of runaways in the swamps, even armed camps of maroons, was not with rebelling but living—surviving from day to day. "In fact, gangs of runaways rarely became so desperate as to attempt a massacre of the whites. Hunger sometimes drove runaways to take life as an incident of procuring food; but in general they confined their activities to stealing, burning, and eluding capture."[21] But in larger swamps such as the Great Dismal, even such "depredations" may not have been entirely necessary. The runaways could, instead, make a living off of their environment. Even in newspaper accounts given to painting a threatening picture of those in the swamps, the domesticity of life there is mentioned as well. Regarding a "'very secure retreat for runaway negroes' in a large swamp between Bladen and Robeson counties . . . the Wilmington Journal of August 14 [1856] mentioned that these runaways, 'had cleared a place for a garden, had cows &c in the swamp.'" The testimony of a captured slave named Moses provides some more insight into the possible extravagance of life in the swamp: in Dover Swamp in North Carolina, eleven houses served a community of thirty to forty runaways.[22] Unlike the temporary shelter provided by the swamp in which Octave Johnson hid, these accounts suggest the long-term commitment and expectation these runaways had for life in the swamp. Not content with sleeping on logs and stealing food when hungry, these maroons set up permanent housing and a self-renewing system of subsistence.

The possibility of living in a swamp in a "civilized" manner is evidenced by the enslaved workers of the Great Dismal Swamp. Better understanding of the material circumstances of the maroon communities may be derived from the example of their counterparts. These are described by Samuel Huntington Perkins, a class of 1817 Yale graduate who had come south to tutor the children of a North Carolina planter. Perkins explains that many of the trees in the Great Dismal are valuable for their lumber, so lumber companies and owners of the land would send Negroes in to work for five months at a time. "They carry several months provisions, and penetrate eight or ten miles, sometimes farther. They are obliged first to make a path, by falling trees. After accomplishing which, and arriving at a suitable place, they erect huts, secured from inundation by being placed on high stumps."[23] Frederick Law Olmsted, in his 1853–54 travels, also witnessed these workmen of the swamps. In speaking with one of them, he learns more of the runaways who "had huts in 'back places,' hidden by bushes, and difficult of access."[24]

Not all of the Dismal Swamp's runaways, however, secluded themselves to this degree. Some, in fact, were open enough to work alongside the still enslaved shingle workers—hired by poorer whites and not turned in to the authorities or their owners because they provided a cheap labor source. One such runaway worked in the swamp before eventually making his way to Canada. There, he offered his testimony of his escape and life in the swamp to abolitionists who were collecting biographical sketches of those they helped. This man had run away to avoid being sold to the Deep South and went to the Great Dismal expressly because a friend had told him he would find work there. At first he boarded with a man who paid him two dollars a month, and later he began working for himself. Besides the opportunity for sustenance that this tale demonstrates, it also gives us a glimpse of the community—the sense of mutual aid—that is formed among the swamp runaways. "Dar are heaps ob folks in dar to work. Most of 'em are fugitives, or else hirin' dar time. Dreadful 'commodatin' in dare to one anudder. De each like de 'vantage ob de odder one's 'tection. Ye see dey's united togedder in'ividually wit same interest to stake. Never hearn one speak disinpectively to 'nut'er one: all 'gree as if dey had only one head and one heart, with hunder legs and hunder hands. Dey's more 'commodatin' dan any folks I's ever seed afore or since." He goes on to describe ventures undertaken as a group for survival, such as making canoes for fishing and joining together to hunt: "When we wanted fresh pork we goed to Gum Swamp, 'bout sun-down, run a wild hog down from de cane-brakes into Juniper Swamp, whar dar feet can't touch hard ground, knock dem over, and dat's de way we kill dem."[25]

The "normality" of life in the swamp can be seen in the mention of Ole Man Fisher, the swamp runaways' preacher, and by the mention of families being raised in the swamp so that some had never seen a white person. Sometimes, however, the day-to-day routines would be shattered by slave-catching expeditions into the region; "sometimes de masters comes and shoots dem down dead on de spot." In particular, he tells of his friend Jacob who one day was surrounded by six men as he was going about his daily affairs. Each of them had a gun pointed at his head, and among them stood his former master who threatened to blow his brains out if Jacob took a step. "Jacob lifts up his feet to run. Marcy on him! De master and one ob de men levelled dar guns, and dar guns levelled poor Jacob. His whole right side from his hip to his heel was cut up like hashmeat. He bleeded orfull. Dey took some willow bark—made a hoop orn't—run a board trough it—put Jacob on it like as if he war dead; run a pole t'rough de willow hoop, and put de poles on dar shoulders."[26] This gives some idea for the reasons this man may have had for moving on to Canada rather than staying in the swamp. But those who remained may have protected themselves by being more cautious in their hiding.

In areas more likely to have unwanted visitors, runaways may have chosen to be less carefree and ostentatious in their habitats; for example, a proper cabin with four walls and a roof may not have been practical. In such circumstances, runaways could disguise their homes. The following examples refer to homes in the "woods." Although we cannot know if by "woods" they mean "swamp," they should serve regardless as examples of possibilities for concealment that were available to runaways. Arthur Greene remembers:

Lord, Lord! Yes indeed, plenty of slaves uster run away. Why dem woods was full o' 'em chile. I knowd one man dat took an' run away 'cause his marster was so mean an' cruel. He lived in a cave in de groun' fer fifteen yeahs 'fo' Lee's surrender. He made himself a den under de groun'; he an' his wife, an' raised fifteen chillun down dar. Ha! Ha! Ha! Had a chile fur every 'ear he stayed in dar. Dis den slopped [sloped] back to keep water from coming in. . . . Dis den was er—I guess 'bout size of a big room, 'cause dat big family washed, ironed, cooked, slept and done ev'ythin' down dar, dat you do in yo' house. Here dis man, Pattin, lived 'til surrender, jes as I done tol' you.[27]

There are numerous tales of slaves hiding in such spaces not in the wilderness but right under the nose of the planter—even in spaces adjacent to his own house. These stories should attest to the fact that a swamp didn't need to be large to conceal runaways. Of course, a small space would require more tactics than just a concealed house, as seen in Samuel Warner's account of a woman who lived in a swamp for seven years with her two children.

When they were eventually found and brought out, the children never spoke above a whisper, as their mother had prevented them from making noise their entire lives.[28]

Nevertheless, much credit can be given to the ingenuity of construction for maintaining secrecy. More detail for a hidden structure is provided in the testimony of the Reverend Ishrael Massie:

> We had one slave dat runned away an' he had a vault in th' woods fixed jes like dis room an' he had a wife an' two boys dat he raised under dar. Waal, ya say, "'Scribe"—ya mean tell how 'twas built? Dar wuz a hole cut in de groun'. I don' cut a many a one an' stole lumber at night to kiver hit over wid. Den dirt wuz piled on top of dis plank so dat hit won't rain in dar. Den he has him some piping— trough-like—made of wood dat runned so many feet in de groun'. Dis carried smoke way away from dis cave. Fer fire used oak bark 'cause hit didn't give much smoke. He had him a hole to come up on lan'. Dar wuz sticks, pine beard, and trash on top to kiver de hole. Ha, ha, ha. Ya could stan' right over dis hole an' wouldn't kno hit.[29]

Although underground houses seem a less likely feature of a swamp than of a forest, many of these same techniques for concealment could be used, especially where there are spots substantial enough for gardening and raising cattle.

The laughter in the above testimony suggests that stories of runaways living in the woods and swamps might be a source of pride and/or empowerment among those who remained on the plantation. But some slaves apparently viewed these runaways as uncivilized and dangerous. Julia Banks of Texas, for example, says: "Some of them runned off and stayed in the swamps, and they was mean. They called them runaways. If they saw you, they would tell you to bring them something to eat. And if you didn't do it, if they ever got you they sure would fix you." Likewise, Green Cumby, who (incidentally) stayed with his old master four years after the Civil War, says: "To see de runaway slaves in de woods scared me to death. They'd try to snatch you and hold you, so you couldn't go tell. Sometimes dey cotched dem runaway niggers and dey be like wild animals and have to be tamed over 'gain."[30] But fear of the runaways did not necessarily mean antagonism toward them. Even where there was fear, it often mingled with sympathy and support. As a little girl, Mary White Ovington marveled at the family of slaves in the wilds nearby: "It was not wise to go near the place, but one might drop a piece of food at the wood's edge confident that it would reach a little hungry stomach."[31] Or fear would disappear to be replaced with curiosity—perhaps envy or wonder. "When we was kids, we used to take keer of cows 'bout four miles f'om home. De runaway slaves used to come

out [from the Dismal Swamp] and beg us for food. At fust we was scare to
deaf of 'em and jes' fly, but after while we used to steal bred an' fresh meat
an' give to 'em. But dey never would let you foller 'em. Dey hid in Dismal
Swamp in holes in de groun' so hidden dey stay dere years an' white folks,
dogs, or nothin' else could fine 'em."[32] Or, given conditions on some plantations, sympathy for those in the bush may have been impossible. Instead,
a barter economy may have developed as described by Octave Johnson, who
supplied those who had remained on the plantation with meat in exchange
for cornmeal.[33]

Ultimately, despite any fear of those hiding in the uncultivated regions
surrounding the plantation, the effect of their existence on those still in the
fields is likely reflected in Cornelia Carney's testimony: "Father wasn't de
onlies' one hidin' in de woods. Dere was his cousin, Gabriel, dat was hidin'
an' a man name Charlie. Niggers was too smart fo' white folks to git ketched.
White folks was sharp too, but not sharp enough to get by ole Nat. Nat? I
don't know who he was. Ole folks used to say it all de time. De meanin' I git
is dat de niggers could always out-smart de white folks."[34] Again we see the
connection between the swamp runaway and the image of Nat Turner, but
this time the image is one of the trickster, using the swamp as a site for out-
witting the white folks.

Carney, born some five years after Nat Turner's Rebellion, touches on
the precise connection between field hand and runaway-maroon that whites
feared most: an infectious, rebellious attitude. Planters may well have toler-
ated individual runaways, waiting patiently for their return and counting on
a good whipping to serve as an example to deter the other slaves. But when
runaways joined together in the bush and began committing "depredations"
on the neighborhood, planters began to worry not only about a violent attack
from these thieves but about the effect the bandits had on the attitudes of
their slaves. At the heart of this fear was the acknowledgment that those in
the bush remained in contact with those on the plantation, as remarked by
Samuel Huntington Perkins: "Their fidelity to each other is almost proverbial.
When one has run away they all take interest in his escape; and though there
are usually 30 or 40 who know where he stays & who supply him with provisions, yet no instance has ever occurred of the most extravagant rewards
inducing one to betray him."[35] Perkins goes on to solidify this claim through
the anecdote of one runaway who was bought by another, apparently more
merciful planter, while still in the bush. The new owner lets the transaction
be known through his other slaves, and within half an hour, the runaway is
in the field working. The upshot of Perkins's story is that the communication
allows the gentry to avoid using the practice of outlawing slaves, which by an
act of the North Carolina legislature made it legal to kill "outlying" slaves.

"Against incorrigible runaways proclamations of outlawry were sometimes published, summoning the slaves to surrender at once upon pain of being shot at sight."[36] By word of mouth, the runaway could be fairly warned of their dangerous new legal status and given a chance to return peacefully.

Because of this communication network among the slaves, the planters could be assured that information on life in the swamp was reaching those in the field. More insidious to the planters, then, than the depredations committed by outlying Negroes was their effect on the behavior of those slaves still at work. In May 1802, one such camp of runaways was blamed for the rebellious actions and attitudes of slaves in Elizabeth City, North Carolina. "The plots and insubordination uncovered among the servile population at that time were attributed to the agitation of an outlawed Negro, Tom Copper, who 'has got a camp in one of the swamps.'"[37] The degree of concern these outliers may have caused is, of course, impossible to gauge and would fluctuate with the times, but a quote dated from Wilmington, January 7, 1831, may serve to illustrate the measures taken when "outlying" slaves seemed to be affecting the behavior of those in the field: "There has been much shooting of negroes in this neighborhood recently, in consequence of symptoms of liberty having been discovered among them."[38] Although this might refer only to the shooting of those who had run away, it appears actually to refer to those still in bondage, who had been inspired with "symptoms of liberty" by the example set by the outlaws.

All of this concern over the plantation slaves' reaction to the goings-on in the swamp suggests that their conception of the swamp is dependent on the existence of maroon societies and temporary runaways using the region as a site of resistance. Slaves, of course, did not need such "outside agitators" to stir them to commit their own depredations. Even those not living or hiding in the swamps (or thinking of escaping through the swamps) made good use of the wilderness. Marrinda Jane Singleton recalls stealing a pig one night with another slave. "We took dis pig, carried hit down to de swamp lands. Killed hit. We got rid of de water whar we don scald him by puttin' hit in de river." Such activities could be typical where the rations allotted to slaves were small and the swamp was accessible. Also, May Satterfield was told by her mother that "de men would go at night an' steal hog and sheep, burry de hair in a hole way yonder in de swamp sommers whar dey knowed de white fo'ks cudden fine it and cook an' eat it."[39] For the most part, then, the swamp was a place where enslaved Africans could seize the opportunity afforded them by the environment to survive and strike back against the institution of slavery. The region certainly could fill them with dread as it would have the planters, yet the spark it must have caused in the imagination would not be one of romantic self-reflection but of possibilities.

Despite this emphasis on the utility of the swamp, it is possible that the fortunate proximity of swamps could fulfill not only a physical opportunity for resistance but a spiritual need. As African Americans most likely adapted to Christianity by fusing African deities with Christian figures and images,[40] so the swamp as a mixture of African spiritual elements may have served to maintain African religion. The composition of a swamp, trees and water (a combination of forest and lake), could echo the significance of those two elements in African religions: "In ceremony after ceremony witnessed among the Yoruba, the Ashanti, and in Dahomey, one invariable element was a visit to the river or some other body of 'living' water, such as the ocean, for the purpose of obtaining the liquid indispensable for the rites. Often it was necessary to go some distance to reach the particular stream from which water having the necessary sacred quality must be drawn."[41] Melville Herskovits sees the Negro Baptist baptism as a survival of spirit possession by African water deities. Similarly, in his research of the Central Guinea Coast, M. C. Jedrej notes that the forest is "a boundary joining yet keeping apart this visible world of human existence and the other invisible world of spirit beings."[42]

Likewise, the American swamp seems a locus for African American magic and spirituality. Often, the plantation conjurer or root doctor is associated with the margins of the community, living in or beside a swamp. Ruth Bass documents the habits of a "tree talker" named Divinity who lives in a swamp: "My grn'mammy brung tree-tawkin' from de jungle."[43] Both practices speak of origins; they are survivals of African practices that perhaps had no place on the plantation proper. If the swamp serves as a place that preserves origins, we must wonder, then, about a folktale that claims that the Negro was made by the Devil who tries to mimic God's creation of man but lacking clay must use materials from the swamp.[44]

As noted in many testimonies of former slaves, woods and swamps served a religious function by providing a space for slaves to meet secretly if they were not allowed to hold open prayer meetings. W. L. Bost remembers part of a slave song that was sung at prayer meetings held in the woods: "We camp a while in the wilderness, where the Lord makes me happy, and then I'm a-goin' home.[45]

Though more directly connected to the image of Moses leading his people, wandering for forty years before entering the promised land, this also suggests the wilderness as a space separate from the cultivated plantation spaces; the wilderness is the home of the dispossessed where they wait for their reward. As such, this space is more their own than the slave quarter provided by the planter. Still, the spiritual aspect of the swamp here is only based in its utility and the necessity to meet secretly. As noted by the nameless Dismal Swamp runaway whose account James Redpath printed, the woods and swamps would provide a suitable substitute for a church. "I b'lieve God is no inspector of persons; an' he knows his childer, and kin hear dem jest as quick in de Juniper Swamp as in de great churches what I seed in New York."[46] In his estimation there seems to be nothing intrinsically sacred in the wilderness.

Harriet Tubman, however, is said to have communed with an invisible force when leading slaves north: "When going on these journeys she often lay alone in the forests all night. Her whole soul was filled with awe of the mysterious Unseen Presence, which thrilled her with such depths of emotion, that all other care and fear vanished. Then she seemed to speak with her Maker 'as a man talketh with his friend.'"[47] Similarly, Zora Neale Hurston records a folktale, "How the Brother Was Called to Preach," in which a man goes into a special praying ground in a swamp to await instructions from God.[48] Old Uncle Louis, as well, "would run away in the latter part of the summer once in every two or three years and come back in time to help dig sweet potatoes." What distinguishes Uncle Louis's occasional running is his intent. Rather than avoiding punishment or being fed up with (mis)treatment, "I does cause de woods seems to call me." He has built a tree house to which he returns, where he sits and communes with nature (not dissimilar to Tubman). In this tree house, "Can't nobody come along widout de birds tellin' me."[49] Again, however, any attempt to solidify these spiritual practices as Africanisms brings us back to the sheer utility of the actions. While Uncle Louis's time in the woods, communing with nature, seems very similar to Bass's tree talker, the fact that the practice allows him to know if anyone is coming makes it seems less an African survival and more a survival technique.

The case for the utility of the swamp can also be made from observing how whites as well as blacks made use of it. When the Yankees advanced on the plantations during the war, the gentry resorted to hiding their valuables in the swamps. J. G. Clinkscales tells of following Uncle Essick who had volunteered to hide the family valuables inside the swamp as Sherman approached.[50] Some family slaves were not so helpful. For example, when one planter hid his horses and mules in the swamp, an unsympathetic slave named Uncle Tom fetched them for the Yankees. His nephew, who relates the story, says of Uncle Tom: "He was jes' mean. He hadn't been much good to massa since de war commenced; lay off in de swamp mos' of de time."[51]

The planter's most innovative use of the swamp, however, came when old massa hid himself there. This inversion of the plantation norm is mentioned in numerous testimonies, but it is captured best in the following song:

> White folks, have you seed old massa
> Up de road, with he mustache on?

He pick up he hat and he leave real sudden
And I 'lieve he's up and gone.

(Chorus)
Old massa run away
And us darkies stay at home.
It mus' be now dat Kingdom's comin'
And de year of Jubilee.

He look up de river and he seed dat smoke
Where de Lincoln gunboats lay.
He big 'nuff and he old 'nuff and he orter know better,
But he gone and run away.

Now dat overseer want to give trouble
And trot us 'round a spell,
But we lock him up in de smokehouse cellar,
With de key done throwed in de well.[52]

Although this song doesn't mention the swamp specifically, it reflects a time when numerous stories are told of white southerners fleeing to the woods and swamps. The joy of this inversion seems to belie the notion that the swamp came to be a sacred place for enslaved Africans; rather, it suggests a joy in seeing the slave owners forced to resort to the slaves' own desperate survival tactics.

It seems likely that the slaves' use of swamps did not change dramatically from the time of William Byrd's expedition to Nat Turner's Rebellion. The number of slaves engaged in such activities as well as the planters' knowledge of uprisings such as those in the West Indies may account for the growing anxiety among whites. No longer satisfied that the gators and snakes would return their runaways for them, the planters grow to fear the image of the slave in the swamp in all its wild and potentially threatening forms. For the African Americans' part, the swamp could come to serve a variety of functions. Certainly for some, the region may have been a place to preserve African traditions, just as for others it was a realm of the wild, savage slaves with which they wanted no intercourse. For the majority, though, it seems likely that the swamp served an important role in both adapting to life as a slave and rebelling against that life. Yes, it could be a foreboding place, but it also was a space that could be theirs, not the white man's.

PART 3

Defining Places in Community Life

11

LIBERTY AND ECONOMY IN LOWCOUNTRY SOUTH CAROLINA

The Case of the Freedmen's Bank

Marland E. Buckner Jr.

THE ROAD TO THE BANK

O N JULY 24, 1868, BENJAMIN RIVERS WALKED into the Beaufort, South Carolina, branch of the Freedmen's Savings and Trust Company and opened a savings account.[1] Rivers, a black farmer in his early twenties from St. Helena Island, South Carolina, had seen three turbulent years pass since the end of the Civil War, seven since Union forces invaded the Sea Islands of South Carolina. If Rivers's life resembled that of many other St. Helena residents, he likely experienced a variety of tumultuous events.

Early on November 7, 1861, fifteen-year-old Ben likely heard his master barking orders that all slaves were to accompany him to mainland South Carolina, beyond reach of threatening Union forces. Along with his four brothers and two sisters, Ben may well have watched his parents, Dolly and Autrum Rivers, openly defy the order, even when confronted with threats that the invading Yankees would sell them to Cuba.[2]

Carts and carriages likely lined the Beaufort streets Rivers strode that July day. Perhaps a cart clattered past him, one similar to those that raced away from "the big house" the day Union forces invaded. If the Riverses' master hastily abandoned their St. Helena home in November 1861, they were not alone. Throughout the Sea Islands rebel authorities demanded residents evacuate to the mainland immediately. For Sea Island plantation slaves like the Riverses, disobeying the Confederate order was relatively simple: they refused to accompany their owners and continued tending crops regardless of what they were told. Not only did many slaves refuse to accompany their owners, many journeyed to Beaufort where they enjoyed the fruits of their labors in planters' summer homes.[3]

Ex-slave Joseph McWright described the scene in testimony before the Southern Claims Commission: "Within a few days before the federals took possession of the town and after most of the people had left, a scouting party of confederate men located at Port Royal Ferry . . . came to Beaufort and seized me and John Ficklin [another ex-slave] bound us . . . gagged us and paddled us. They then sent us to Gillisonville Jail and kept us in irons. This was done because we did not obey the order to leave town."[4]

For thousands of Sea Island slaves the Union invasion signaled the end of their bondage. Many, however, remained human chattel for several more years. Sam Polite, a St. Helena slave, was one such unfortunate: "W'en war come, Missis tek me and two more niggers, put we and chillen in two wagon and go to Baarnwell. . . . We stay in Baarnwell all enduring de war. . . . W'en Freedom come, Missis didn't say nutting, she jest cry. But she gib we a wagon and we press a horse and us come back to St. Helena Islant. It tek t'ree day to git home. W'en we git home, we fine de rest ob de nigger yere been hab Freedom four year befo' we!"[5]

Perhaps Ben Rivers had heard stories like these from friends and family. His recollections of the war years were likely much different. As a member of the Thirty-third South Carolina volunteers, Rivers experienced the horror of war firsthand. He may not, however, have willingly chosen to serve the Union cause. Some plantations on St. Helena saw the wholesale desertion of the male population when Union soldiers came to call. Rivers might have fled to the woods as many field hands did. He may have done so because he was uncertain about Union soldiers' intentions. If so, endless hours of marching and drilling at Camp Saxton on Port Royal Island and long hours marching and drumming with C Company of the Thirty-third Regiment likely made him painfully aware.[6]

Rivers's mind may have been full of images as he made his way to the Beaufort bank. Perhaps he remembered his military service with pride. Perhaps he recalled the last three years with bitterness and disappointment.

The path Ben Rivers and other lowcountry African Americans trod after April 1865 must have seemed chaotic. Hope, anticipation, fear, disappointment, and anger likely followed on each other's heels.[7] Like African Americans throughout the South, lowcountry residents grappled with the precise meaning of freedom. But the distinctive characteristics of lowcountry slavery provided a unique context in which to fashion freedom. The intersection of ethics and practices in slavery and events during Reconstruction were defining elements for black patrons of the Freedmen's Bank.

LIFE AND LABOR IN LOWCOUNTRY SOUTH CAROLINA

Seventeenth- and eighteenth-century lowcountry settlers found themselves situated in a region tailor-made for rice production.[8] Rice required only efficient irrigation and disciplined labor; inland swamps provided the former, African slaves the latter. With rice cultivation came prosperity, and by the last two decades of the eighteenth century, after the addition of long-staple cotton production, Sea Island planters would rank among the wealthiest American nabobs.[9]

The central and unique feature of slave life on lowcountry plantations was the task system. The task system was instrumental in helping shape the social experience upon which lowcountry blacks would draw during emancipation.[10]

Though the task system began on mid-eighteenth-century rice plantations, by the late eighteenth century planters adjusted it to accommodate cultivation of Sea Island cotton as well as rice. When slaves completed their assigned tasks, they were frequently allowed to pursue their own interests. An industrious slave might complete a task by noon, leaving the afternoon for personal use.

By the nineteenth century tasks measured not only labor requirements but distance and even time. A task became such a standard unit that slaves and planters could refer to distances between various locations as so many "tasks" apart or report that an event took a given number of tasks to complete. "Tasking" gave slaves greater control over their own time. Most cultivated personal or family garden plots to augment whatever rations were distributed by their masters.[11]

Independent time management opened other doors for lowcountry slaves. Since nearly all lowcountry slave owners allowed their chattel to own and control property, many participated in market relations. Lowcountry slaves bartered, bought, and sold goods not only among themselves but with all lowcountry residents, including their own masters.[12] Slave ownership of property spanned the lowcountry region, and it spanned generations. Many inherited property, which imbued recipients with an understanding of property as security.[13]

Even as Americans debated and fought over the nature of the national economy, lowcountry slaves quietly cultivated gardens, raised livestock, and bought, sold, exchanged, and bequeathed property within their legally proscribed economic world. By producing commodities for consumption and trade, lowcountry slaves established patterns of individual and familial economic participation early and often. Since the slave regimen severely limited opportunity to earn additional income, these patterns of participation developed slowly. Economic activities were nonetheless a critical part of the process by which lowcountry slaves sought to distance themselves from their

owners' economic paternalism.[14] Unique conditions, such as extensive property ownership, market relations, and experience with disposable income,
gave lowcountry slaves a taste of what liberation might bring.

Though many lowcountry slaves had experience with property ownership
and market relations, most field hands did not earn regular wages. Still, many
slaves worked for themselves. Sam Mitchell, an ex-slave from Ladies Island,
described arrangements on his plantation. "De slave had 'bout two task ob
land to cultivate for se'f in w'at called Nigger field. Could raise one pig," he
remembered. Economic opportunities extended beyond land allotments.
Mitchell recalled: "My father hab a boat and he gone fishing at night and sell
fish. Master let him cut post and wood at night and sell, too. He had to do dis
work at night 'cause in daytime he have to do his task."[15]

Though arrangements for urban slaves differed from rural slaves, they
too pursued economic opportunity. Joseph McWright was one such individual: "I was a slave . . . but paid for my time. I was free to buy and own property and control it." When Southern Claims commissioners asked McWright,
"Did you have a great deal of prosperity when the war broke out?" he
responded, "I did."[16]

As a young slave Benjamin Rivers probably did not own property. Ben
Rivers's parents, however, very likely did, perhaps in the form of livestock or
surplus produce. Beaufort District resident Mooney Sinclair described what
many lowcountry planters and slaves understood as a way of life: "I was a
slave . . . at the beginning of the war. I owned the property before I became
free. I raised hogs before and during the war and made provisions in my spare
time." Andrew Jackson bemoaned Union confiscation of his holdings in
1865: "I had cattle, hogs and poultry when Sherman's army came through
here. I had five head of cattle."[17] Sherman's incendiary march to the sea
stripped Jackson and hundreds of other lowcountry slaves of property they
had struggled to obtain.

Lowcountry African Americans understood the value of property. Their
understanding was fashioned, however, in a cultural context where economic
advancement and upward mobility were proscribed by color and caste. This
meant ambitious slaves had a much longer ladder to climb than other
Southerners. And yet slave success stories do exist.[18] Slave ownership of property spanned the region, and it spanned generations. Many slaves inherited
property. Inheritance gave recipients an understanding of the relationship
between property and personal and familial security. The means to this security demanded careful supervision, as William Riley recalled: "My animals
were all worked the same as my master's animals—I did this so as to prevent
other persons from taking them."[19] Slaves valued property and cash, but

because they were their own. As Sim Greely of Spartanburg District was quick to point out: "Everybody buried dere money and sometimes dey forgot where dey put it. . . . Lots of money buried somewhars, and folks died and never remembered whar it was."[20]

Individual effort gave lowcountry slaves opportunities to create wealth for themselves. These experiences during slavery made the lowcountry African American community as a whole acutely aware of the Civil War's meaning and the economic potential of freedom. Liberation did not diminish or change the basic values that lowcountry slaves held dear; it gave them greater opportunity to act in accordance with those values.[21] Although war brought liberation, liberation brought opportunity for only a select few. Most African Americans would have to create their own opportunity, unsure if the promise of freedom would be the promise of land ownership.

African Americans made 347 land purchases on St. Helena Island by June 1865, and by the following year they owned much of the land on the island. Thousands more throughout the region, however, believed they owned the land they worked since Sherman's Field Order 15 gave "possessory title" to some 40,000 African Americans living on "the Sherman Reservation." Lowcountry African Americans soon found their possessory titles in danger of being revoked when Sea Island planters returned, armed with presidential pardons.

Government policy regarding the validity of possessory titles was at best makeshift. Some land was finally granted to ex-slaves in the Sea Islands but only under stringent conditions. If property had been cultivated by an individual before October 17, 1865, and that property was part of the plantation named in the possessory title, then the title was considered valid. About 1,500 landowners fell into this category. In 1867 the federal authorities granted confiscated land in the central Sea Islands to these individuals.[22]

African Americans held high hopes for lowcountry land during 1865 and early 1866. It quickly became clear, however, that little hope for large-scale federally sponsored land redistribution existed. In 1865, when unreconstructed Carolinian legislators passed the "Black Codes," an apartheidlike set of regulations governing black life, some lowcountry African Americans took matters into their own hands. Thousands refused to make labor contracts with their ex-masters.[23] Some went so far as to arm themselves in order to expel federal authorities attempting to evict them from what freedpeople believed was their land.

Since federal intervention on behalf of African Americans did not materialize, most freedpeople finally were forced to submit to contracts regulating plantation labor. It was not unheard of for federal authorities to force freedpeople, ofttimes at gunpoint, either to contract with former rebels or to face

eviction. Even as rumors continued to circulate regarding federal land redistribution policy, military authorities forced most freedpeople to return to the
same labor they had performed while slaves.

And yet they were not slaves. Freedpeople had a wider corridor of choice
after liberation. In principle they could refuse terms of contracts read to them.
In practice, however, such refusals generally meant freedom to starve. Bad
weather, poor crops, and planter collusion in establishing labor contracts
combined to put many ex-slaves in an untenable situation. The 1865 harvest
was so poor that by early 1866 it appeared to most freedpeople that they had
little choice but to accept labor contracts proposed by ex-Confederates and
sanctioned by the Freedmen's Bureau.[24] At bottom, freedom meant work.

By the spring of 1866 more than 100,000 Sea Islanders had contracted
with ex-Confederate landowners. Under the watchful eye of the Freedmen's
Bureau, freedpeople who still refused to contract were forcibly removed from
lands they believed their own.[25]

Freedpeople in the South toiled under a variety of labor arrangements
after the war. As in slavery, lowcountry residents, especially Sea Islanders,
enjoyed far greater labor autonomy in liberty than other ex-slaves. The "two-
day" system was the labor arrangement of choice among many lowcountry
residents and the primary arrangement among Sea Islanders. This system wed
freedpeople's desire for land with planters' desire for a stable labor supply.
Workers contracted to provide two day's labor in exchange for several acres
of land to cultivate during the rest of the week. Labor requirements were still
measured in tasks. Planters paid cash to workers for tasks beyond those performed on contracted days. These arrangements gave freedpeople labor
autonomy and some benefits of landownership even if they could not afford
to purchase the land themselves.[26]

By 1868 social stability returned to the lowcountry. Though the Johnson
administration shattered freedpeople's dreams of wholesale land redistribution,
Sea Islanders had tasted what ex-slaves elsewhere in America could only
dream of: a government-sanctioned plan for African American landownership.[27] Though the government nullified Sherman's grant, thousands of
African Americans saw at least the possibility of landownership in the future.
Thousands, like Ben Rivers, hoped to see their dreams materialize through
the Freedmen's Savings Bank.

That African Americans opened bank accounts on the heels of centuries-
old bondage urges historians to contemplate attitudes and sensibilities under-
girding the banking experience. The bank cards reveal substantial social
diversity within African American communities. For example, the bank cards
indicate that residence, occupation, gender, and complexion factors intersected
and helped to define constituencies or subgroups within the group of depos-

itors as a whole. One crucial factor appeared to unify or homogenize patrons, regardless of complexion, residence, occupation, or gender: the vast majority of bank patrons were illiterate.

What motivated depositors to open accounts? Clearly, an undeniable economic self-consciousness—though perhaps embryonic compared to other aspects of African Americans' lives in liberation—unified bank patrons regardless of their social circumstance. At some level patrons, whether encouraged, educated, or even indoctrinated, must have believed that banking served their needs.

THE FREEDMEN'S BANK

When the Union mustered out Ben River's regiment on Morris Island during February 1866,[28] it likely sent him home with some money in his pocket. Though Ben certainly learned about the value of property early in life, he probably never had money of his own till he enlisted. Rumors that land was to be given to ex-slaves swirled during the closing months of the war. Perhaps Rivers hoped to buy some land for himself and his family. Perhaps he hoped to raise his son, Benjamin Jr., on that land. Perhaps the Union veteran hoped to pass it on to his son as other lowcountry parents passed their livestock and belongings down to their children. Perhaps his trip to the bank attested to his hopes for economic advancement in a free-labor economy.

Scores of thousands of freedpeople opened accounts at Freedmen's Banks throughout the South.[29] General Rufus Saxton established the Beaufort Military Savings Bank in the town of Beaufort in 1864. He created the bank out of both necessity and a philanthropic spirit common to many New Englanders who came to the lowcountry during the war.[30] Saxton promoted the military bank as a means to achieve stability, self-sufficiency, and prosperity for African American soldiers.

Saxton enlisted other Northerners in the region to advertise the bank's rapidly expanding services among all lowcountry African Americans. By August 1864 Saxton's brainchild contained $180,000 of freedpeople's deposits.[31] Northern teachers and missionaries quickly followed Saxton's lead and worked to inculcate habits of "thrift and industry" among ex-slaves. Though Saxton's project was not part of a regional or national institutional structure, other department commanders noted it, and two other banking concerns sprouted up, one in Norfolk and another in New Orleans.[32]

The first attempt to unify these small concerns occurred in 1865 when a Union paymaster sought to amalgamate the three institutions. Though this attempt failed, Northern abolitionists and philanthropists quickly seized upon the idea that ex-slaves needed banks. A group of New York businessmen-philanthropists, inspired by Saxton's example, took steps to establish a national bank for freedpeople. Led by John Alvord, this group quickly drafted a proposal. Congress passed legislation and formally incorporated the bank on March 3, 1865, the final day of its thirty-eighth session.[33]

Northern philanthropists established the bank as part of a larger plan to help African Americans impose order on what many Northerners saw as the chaotic transition from slavery to freedom. Military service or plantation labor in Union-held territory created new responsibilities and opportunities for African Americans during the war. Because it was an institution supported by Freedmen's Bureau head General O. O. Howard and by Abraham Lincoln himself, the bank's founders hoped it would be an organizing force in the economic lives of newly freed African Americans.[34]

In addition, the founders hoped to foster strong republican values among ex-slaves. They intended the bank to function as a crucible within which a virtuous African American citizenry would be molded. This unshakable imperative, critical to the bank's founders, connected economic advancement with moral progress. Hard work, thrift, and sobriety, the founders argued, would remove slavery's chains on African American morality and bring them into mainstream American life.[35] For lowcountry freedpeople, the bank provided the opportunity to extend the experience many had tasted in slavery but could attain only through liberation.

WORK AND FAMILY IN TOWN AND COUNTRY

Ben Rivers's crops probably did not suffer because of his midsummer banking excursion to Beaufort. He likely had finished spring planting well before his trip, and harvest was at least a month away. When Ben returned from Beaufort, he came back to the same St. Helena cotton fields where he had grown up. He also returned to work similar to that of his slave forefathers. While liberation gave Ben charge of his family, his routine daily work differed from slavery only in that the threat of potential starvation and debt replaced the driver's whip.

Lavina Palmer came from a far different life than Ben Rivers. Born, reared, and residing in Beaufort, Lavina had but a short trip from her Orange Street home to the bank on March 23, 1869.[36] Bank clerks listed her complexion as light, which suggests one of her parents, David Myers and Sally Gourdine, may have been white. Lavina married and bore one child who died in infancy. After the death of her husband and first child, Lavina adopted Mary Anne Allston. This forty-eight-year-old urban nurse and single mother probably never experienced Ben's daily farm routine.

Though barely a year apart in opening their accounts, Ben Rivers and Lavina Palmer were, in many ways, worlds apart in their social origins. Lavina was a middle-aged widow; Ben was new to family responsibilities and demands. Lavina was an urbanite probably inexperienced in tasks, hoeing, or cotton picking; Rivers's life was agrarian.

Lavina Palmer and Ben Rivers exemplify the remarkable breadth in social circumstances among Beaufort bank patrons. Their lives illustrate the racial and occupational gap separating urban and rural patrons.

The majority of urban males either farmed or labored. Women, however, overwhelmingly chose domestic service. Many urban patrons were self-employed.[37] Rural patrons' job patterns were far more uniform than urban patrons', regardless of gender and race. Over 90 percent of the rural depositors were self-employed farmers, though some listed additional occupations, usually carpentry or some other trade.[38] Varied social circumstances demonstrate the extensive support African Americans gave the bank.

Only ten women from St. Helena are listed as having opened bank accounts. Radical differences in their social circumstances suggest interesting possibilities. Six were self-employed farmers. The only woman listed as a domestic was thirteen-year-old Celia Brown, servant to the prominent Northern educator Laura Towne.[39] Three of these St. Helena women were married, four had children, and four were widows. Celia Brown was the only female depositor from St. Helena under the age of thirty. Signature cards list another woman as thirty years of age, but the remainder were all listed as over fifty years.[40]

By 1868 the Johnson administration had made it abundantly clear that African Americans would not be given land outright. It seems likely, therefore, that younger farmers would save to buy land. Younger farmers, now responsible for feeding and clothing their families, had time to save funds required to purchase portions of government-confiscated plantations. But average life expectancy was relatively short on the Sea Islands, yet elderly widows from St. Helena opened accounts.

Elderly widows' deposits represented an investment in their future even at a relatively late stage in life. As farmers, perhaps they, like so many others, hoped to purchase land. What seems more likely, however, is that their accounts were meant to provide security in their declining years. Either way, opening bank accounts was a tangible expression of liberty and a practical, sensible course of action for women whose lives probably had been spent in slavery.[41]

Patrons from the town of Beaufort contrasted sharply with rural depositors. Though occupational distribution was broad, many Beaufort patrons worked as domestic servants. Cooks, waiters, and housekeepers accounted for nearly one-third of these urban depositors. Laborers and farmers composed nearly half the town's patrons. Artisans and white-collar workers made up the remainder.

Though they both listed farming as their occupation and closely resembled each other in age, rural Sea Island farmers and farmers from Beaufort probably led substantially different lives. Although part of the same occupational group and similarly complected, these men's signature cards suggest further differences in social structure between town and country depositors.

Since they were overwhelmingly self-employed, farmers from Beaufort likely lived in town and worked on farms in the surrounding area. As Simon Gallman, an ex-slave from Spartanburg County, put it: "When freedom come, de slaves hired out mostly as sharecroppers. A little later, some got small farms to rent. Since dat time dey have worked at most anything dey could get to do. De ones dat moved to town worked at odd jobs, some at carpenter work, janitor work or street work; but most of dem worked in fields around town."[42]

Perhaps these individuals hired their time as day laborers or for some other form of wage but chose to list themselves as self-employed farmers. These "urban farmers" also were less likely to have children than their rural counterparts, which suggests that residence had more impact on social structure than occupation among those who listed farming as an occupation. Those in rural areas who listed farming as their occupation probably were involved in a lifestyle quite different from that of farmers listing Beaufort as their home. Farmers in rural areas lived on the land they cultivated while urban farmers did not. Rural Sea Islanders, tasked during slavery, viewed freedom as an opportunity to expand their agricultural enterprises. Sea Islanders farming in freedom likely required larger families to meet increased labor requirements. Farmers living in Beaufort would not have required the additional labor necessary to maintain a rural residence. This may account for the higher incidence of children among rural farmers.

With the exception of those who farmed, urban women depositors tended to be in their late twenties or early thirties. The average age for the few urban farm women and laborers was thirty-eight. Among women engaged primarily in service professions, most claimed to be self-employed. As with nearly all other depositors, most urban women had siblings and came from families of between three to five children. Interestingly, these women were far less likely than any other depositors to have children, and those who did rarely had more than two. Unlike many rural female depositors who were widows, virtually all urban women were married.[43]

The differences in lifestyle between an urban domestic servant and a rural farmer raise the issue of characterizing depositors' motives. Did urban and rural women share similar goals, when their lives were so different? It would seem unlikely that urban domestic servants would be saving money to buy land, but for many rural women landownership may well have been a goal. How should these differences be interpreted? How can the choice to open a bank account be explained given these wide-ranging experiences and social circumstances?

The specific goals of elderly St. Helena widows almost certainly differed from the goals of younger women from Ladies Island. St. Helena women likely had extensive experience in market relations as they probably lived most of their lives as tasked slaves. Given the commonality of property owner-ship and market relations among Sea Island slaves, these women likely had experience with disposable income in some form.[44] Opening bank accounts represented another method of handling disposable income, a new arena and a new form of financial management. The meaning of these particular deposits, however, was rooted in the generations-old internal economy devel-oped by lowcountry slaves.

For older patrons who lived nearly all their lives as slaves, bank accounts could translate into self-reliance and self-respect just as property ownership did during slavery.[45] Many younger women throughout the Sea Islands, such as Ben Rivers's wife, did not have accounts. That these elderly women did suggests that ideas about independence and self-reliance cut across gender and age lines.

Underneath these different goals lay a strikingly similar sensibility. Lowcountry African Americans shared a history and an ethic of saving, regardless of gender. Thousands of slaves saved proceeds from sales of garden produce and livestock to acquire other commodities. These exchanges and acquisitions often took place after long periods of accumulating funds. Slaves practiced the process of immediate denial for future gain.

Task labor allowed lowcountry slaves to acquire goods and capital, thereby decreasing economic dependency on slave owners. It would seem, then, that accumulation and exchange served, at the very least, as niches of self-reliance in an oppressive system. During emancipation elderly female depositors clearly acted on experiences and beliefs formed during slavery.[46] These beliefs also informed other developments in lowcountry life during emancipation.

ILLITERACY

Though freedpeople undoubtedly brought inestimable hopes and dreams to the Beaufort bank, almost none could have written about them. Although residence and occupation indicate that bank patrons lived remarkably dif-ferent lives, illiteracy festered among depositors regardless of other social characteristics. The level of illiteracy among depositors provides a crucial final element in understanding Beaufort bank patrons. Beaufort bank cards show most depositors lacked sufficient literacy training to sign their names. Despite Freedmen's Bureau and other philanthropic relief efforts, illiteracy plagued most depositors, regardless of complexion.[47]

Ex-slaves' surging desire for education after the war suggests the importance they attached to literacy. They appreciated the need for education, as
well as its potential, and continued to emphasize these needs well into the
twentieth century. Ezra Adams, a former slave living near Columbia, South
Carolina, in the late 1930s stated this clearly: "What does I think the colored
people need most. . . . I thinks dat good teachers and work is what de colored race needs worser than anything else." During emancipation freedpeople
demanded and directed organized educational efforts.[48]

Educational efforts and the Freedmen's Bank were inextricably linked. John
Alvord, founder and bank president, served simultaneously as general superintendent of schools for the Freedmen's Bureau. Though technically unrelated
to the Bureau or any other federal agency, the bank's directorate shared an
agenda with other Northern missionaries and reformers. They sought to impart
a particular type of education to ex-slaves. They hoped the bank would serve
as a location where habits of thrift and self-sufficiency could be developed.

Though liberation spawned widespread educational efforts among
African Americans themselves, it also flooded the lowcountry with missionaries and educators from the North. The Reverend William Peck of Massachusetts opened the first Sea Island school in Beaufort on January 8, 1862.
African Americans operated and supported the "Billaird Hall School."
Missionaries taught African American teachers who, in turn, taught the
school's pupils. The five-cent weekly tuition fee proved undaunting to many
poor African American families whose children composed the school's 101
students by March 1862.[49]

The campaign for literacy gathered steam in the Sea Islands during the
early 1860s. Educational efforts expanded rapidly even before Lincoln's
Emancipation Proclamation. Missionaries sought to bring "civilization" to
the region's ex-slaves through education. Ex-slave Sam Mitchell remembered
Northern efforts on his Ladies Island plantation: "De Yankee open school
for nigger and teacher lib in Maussa house to Brickyaa'd."[50]

Freed Sea Islanders also attended Sabbath schools. These institutions
gave many African Americans, regardless of age, their only opportunity at
basic education. African American teachers stressed Bible literacy and
Christian values. These schools existed throughout emancipation and provided
education to those in remote areas. In June 1862 Treasury Department special
agent E. L. Pierce reported that some 300 African Americans attended the
Sabbath school held at a church on St. Helena.[51] In addition, missionaries
established day schools from which children benefited.

Northern educators may well have used bank literature to educate freedpeople in both literacy and civics. As students learned to read and spell the
word *bank*, Northern teachers preached the gospel of hard work and

patience required for saving and financial success.[52] Ultimately, however, Northern educators simply attached labels to the values many lowcountry African Americans had lived by in generations of old local economies.

While the number of depositors grew during the early 1870s, illiteracy continued to plague most bank patrons regardless of race, residence, or gender. Nearly three-quarters of all bank patrons were illiterate. Though complexional, residential, and occupational distinctions existed, bank patrons were remarkably homogeneous in their illiteracy. Even though Sea Island African Americans and missionaries gave education high priority during the war, the bank cards suggest that by the late 1860s and early 1870s widespread literacy, defined as the ability to sign one's name, was still far off. Though men signed their names more frequently than women, overall illiteracy affected all groups of depositors.

To understand the meaning bank accounts had for freedpeople, scholars must recognize the critical role illiteracy played in social structure. One might expect "educated" (literate and "civilized" in contemporary Anglo-European terms) African Americans to understand and embrace banking as a means to independence and autonomy. Most patrons, however, were illiterate. This suggests that bank deposits ought to be considered as acts of economic self-consciousness, distinct from broader participation in "civilized American culture" as it was then understood by Anglo-Americans. Clearly, African Americans had a sense of economic self-interest not necessarily derived from Anglo-European acculturation—wherein literacy played a central role—but from African American culture.

A flood of freedpeople hoped to become literate at the end of war. Bank deposits indicate that by 1874 these hopes remained essentially unrealized. Signature cards do, however, reveal pockets of educational growth among patrons. Overall, illiteracy among male patrons seemed on the decline. Men able to sign their names were, on average, more than a decade younger than their illiterate counterparts. Women able to sign were uniformly in their midteens. This trend suggests African Americans concerned themselves with their community's future: young people. The investment in educating youth was apparently being made without regard to sex. The education of young people regardless of sex suggests African Americans hoped to provide all their children with opportunities denied during slavery.[53]

Liberty provided freedpeople with choices largely defined by the social circumstances of slavery. Participation in different forms of economic life was important for lowcountry freedpeople, but generations of experience informed these activities. Choosing to save money in a bank was not altogether unlike burying money in the ground. Though the mechanics of opening a bank account differed from burying money, the intent did not.

A Sea Island slave could bury money in the ground without censure. A slave could buy, sell, and trade with virtually anyone, without censure. Sea Island slaves could not, however, send their children to school. Thus the social dynamics of education, encouraged by the Freedmen's Bureau, differed markedly from the social dynamics of stealing education during slavery. Economic self-consciousness must, therefore, be understood as distinct from other areas of autonomy freedpeople were slowly beginning to discover. These enterprises must be distinguished from choices African Americans made which were qualitatively different, choices which were new.

Patterns of illiteracy in the signature cards reveal a crucial distinction. Sea Islanders' economic self-consciousness was rooted in the slave experience, especially among slaves over sixteen in 1865. The low number of patrons capable of signing their names at the time of their deposits indicates economic self-consciousness drew on a different reservoir, or cultural legacy, than the desire for literate culture. The low ratio of signatories suggests far more widespread consensus among African Americans regarding the value of bank accounts than the value of literate culture. This is not to say freedpeople valued banking more than literacy. Evidence simply suggests that there may have existed, because of cultural experience, a cultural predisposition to banking.

This suggests a sharp contrast with the argument that ex-slaves drew their economic self-consciousness from an Anglo-American model or example, or that they absorbed an Anglo-American Protestant work ethic. Freedom to bank was understood differently than the freedom to educate. Widespread educational efforts were a completely new experience for low-country freedpeople. Literacy training was a new opportunity with barely any historical precedent among slaves. It drew solely on the hopes and aspirations of freedpeople in the midst of the upheaval of war and emancipation. Banking, while new in practice, drew on old, established traditions and experiences throughout lowcountry African American communities.

EPILOGUE

More than 100,000 African Americans deposited their hopes and dreams when they opened bank accounts. They came out of abject poverty, in a climate of violent racism, to the doors of Freedmen's Banks everywhere in the South and put their trust in what they thought was a national institution.

On July 2, 1874, the bank closed its doors. Pressures from an economic depression and gross impropriety on the part of its leadership doomed the Freedmen's Bank. The original bank charter required that its investments be confined to U.S. government securities. In 1870, however, the charter was amended, permitting its directorate to underwrite a variety of speculative real estate ventures in Washington, D.C., and elsewhere.

When financial panic struck in 1873, the bank was forced to bear the burden of property devaluations and loan defaults. After several runs and a brief period of restructuring, the bank was forced to close permanently, nine years after it opened. Patrons never recovered their deposits.[54] The failure of the Freedmen's Bank foretold the ongoing poverty and disenfranchisement of millions of new American citizens. They were banking on freedom, but liberation's legacy was grim.

12   THE PRAISE HOUSE TRADITION ON ST. HELENA ISLAND, SOUTH CAROLINA

Vanessa Thaxton

PRAISE HOUSE OR PRAYER HOUSE is a place of worship that was originally constructed in the 1840s by white plantation own- ers. These unique structures were built primarily in the Sea Islands for the use of African bondsmen. Planters constructed praise houses on their property because they were trying to control their slave property. Some planters were genuinely interested in providing religious instruction for their bondsmen; however, it was not for the salvation of the slave. They were more interested in developing a sense of fear in the bondsmen so that they would not run away or rebel against their captivity. The planters taught catechism or Scriptures from the Bible that carried the message of passivity. This type of biblical instruction helped to maintain control over the bondsmen and to perpetuate the belief that whites were superior. Another reason that the planters put praise houses on their plantations was because of the hardships experienced with transporting people on and off the island. The landscape included many waterways, and the vegetation in the area was very dense. The planters could not travel as often as they would have liked although they had several churches and other outlets in the area. Even though the planters allowed their bondsmen to attend church services at the white church in Beaufort or the Brick Church on St. Helena Island, built in 1855 by slave labor, or the Episcopal Church, also on St. Helena, the bondsmen were made to sit on the back row or in the balconies.

One leading advocate who brought Christian religious instruction to the bondsmen was Richard Fuller, a Harvard-educated attorney with plantations on both St. Helena and Cat Island as well as the mainland. Fuller was "greatly moved by the reformer's cry to instruct the slaves and was largely responsible for the comparatively phenomenal growth of the Beaufort Baptist Church." The United Methodists had already come into the Sea Islands to convert the bondsmen. However, they did not convince them to join the Methodist Church because the people preferred the preaching styles of the Baptists. Fuller was known for his ability to preach which helped him to develop good relations with the bondsmen. He also further developed his relationship with the Africans because he spoke selectively about better treatment for them. However, Richard Fuller still "upheld American slavery as a white man's right."[1]

Richard Fuller wanted to expose the black population to Christianity but often found resistance among many of the whites. "In the Beaufort Church, it led to the creation of an entrance to the galleries from the outside."[2] Many whites did not want to associate with their slaves in a social manner no matter if it meant "saving souls." We will never know if Richard Fuller had a choice in whether or not he really believed in better rights for the Africans, but many of his writings imply that he kept himself aligned with the sentiments of the majority of white Christians. Fuller wrote:

> Removed so large a number are, every Sunday from the control and discipline of the plantation, and impossible as it is for the church to know and control their conduct, they use the liberty in ways and purposes adverse to their morals. Nothing seems to me more essential in order to their becoming a religious people, than that they be subjected to the supervision of the plantation, of the minister of a church, that will investigate and correct their wrong views and bad habits. It is owing, I think, to the want of religious instruction and discipline on the plantations that the influence of religious instruction and the spirit of subordination among the negroes is so little seen and felt.[3]

Richard Fuller was primarily responsible for the establishment of a praise house on each plantation. The praise house would essentially be used to control the movement and religious expression of the bondsmen. Kenneth Doe states, "A generally positive institution, the local church, is used for negative purposes, the control and discipline of slaves."[4]

However, in the praise house the African bondsmen were able to worship freely, often incorporating rituals from their homeland. They were able to praise God in the lowcountry in a manner that they were accustomed to. Praise houses, simple wooden structures, had and still have a power over the community. There were over forty-five plantations on St. Helena Island, and usually there was a praise house on each one. Historians have found that as late as 1932 twenty-five praise houses existed on St. Helena Island, which is one of the most noted Sea Islands. Currently, there are four praise houses left on the island, and they have all been designated historic landmarks by the National Trust.

This chapter describes the St. Helena Island community; other Sea Island communities that used to have praise houses; the exterior and interior of the praise houses, primarily the two that are still in use; and the Penn Center and its role in Sea Island preservation, education, and retention of Gullah culture. Also, the importance of the praise house to the African bondmen and the community today is reviewed. I offer my opinion on the sustenance of this institution and its importance to the community in the midst of the encroachment of development that is found on most of the islands in the lowcountry. This is done through my personal recollections, interviews with St. Helena Island residents, and a small sampling of the massive research done on African American Sea Islanders.

St. Helena Island is one of the largest of the Sea Islands in coastal South Carolina. Located in Beaufort County, St. Helena is situated approximately fifty miles southwest of Charleston, South Carolina, and forty miles northeast of Savannah, Georgia.[5] Hilton Head and Daufuskie Islands are also located in Beaufort County. These two islands are major resort areas and have very elegant retirement and vacation homes for the many whites who love the weather and the beaches. Many of the old cemeteries that belonged to generations of African American descendants have new luxury homes built on them or are enclosed within the confines of gates manned by security guards. It is amazing that the four praise houses located on St. Helena Island are still intact and standing where they were built over one hundred years ago.

Each of the four praise houses is located on a former plantation and carries the name of the planter who owned the land. After the Civil War the plantations were still named for the owners even though the land had been sold to the now free Africans. The term *plantation* eventually became *community*. The unique shape of St. Helena Island and all of the waterways and vegetation made for an interesting division of land. Historian Theodore Rosengarten describes St. Helena Island as shaped like a "blue crab" with the majority of the plantations around the perimeter of this shape. Also, he recounts that there were many creeks, ditches, wooded areas, and fences separating the land and only two roads central to the island.[6]

St. Helena Island was a very marshy area. With few roads and with plantations located in areas connected only by intervals of wooden causeways, it was difficult for both whites and their bondsmen to travel frequently. Most of the institutions for white society during this time—the churches, general store, and other conveniences—were located in the center of a town known then as St. Helenaville.[7]

This region, often referred to as the lowcountry, is known by many as one of the most important areas where aspects of African heritage can be found in the United States. Many scholars believe that because of the isolation of the island and the marshy land, as well as the other difficulties that Rosengarten described, the majority of the African bondsmen were able to maintain many of their African customs. In addition, there was not always a large population of whites living on the island because the conditions of the area bred mosquitoes and disease that the whites could not tolerate. These conditions caused many whites to serve as absentee owners, and in many instances blacks were left to serve as overseers, as seen in one of the paintings by Sam Doyle, who was a folk painter from St. Helena Island's Wallace Community.

In 1861 Northern troops gained control of St. Helena Island, banishing the plantation owners. Over 10,000 bondsmen were left on the island. Other bondsmen heard of the freedom found on St. Helena and ran away to this land of freedom. Northern missionaries also came to St. Helena and began to aid in the transition from slavery to freedom. Willie Lee Rose wrote *Rehearsal for Reconstruction: The Port Royal Experiment*, an excellent resource on reconstruction efforts on St. Helena Island and the first school for the freed Africans. Penn School was founded in 1861 by two white ladies, Laura Towne and Ellen Murray. A free African American, Charlotte Forten, also joined Towne and Murray, even though she is not mentioned in Laura Towne's biography except once as a black teacher. They educated many African American Sea Islanders. Towne and Murray were at Penn School for over forty years; Forten left after three years because of ill health. Penn School was later managed by two white teachers from the Hampton Normal and Agricultural School located in Hampton, Virginia. The two ladies, Miss Rossa Cooley and Miss Grace House, were also at Penn School for forty years. Many students from Penn School attended college at Hampton, and black teachers also came from Hampton to teach at Penn.[8]

Penn School served the islanders from 1861 until the 1950s when St. Helena High School, the first public school for blacks, was established. St. Helena High School is now an elementary school. Penn School changed its name to Penn Center Community Services and continued to serve the African American community not only on St. Helena but also on John's Island and other islands in the Charleston area. Penn Community Services also had an effect on the Georgia Sea Islands. Penn's work spread even farther than the Sea Islands, as indicated by the frequent visits of Dr. Martin Luther King, Jr., who used Penn for retreats and voter registration training. Penn was and still serves as a training ground for the Peace Corps and was a home for conscientious objectors during the Vietnam War. It was the only multicultural place on St. Helena Island where groups of different ethnic and religious faiths could meet. Today, Penn Center, Inc. continues to work to educate Sea Islanders and visitors about the history and culture of the area. Its primary purpose is also to continue the tradition of teaching the community how best to live and sustain itself with the changing times. Through the work of Penn Center and other organizations, like the McIntosh Shouters of Brunswick County, where St. Simon's Island is located, and the efforts of Mrs. Janie Hunter and Septemia Clark from John's Island in Charleston, the Sea Islands have become a breeding ground for researchers interested in the "peculiar people" known as the Gullahs.

The people of the Sea Islands, particularly St. Helena Island, have fascinated scholars for years. Lorenzo Dow Turner, one of the first African American linguists, studied the language of the people and compared it to West African syntax and language patterns during the first half of the twentieth century. In his book *Africanisms in the Gullah Dialect*, published in 1949, he documented words and sounds that remained intact through the transatlantic voyage. Others have studied the region's music, extensively documenting the spirituals and often making recordings and extensive transcripts of the music and the words.[9] Carter G. Woodson wrote on African American Sea Island families and their living conditions. During the three years that I worked at Penn Center as coordinator of history and cultural affairs, there were numerous scholars working in the area. They visited the center researching the music, language, material cultural retentions like basket weaving, fishing patterns, knowledge of herbal medicines, voodoo, and religious practices. Scholars like Margaret Washington Creel, who wrote *A Peculiar People*, Joseph Holloway, *Africanisms in the Sea Islands*, and rising scholars like Beverly John and Theophus Smith, and so many others who have updated and expanded on the work of the pioneers like Eugene Genovese came through the center. One scholar, Joseph Opala, worked in Sierra Leone, West Africa, when he was with Peace Corps. The Krio language that he heard there reminded him of the language he heard spoken among the Seminole Indians in Oklahoma and led to years of research in the Carolina Sea Islands. He and several West African professors who were at the University of Charleston, Alpha Bah and his colleagues, studied the Gullah language and helped to confirm many connections. This research resulted in an exciting event. The former president of Sierra Leone, H.E. Major General J. S. Momoh, and his delegation visited the Sea Islands in 1988. In 1990 a delegation of Sea Islanders, headed by the director of Penn Center, Mr. Emory S. Campbell, visited Sierra Leone. This exchange serves as an example of how strong the connections to Africa are. Penn Center and the residents of St. Helena are proud of their ties to Africa. It is not surprising that the unique structure, the praise house, has survived for over one hundred and fifty years on this particular island. Because of the limitations of this study, two of the praise houses—Croft and Mary Jenkins—are referred to the most.

Early accounts of the praise house most often describe the building as a little chapel, a barn, or a cabin. Harriet Ware, as cited in Mechal Sobel's *Trabelin' On: The Slave Journey to an Afro-Baptist Faith*, described a little chapel she saw in the 1800s as "being made very roughly of boards white washed, covered with straw."[10] Another account describes "a paintless, cheerless-appearing building of boards that looked as if a heavy gale might lay it low."[13] Theodore Rosengarten explains how plantation lifestyles changed between 1795 and 1845 because of changes in the Sea Island cotton crops. His account helps to create a visual image of where many of these praise houses were placed on the plantation in relationship to the planter's home. From his descriptions, it is possible to surmise that on a number of plantations, when things were not well with the cotton crops, the plantations deteriorated, and the view of the slave quarters became more obscure from the big house: "In 1795 . . . the planter's family lived in an old plain, low house. . . . A porchless front facade looked out on an irregular row of Negro houses. . . . Fifteen years later . . . new Negro cabins and stables sat further from the planter's new residence than they had from his old one . . . by 1830 . . . one sign of tight economic times was the dilapidation of the Negro cabins, now shielded by bushes and trees from the right side of the Big House."[10] This description may explain why many Northern missionaries to St. Helena Island were upset after seeing the condition of the "Prays" or praise houses. They observed that "the owners furnished a better stable for his horse than a house of worship for their sons and daughters." Most often, the praise house would be the first cabin or structure located in the slave quarters, or, as the Gullahs call it, "the street."[11]

Today, the descriptions of the praise house are not much different as the four buildings that still stand on St. Helena have been on the same plantation used by generations of African American Sea Islanders. With the exception of a fresh coat of paint, the addition of modern conveniences such as electricity, and minor repairs, the buildings are essentially the same.

All four praise house structures are about the same size, measuring about 14 by 18 feet. The Croft Praise House and Mary Jenkins Praise House are the only two that are still in use. Both of them have caretakers and are used the first Sunday of every month, with services alternating between the two because of the low attendance. One of the others, Eddings Point, is located about two miles away from the Mary Jenkins Praise House. Because this structure is no longer in use, access to any other information except for a general description of the exterior was not available. I did find out that the building falls under the jurisdiction of Ebenezer Baptist Church located on St. Helena. The Coffin's Point Praise House structure is a little different from the others in that there are handrails and windows on either side of the door. The Coffin's Point Praise House leader could not be identified, nor could the church affiliation. The Croft Praise House is under the jurisdiction of St. Joseph's Baptist Church, and the caretaker or leader is Deacon Garfield Smalls, who is a long-standing and well-respected member of St. Joseph's.

The Croft Praise House has five small windows, with two on each side of the building and one in the back. The first window on the right side of the building has a wooden shutter. When asked why, the caretaker, Deacon Smalls, replied, "I have not been able to find glass for that window yet."[12] The other four windows have glass panes. The roof was upgraded a couple of years ago. Many of the materials used in the upkeep of the praise house are donated items from the community members who attend. There is only one entrance and exit in the front, which is large enough for one person to enter at a time. There is no porch, only one step to gain entrance directly into the worship area. The Mary Jenkins Praise House, located about three miles from the Croft Praise House, is structurally the same. Deacon David Henderson is the leader of this meetinghouse. Henderson is a deacon at the Ebenezer Baptist Church, also located on St. Helena Island; therefore, the Mary Jenkins Praise House falls under the jurisdiction of Ebenezer.[13] The words "Praise House" with small flowers on both sides have been painted across the front of the building in red. Deacon Henderson said that volunteers from a United Methodist church located in Aiken, South Carolina, painted the sign when they made minor repairs to the structure. The sign helps to identify the function of this and the other little unobtrusive wooden buildings that are sporadically spaced on the side of the road. Deacon Henderson lives directly across from the Mary Jenkins Praise House. When home, this spry man in his seventies will stop picking pecans in his yard and talk with you about the praise house, religion, and the changes he has seen since returning home from New York. The Mary Jenkins Praise House has become a part of the tour given during the annual Beaufort Gullah Festival. Van loads of people come, escorted by a guide who has a key to let them enter the praise house, often without a person present who attends services there. This seems like an odd function for a praise house. Otherwise, the praise house is used both by members of St. Joseph's and Ebenezer.

One woman who used to attend the Mary Jenkins Praise House is Mrs. Julia Reynolds. Mrs. Reynolds was born in Savannah and moved to St.

Helena Island when she was a child. Both of her grandfathers owned adjoining land on the Mary Jenkins plantation on St. Helena Island. Mrs. Reynolds recalls that the Jenkins Praise House was "located right on the corner here, the big highway on Mary Jenkins's plantation." Mrs. Reynolds also recalls, "As long as I can remember . . . it's the same building, but a lot of repair work had been done, you know, remodel—take down the old and replace with new one."[14] Deacon Smalls also reflected that the Croft Praise House is still in the same place. Both of these praise houses are located off the major road that connects the three adjoining plantations: Croft, Mary Jenkins, and Eddings Point. The road or the community is named Eddings Point even though when they were formal plantations, they were considered three separate areas.

When I used to pass by the praise house in Eddings Point to visit my best friend, I often wondered what was inside the structure. I thought the buildings were so small and cute, and I could not imagine what was inside and how all of the people I had read about could fit inside. There has been extensive documentation of what happens inside the praise house. Usually, the "ring shout" is the focus of discussion (for example, see Sterling Stuckey's work and other works about African American music). However, I was interested in finding out more information about the actual buildings, such as whether the inside was set up like the larger churches. As a museum curator, I also wondered what an exhibition on praise houses should contain, and what objects were inside the praise house.

Margaret Washington Creel describes a post–Civil War praise house that could be the interior of an antebellum praise house or even the interior of a praise house in the 1920s: "It was a small one-roomed cabin. . . . The room was filled with rough backless benches, and at one end was a little table for the leader. Behind this stood a long bench where several men, officers of the Praise House, sat facing the people in motionless silence—with half-closed eyes and bowed heads."[15] The Croft Praise House has a new podium purchased from a store with a small collection of commercially woven baskets stored inside of the podium. There are cardboard fans of the type that African American funeral homes give to churches and some papers stored inside of the podium as well. Since a section had been added to increase the size of this praise house, the podium is slightly elevated. There are wooden benches on each side of the building. Old discarded school desks are arranged in the middle of the floor space. The Croft Praise House has acquired two rows of beautiful antique benches that reminded me of the type that might be found in an old bus or train station. They stood grandly in the front two rows. A small gas heater is located on the right side of the building near the front. In earlier accounts of the praise house there was no heat inside. A fire would be made on the outside of the structure, and the participants would go outside to get warm and then return to "Praise." There is a rectangular-shaped electric clock, trimmed in black with the traditional portrait of the "Lord's Supper" painted on the front. Deacon Smalls remembered that when he first attended the Croft Praise House, "they did not have heat inside, so they left the door open and warmed themselves with a fire that was burning outside of the building."[16]

The interior of the Mary Jenkins Praise House is closer to the description of the post–Civil War structure that Margaret Creel describes. Moving through the room from back to front, the Mary Jenkins Praise House has a long wooden bench on the back wall. It is highly probable that the bench is used by the officers waiting to participate in the service. There is a large impressive wooden cross on the back wall. Instead of a table, there is a small hand-crafted podium covered with a plastic flower-print table cover that does not drape very far over the edge of the top. Wooden benches are placed against the walls of both sides of the building. Old discarded school desks, about four per row, are placed in the middle of the floor in about four or five rows. There is a gas heater and a fan in the rear. The windows are decorated with a print curtain that does not match the cloth on the podium in the way you might expect in a more traditional church. The floor seems to be corrugated wood. Julia Reynolds remembers that "they worshipped by lamplight," when she was a child attending the Mary Jenkins Praise House.[17] Samuel Miller Lawton, who studied and worked among the Gullahs of St. Helena Island during the late 1930s, found that the leader was supposed to arrive at the praise house first and light the lamp. He also noted that there was at least one hymnal in every praise house.[18]

For the African bondsmen, the praise house became a place of worship and fellowship and a training ground for religious instruction. It was further a means to maintain discipline, harmony, and bonding within the slave community. Basically, this crude building became for the bondsmen the complete opposite of what the planter intended. The bondsmen had already established their own religious and community base, and even though the planter erected these crude structures as a means of controlling the movements of the bondsmen, they were able to make them their own. The white planters did not anticipate that they were actually assisting the bondsmen by giving them their own place to worship. There was a large number of "Black Societies" believed to have descended from prototype African societies which continued a process of amalgamation with the Christian church.[19] Therefore, St. Helena Island and many of the other isolated Sea Islands experienced a unique phenomenon where the religious practices were not African nor wholly Euro-Christian:

Within these societies Gullahs practiced their own version of Christianity, and created their religious folk culture. Baptist planters apparently intended to alter the "corrupt" elements within these slave associations and use them to promote a Christianity suitable to their own ends. Slaves' familiarity with concepts of secret society membership and social regulations suggests a relationship to African institutions that Christian ideas of community reinforced. For many years, Gullahs heard of "Christianity" mainly from black rather than white teachers, and this contributed to the persistence of African norms, thought, and ceremony.[20]

The bondsmen created their own form of Christianity as the whites supervised from a distance. Lawton stated that "the church held the Praise House accountable for the good behavior of all church members."[21] The slaves accepted accountability of their own because this contributed to a continuing sense of community that was already solidly based on the African societies.

Even after slavery, the praise house remained important to the Gullahs. It continued to hold together the community, which was made up primarily of families who had either lived on that plantation as bondsmen or who had been relocated there when the land was sold after the Civil War. Everyone was accountable for one another. Not only was this a place for the Gullahs' spiritual well-being, but it was a way to keep the community together.[22]

One way the praise house kept the community together was through its function as a courthouse. The praise house is where the "just law" was practiced. The praise house served almost like a court, holding its members responsible for their behavior and punishing the offender accordingly. When asked about the praise house serving as a court, Deacon Smalls stated: "You got to apply yourself within, the spiritual way, so if I got to counsel you, knowing you by you in the community, you gonna have the devil on your hand. And if placed them . . . you place them on the back seat."[23] The praise house served as courthouse for anything from a minor crime to marital disputes. These cases would be examined by the leader and/or committee, and a ruling was given. Today, disputes are not taken to the praise house but to the local magistrate.

The ten to fifteen people who regularly attend the Croft and Mary Jenkins Praise Houses see these two simple white buildings and the events that occur within them as a source of strength and as a place where they can practice their "old-time" religion. They also serve as a training ground for deacons and other church leaders. It gives an individual who does not lead in a regular church service an opportunity to participate because everyone is welcome to lead a spiritual or a prayer.

It seems that the function of the praise house has remained similar in its social implications for the bondsmen of the past and the Gullah today. Primarily, the praise house defined one's position within the community. Early records indicate that when the Baptist planters first began the praise houses, they appointed men from the African community as "elders" or "watchmen" to be the leaders. A majority of the bondsmen felt that these chosen men supported the mission of control that the planters desired; nonetheless, they were still treated with respect.

There was another type of leader from the African community that was not assigned or sanctioned by whites. The individuals in this category were given the utmost respect by the slave community. Both men and women, they were known as "spiritual fathers" and "spiritual mothers." They were often feared by the whites because they continued African traditions. They were not as likely to incorporate Christian elements into this new religious experience. These special leaders were often the root doctors and conjurers, serving to bridge the old and new tradition.[24]

Laura Towne, the founder of Penn School, met a woman in 1864 who was named Maum Katie. Towne described Maum Katie as "an old African woman, who remembers worshipping her own gods in Africa. 'Over a century' old, she was a 'spiritual mother,' a fortune-teller or, rather, a prophetess, and a woman of tremendous influence over her spiritual children." Even though the watchman was not looked upon in the same manner as a spiritual parent like Maum Katie, he was still an important figure in the community. His duties included advising on spiritual matters, opening and leading prayer meetings, counseling, and generally setting a Christian example for the slaves.[25]

Deacon Smalls surmised that the praise house leader always has to be cautious, "just like a stoplight." Today the elders, or leaders as they are called, are still primarily men. However, women are important figures in the praise house tradition. There have been instances when there was a female leader. Deacon Smalls indicated that though he does not exactly agree with women leading in the praise house or preaching in a church, he did recall that when he first "came down here" there was a woman who was a leader.[26] Today, the female participants are primarily responsible for keeping the building clean, leading spirituals, and occasionally leading prayers and testifying. Deacon Smalls's childhood memories of the females' role in the praise house are very similar to what he believes today. He remembers the women leading spirituals and bowing their knees occasionally to pray. But they never got to the desk, the podium.

Julia Reynolds, who attends the Mary Jenkins Praise House, feels that praise house rules may differ by church or community affiliation: "The lead-

ers are all men. There is a committee. It can be women. I was a committee
member. . . . They go out and do missionary work—go pray for the sick that
can't tend 'Praise.' . . . No, missionary in the church . . . committee in the
Prayer House." In the five praise house services that Lawton attended in the
1930s, "there were three times when the one leading the service led a prayer
himself, two times when he called on someone. . . . In none of the five Prays
house services attended was a woman called by name to lead in prayer."[27]
Men and women have certain roles in the praise house today. Lawton's summary of the five services in the 1930s indicates that the leader is an important
figure in the community. Women are also important because they often
become the primary bearers of the songs and serve as true missionaries.

Everyone that I spoke to attended "Praise" as a child. Children accompanied their parents when Deacon Smalls and Mrs. Reynolds were children.
Both of them seemed disappointed that the younger people today were not
attending the praise house services often or at all. Mrs. Reynolds's daughter,
Sara Wilson, who is in her early forties, remembers attending services as a
child. For her, the praise house was a place to be with family members. She
felt that it made the community stronger and more cohesive. A closeness and
kinship developed walking down the road to get to the praise house, listening
to the spirituals and hymns, then returning home in the dark. These memories
fill her with a warmth that seems to be missing in services in the church today.

Unfortunately, there are only two teenagers who attend the praise house
services now. Because of changing times, many of the young people have left
the island and moved up north to work. Others who stayed leave early in the
morning to go to work on Hilton Head or Daufuskie Island. They usually do
not return home until late in the evening and must soon retire to get up in
the morning to return to work. For instance, Sara Wilson is not able to attend
the scheduled praise house services because of her time constraints with work,
home, school, and other community volunteer obligations. However, in an
effort to incorporate praise house traditions with the church, Ebenezer Baptist
Church requires that new converts attend the praise house to receive the
"right hand of fellowship." For many, the praise house is a house of worship,
music, community, and tradition. It is a social activity and a source of relax-
ation for others. Deacon Smalls feels that the tradition will continue. So does
Deacon David Henderson. Julia Reynolds feels that if no young people come
to learn how to conduct "Praise," the future is not promising.

Pastor Kenneth Doe, the minister of St. Joseph Baptist Church and a
native of Beaufort County, completed his doctoral dissertation on "The Praise
House Tradition and Community Renewal" in 1991. Through his research,
his knowledge of his "homefolk," and his ministry, he has aided in renewing

the memories, traditions, and religious training of the praise house. Usually every Sunday, the Reverend Ervin Green, the pastor of Brick Baptist Church, begins with one of the "old-time" spirituals recalling the words and emotions attached to the praise house. Ebenezer Baptist Church's practice of having new converts attend the praise house is important because people are being reminded of praise house concepts.

Also, because of the way the community is structured, family members, particularly the elders, are able to pass on the traditions and memories of this meetinghouse. Most families live on inherited property in a communal type of setting. The property is arranged basically like an African compound. The great-aunts, grandmothers, children, and their children's houses are normally in close proximity to each other. Therefore, the great-aunt or grandmother can take care of the children when the parents are away at work. That is the time that not only praise house traditions may be passed on but other cultural traditions such as language, stories, foodways, and fishing and farming techniques.

Penn Center and its work to educate, preserve, and document African American history and culture has contributed significantly to continuing the praise house tradition. Through monthly community sings where the old songs are raised and through the Annual Heritage Celebration where praise house services have been incorporated into the sing, not only are residents of St. Helena Island exposed to these rich traditions, but outsiders are given the opportunity to partake of the rich chords and verses of a spiritual like "De Old Sheep Done Know de Road, De Young Lamb Must Find de Way."

The warmth that Sara Wilson expressed came from the spirituals and the sense of community that the services created. As a teenager, Mrs. Wilson felt "that the Praise House service was more interesting. The music was better and it was fun to watch the older people shout."[28] In the praise house the bondsmen, the freedmen, and the elderly men and women of a rapidly changing community can practice their "own" religion in its purest and most basic form.

Here, tradition is stronger. At a typical praise house service, activities found in 1840 still can be found in the 1990s. There have been some minor renovations to the buildings, and occasionally even a woman might "be at the table," but the commonality of the service throughout the years has remained the same. For example, Lawton describes a praise house service in the 1930s: "Prays house activities of today include an evening devotion three times a week of bible reading, prayer and singing, a speech of exhortation and instruction; a period of free religious expression; and occasionally the shout, affording social pleasure with a degree of religious."[29] The description of a praise house service conducted at St. Joseph Baptist Church in conjunction with the Fifteenth Annual Penn Center Heritage Days held November

11–13, 1993, illustrates how the community is trying to ensure that aspects of the praise house tradition are kept alive. Deacons from the church led the service as visitors from all around the United States attended this event.

Deacon Prince LeGree served as the leader. He asked Deacon Smalls and a younger deacon to serve as his committee. First, Deacon LeGree asked for two spirituals from the audience. A voice rang from the audience leading a slow-paced spiritual first, and then a happier spiritual, "I Love to Praise Him," followed in the call-and-response pattern. Deacon Smalls led a lined hymn, Number 531, Common Meter, "For I Must Go with Him," after which the young deacon read the Scripture. A prayer by a church elder, Deacon Eddings, followed. Another spiritual was "raised," and then the younger deacon was asked to explain the Scripture he read. After this, Deacon LeGree informed the congregation that they could do what the spirit led them to do and that the service was open. Unlike what may have happened in the praise house, the shout did not occur that evening.

Some of the elders felt that there were some problems in conducting a praise house service in the church. I feel that the problem may not have been so much in having the service in the church but in the difficulty of conducting a service that is foreign to outsiders without "presenting" it as a program. The service was presented to teach outsiders about the praise house rather than letting the service happen naturally. It also seems that St. Helena Island natives do not attend the Heritage Days praise house service as much as they used to; therefore, there are not enough people who understand the tradition to keep the service going. For example, there was a problem in "setting" the song to tempo in order to obtain the unique syncopated multirhythmic style most often associated with St. Helena Island residents' music.[30] Now, gospel music is preferred in the church services because the churches are also changing with the times. With cable television now accessible to island residents (it was only approved because more whites moved into the area), programs like the Bobby Jones Gospel Hour and all of the latest African American gospel stars are receiving more exposure on the island, and traditional a cappella spirituals may not be as inviting as they once were. However, many churches still have a devotional service before the regular service begins. That is the time many of the old songs and hymns are sung. Penn Center also requests that all groups that sing during the community sing perform a cappella. In addition, Penn staff and older residents of St. Helena Island teach the children who attend the afterschool program at the center many of the old songs.

Julia Reynolds recalls attending "Praise" when she was a young woman when the old songs and rhythms were used during devotion: "I used to go Sunday night, Tuesday night, and Thursday. We had prayer service. We sung a few songs—had a prayer—testify for a short while. Then we go to the main service. . . . Spirituals come first. We sing two spirituals when you get started. Have a prayer. The committee, or the deacon he's the one. Mostly, the committee ask if you would like to lead the service tonight."[31] After the devotion ended, the wooden benches would be pushed to the side, and the shout would commence. By this time the participants would be "feeling the spirit" and would want to relax by participating in the shout. The shout served as a social outlet.

Charlotte Forten, the first African American teacher at Penn School, kept a diary of her three years on the isolated island during the 1860s. When Forten, a free mulatto, first came to St. Helena from Philadelphia, she was shocked to see the shout. However reviewing the entries in her diary makes it evident that she began to appreciate this foreign religious expression:

> Sunday, May 3 . . . The people, after "Praise" had one of the grandest shouts, and L[izzie] and I, in a dark corner of the Praise House, amused ourselves with practicing a little. It is wonderful what perfect time the people keep with hands, feet, and indeed with every part of the body. I enjoy these "shouts" very much.

> Thursday, July 2 . . . We had a pleasant talk on the moonlit piazza, and then went to the Praise House to see the shout. I was delighted to find that it was one of the very best and most spirited that we had.[32]

Several types of shouts occur on various occasions. There are shouts for Christmas, New Year's, baptisms, and other social occasions. For instance, shouts for new converts help create another type of social stratification within the community. According to Lawton, only members of the praise house could participate in the shout. Often, the young converts could not wait until they could "show off" their techniques as well as their singing abilities. When it was time to push back the benches and form the circle or "ring," they were willing and able, often creating a real sweat. Albert Raboteau quotes an account of the ring shout printed by W. F. Allen in the May 30, 1867, *Nation*:

> The true "shout" takes place on Sundays or on "Praise" nights throughout the week, and either in the praise house. . . . Very likely more than half the population of the plantation is gathered together. . . . But the benches are pushed back to the wall when the formal meeting is over, and old and young men and women . . . boys . . . young girls barefooted, all stand up in the middle of the floor, and when the "sperichil" is struck, begin first walking and by-and-by shuffling round, one after the other, in a ring. . . . It is not unlikely that this remarkable religious ceremony is a relic of some African dance.[33]

Julia Reynolds said that they do not shout at the Jenkins Praise House much now, because everyone is too old. She put down rug remnants to cover the cracks in the floor because the members did not need the wooden floors to keep time anymore. Ebenezer Baptist Church through the encouragement of Penn Center and an alumnus of Penn School, Mrs. Lula Holmes, hosts monthly shouts in the church fellowship hall. Here old and young learn many of the "speritichals" and how to "set" the song. They learn how to clap and keep rhythm in the syncopated style that sets up the shout.

When I first wrote this chapter, I felt that the four structures—Croft, Mary Jenkins, Eddings Point, and Coffin's Point Praise Houses—would continue to stand because they were designated historic landmarks. I still feel that is true. I also felt that the leaders of the praise houses and the few members that attend have a commitment first to God, then to their forefathers who struggled to maintain these buildings, and to their present-day community to continue as "long as they have breath" to keep the praise house going. I still feel that is true.

I also believed that although the youth do not attend praise house services as in earlier days, through the work of Pastor Doe, Penn Center, and the long memories of the people the praise house traditions would continue. However, I now have to wonder if the function of the praise house in the community and the religious expressions that take place within it will continue with the influx of newcomers and the development that is all over the island. I have returned to St. Helena Island at least twice a year since I left in 1991. The changes that have occurred on St. Helena and the surrounding area are unbelievable. Whites are moving into areas of the island that were unheard of five years ago. You used to be able to safely say that wherever there was water, that's where they would move. Now, they are moving in very isolated areas of the island, for instance, the Eddings Point area where three of the praise houses are located. They purchase the land and build homes, and within six months the "For Sale" signs go up. It seems that areas that were once beautiful wooded spaces, creating a sense of privacy, are quickly being cleared.

Along with this new trend, it seems that the African American residents who live in these areas are beginning to emulate the practices of the whites. They are clearing their land as well. It seems that they are opening the door for more whites to gain more access. Also, as in Sara Wilson's case, the majority of the young folks are leaving early to work in Beaufort, Hilton Head, or Daufuskie Island. After returning from the long, taxing days, they are not able to attend the service at the praise house or even the programs offered at Penn Center to promote the traditions of the Sea Island. As Bernice Johnson Reagon wrote in the afterword of *Ain't You Got a Right to the Tree of Life?*

The People of Johns Island, South Carolina—Their Faces, Their Words, and Their Songs: "The questions and fears are for the youth and their future. Their voices are heard only as whispers in the minds and hearts of their parents. The questions are: Will they continue? And how and where and what of this rich legacy will they harvest to pass on?" Despite all of the efforts of the preservers of the St. Helena Island praise house traditions, in the midst of rapid development and encroachment of whites, how much will be left to harvest?

13 "TRASH" REVISITED

A Comparative Approach to Historical Descriptions and Archaeological Analysis of Slave Houses and Yards

Ywone D. Edwards

> To "read landscape," to make cultural sense of
> the ordinary things that constitute the workaday world
> of things we see, most of us need help. . . . What we needed,
> I concluded, were some guides to help us read the landscape.
> —Peirce F. Lewis, "Axioms for Reading the Landscape: Some Guides to the American Scene"

> The landscape is an enormously rich store of data about
> the peoples and societies which have created it,
> but such data must be placed in its appropriate
> historic context if it is to be interpreted correctly.
> D. W. Meinig, "The Beholding Eye: Ten Versions of the Same Scene"

THE ANALYSIS OF CONTEXT AND MEANING of parts of the past material world, formerly viewed as "trash" by African Americans and Euro-Americans alike, can bring new understanding to African American culture. It is possible to study slave houses and yards and their trash as products of racial, social, and economic exploitation. During slavery in the American South, trash was a complex phenomenon; it embodied African American culture in the form of landscape traditions, perceptions of "naturalness," and beliefs about the supernatural world. Trash also involved the treatment of discarded materials and waste and improvised performance using recycled and found materials. It was the prescribed material that formed the structures and contents of slave houses and yards.

The *American Heritage Dictionary* defines *trash* as "worthless or discarded material or objects; . . . something broken off or removed to be discarded." The trash of slave dwellings should not be interpreted solely within this definition, because meaning should be sought within different cultural settings. Studies have shown that different cultural groups categorize as trash things in different stages of production and use. The life cycle of goods is generally understood as the way goods are used and how their use changes over time, culminating at a point when they are considered useless.[1] Material items in the later stage of the cycle are usually discarded in recognized areas of refuse disposal; for example, in trash pits, privies, dumps, and yard areas. Social categories, however, are continually redefined, and this process profoundly influences the acquisition, use, and discard of material items.

During slavery African Americans used and reused different items in ways that fixed or challenged other public meanings and use of these things.[2] Both enslaved and free blacks interacted with other racial and cultural groups and were active in the social construction of distinctions about the materials considered trash.

Increasingly, scholars of the African American past are using data from disciplines such as art history, geography, anthropology, archaeology, and history in their work.[3] Throughout this chapter I rely on evidence from several disciplines to show that a more comprehensive picture of the past can emerge from looking at trash across time and space and to note the ways in which seemingly unimportant objects played key roles in slaves' lives. Studies of slave societies in the New World and traditional and present-day African and African American cultures are also pertinent to my study of trash. Documentary and archaeological records relating to the trash of slave sites in Virginia in the United States and sites in the Caribbean island of Jamaica are the main evidence for this study. Special focus is on the slaves' intellect and intention in the creation of the material world. This approach assumes that slaves defined their existence through the daily use of things, within different contexts, wherein meanings were constantly created and re-created. Continuities and changes in the diaspora as well as African American creativity in, and as responses to, the new settings in the Americas are highlighted. The struggles, misfortunes, and triumphs of Africans and their descendants in the New World were both individual and communal responses to a variety of factors and relationships.

Several aspects of African American creativity and survival strategies have been documented. One area that is relevant to the study of trash concerns communication. Many slaves communicated specific messages to other slaves while they were in the presence of slaveholders, and many slaveholders were unable to decode these messages. The nature of African American communication networks and approaches to the material world made this phenomenon possible.[4] Today, in spite of the concerted effort of scholars from several disciplines, some aspects of the past cultural world of slavery continue to elude our understanding.

But trash can be revisited and reanalyzed giving full consideration to its contents and contexts. It can be viewed as part of the system of slavery that impoverished blacks economically and socially, but not culturally. How trash related to African American values and beliefs in the American South and other areas of the African diaspora is another main theme for this study. The material culture of African Americans, in part, was a tangible expression of their values and beliefs. Particular objects on slave sites, however, epitomize the oppression of blacks. For instance, tools seen in and around slaves' dwellings represent their endless toil for someone else's profit. Yet through the slaves' initiatives these objects were used in farming and livestock production, activities that helped to ameliorate the slaves' living conditions. Other materials were derived from slaveholders' provisioning of slaves. Overall, slave access to different goods was affected by local and environmental conditions and social factors such as the slaveholder-slave relationship. Further, the different social connections that arose among slaves influenced the contents and contexts of their material world.

The trash of slave yards and houses included more than what fits a normative definition of discarded, reused, and improvised material. Some trash was deliberately buried underground. Other materials on the ground in plain view that appeared to outsiders to be trash may have been used by African Americans to invoke supernatural aid in harmful, protective, and healing rituals. In an article entitled "Tradition and Innovation in African American Yards," Grey Gundaker explains that "some African Americans decorate, dress, or work their yards using a flexible visual vocabulary that creolizes and revitalizes American, European, and African traditions through everyday materials."[5] Plantation slaves, as occupants and "dressers" of slave yards and sometimes builders of slave houses, used similar concepts to work or decorate their houses and yards. The rest of this chapter concentrates on how several objects which were viewed as no longer valuable to a mainstream American culture were used as "dressings."

Decorating, working, or dressing yards and houses included activities such as burying objects to engender protection and creating art as public display. When slaves dressed, decorated, or carved out their living spaces on plantations, they gave new meanings and functions to natural and cultural materials.

Objects help to create and maintain social relationships; nevertheless, they can be used to mask relationships, for the choice or use of items "creates certain patterns of discrimination, overlaying or reinforcing others."[6] Some slaveholders created or increased the social distances among slaves. For example, they treated some slaves as favorites. This practice influenced different levels of slaveholder-slave interactions. At times, it resulted in the unequal allotment of goods and services to the slaves. Appreciating the complexities and inconsistencies of life and exchanges between different cultural groups enhances our knowledge of the possibilities in peoples' creativity.

Ethnohistorical descriptions, such as travel accounts of life in the American South and the Caribbean during slavery, contain stereotypical depictions of blacks. Roger Abrahams and John Szwed advise that

> in using observers' accounts, one must always bear in mind that the practices which came to the notice of these Euro-American observers were selected by them not just because they were different but also because they often confirmed the white stereotype of blacks. There may then be an over-focus on the kinds of events which confirmed this convenient European ethnocentric perspective. . . .
>
> If one is to understand the nature of the Negro practices which were and are observed by Europeans, one must consider at all times the possibility that some characteristics of these occasions may have arisen in response to this Western value system in its stereotype dimension.[7]

From reading slaves' and free blacks' trash, observers received private and intended meanings, but the level of information observers gained depended on their knowledge of African American culture. Material objects are a part of the social world of communication, and meaning is intrinsic to communication. However, it is not always apparent. Mary Douglas and Baron Isherwood have highlighted the importance of goods in communication and in the creation of self-identity. They note that "goods assembled together in ownership make physical, visible statements about the hierarchy of values to which their chooser subscribes." But in studies of the African American past, the meanings of trash can be unclear and evasive. One way to decipher meanings is to focus on rituals enacted with objects and through the manipulation of the landscape. This is important to the effort to understand how different people in the past viewed their social settings. Focusing on relationships and assemblages is a more fruitful approach than concentrating on individual items outside of their contexts.[8]

The concept of "trash" and the ambiguity in deciphering meanings in the material world appear as issues in modern African American literature. One outstanding example is Toni Morrison's novel *Song of Solomon*. In this novel Morrison is concerned with "rooting" or "planting" the Deads in the African American past and the present of the early twentieth century. In doing so, she clearly distinguishes the "wilderness" versus the "cultured" areas of the town where Macon Dead and his sister, Pilate Dead, live. Morrison beautifully blends her knowledge of the African American past with her understanding of African American culture through the narrative genre of the novel. Macon Dead, the economically better-off brother of Pilate, lives in a big, dark house of twelve rooms. Pilate is portrayed as living closer to nature and is depicted as a person with some knowledge of the spiritual world. For instance, she gives Ruth, Macon's wife, "trash," "some greenish-gray grassy-looking stuff," to put in Macon's food to ensure that another child would be born to the family.[9]

Pilate's house fits historical and archaeological evidence of slave houses, and it displays African American organizational principles. The house and its furnishings incorporate a "double-talk" of sacred and secular possibilities. Pilate's house is "backed by four huge pine trees, from which she got the needles she stuck into her mattress." Inside, the house "looked both barren and cluttered. A moss-green sack hung from the ceiling. Candles were stuck in bottles everywhere; newspaper articles and magazine pictures were nailed to the walls. But other than a rocking chair, two straight-back chairs, a large table, a sink and stove, there was no furniture. Pervading everything was the odor of pine and fermenting fruit." The residents of Pilate's house are as "disorganized" as their house when viewed from the perspective of American "mainstream" culture. They never sit down to a planned meal, and for them time is not linear but circular; the past is always present in the form of memories and objects, and the present is inextricably linked to the past. Several objects in Pilate's house are used creatively, and "most everything in the house had been made for some other purpose."[10] Things are placed in new contexts of use wherein they acquire new meanings.

The structures and contents of slave houses and yards incorporated aspects of African American cultural practices. These practices, in part, combined elements of European, African, and American cultures. Slaves' creativity and resilience were fueled by "remembered" and "invented" African cultural traditions. Some slaves had more opportunities to interact with other slaves, and scholars have attributed the strength of black family allegiances, community life, and the emergence of African American culture to such interactions.[11]

Oral tradition and improvisation are important concepts and practices that have been incorporated in studies of African American material culture. For instance, scholars of African and African American music, such as Hildred Roach, believe that oral tradition accounts for improvisation, or improvised variation, one of the most exciting aspects of African American performance. She described rhythm as the most basic characteristic of African lifestyles and said that it imitated various human activities.[12] Her findings have strong implications for other areas of African American culture, including dressing the house and yard. African American houses and yards also embodied complex and simple rhythms of time, space, energy, and change during slavery, as they do today. When analyzed as improvised and planned trash, slave houses and yards were complex in organization and performance.

Slaves were renowned for "making do" as they created and changed their

material world from trash. They worked with available materials, embell-
ished the functional, and created various things to improve their lives. Slaves'
accomplishments reflected their concerns for aesthetics. Archaeologists are
prominent among scholars who have contributed to knowledge of the material world of African Americans and information about African Americans'
concerns for aesthetics. For example, archaeologists have analyzed decorated
pewter spoons and the waste material that had been trimmed away from
molded spoons. The materials were recovered during archaeological excavations of the slave quarters at the Garrison plantation in Maryland.[13]

In the Chesapeake area of the southeastern United States, locally manufactured clay tobacco pipes, recovered from seventeenth-century archaeological sites, have been attributed to slave skills. These pipes, also manufactured
by Native Americans and probably European Americans as well, are thought
to exhibit African-influenced designs. Archaeologist Matthew Emerson found
that several decorations on these pipes are identical to designs during the
same period in the art and crafts of Ghana, Nigeria, and Senegal-Mali.
Emerson concluded that the pipes display a combination of European form,
American material, and some African art. The smoking of tobacco pipes was
commonly practiced among slaves. Archaeologists have recovered similar
pipes from slave burials in Virginia and in the Caribbean, and their occurrences in these contexts have been interpreted as evidence of slave rituals.[14]

Slaves created objects and fashioned their landscape in ways that revealed
their need to interpret and negotiate with the sacred and secular world. Annie
Wallace, a former slave in Virginia, described "how she had learned to knit
on broom sedge straws. She had been taught to piece quilts too from the
scraps her mistress had left from clothing she made for folks. . . . 'I used to
get the scraps from the pants she made for the men and cut 'em into pants
and sew 'em up and put 'em on forked sticks I used for dolls. I didn't never put
any shirts on 'em because I never could get no scraps for 'em,' and she chuck-
led at the memory of those shirtless dolls."[15]

In the sphere of entertainment slaves improvised, as former slave Nancy
Williams remembered: "Anyhow we'd go to dese dances; ev'y gal had a beau.
An' sech music! You had two fiddles, two tambourines, two bango [banjo],
an' two sets o' bones. Dem deblish boys 'ud go out'n de wood an' git de bones
whar de cows done died."[16] Apparently, discarded animal bones were reused
in foodways as well. One eighteenth-century observer of slaves in Jamaica was
surprised to see the "mean Shifts to which these poor Creatures are reduced:
You'll see them daily about 12 o'Clock, when they turn in from Work, till
Two, scraping the Dung-hills at every Gentleman's Door for Bones, which, if
they are so happy as to find, they break extremely small, boil them, and eat
the Broth."[17]

In spite of the general poverty of slave life, improvisation, not poverty, was the hallmark of slave culture. Improvisation serves as a better explanation of how slaves established and sustained identities through material forms. It also offers opportunities for deciphering the trash of slave dwellings.

Several scholars have found cultural practices that are similar to other conventions within the diversity of African American experiences. They have identified the practices as connections between Africans and their descendants in the Americas. For example, Paul D. Escott describes the slave culture as involving "different relations to the spiritual world, different attitudes toward nature and its powers, and a remembered connection with Africa." Following a similar approach, Robert Farris Thompson and Grey Gundaker identify several themes and practices relevant to the study of slave yards and houses.[18]

Among the themes and practices that these scholars have noted are occurrences of the Kongo cosmogram, graveyardlike decorations including shells, broken glasses, and ceramics, plantings of protective herbs, color symbolism, and tying and wrapping. In addition, they have named other general themes such as using object puns like shoe soles to stand for the human soul and using filters like brooms and bean seeds to ward off unwelcome visitors. One type of filter with important implications for the study of trash is the use of irregular paths and patterns to confuse evil spirits, as some Africans and African Americans believed that these spirits travel in straight lines and are thrown off course by random designs. That some of the ceramic objects found on slave sites are mixed and varied in colors, probably resulting from slaves' preferences, based on their beliefs, and not from an inability to acquire matched sets of things.[19]

Some African Americans' cultural practices drew upon African religious traditions. Many of these practices have incorporated the use of trash or trashlike materials such as shells and broken pottery that were used in funeral and mourning rites. Many of these practices have been linked to particular cultural groups in Africa such as the Bakongo, who were well represented among the Africans imported to some areas of the American South. This group traditionally occupied western and central areas of Africa. The Bakongo perceived death as an ongoing relationship between the living and the dead. They practiced procedures such as burying the dead properly and using charms to cultivate good relationships with spirits and other activities to prevent newly dead spirits from roaming. The Bakongo depicted the dead as occupying a watery, upside-down, white world underneath the world of the living. This idea is alluded to in the Kongo cosmogram, a visual representation of their worldview. Frequently shown as a cross enclosed in a circle, the cosmogram charts the connection between life and death.[20]

Negotiations with the spiritual world required knowledge of the power of trashlike objects such as those forming charms. The *nkisi* (plural *minkisi*), a Kongo charm, is an object endowed with spiritual energies which could be used to harm or to aid. Bakongo and later African American charms were made with shells, nails, glass, grave dirt, and other substances allegedly endowed with medicines, especially when they are together in containers. Tying and wrapping were common ways to enclose these charm materials and to guarantee results. In the landscape tying and wrapping took such forms as growing herbaceous borders at boundaries, separating the wilderness from the cultivated areas with fences and objects, and by clearing some areas of the yard by sweeping.[21] Aspects of the Bakongo culture concerning spiritual and ritual beliefs have influenced various groups in Africa and the New World.

Using certain colors such as white and red and asymmetrical or busy patterns were methods that Africans and their descendants in the New World deliberately employed to confuse evil spirits. Because it was believed that evil spirits first had to decipher these codes or patterns before they could harm the living, more protection was guaranteed by using more random designs. The asymmetrical designs of some African cloth, and later African American quilts, have been interpreted by various scholars as materials that encode protective elements.[22] Specific practices that included trash are among several cultural applications that have been documented as important to blacks' spirituality in the Americas. These practices reached their zenith in voodoo, obeah, and hoodoo, all religious forms with strong connections to Africa.

Today scholars from several disciplines are becoming more aware of how meanings are encoded in many forms and in approaches to the material world. My emphasis on multiple sources, changes, and continuities benefits from using a multidisciplinary perspective. The trash in slave landscapes took different forms, but some materials and their interpretations exhibit clear parallels throughout the Americas, suggesting individual and communal intellectual responses derived, in part, from connections to Africa.

HISTORICAL ACCOUNTS: THE SLAVE LANDSCAPE AND "TRASH"

According to Frederick Law Olmsted, "There were in them [the slave cabins] closets, with locks and keys, and a varying quantity of rude furniture. . . . In the rear of the yards were gardens—a half-acre to each family. Internally the cabins appeared dirty and disordered, which was rather a pleasant indication that their home-life was not much interfered with, though I found certain police regulations were enforced."[23] Slaves' houses, yards, and their surroundings were more than environmental or visual scenes. These areas were consciously created or prescribed and intentionally and unintentionally contrasted with the slaveholders' landscape. Several scholars have treated the slave quarters and work areas as "informal" areas of the plantation. They have studied structures such as the "big house," kitchen, laundry, dairy, and stable and features such as the ornamental gardens as parts of the "formal" landscape of slaveholders. Folklorist and historian John Vlach claimed that the slave landscape was founded more on behavioral connections than on specific material manifestations; it was a landscape that reflected slave cultural practices.[24]

The study of slave landscape has benefited from the work of archaeologists. For example, Larry McKee, who has worked on African American archaeological sites in different areas of the American South, suggested that slaveholders used the landscape as part of social control strategies and that this management practice was meant to instill a message that slaves were inferiors.[25] McKee described the difference between the usually larger, towering houses for slave owners and the smaller houses for slaves as significant to slaveholders' effort to control their slaves. According to McKee and Vlach, slave houses frequently were closer to their working areas and usually at a distance from the planter's house to prevent the slaves from being nuisance. The location of slave houses was part of plantation management strategies to maximize slaves' time and labor, to underscore that slaves were considered subordinates, and to police other areas of their life. Planters generally viewed their slave quarters as smelly, noisy, dirty places. McKee and Vlach argued that the slaves fashioned their own landscape through behavioral association and material culture; they did not bend, at all times, to the message of inferiority. Both writers attributed the slave landscape, which was formed within informal and mostly hidden aspects of the planter's formal landscape, to slaves' improvisational responses to European and American cultures and to slaves' beliefs that drew on the African cultural connections.

In seventeenth-century Virginia, however, some slaves lived under the same roof as the master and white servants and did not have a landscape distinguishable by separate housing. The continuing friction between white servants and their masters, and the increase in the slave population and other changes in the society, contributed to the separation of slaveholder and slave living spaces. Many slaves were moved into their own quarters or to live where they worked, in kitchens, stables, laundries, and dairies. In some instances slaves had less access to the planter's house.[26] Some domestic slaves, however, were allotted particular sections in the big houses for sleeping so that they were always close by for service.

A variety of building materials and styles were used in the construction of slave houses. Some were small, while others were much larger, particularly the ones that housed several families. These cabins usually had fireplaces, and in some areas of the American South, they had brick or stick and mud chimneys and dirt or board floors. Some quarters were better built than others, even when they utilized elements of trash such as poor-quality building material and stick and mud chimneys; such chimneys sometimes caught fire and could be pushed away from the cabin before fire consumed the whole structure. The poor construction of many slave houses suggest that even some wealthy slaveholders economized on labor and materials.[27] Baily Cunningham, a former slave, remembered that the slave quarters were "log cabins, some had one room and some had two rooms, and board floors. Our master was a rich man. He had a store and a sawmill on the creek. The cabins were covered with boards, nailed on and had stick-and-mud chimneys. . . . We had home-made tables and chairs with wooden bottoms. . . . The cabins were built in two rows not very far from the misses big house. My mother kept house for our misses and looked after the quarters and reported anything going wrong to the misses."[28]

Some slaves sought privacy in their living arrangements. They requested that their cabins be placed near trees or in specific locations such as those described for the Georgia rice coast, "in some secluded place, down in the hollow, or amid the trees, with only a path to their abode."[29] Some slave quarters were grouped resembling villages, and some were arranged in grid patterns.

Historian Mechal Sobel wrote that for most of the eighteenth century, poor or "middling" white houses were only slightly larger than slave cabins. Apparently many whites were living in small and temporary dwellings up to the last decades of the eighteenth century and for some time in the nineteenth century. Their material possessions were similar to those of slaves, simple and limited. A visitor to Virginia in 1780, the chevalier de Chastellux, described the living conditions of some whites who resided in the areas he visited. He found that "among [the] . . . rich plantations where the Negro alone is wretched, one often finds miserable huts inhabited by whites, whose wan looks and ragged garments bespeak poverty."[30]

Europeans and Euro-Americans criticized some of the dwellings of the white population in the American South. They compared the homes of whites with those of slaves. Solon Robinson's nineteenth-century description of the slave cabins on Joseph Dunbar's plantation in Jefferson County, Mississippi, is most revealing about this phenomenon.

> His negro quarters look more like a neat, pleasant, New England village than they do like what we have often been taught to believe was the residence of the poor, oppressed and wretched slaves. I did not give them a mere passing view, but examined the interior, and in some of them saw what might be seen in some white people's houses—a great want of neatness and care—but, so far as the mas-

ter was concerned, all were comfortable, roomy and provided with beds and bedding in abundance. In others there was a show of enviable neatness, and luxury; high-post bedsteads, handsomely curtained . . . with musketo netting, cupboards of blue Liverpool ware, coffee mills, looking glasses, tables, chairs, trunks and chests of as good clothes as I clothe myself and family with.[31]

Former slaves also described the appearance of plantations. Booker T. Washington in his autobiography, Up from Slavery, noted the rundown state of the plantation where he had lived as a slave boy, for apparently the slaves did not bother to sweep the yard or repair structures: "The slaves, of course, had little personal interest in the life of the plantation. . . . As a result of the system, fences were out of repair, gates were hanging half off the hinges, doors creaked, windowpanes were out, plastering had fallen but was not replaced, weeds grew in the yard."[32]

During his travels through the South in the nineteenth century, Olmsted described slave cabins near Richmond as well made from log, "about thirty feet long by twenty wide, and eight feet tall," with a loft and shingle roof. These cabins were divided in the middle, with "a brick chimney outside the wall at either end," and had windows "closed by wooden ports, having a single pane of glass in the centre." They were built to house two families. In the southeastern areas of Virginia, archaeologists have uncovered the remains of two-room cabins with central chimneys that date to the eighteenth century.[33]

The cabins Olmsted saw in eastern Texas in the nineteenth century were not so well made as some slave houses in Virginia. His descriptions of the cabins suggest that they were made from and maintained with trash: "The negro-quarters here, scattered irregularly about the house, were of the worst description, though as good as local custom requires. They are but a rough inclosure of logs, ten feet square, without windows, covered by slabs."[34] Nineteenth-century slaveholders responded to the ferment of social reform and tried to improve the lot of their slaves by building better houses for them.

Some slaveholders ordered the construction of pier-supported houses for their slaves because raising the houses off the ground was one means of preventing slaves from having "hidey holes," storage areas commonly known as root cellars, beneath the cabins. This practice was another measure to stem the alleged large buildup of trash at the slave quarter and to preserve the health of slaves. Nevertheless, slaveholders had to negotiate change with their slaves. Archaeologists have found evidence that some nineteenth-century slave housing contained a considerable amount of trash.[35] Apparently, slaveholders compromised on issues surrounding the use of yard areas, the construction of slave houses, and slave trash.

Other slaveholders in South Carolina and Virginia knew that slaves had valuable possessions. These slaveholders ordered locks placed on the doors of the slave cabins. Historical evidence alludes to the practice of slaves stealing from other slaves. Notices for the return of runaway slaves sometimes detailed the various items of clothing and tools slaves owned, or fled with, and apparently some of these items were taken from planters and their families, as well as from other slaves.[36] Some slaves took other measures to protect their possessions; they employed their dogs to guard their cabins.[37]

ARCHAEOLOGY, HISTORY, AND "TRASH"

Archaeological studies of artifacts and foundations are providing more insights into slaves' and planters' concerns about sanitation and perceptions of the order of things in the past. From their studies of the African American past, archaeologists are finding that "fragments of pots, the outlines of houses, and so forth represent a past material world that not only provided tools for cooking and shelter, but also served as symbols that reinforced people's views of themselves as culturally distinct from others."[38] Most archaeologists seek to understand trash and the occupants at a site within broad social and cultural frameworks. Usually their studies are based on theories of culture change and economic and social differentiation. Similar to researchers from other disciplines, archaeologists have found the interpretations of the material evidence of New World slavery challenging. For example, some fragments of ceramics determined to be expensive wares are treated as evidence that some slaves "were using ceramics, much as did whites, as status markers within their *own* community."[39]

The consumption of these items probably had different meanings for slaves and slaveholders. Historical documents allude to slave practices that slaveholders viewed as socially appropriate and fashionable behavior. Some skilled and other household slaves, as well as slaves who provided services that were considered relevant to the survival of the slave community, most likely had a wider assortment of goods than other slaves. Nevertheless, archaeological studies have shown that field slaves had as wide a range of material goods and identical "perceived high quality goods" as household slaves.[40] The composition of the slave household was another factor that influenced the material world of slaves.

Archaeologists value trash because the forms and contexts of things, including changes to the landscape, are important clues to the study of people and the past. People are linked to the material world by the things they acquire, use, and discard. In the past they created trash when they broke things and swept them aside. Fragments of things were eventually thrown in pits with other refuse.[41] On plantation sites some things were broken in the process of disposal, while other trash was scattered throughout the yard areas. Archaeologists have classified the accumulated scatter of trash in yards as sheet refuse. In colonial times household trash was routinely deposited close to living areas in yards, near doorways, and occasionally in holes in the ground. Trash provides archaeologists with materials to study the occupants of households and their behavior because refuse was usually deposited very near to the place where it was generated.[42]

Archaeologists Julia King and Henry Miller, who worked in Maryland, claim that "refuse disposal at most British colonial sites in North America occurred primarily in surface middens located around structures and only secondarily in so-called trash pits or other features." Another archaeologist, Mary Beaudry, cautions that "the emphasis on trash deposits *per se*, however, has distracted far too many archaeologists' attention from a very important issue, namely, what was the *primary* function of holes in the ground that became trash receptacles only when they no longer served as wells, privies, borrow pits, and so forth?"[43] The investigation of archaeological material from slave houses and yards, as this study of trash illustrates, will need to go beyond an examination of "trash deposits *per se*" to explore social and cultural approaches to the material world.

King and Miller studied trash on a colonial Euro-American home lot in St. Mary's City, Maryland.[44] They found that garbage was deposited near the dwelling and close to the main entrance of the property. In the seventeenth century occupants of the site deposited refuse in public areas, particularly in roadways and paths. Apparently those areas were considered acceptable places for garbage, unlike the spaces that were considered private; these places were kept clean. King and Miller used archaeological and historical evidence to substantiate their claim that a fenced area on the northern part of the property was probably used for family and private activities. They suggested that the fenced outdoor space near the house probably related to its owner's Dutch background. In the seventeenth century, evidently, one Dutch tradition was to use arbors or outdoor locations for drinking, feasting, and relaxing. The owner of the Maryland site kept a lodging house close to a well-traveled street. This also may have contributed to his need for a private outdoor area for his family and elite customers.

Other archaeologists have investigated the social use of space and trash disposal patterns on colonial sites. Douglas Armstrong discovered that the archaeological evidence supported historical descriptions of the slave living area with respect to the various activities that took place in the front yards.[45] From his study of slave houses and yards at Drax Hall plantation, Jamaica,

Armstrong claimed that there were higher concentrations of trash in the yards behind the houses than in the front areas. Armstrong inferred that this factor may have resulted, to some extent, from the slaves' practices of having cooking areas and garden plots for fruit trees and medicinal plants in the backyard areas.

Several archaeologists have produced useful studies that described how African Americans used, preserved, and discarded food. In addition, they have provided more details about the activities that resulted in trash and produced odors at the slave quarters. Archaeologist Steve Mrozowski contended that it is not surprising to find a high density of trash associated with intensively used houses and yards.[46] From his studies of sites in Boston, Massachusetts, and Newport and Providence, Rhode Island, Mrozowski found that the yards in many urban households served as areas for activities such as food production and waste disposal, and also for commercial activities. On these sites trash accumulated in the yards and in places such as privies and trash pits. Mrozowski's study is relevant to the study of slaves houses and yards, for like urban sites, sections of slave yards were used as work spaces, as kitchen gardens, and for keeping animals such as pigs. Several factors including population density and the intensity of land use contribute to problems of sanitation and health. Keeping pigs in yard areas, for example, raised the potential for the residents of the yard to become infected with parasites carried by these animals. Slave houses, too, were occupied by a large number of residents, and it has been documented that animals were kept in slave yards. Mrozowski's idea that there is some correlation between the occupations of residents and the way yard spaces are utilized is useful to the analysis of slave houses and yards.

One source of trash in plantation excavations is the root cellar. Archaeological studies of eighteenth- and nineteenth-century slave quarters in Virginia show that several of these structures had root cellars. These subterranean caches were used to store a wide range of goods, mainly root crops, and frequently were located in front of fireplaces. Some pits were dug at various places in the floors of cabins. These pits were either reinforced with clay or were lined with wood or sand. When excavated, many of these cellars contained refuse that was generated during the occupation of the site. Some cellars were backfilled slowly over time, while the site was occupied, and contained debris such as storage containers, useful tools, and remains of fish scales and bones. The animal bones presumably are the remains of diet, and in some instances this trash has been described as "raw garbage." Some items considered illegal for slaves to possess have been found in root cellars.

Some slave cabins at Kingsmill, Carter's Grove, and Rich Neck plantations in tidewater Virginia had multiple cellars.[47] The slave quarters at Carter's Grove and Rich Neck plantations were excavated under the auspices of the Colonial Williamsburg Foundation. The artifact assemblages of domestic and personal goods and tools are curated by the foundation. A slave quarter complex has been reconstructed at the Carter's Grove site. The complex consists of a double log house, a single log family dwelling, a gang house, and a corncrib, small garden plots, and chicken pens. These are built around a courtyard and represent the living spaces of a small slave community of 1770.[48] The reconstruction and furnishing of the cabins were fueled by the interdisciplinary effort of archaeologists, architectural historians, historians, and curators. The furnished cabins contain reproductions of items that were recovered from the trash found during the excavations at the site. Both the archaeological and the later reproduced items include examples of imported and locally manufactured ceramics, utensils, personal items, and plantation tools.

The presumably two-room slave quarter at the Rich Neck plantation in Williamsburg was represented by the remains of a central brick chimney base and several root cellars. In addition to the numerous ceramic and metal objects, archaeologists recovered a huge quantity of fish remains which suggest the importance of fish in the slave diet and to other social and economic exchanges. Botanical remains of seeds and plants helped archaeologists to reconstruct foodways and other uses of the environment. Earlier, at the nearby Kingsmill plantation, archaeological excavation uncovered the remains of a late eighteenth-century double-sided slave quarter with a central chimney and an additional shed extension.[49] The quarter had about eighteen small cellars in the interior floor, and each was filled with cached tools and personal items mixed in with, presumably, kitchen trash.

Plantation tools found at archaeological sites were probably the result of the slaves' effort to lower their production and to shorten their workday by hiding useful tools. Historical evidence supports archaeological interpretations of trash. Slaves created trash of useful items and discarded them in places which were not intended to receive trash. In 1774 a Virginian planter had his well cleaned and noted in his diary the

> abundance of trash, mud and things tumbled and thrown in, Particularly a Plow gardiner Johnny stole 3 years ago and offered to sell that and another to Robin Smith, who being a Penitant, Advised him to go and Put it where it might be found; but Johnny being suspected got whipped for them and threw them both in the Well as he told Robin Smith. I fished and got up one, but the other could not get till now. Found also the 2 bows of a pair of handcuffs, but the bolt we could not find. Joe had been Ironed in them and got his little brother Abraham to swear he saw black Peter take them, and carry them behind the Kitching; but the rascal threw them into the

well, and I do suppose sold the bolt. A good whipping both Joe and Johnny shall have and Abraham for lying tomorrow.[50]

Apparently slaves discarded items that were used to oppress them and other objects that would implicate them with insubordination.

Archaeological study of the eighteenth-century trash from a slave dwelling called the House for Families at George Washington's Mount Vernon estate supports the thesis "that slaves carved out a subsistence within the context of their own circumstances."[51] The analysis of dietary remains of animal bones recovered from a brick-lined cellar beneath the dwelling alludes to the diversity of slave diets. The slaves added to plantation rations and changed their diets with wild and domestic species. The archaeological assemblage includes remains from both large and small cuts of meat from pigs, fish, deer, and chicken and other birds. The bones were mixed in with ash, charcoal, oyster shells, and other trash that was deposited in the cellar. The trash was deposited in the cellar while the house was occupied. This evidence strongly suggests that a root cellar was considered an acceptable place for trash at the House for Families.

The production and use of goods resulted in trash around slave houses. Colonoware, a locally manufactured coarse earthenware ceramic, has been associated with slave sites, particularly in Virginia and South Carolina. A growing body of evidence substantiates that slaves, as well as Native Americans, made this type of ceramic, and it is mostly found as utilitarian wares in the forms of pots, basins, and jars. Archaeologist Leland Ferguson maintains that colonoware was useful in African American foodways for it influenced slaves' cultural autonomy.[52] Ferguson studied the marks found on colonoware sherds and discovered that most marks were simple crosses or Xs. But some were more complicated, and in some cases a circle or rectangle enclosed the cross. Ferguson proposed that the marked colonoware was connected to rituals which included elements of Kongo religious principles. More marked bowls have been recovered from rivers adjacent to old rice plantations than from around former slave quarters.

Archaeological studies of slave living areas at Monticello, Thomas Jefferson's piedmont Virginia plantation, 1770–1825, have provided more information for interpreting trash and how it was produced.[53] Some of Jefferson's slaves lived in quarters that were located next to farming areas and at a distance from the main house complex. These slaves presumably had less contact with whites. The slaves who resided closer to the main house or along Mulberry Row, a main street area with several outbuilding for housing slaves, animals, and various craft activities, had more contact with whites.

Archaeologists found evidence for craft and trade activities at Mulberry

Row. The archaeological remains suggest that activities of sewing and bone-button manufacture occurred at this site. In addition, tools, materials, and products of ironworking, particularly nail making, were found. Slaves probably netted monetary payments and other rewards from manufacturing nails and other activities that were sources of trash at slave dwellings. Some of the slaves at Monticello passed on their trade skills to family members.

Among the diverse artifactual assemblages that have been studied by archaeologists are several objects such as pierced pewter spoons, coins, and bones, as well as colored beads and cowrie shells. These objects have been interpreted as associated with African American rituals.[54] Cowrie shells, for example, are Indo-Pacific artifacts used in various rituals, in craftwork, and as currency in Africa. They have been found on slave sites in Virginia and in the Caribbean. Their recovery from contexts such as burial sites have led archaeologists to believe that probably they were significant to slave belief and religious systems in the New World. Presumably pierced objects of different materials were strung together. Documentary evidence depicts slaves wearing beaded or shell ornaments around their arms, feet, waist, and necks.[55]

At the Levi Jordan plantation in Texas, archaeologist Kenneth Brown uncovered evidence of Kongo-influenced rituals practiced by American slaves and tenant farmers.[56] Brown found trash that was purposely buried. He believed that the locations of these materials, beneath the hearth and near the doorway of a shaman's cabin, were as significant as the fact that they were intentionally buried. The trash included several cast-iron kettle bases, cubes of white chalk, bird skulls and an animal's paw, sealed tubes of bullet casings, coins, ocean shells, small dolls, nails and spikes, knife blades, stone scraping tools, patent medicine bottles, and a thermometer. Presumably the materials that were found beneath the hearth were placed there while the hearth was still being used as a cooking place and a source of heat for the cabin. Brown suggested that curing/conjuring rituals were enacted in the cabin and that the trash was related only in part to Euro-American culture.

Other researchers working in Maryland have found a similar ritual kit. A collection of artifacts consisting of quartz crystals, polished stones, bone disks, and pierced coins was found in a dark corner of a basement workshop in the home of Charles Carroll in Annapolis, Maryland. Carroll influenced the politics and society of eighteenth-century America. The cache, probably buried by a slave, contained more than twenty items covered by a bowl with a marking similar to an asterisk. The symbol painted on the interior surface of the bowl suggests affinity to the Kongo cosmogram. The researchers associated with this Maryland project believe that the kit is evidence of African-derived religious practices that were part of the lifestyles of African Americans in Annapolis.[57]

Other examples of ritually interpreted archaeological material have been found in Virginia. A whole bottle was uncovered beneath a freestanding cross wall in front of a fireplace at the Willcox plantation kitchen at Flowerdew Hundred, Prince George County, Virginia. Archaeologist James Deetz, who has worked on African American sites in both the North and the South, suggested that the bottle was deliberately placed there. The exact date of construction of the kitchen is unknown, but the inner cross wall was built after the kitchen was erected. The bottle enabled the researchers to date the construction of the wall to the 1830s. The kitchen at Flowerdew Hundred was a wooden two-room over two-room structure with brick chimneys at both ends. The lower rooms probably were used as cooking and laundry areas, and the upstairs rooms likely served as housing for slaves. Deetz writes that "the kitchen marks the place where the world of the Willcoxes and that of their slaves abutted one another. It is, in a sense, the mediation between the two worlds where the residents of the slave quarter, and possibly of the kitchen itself, worked to feed the planter and his family and to provide other amenities as well."[58]

Archaeological evidence suggests that amid the clutter of slave yards, there was some planned disposal of garbage. There is some evidence to indicate that on some archaeological sites significant trash pits are usually found at the rear of buildings and, for some slave housing, in areas away from the formal landscape of planters. At the Willcox plantation Deetz found that the yard areas surrounding the kitchen, visible to the planter, were free of rubbish. This was unlike the area away from the planter's view, which had a "vast and deep deposit" of trash. Deetz treated the kitchen as a "cross-road," for he described this junction as an interplay "between the ordered and manicured world of the planter, which enhanced his social standing, and the more cluttered world of the working plantation, which made his wealth and social standing possible in the first place."[59]

The remains of a nineteenth-century slave house also was uncovered at the Willcox plantation. The house had stood on seven brick piers with a chimney at its northern end. The cabin falls into the category of prescribed quarters as advocated in the nineteenth century. For example, the wooden floor would have been on piers, resulting in a crawl space beneath the building. The entry to the cabin was on the west side, but, more importantly, "a rich deposit of artifacts and animal bones was located at the rear of the cabin on the eastern side."[60]

Some slave owners tried to control slave trash and sought to change slave dwellings and the yards around them. They were concerned with the accumulation of garbage and the use of the yard. One nineteenth-century description of a slave yard emphasized differences in practices of slaves and slaveholders:

"On every side grow rancorous weeds and grass interspersed with fruit trees, little patches of vegetables and fowl-houses effectually shading the ground and preventing that free circulation of air so essential to the enjoyment of health in a quarter."[61] McKee explains that "the complaints of planters about the unkempt appearance of slave homes focused on how this showed the sub-human nature of the race, rather than on the fact that this was physical evidence of the slaves' ability to resist and ignore their masters' programs of plantation order."[62]

Most archaeologists have recognized that reuse must be considered in any interpretation of bottles found on archaeological sites. The history of bottle reuse is part of the history of trash disposal.[63] Frequently, empty bottles and their values were listed on inventories of slaveholders. Archaeological analyses of bottles from plantation sites reveal that sometimes bottles were kept for years before they were discarded. The same bottles were used by different people over time. Wine bottles, for example, have been found on numerous slave sites, but this factor probably is not an indication that wine was consumed at these sites. At some rural domestic sites, some bottles had more reuse value than in urban areas where most likely they were returned to entrepreneurs who needed bottles to market their products and gave cash or goods for new and old bottles.

Some of the trash, such as shells, bottles, ceramics, and pierced objects found in root cellars and around slave quarters, resembles the trash used to dress or medicate the yard, thus protecting the inhabitants and their property. For example, dressing the yard could involve such activities as inserting bottles in foundations and burying charms in doorways. Former slave Henry Rogers remembered that his parents hid a bag containing a mixture which included cotton stalks under the front of their cabin. This buried trashlike charm was to render those who came up the steps friendly and peaceful regardless of their original intentions.[64] Both historical and archaeological studies have shown that slave houses and yards with their clutter encoded knowledge that empowered their occupants to resist the evils of the spiritual and the secular world.

ON MEANINGS: TRASH, SLAVE HOUSES, AND YARDS

One nineteenth-century observer noted: "A negro loves the sun—it is his element, and he basks in its ray 'con amore'. His quarters should be on the south side of a hill, and never in the shade. No tree should be allowed to stand very near them. He is a filthy creature and has a proclivity for collecting all manner of litter about his residence, and every means should be used to keep his quarters well dried and well ventilated."[65]

The structures and contents of slave houses and yards spoke of slaves' needs to link place, time, and people. Objects among the clutter of slave dwellings perhaps commemorated loved ones who had been sold or had died. The presence of these objects served to continue these linkages. Amid the clutter there was organization that could be accessed if one knew how to do so. Oral tradition and practice taught slaves and their descendants the network of activities for mediating and understanding nature and the ways of the spirits. Objects and structures sometimes had multiple meanings and helped their organizers and creators establish their claims to knowledge of both the spiritual and the secular world. Seemingly insignificant objects were connected to each other in configurations made significant by slaves' values and beliefs.

Perhaps if contemporary observers had looked more closely and with better informed eyes, they would have noticed that slaves selected certain objects to be part of their clutter and excluded others. For example, the archaeological evidence points to oyster shells as common finds at African American sites. They definitely were chosen to be part of slave lifeways, and at times as the remains of slave diets, they were used in many contexts, as utensils, tools, inside wrapped charms, as decorations on graves, for paving paths, for footing buildings, flooring, and as part of a masonry material called tabby, "a mixture of oyster shells, lime, and sand," used for chimney construction.[66]

In 1782 one runaway slave allegedly was frequenting the marketplace in Williamsburg, Virginia, selling cakes and oysters.[67] Oyster shells, useful in foodways, also illustrate slaves' material impoverishment. As historian Eugene Genovese notes, "Where possible, they collected mussel or oyster shells to serve as spoons and knives. They raised gourds, which they dried, processed, and converted into bowls, dishes, ladles, jugs, and anything else their ingenuity and skill could shape."[68] Many objects were substitutions for other items. Plantation slavery operated to marginalize and deprive slaves socially and economically and to deny slaves' ownership of many basic material goods. In this context of enslavement, slaves' effort to dress and decorate their living spaces assumed different forms from those intended, as when a gourd replaced a cup, and oyster shells were used as spoons.

Oyster shells were collected and discarded in and around buildings in no apparent order, as Fanny Kemble observed in the 1830s, at Hampton plantation on Saint Simons Island, Georgia: "The shells are allowed to accumulate, as they are used in the composition of which their huts are built, and which is a sort of combination of mud and broken oyster shells, which formed an agglomeration of a kind very solid and durable for building purposes; but, instead of being all carried to some specified place out of the way, these great heaps of oyster shells are allowed to be piled up anywhere and everywhere, forming the most unsightly obstructions in every direction."[69] Yet the shells, when scattered around slave dwellings, probably served as an effective warning system signaling the approach of a person or an animal. The slaves would have heard the crunching of feet walking over the shells.

Slave yards and houses would have contrasted negatively with the "order and formality" of the planter landscape. Even when hidden, planters were still aware of the slave landscape, and at times for some planters this may have been a cause for discontent; slave cabins and yards were anomalies in the formal landscape of the plantation. Slaves appropriated their dwellings and yards, and for many of them these areas became a wilderness, the places where they had power and could be alone with their own kind and their ancestors. Mechal Sobel points out that "traditional African peoples accepted the spirit power of the forefathers who lived in time past. Africans believed spirits and forefathers affected their destiny, although a spirit worker might use power to counteract power."[70]

The African American wilderness of the slave quarters resonated with the slaves' thwarted aspirations. From this perspective the quarters and their adjacent surroundings became the graveyards of the slaves. These could be decorated and dressed like graves. Perhaps when yards were paved with oyster shells, they were reminders of the transparency and the whiteness of the watery world of the dead, thus serving as reflections of the potentials of the inhabiters of these yards. Surrounding themselves with certain objects linked to ancestral and other spiritual power probably served to bolster slaves' courage, helped to keep their thoughts clear of potentially dangerous intentions, and renewed their hopes. The planting of herbs and allusion to burial places suggest the power to heal, especially important to a people who valued their ancestors.

But the wilderness of the cluttered slave quarter freed the slaves; it was a resistance against slaveholders' consistency as opposed to slaves' random organization. The wilderness was wild and unkempt, it was for a free spirit, and it was not to be tamed. It was the context and the content of slave songs. Former slave Frederick Douglass described these "wild" songs as reverberating through the woods. He states that "the songs of the slave represent the sorrows of his heart; and he is relieved by them, only as an aching heart is often relieved by its tears." W. E. B. Du Bois asserts "that these songs are the articulate message of the slave to the world. . . . They are the music of an unhappy people, of the children of disappointment; they tell of death and suffering and unvoiced longing toward a truer world, of misty wanderings and hidden ways."[71] These sorrow songs were sung at the slave quarters and at the slave churches or bush arbors in the wilderness.

Particular trash in slave yards was probably a miniature wilderness for it would have contrasted with the order elsewhere in the yards.[72] This practice is reminiscent of practices in traditional African societies and in the Americas. In Kongo the wilderness is associated with the cemetery because traditionally some burial grounds once were villages. In the West and Central Africa past, specific times and places were considered sacred. Mechal Sobel writes that "soil and bones, burial grounds and village locations, and even village plans were seen as holy. Streams and rocks harbor spirits, and certain places were particularly close to the gods. Soil and herbs growing in these places made charms efficacious. Place was thus sanctified and inextricably bound to time."[73]

Slaves' narratives and interviews and other historical and archaeological evidence clearly support these conclusions.[74] The planting of trees at the heads of graves was practiced by slaves. Presumably these trees were symbols of ancestral roots and of the soul's movement to heaven. In the former-slave narrative *Incidents in the Life of a Slave Girl*, when Linda Brent (pseudonym of Harriet A. Jacobs) decides to run away from slavery in hopes that her master would sell her children to their white father, she goes to the wilderness, to her parents' graves. The graves were marked: "The graveyard was in the woods, and twilight was coming on. Nothing broke the death-like stillness except the occasional twitter of a bird. My spirit was overawed by the solemnity of the scene. For more than ten years I had frequented this spot, but never had it seemed to me so sacred as now. A black stump, at the head of my mother's grave, was all that remained of a tree that my father had planted. His grave was marked by a small wooden board, bearing his name, the letters of which were nearly obliterated." The syncretic nature of African American culture is illustrated in Linda Brent's action: "I knelt down and kissed them [the markers], and poured forth a prayer to God for guidance and support in the perilous step I was about to take. As I passed the wreck of the old meeting house, where, before Nat Turner's time, the slaves had been allowed to meet for worship, I seemed to hear my father's voice come from it, bidding me not to tarry till I reached freedom or the grave. I rushed on with renovated hopes. My trust in God had been strengthened by that prayer among the graves."[75] Earlier Brent described the church in the wood as built by the "colored people" with their burying ground around it. She further stated that the slaves had no higher happiness than meeting there and singing and praying, before it was destroyed in the aftermath of Nat Turner's insurrection.

During slavery the commemorative service for the deceased, freed-by-death slave frequently was separated from the time when the body was interred. Grey Gundaker notes that "just as there is room in African

American tradition *temporally* to distance interment of the body from the commemorative funeral service, so there is room *spatially* to distance the place of burial from the material commemoration of the lives of individuals and ancestors. While the body rests in the graveyard personal items like dishes and pitchers may be arranged in a special commemorative area of the yard or the interior of the house."[76] Perhaps this practice was important to slave time management strategies, to commemorate and maintain the link with the ancestors and to deal with the distance of burials, especially as the lengths of time slaves could use as their own were so short.

Slaves' cultural practices are most significant for some archaeologists who have mainly interpreted ceramics and glass recovered from slave sites as part of foodways. These archaeologists generally have shied away from interpreting objects and features on archaeological sites as relating to rituals. These rituals included the practice of using pottery and glass as deterrents against theft of slaves' livestock, garden produce, and other objects. Many of these objects, especially utensils, were broken and left on graves with shells and other objects as decorations. This practice has been documented for traditional West and Central African societies and in the postslavery American South.[77] Archaeological excavations of the African Burial Ground in New York have uncovered coins and beads that were buried with the corpses. Excavations of a slave cemetery in Barbados produced clay pipes, beads, cowrie shells, drilled dog teeth, and fish bones that had been part of a slave burial.[78] Trash and trashlike objects appeared in many forms and contexts on slave sites.

The morals and ethics that governed slaves' lives are significant factors that affected their living areas. These conventions include "mother wit," advice given by mothers, surrogate and real, to children or the younger generations. Ida B. Wells, whose mother was a former slave, taught her children "how to do the work of the home."[79] During slavery the social and economic impoverishment of blacks affected their material world profoundly, but poverty should not be equated with dirt and untidiness among slaves.

Perhaps some of the smells that emanated from slave quarters resulted from preserving and using preserved meat. Many slaves did not have separate areas for food preparation, storage, and consumption. Having livestock and supporting structures for their maintenance also added to the myriad smells in slave houses and yards. Particular smells, objects, and activities around the slave quarters in the Americas most likely were linked with controlling pests, a practice perhaps reminiscence of African ways. Olaudah Equiano, a West African captured and sold into slavery in the New World, described houses for sleeping in his village as "always covered, and plastered in the inside with a composition mixed with cow dung, to keep off the different insects, which annoy us during the night."[80] In his nineteenth-century travel memoirs, Olmsted recorded one African American's effort to rid his quarter of fleas:

> An Ingenious Negro.—In Lafayette, Miss., a few days ago, a negro, who, with his wife and three children, occupied a hut upon the plantation of Col. Peques, was very much annoyed by fleas. Believing that they congregated in great numbers beneath the house, he resolved to destroy them by fire; and accordingly, one night when his family were asleep, he raised a plank in the floor of the cabin, and, procuring an armful of shucks, scattered them on the ground beneath, and lighted them. The consequence was, that the cabin was consumed, and the whole family, with the exception of the man who lighted the fire, was burned to death.[81]

Other examples of pest control were documented in Jamaica. An eighteenth-century visitor to the island related that "as rats are very numerous and rapacious, the negroes guard against their devouring the meat, fish, and other provisions, which they hang over the fires in the middle of their huts, by placing a little above the same, an half cylinder of bark with the round side uppermost, the rope to which their food is appended passing thro this up to the ridge pole."[82]

The trash of slave cabins probably spoke of slaves' skills at hunting and their involvement in activities that implied prowess and perhaps protection as well. Some slave houses were decorated with trophies, broadcasting the skills of their occupants. The skins of raccoons and other animals were used to decorate the cabins.[83] This practice also was recorded in Jamaica during the eighteenth century: "The underparts of the eaves (which projects to shelter the walls from rain) afford places for bestowed sticks, pipes, whips, hunting and fishing gears, cutlasses, and other implements. I have seen the back-shells of river crawfish clasped round the rafters as a token of the owners prowess and good cheer. Tusks of the wild boars are deposited in the same places on the same account."[84] Some slaves tried to change the appearance of their cabins by dressing them. Women sometimes collected flowers to decorate their cabins and tried to keep them neat.

It is important to understand the conditions of slave houses and yards by looking at the time available to engage in housework, considering too that at times there was no great distinction between the house and the yard so far as the activities that took place there. This was particularly true because the quarters were so cramped that most activities took place outside among the poultry and other animals. Eugene Genovese in his extensive study of slave living conditions elaborated on the physical demands of daily labor, as well as the time it took to control insects, poultry, and small animals which were almost part of the household. He found that it would have been very difficult for many slaves to have kept clean and "well-ordered" cabins.[85]

Some slaves made trash of their work to allow for more time of their own. In 1770 a Virginian planter noted his loss of tobacco caused by his slaves: "Where there is a large Crop, which people are obliged to stem in the night the Negroes in spite of our teeths will throw a good deal of their task away. . . . I will endeavor to prevent it by making each person keep their stemms by themselves till the morning inspection and a proper correction. . . . By the heaps of stemms many bundles were thrown away by the negroes to have it said there task was finished besides a pretty great bulk quite spoilt when the remainder of the barn was blown down."[86] In spite of restrictions such as insufficient time to engage in activities to benefit themselves, some slaves built extensions to their cabins and expanded their living spaces. They also made structures to keep pigs and chickens from roaming freely in yard spaces.

Slaves' efforts to insulate their living areas from changing weather conditions have been interpreted as harboring trash near their dwellings. Because they usually lived in drafty cabins with large chinks between the logs, slaves resorted to various ways of filling open spaces in the walls of their cabins, as this nineteenth-century reference indicates: "When the houses are built of logs (which is generally the case) they should be hewn and all the bark taken off. The cracks should be neatly lined inside and out. If this is not done, the negroes will soon have them filled with dirty rags, old shoes, coon skins, chicken feathers and every other description of trash. They should not be permitted to indulge in these filthy, though very natural, propensities. Nor should they be allowed to have bundles of rags and dirty clothes stuffed above their beds. This they will certainly do if not prohibited."[87]

Daubing and filling in the spaces between the logs with clay were perhaps too much an expected "straight" pattern. Olmsted writes that "the great chinks are stopped with whatever has come to hand—a wad of cotton here, and a corn-shuck there. The suffering from cold within them in such weather as we experienced, must be great."[88] Working with various materials would have resulted in a more random design and would have allowed for the inclusion of special colors that had ritual significance such as red, blue, and white or just the use of things with bold colors. Perhaps slaves used the various materials that have been interpreted as the clutter of their landscape for protecting their houses. The practice of using newspaper as wallpaper in traditional African American houses falls in the category of confusing evil spirits.[89]

The varied materials used between the logs of slave cabins undoubtedly were useful for protection, at least from the adverse weather.

The reconstructed slave quarter at Carter's Grove plantation provides one setting to examine how African American history is re-created and presented and the interplay of trash with values and expectations in the American South today. The filling between the logs of the cabins is smoothed to a concrete consistency. In the eighteenth century slaves at Carter's Grove probably stuffed whatever they could find into chinks to keep their cabins warm. Special objects may have been deliberately stuffed between the logs of these cabins, likely serving as codes for runaways or other slaves who would have deciphered the codes, understood that they were on friendly ground, and known how to proceed.

Today, the yards in and around the cabins are covered with oyster shells, but there is little other trash. The quarter abuts woods and ravines and is excluded from the formal landscape of the big house. In colonial times a similar landscape probably allowed slaves to dress the yard and cabins to their liking. The quarter probably teemed with both visible and invisible dressing. Objects of certain colors as well as their locations in the yard likely contributed to a communication network.

CONCLUSION

Slave houses and yards, essential aspects of the slave landscape, represented slaves' efforts to make a world for themselves in the harsh regime of plantation society. Slaves surrounded themselves with objects that commemorated their abilities to survive and with others that spoke of concerns for natural things and their link to the past. Trophies of their hunting skills became keepsakes, further establishing the slaves in time and space. Some objects were held in memory of loved ones who had died or had been sold. Other objects were placed to communicate with other slaves who needed assistance in the quest for emancipation from the chains of slavery. Yet some trash was buried and protected the inhabitants of slave dwellings, while other trash was a deterrent to potential thieves and other pests. Many European and American objects were used in ways that were strongly African and African American.

The slave landscape incorporated both the apparent and the hidden. It was consciously created and appropriated by the slaves as a place where they had some autonomy. Slaves refused to shackle their expressive and dynamic characteristics in their fight to survive the inhumanity and cruelty of slavery; they created their own world based on individual visions and communal ideals. Trash and stories and songs about trash in the slave landscape were incorporated in slaves' attempts to heal their wounds, the wounds of an oppressed and exploited people. Songs and stories were important to slaves, for they were vital to the oral tradition and practices that linked generations, and those songs and stories kept the slaves and the past alive. The slave landscape was not trash, but like slave songs, trash articulated music that spoke of the present and the past.

14   RACE AND THE POLITICS OF PUBLIC HISTORY IN THE UNITED STATES

Patrick Hagopian

WHEN ANDREW GOODMAN, Michael Schwerner, and James Chaney, the three civil rights activists, disappeared in Mississippi in 1964, the victims of Klan violence, the authorities began to drag the swamps in search of their bodies.[1] Soon, a body emerged from the dark waters, the body of a black man—but not that of James Chaney. In the days that followed, one unsought body after another, every one the body of a black man, came up from the depths. These men had vanished without a trace, the local police dismissing the disappearances by explaining that they had probably moved out of state. Finally, a tip-off led the authorities to the place where the three bodies they sought were hidden, thus sparing the local police, and the nation, the further embarrassment that the apparently endless parade of corpses was causing them.

The unintended exhumations brought to light some uncomfortable facts: first, that a black man's violent death in Mississippi would raise no outcry, would scarcely raise a ripple in the minds of the state's police and its white public; second, that Chaney's body, too, probably would have been lost with the others had the federal authorities not been compelled to act by the disappearance of his northern white companions. And yet, although the nation may have lost no sleep over the unknown dead in their unmarked graves, their families had not forgotten them; nor could any African American in the South have been oblivious of the presence of the untended graves in their midst and the silent threat that beckoned from the ground.[2] The bodies the waters yielded were monuments to white Americans' treatment of their African American neighbors; so too the undiscovered bodies lived long in some memories, where they still lie unforgotten.

In subsequent decades the exhibitions and interpretive programs in mainstream historical institutions have devoted increasing attention to African American history, corresponding to an increased acknowledgment of racism in the American past and present.[3] In the 1960s television screens were filled with images of fire hoses, police dogs, batons, and defiant southern governors. A public sensitized by such televised images could now view museum exhibitions displaying slave shackles or a whipping post as representations of an undeniable history, not as evidence of the bad taste of the curator; nor could such displays be viewed complacently as benchmarks against which American social progress could be measured. The violent racial oppression in America's past became visible in historical institutions as contemporary racism moved into the mainstream of public discourse.

Over the years increasingly vexatious aspects of the nation's history have been brought into the public gaze, but this process of incremental exposure seems to have hit some sort of unseen limit. At first, African American activists were united in demanding that the presence of an African American population and the history of racial oppression be represented adequately in historic sites. Lately, an opposition to the successive representation of one aspect after another of the history of slavery has arisen among some African Americans in civil rights organizations. In the argument about the reenactment of a slave auction in Colonial Williamsburg, the conflict does not boil down easily to one between whites and blacks or racists and antiracists. Nor does the question easily reduce to the terms most frequently used by scholars of social memory. This chapter explores what was at stake in the argument about the reenactment, and at the same time it offers a new account of debates about historical representation that attempts to address the failings of the explanatory schemata available in current scholarship.

Most scholars of public history, social memory, and their synonyms treat every argument about the representation of the past as a version of the question, Who owns the past? The last few years have seen one case after another in which the protagonists are presented as groups with contending social interests; these groups see the world in distinct ways and wish history to be represented accordingly; generally the contest is between a party of repressive power and a party of historical truth, and the truth is almost inevitably compromised by the imposition of power. Tragic and moving though these accounts may be, I think they are inadequate to explain the controversy about representing the history of race and slavery. Should a reenactment of a slave auction be included in the public repertoire of a living-history site? The question would be easily answered if it were treated as one more variant of the incessant battle between historical truth and the oblivion of repression. The difficulty of the question, though, indicates the inadequacy of this recurrent interpretive schema.

Here, I argue that shared memories are not just those that are brought to the surface, into public view. A shared experience of the past can also inhabit a subterranean stratum, visible to some but concealed from others. A group of people's common memory of the past may, indeed, inhere in their sharing what is occluded from the gaze of others and knowing that only their fellows possess that covert knowledge and feel its emotional charge. Ownership of the past sometimes does involve contesting the space of public representation and determining the content of what takes that stage; it may also involve, however, deciding what should remain proprietary and protected from the gaze of outsiders. For African Americans, once deprived of all possessions except their secret pain, decisions about what should and should not be brought within the horizon of representation have a special sharpness.

Under the peculiar conditions of slavery in the British colonies of North America and in the United States, African Americans developed expressive strategies characteristic of the conditions of servitude and political oppression. African Americans needed to be acutely attuned to the nuances of the slaveholders' speech and conduct in order to glean intelligence bearing upon the conditions of their own lives. For slaves who worked in the plantation houses, sharp ears and doors left open were tactical instruments to this end. And among themselves, African Americans developed coded and cryptic means of communication that enabled them to express ideas and feelings and to exchange information unbeknownst to the planters and overseers whose prying eyes and ears they could not escape at will. This pattern—of simultaneous attentiveness and secrecy—demanded proficiency in more than one communicative code. Enslaved people needed to be able to discern both secret signs that were intended for them and telltale ones that were not. As a people whose political and social emancipation has been neither quick nor easy, African Americans have continued to elaborate and practice expressive strategies in which a keen sensitivity to the privileges and protocols of knowledge has remained an important part.

MAKING THE INVISIBLE VISIBLE

Among the most popular tourist attractions in Virginia are the homes of the Founding Fathers who fought the Revolution against the British, framed the Constitution, and ruled the nation as its presidents. Visitors to Washington, D.C., can take a short journey into Virginia to visit Mount Vernon, the home of the Founding Father who lent the capital his name. A set of slides purchased from the gift shop on the site shows a number of views that comport with an official—although now outdated—view of a historic house museum, showing the magnificent exterior of the building and, inside, Mrs. Washington's elegantly presented tea service and George Washington's study and bedchamber. Lest we think that General and Mrs. Washington were the sole inhabitants of Mount Vernon, we can also see the building that one slide label identifies as the servants' hall, a simple living quarters outside the mansion building, a kitchen garden, and the spinning room.

This slide set has not kept up with the times, though. Archaeologists have uncovered evidence of the hidden history of the life of the enslaved inhabitants of Mount Vernon, as they have at other historic homes around the United States. Archaeological excavation revealed the foundations of the Mount Vernon slave quarter to which George Washington referred as the "house for families," which housed over sixty household slaves between 1760 and 1793. On this recovered ground, curators have introduced new signposts and text labels outside and inside the buildings. In the remade interior of an overseer's room, identified in the gift shop slide set as a spinning room, the cheerful red coat is gone and the rocking horse has been replaced by a text label referring to the work performed by slaves on Washington's estates.[4]

A number of sites outside the mansion building now have new labels and, in some cases, new artifacts revealing the presence of slaves at Mount Vernon. For example, the slide set labels an interior scene, "West Quarters Building," and the photograph reveals no interpretive labels identifying those who worked in the quarters. This interior has now been considerably transformed and relabeled, with a large gang-label identifying the building as the "Greenhouse Slave Quarters."[5] The new exhibit labels appeared as a result of pressures affecting not just Mount Vernon but other historic sites across the nation. In the decades since African Americans revived their struggle for racial justice, museum curators and trustees have increasingly found themselves under economic and political pressures. As the proportion of African Americans in the populations of major cities increased in the post–World War II period, museums discovered they needed to reach out to this potential audience; moreover, state and federal grants began to require museum programming targeted at minority audiences.[6] In line with these trends, the curators at Mount Vernon have recognized, first, that most of those who lived at the estate were African Americans and, second, that they were not "servants" but slaves.[7] As a result of proddings from the local African American community, the Mount Vernon Ladies' Association, which owns and operates the site, unveiled a memorial there in 1983 to replace a small marble tablet, overgrown with weeds, honoring the hundreds of African Americans buried there who lived and worked as slaves at Mount Vernon. Although there are no African American administrators or regents at Mount Vernon, in 1990 the Ladies' Association hired an actor to portray a black slave overseer during Black History Month. In his performance he greets visiting groups of schoolchildren as though they were newly arriving slaves needing instruction in the rules and regulations of the estate.[8]

The same pattern of a widening horizon of representation is evident at another Virginia historical site, Colonial Williamsburg. Colonial Williamsburg is run by a private institution, the Colonial Williamsburg Foundation; unlike Mount Vernon, it is not a single estate but a complex of buildings and streets covering a several-block area at the center of Virginia's eighteenth-century capital; and its portrayal of history is animated by "People of the Past"—costumed interpreters who play historical personages and types of the colonial era.[9] Founded in 1926, with the backing of John D. Rockefeller, Jr., the historical reconstruction had a lily-white coloration in its first few decades. In the 1960s and 1970s, critics began to demand revisions to make the history portrayed more accurate and inclusive. Half of the eighteenth-century population had consisted of free and enslaved African Americans, yet the population of costumed interpreters was virtually all white. Moreover, the work of preservation and restoration focused on the dwellings and institutions of the high and mighty, not on those of the craftspeople, housemaids, and manservants on whose work they depended. Williamsburg, one critic noted, was "a fantasy in which the more pleasing aspects of colonial life are meticulously evoked, with the omission of smells, flies, pigs, dirt, and slave quarters." It was "history homogenized, cleaned up, and expurgated . . . an entirely artificial recreation of the imaginary past."[10]

In response to such criticisms, the Colonial Williamsburg Foundation discovered slavery in eighteenth-century Williamsburg. Beginning in the 1970s, African American costumed interpreters have been hired and currently number around seventeen;[11] the schedule of interpretive programs has begun to include aspects of African American life in Williamsburg. Visitors today can witness "jumping the broom" ceremonies in which enslaved people uttered their marriage vows; they can see vignettes, initiated by curator Christy Matthews, in which the sexual relations between white masters and female slaves are dramatized; they see African Americans not simply in relation to whites but conducting active spiritual, emotional, personal, and collective lives of their own.[12] Today we can see both the mansion house and the slave quarters at Carter's Grove, a nearby plantation administered by Colonial Williamsburg, where the same costumed interpreters work. The view of life presented at Colonial Williamsburg is often happily nonconflictual, though, as in the depiction of African American drumming and dance in which the largely white audience is invited to participate.[13] Presented in the spirit of inclusiveness and goodwill, the African American experience is shorn of struggle and violence.

Costumed interpreters hired to play Williamsburg's black population do
not just play African Americans. Until 1995 they were all African American.[14]
This principle of casting proceeded from the expectation that visitors to
Colonial Williamsburg might be confused by "nontraditional casting."
Consequently, because African Americans in eighteenth-century Virginia did
not enjoy social equality or hold legal and political offices, African American
costumed interpreters are permanently consigned to play lowly members of
a colonial society without even a nominal commitment to equal opportunities. And arcing across the gap between the eighteenth century and today are
some uncomfortable facts about racism today and yesterday.

While white actors can frequently be seen in their off-hours shopping or
walking around town in their costumes, African American interpreters do
not feel comfortable wearing their costumes off-site and take them off at the
first opportunity. Although this is not evident to the audiences of the interpretive programs, playing the part of a slave to a largely white audience
exacts a psychological toll on the players.[15] Sometimes obnoxious visitors, a
perennial problem at living-history sites, try to tease the actors into breaking
character; sometimes visitors enter a little too spiritedly into the eighteenth-
century milieu. In a dramatic setting that is at once auditorium and stage, it
is all too easy for an audience member to bound into the action or to try to
drag the player back across the notional footlights. Nor is it easy to distinguish between appropriate audience interaction and heckling. What happens
if a white audience member begins to address a costumed interpreter in a
haughty way? Such an interaction hits close to home in a southern state in
which any visitor to a cafeteria immediately can see that relations of service
and patronage are still organized along racial lines. Thus, although the interpretive programs never make an explicit connection between past and present, the insulation between these eras is always liable to short-circuit because
of the perdurance of racial oppression in both eras.

A scholarly article on the interpretive program at Colonial Williamsburg
predicted that while music, religion, and work were all worthwhile subjects
for interpretation, an "equally important subject, slave whippings, could not
be feasibly re-created. . . . slave auctions and the daily humiliations masters
visited on slaves would probably never be shown because they would be
unpleasant for the staff members who re-created them and because they might
alienate visitors."[16] This prediction, borne out by subsequent events at
Colonial Williamsburg, was amplified by the controversy about the Disney's
America historical theme park unsuccessfully planned in Manassas, Virginia.
The plan was to establish a park within easy reach of Washington depicting
several different geographical areas and historical periods, but after a pro-
longed outcry by local residents and historians, the plan was abandoned.

One of the unfortunate events that sank the theme park was the statement by a Disney executive that the history park would be valuable because it would allow the public not just to see but to feel what slavery was like.[17] Not just to see but to feel what slavery was like: this statement from a Disney executive tested the plausible limits of visitors' capacity to transcend different experiences. What did the Disney Company plan? Did it intend to subject the visitor to whippings and strenuous labor in the fields? How, short of this, could the company convey so vividly the experience of slavery? And would such a display send visitors out "with a smile on your face," as the general manager of Disney's America announced as his aim?[18] To such awkward questions, the Disney Company rejoined that the vice president who made the offending statement was not an authorized spokesperson; the damage was done, however, and the statement came back to haunt the company every time an academic historian or Civil War buff criticized their plans. Either the history would include slavery, in which case how would it represent the slave's point of view? Or it would evade the issue, in which case the company would be accused of performing cosmetic surgery on the past.

Part of the problem with the Disney proposal was that many historians and press commentators did not trust the Disney Company to present an honest version of the nation's history. Although some historians argued that Disney could reach an enormous number of people not otherwise exposed to history and that professional historians should therefore climb aboard the bandwagon, others were not so sanguine.[19] Their mistrust of Disney's version of history was based not on prejudice but on observation of the historical components of Disney's existing theme parks, which tended to celebrate a mythical small-town American past with all the nasty bits, such as labor conflicts and gender and racial oppression, taken out.[20]

In discussing the ratio of "fun" and "facts" at Colonial Williamsburg and the planned Disney's America theme park, a chief designer for Disney's America stated that Williamsburg had what the Smithsonian shared but that Disney's America never would possess: "real history." "You can't compete with living history," declared Thomas Jefferson, as played by Colonial Williamsburg's costumed interpreter, dismissing the competition of the "audio-animatronic" robot Jefferson planned for Disney's theme park.[21] At a meeting in Williamsburg, Ann Crossman, of the Association for the Preservation of Virginia Antiquities, asked how visitors to Disney's America would be able to distinguish its "imitation history" from the authentic displays at other sites (presumably including the meeting's location).[22] Her assumption must have been that a museum such as Williamsburg was, somehow, real history, of which Disney's park would be only a debased replica. Many of the attempts to contrast Disney's America with other representations of history served similarly to reveal a naive faith in the authorized media of guild history. Whether any unenslaved citizen can feel what it was like to be a slave and whether there is any such thing as an authentic historical representation are not questions for Disney alone. Unable to address the questions that the controversy raised—about the irreducible reliance of history on representation and the inevitable dependence of edification on audience appeal—defenders of the sacred Manassas battlefield resorted to Mickey Mouse trivialization, snobbery, sentimentality, and elitism.[23]

THE PROBLEM OF PROPRIETY

Would the mistrust of Disney's America also apply to Colonial Williamsburg's rendering of the slave auction? If, through the magic of an imagineer's epistemology, Colonial Williamsburg could be the "real," against which Disney's America would play the replica, this was not CW's only credential. By the mid-1990s CW had established a sound academic reputation. It had an active research program occupied by curators with strong scholarly credentials; it had links with the College of William and Mary and the Institute of Early American History and Culture. Moreover, its growing African American history department was successfully running programs for a diverse audience and was forging links with organizations such as the local NAACP group that was pleased to see a fuller representation of history in Williamsburg. By September 1994 the newly appointed director of the African American department, Christy Coleman (now Matthews), had decided to broaden the scope of her department's programming first by "re-educat[ing] the public" to hear African American history from white costumed interpreters and also by dramatizing an eighteenth-century slave auction.[24]

The nearby Jamestown Settlement, a living-history site independent of CW, coincidentally staged a prelude to the auction the previous summer: a commemoration of the 1619 landing of the ship of the first Africans at Jamestown, the initiating event for the history of African American presence in British North America.[25] Unlike this heavily promoted event, however, the planned auction in Williamsburg was not independently advertised. News of the event was spread by word of mouth, in order to limit the size of the audience and the potential repercussions. The Williamsburg branch of the NAACP supported Christy Coleman's plan. Opposition from the state office of the NAACP in Richmond created a controversy, however, which became the subject of numerous local news stories. The press and television coverage of the controversy spread the news about the event so that a larger-than-usual crowd gathered for the auction in October 1994.

The expectant audience and protesters waited through an unexplained delay under the eye of the attendant TV cameras. Christy Coleman finally emerged from negotiations with the Southern Christian Leadership Conference and the NAACP and pleaded to be allowed to represent the whole of what she, as an African American woman, called "the story of our mothers and grandmothers."[26] But, equally vehemently, Jack Gravely of the NAACP told the impatient crowd of his long years in the civil rights movement.[27] He had not seen his race come so far, he said, to allow the performers to make an entertaining spectacle out of the history of their enslavement. He and other protesters intended to prevent the event from taking place, he said, and demanded to be arrested.

What makes the live-action portrayal of slavery different from the display of an auction block, which has occurred in museum exhibitions without any complaint? Why should a painting of an auction (also displayed in museums) or a filmed representation (as in *Roots*) not excite the same condemnation? Regardless of the medium, none of these representations can escape the charge, sometimes directed at historical representations by African American critics, that they focus on the negative and that public displays should be uplifting. If one accepts such premises, it may be the unusual vividness of a live reenactment that pushes disapproval over into active dissent. But three other contingencies must be kept in mind: (*a*) the use of African American actors; (*b*) the character of the audience and the context of the performance; and (*c*) the purposes of the performance.

The use of African American costumed interpreters is one particularly sharp instance of the problem I alluded to earlier. If racial identity certifies one's qualification for certain roles in the historic site, then the reenactment of a slave auction reopens an unhealed wound for those who feel their bodies marked with a stigma of shame and humiliation. If race matters in this way, it creates a triangular relationship between the people enslaved in colonial Virginia and African Americans today, with the actor on the auction block at the vertex. If the performance were intended to garner income for the performers or their employers, this might make the economic transaction portrayed all the more disturbing, since the historical transaction would be amplified by contemporary commerce, with both dependent on the presence of the black bodies on the block.

The audience for the slave auction performance did not pay to see it, though. Normally, performances at Colonial Williamsburg are advertised in the freely distributed *Visitor's Companion* and are accessible to those who have a pass identifying them as paying visitors. For some performances an additional fee is charged. Even when there is no additional charge, though, visitors must often book places and receive tickets for a given performance, in order to control audience sizes. The slave auction was neither advertised nor ticketed, though, removing it from the normal cash nexus of visitation at Colonial

Williamsburg. This might justify the demarcation between education and entertainment that both supporters and opponents of the performance attempted to make.[28] But is any absolute distinction between the two possible?

Because visitation is voluntary, Colonial Williamsburg must be able to attract an audience, just as Disney's theme parks must. And while the content of Disney historical components might differ from Colonial Williamsburg's, they all must interest as well as inform the audience. I do not believe it would be possible to produce any definition of *interest* that would exclude "entertainment." As any teacher knows, if one bores an audience, one will find it more difficult to instruct them; in this sense, the charge that any display at Colonial Williamsburg is intended as "entertaining spectacle" is, generally speaking, banal and meaningless, since this appears to be an inescapable part of the museum's mission. Nevertheless, the charge is undeniable; nor can it be disputed that historical tourism is the economic heartbeat of the local economy, around which craft shops, hotels, restaurants, tourist attractions, and the real estate industry thrive.[29] The fact that Colonial Williamsburg's fortunes rise or fall with its capacity to entertain, as well as enlighten, makes the propriety of the display the more questionable.

"Propriety" means ownership as well as moral rightness. Whose property is the pain of the slaves on the auction block? Because Christy Coleman is an African American, does that mean that the history she wishes to portray was a birthright inherited from her mother and grandmothers, of which she could dispose at will? But if it was "hers," was it any the less Gravely, the civil rights leader's, in which case didn't his ownership give him a right of veto over the presentation of that history to those who do not own it?

By what right did the audience deserve to witness the re-created auction? What would protect the history displayed from trivialization, from being a mere curiosity, from being sentimentalized, from being rendered spectacular? What might prevent its being used by a publicity-hungry historical site? What might ultimately prevent its being "normalized," by becoming simply a regular part of the routine at Colonial Williamsburg, something to see between visits to the blacksmith's shop and a meal at a nearby tavern?

The majority of the audience clearly sided with Coleman and were there to see the auction. Finally, a compromise was reached such that the protesters could make a statement about their reasons for opposing the event. No one was arrested; the auction was portrayed. What was unnerving about the event was not the conflict between the two positions but the reaction of the audience. They were growing impatient and had come to witness the auction, not a debate about public history and civil rights. Growing restive, members of the largely white crowd heckled Gravely as he spoke. Someone called out, "Get on with the show!" Gravely's words reminded the audience of the long history of racial injustice that intervenes between the past event and the present; he also reminded the audience of a third moment, of struggle for freedom and justice, separating as well as uniting past and present. The crowd's reaction was sufficient to remind me that this struggle is not yet over; and much as I sympathize with Christy Coleman's position, I could not help but feel that there was more than one tragic history being played out on Duke of Gloucester Street that day.

The auction of "slave property" was the last in a series of lots sold under the hammer on the steps of a Williamsburg tavern. The first sales involved real estate and movable goods and helped to settle the audience by familiarizing them with the main characters in the drama and instructing them in the conventions of the commercial transaction they were witnessing. It was clear that not every costumed interpreter had the right to participate in the auction as a bidder, and those whose credit was uncertain had to provide letters of credit to establish that right. Banter concerning one prospective bidder revealed the class differentiation in the society.

The slave auction itself cleverly manipulated the reactions of the audience. The audience did not join in with catcalls or unscripted bids, as the organizers had feared and had prepared for. Onlookers did, however, become absorbed in the personal dramas played out through the bidding. A planter had bought one member of a slave couple, the husband; his wife was fearful because she was being sold separately. The audience overheard the dialogue of the couple and thus learned of their anguish at the thought of separation. The planter bid for the wife, too, but there was a competing bidder. As the sale proceeded, therefore, the audience was on tenterhooks, not knowing if the couple would remain together or would be dragged apart. One young girl in the audience encouraged the first planter, speaking quietly to herself, not catcalling. When the second planter's final bid succeeded, the crowd sagged with disappointment at the outcome. This reaction contrasted with the relief the audience felt in an earlier sale, in which a free black man successfully bid to be reunited with his wife, a slave. In both of these vignettes, the drama had cleverly seduced the audience into a vicarious and approving identification with one of the bidders in the auction as well as with the people on the block. The palpable tension that the audience felt in witnessing these sales, evident in the vocal encouragements of one young onlooker, indicates the success of the event—but also one of its limitations. Because the slaves occupied a passive role in the auction, the audience's hopes for them were necessarily articulated through an engagement with the active protagonists, the bidders. This manipulated audience identification with the bidders in the auction could have been used to create a sharp-edged irony. The opportunity was ignored, though, leaving the audience's emotions invested most immediately in the hope for a humane outcome to the auction. One could, I suppose, have come away with a greater outrage at the institution of slavery itself, but this result would derive from a historical extrapolation, not from the excitement that the reenactment cleverly provoked.[30]

"BLACK KNOWN AND UNKNOWN POETS ♦ ♦ ♦ HOW YOUR AUCTIONED PAIN SUSTAINED US"

Thus far, I have focused on the issue of representation as visibility: who should have the right to determine what is portrayed, what should be included and what left out. There is much that is useful about the set of investigations under the rubric, Who owns history? but a number of encounters in the last few years have made me begin to wonder if I and others like me weren't missing something, and whether there might be something ethnocentric about defining social memory in terms of visible representations in sites of public history such as museums. What might we not see by focusing on visibility? It was in the context of this thinking that my teaching responsibilities charged me with reading Maya Angelou.

In her autobiography, *I Know Why the Caged Bird Sings*, Maya Angelou writes: "If we [African Americans] were a people much given to revealing secrets, we might raise monuments and sacrifice to the memory of our poets, but slavery cured us of that weakness. It may be enough, however, to have it said that we survive in exact relationship to the dedication of our poets (include preachers, musicians, and blues singers)."[31] The whole of this chapter can be considered an extended gloss on this passage from Angelou's text. Since the time of slavery, secrecy and indirection allowed enslaved people to construct shared intellectual and emotional responses to the world, preserving their own conceptions of self and community under the eyes of slaveholders but without the knowledge of these inescapable onlookers. If the slave-owning class refused to sanction slave marriages unless these unions suited the planters' purposes; if they could separate slave families at will, if they could restrict the economic and political activities of those they held in captivity, if they were able to contain and suppress most forms of organized resistance, and if they were able to foreclose many of the platforms and media through which collective communications are conducted and shared identities are forged, still they were never able to eradicate the will among the enslaved to express their joys and sufferings to others and hence to create, share, and preserve a sense of community. This collective identity is not counterposed to individuality in Angelou's account but is a condition for the life of individuals, a means by which they can throw off the blanket of oblivion which otherwise would enshroud each and all.

"Slavery cured us of that weakness"—the weakness of revealing secrets by raising monuments and engaging in public rites of sacrifice. In the time of their enforced servitude in North America, enslaved people were unable to raise or preserve the kind of visible markers that most Europeans and European Americans know as monuments. Enslaved people learned to honor their heroes and to preserve their memories covertly, just as they often practiced religion and social ceremonies secretly. Visits between plantations took place surreptitiously, evading the slave patrols; slaves consecrated places in the woods away from the master's and mistress's eyes in which to celebrate rites of marriage and burial.[32] African Americans sought protection against the forces ranged against them by planting canes between the walls of their masters' houses and used "mojos" or luck balls for power or divination. African Americans used semiotic markers such as broken crockery, polished, reflective objects, and geometric patterns to mark certain places as distinct and to embody cosmological ideas about the relationship between material and spirit worlds.[33] Lamps, pitchers, pieces of glass and of quilts, and wooden figures were used to mark burials and can be seen in twentieth-century photographs, as well as being commented on by sharp-eyed nineteenth-century observers.[34] Some such signs are recognizable only to those familiar with the semiotic code but remain unremarked by others.[35] A tree might be just a tree to a white southerner; to a former slave, though, it might mark a place of burial, or it might be remembered as the place where people were bound and flogged.[36] A world becomes full of sites of palpable feeling for those who live and die and suffer in it, so that ordinary places become part of their commemorative mental maps.

"Let us say that we survive in exact relationship to the dedication of our poets (include preachers, musicians and blues singers)." This finely balanced statement is the correlate to the impossibility of a slave-created monument, in the sense that many would understand the term monument, indicating a prominent and widely comprehensible public artifact. In Angelou's formulation the people do not dedicate monuments to their poets; inverting this relationship, the poets dedicate their acts of creation to the survival of a people. Their creations are not composed of stone or polished metal on pedestals; they are vocal, verbal, musical expressions. The survival of African American communities testifies to the efficacy of verses, hymns, and rhythms, because these expressions of pain, Angelou tells us, sustain their listeners, ease their loneliness, and make hunger endurable.[37] The people themselves thus become a testament—a monument—to the poets' creation.

This concept of monumentality is quite distinct from that usually considered under the rubric of commemoration, in the European American tradition. Indeed, the relevant term would be *testimony*, not *monument*, because the commemoration is inscribed in textuality. Shared acts of commemoration, in this account, occur not just when groups of people gather in front of stone monuments but also when people share privileged knowledge in the way they use their words so as to partake of a tradition and bring it into the present.

Angelou expresses the inextricable communion of audience and speaker, community and poet, in her own writing. Angelou's autobiography is both an account of, and the result of, her assumption of her own voice, literally as well as figuratively, since she is, for a spell, terrified into silence before a teacher restores her power of speech; resuming the capacity for verbal expression, she adds her voice to a form, autobiography, that had long registered "the timbres of the African American narrative voice."[38] Angelou's voice is suffused with the voices of the others who find a renewed life through hers. Angelou's assertion of the role of African American poets comes at the end of a chapter in which she describes the demoralizing effect that the words of a white politician have on a black graduation ceremony audience, and the way the audience is revived by a collective performance of the Negro national anthem, its words composed by poet and NAACP founder James Weldon Johnson. Angelou's invocation of the "Black known and unknown poets" whose "auctioned pain" sustained a people is a reference to James Weldon Johnson that pays homage to his work as well as to the unnamed minstrels and prophets his poem honors. Her title, *I Know Why the Caged Bird Sings*, is a reference to Paul Laurence Dunbar's poem "Sympathy."[39] These allusions typify an autobiography filled with reference to songs, ceremonies, and black storytelling—as well as comic strips, Horatio Alger's stories, and English novels—the stuff from which Angelou's awakening self-awareness was made.[40]

Slavery could not eliminate the practice among African Americans of intertextual verbal and musical expressions filled with allusion and borrowing, a creative tradition to which Angelou contributes as well as defers. All acts of expression are capable of multiple readings, and every tradition is malleable, but these irreducible semiotic facts were transformed into creative strategies, perforce, in the production of narratives readable in different ways by different people. Trickster narratives and other folktales might be heard as innocent stories by some listeners, and they also could be heard as expressions of a critical cosmology and an acerbic account of social relations by others.[41] So too with the shared verbal repertoire of a vernacular culture, such as hymns, proverbs, catchphrases, and ways of talking, each of which could shift in meaning depending on the situation in which it was expressed and could link to a whole chain of references. Along with various forms of performative behavior that operated in the interstices of power in order to gain some secret advantage, such verbal strategies grew out of, and carried the covert sign of, the slave experience.[42]

When Angelou explains this idea, she uses a proverb to explain her own mother's "African-bush secretiveness and suspiciousness . . . compounded by slavery and confirmed by centuries of promises made and promises broken." The proverb pronounces: "If you ask a Negro where he's been, he'll tell you where he's going." Angelou comments: "To understand this important information, it is necessary to know who uses this tactic and on whom it works. If an unaware person is told a part of the truth (it is imperative that the answer embody truth), he is satisfied that his query has been answered. If an aware person (one who himself uses the stratagem) is given an answer which is truthful but bears only slightly if at all on the question, he knows that the information he seeks is of a private nature and will not be handed to him willingly. Thus direct denial, lying and revelation of personal affairs are avoided."[43] The use of encryption is thus part of a strategy of communication in which different people can participate to differing degrees, and one that also allows a measure of grace and art in the respecting of boundaries and the private acknowledgment of the unsaid.

"GLORY"

If a complex verbal etiquette was one legacy of enslavement, the incomplete emancipation at the end of the Civil War era created another possibility. Emancipation offered at least the momentary hope that African Americans could demand a place and a say in museums and public monuments and that their history could be acknowledged as a constitutive element of the nation's past. The presentation of an African American past in the United States in this century occupies the terrain marked off by two strategies: the cryptic strategies for sharing knowledge and experience that emerged during slavery time and the open contestation of public space made possible by the incomplete emancipation process of the late nineteenth century and renewed as a part of the social movements for black liberation in recent decades. These two approaches do not exclude one another. In addition to the public debates about the visible representation of slavery in museums and historic sites, there are other lines of transmission of shared memories that go on through, around, and sometimes quite apart from the most overt forms of social contestation. Beneath the recent high-pitched clashes about African American representation in public institutions, a deeper sound, resonant with the past, has continued, a bass line at a "lower frequency" not everyone can hear.[44]

For example, recall that 180,000 African Americans enlisted in the Union forces during the Civil War, attempting to play their part in the liberation of their people, particularly after the Emancipation Declaration freed the slaves in territory controlled by the South. These African Americans have been elevated to heroism in the feature film *Glory* and were honored in the monument to the Fifty-fourth Massachusetts by Augustus Saint-Gaudens, named the Shaw Monument after the regiment's white officer.[45] Southern slaves served their masters on the Confederate side. Never armed by their military leaders, as some African Americans in the Union forces were, these southern blacks served the Confederacy in the menial capacities to which whites restricted them, in the baggage train, hauling, cooking, and cleaning, or providing personal services to officers.[46] In the 1900s the Confederate advocacy groups, the United Daughters of the Confederacy and the Sons of Confederate Veterans, proposed to dedicate a memorial to the "faithful slaves" who served their white masters and mistresses during the Civil War. "Erecting this monument would influence for the good the present and coming generations, and prove that the people of the South who owned slaves valued and respected their good qualities as no one else ever did or would do."[47] The memorial was intended thus to honor the old way of life of the plantation South by promulgating the myth that African Americans were happy in the condition of servitude.

Although at first the Confederate organizations were uncertain how a faithful slave memorial would be received and decided not to proceed, by 1920 they were prepared to go ahead and chose Harpers Ferry as the site for the proposed memorial.[48] This was symbolically an important site, as the place where, in 1859, the emancipationist John Brown carried out a raid on a federal arsenal that was intended to set off a revolt of southern slaves but succeeded only in increasing the tensions between North and South.[49] After fighting local forces, Brown's company took refuge in an enginehouse that has since come to be known as the John Brown Fort. The raid was ended by a detachment of Marines led by Lieutenant Colonel Robert E. Lee, uncannily the same Robert E. Lee who led the Army of Northern Virginia in a series of successful campaigns for the Confederate cause, whose defeat at Gettysburg marked a turning point in the war, and whose surrender at Appomattox ended the military hopes of the Confederacy. After the war Harpers Ferry became the site of Storer College, an institution designed in the early, hopeful years of Reconstruction to train African American teachers. Harpers Ferry was also a frequent site of pilgrimages by African Americans who saw Brown as a hero, unique among emancipationists in his willingness to fight and sacrifice his life for the cause. Storer College obtained the John Brown Fort, moved it onto the college's grounds, and turned it into a museum, with a plaque commemorating the sacrifice that Brown and his followers offered for the sake of a new birth of freedom for the nation.[50]

The president of Storer College was an admirer of John Brown. Together with the local NAACP branch, he delayed the erection of the so-called faithful slave memorial in Harpers Ferry for a decade. The Confederate organizations purchased a stone tablet and wrote the text of an inscription, including the inflammatory phrase, "The negroes of this neighborhood, true to their Christian training, would have no part with those who offered PIKES and STAVES for BLOODY MASSACRE."[51] After this wording was removed, the monument was dedicated on October 10, 1931—sixty-three years to the day before the reenacted slave auction at Colonial Williamsburg.

The stone marker purports to honor Heyward Shepherd, an African American railroad employee in the town who was among the first victims of the raid. In the years following the end of the Civil War, apologists for the Confederacy who denounced Brown as a wild, demonic villain never tired of pointing out that Shepherd was black. Inconveniently for the purposes of a "faithful slave" memorial, though, Shepherd turned out not to have been a slave at all but a freeman, so some rhetorical work was required to make the appropriate point. While paying tribute to Shepherd's industry, which one might have supposed would be an affront to those who considered African Americans best employed under conditions of servitude, the United Daughters of the Confederacy extended the praise to the faithful slaves who resisted temptations during the years of war. This extraordinary piece of rhetoric not only praises slaves who did not run away to the Union side (as many did)[52] but uses their loyalty as a vote of confidence in the slave system itself. In praising Heyward Shepherd for the inglorious act of stopping a raider's bullet, the UDC actually applauds its own members, since the loyalty of southern slaves does honor not just to the slaves but to their masters and mistresses.

The Heyward Shepherd memorial became something of an embarrassment to its most recent stewards, the National Park Service, who removed it for storage during the restoration of the park's buildings in 1975. Members of the local community threatened vandalism and defacement if it was redisplayed, and consequently the memorial was replaced in a protective crate. This had the double virtue of protecting the memorial from damage and protecting the sensibilities of those who preferred it to remain out of sight. In 1981 the park superintendent met with the United Daughters of the Confederacy, the Sons of Confederate Veterans, the NAACP, and park employees, but they were unable to agree to another resolution of the impasse.[53]

The fate of the Heyward Shepherd memorial would have been more easily settled and the memorial itself less embarrassing were it simply a historical curiosity, reminding contemporary audiences of the proclivities of those who had gone before. However, as recently as 1993, a local NAACP representative found himself having to beat back a proposed monument in Nottoway County, Virginia, that would have expressed sentiments similar to those on the Heyward Shepherd memorial. The wish to redeem the Lost Cause, it seems, always threatens to exceed the container to which it is consigned, be it a wooden box or a textual frame. In August 1993 a local Virginia newspaper announced that the Sons of Confederate Veterans organization planned to add a commemorative marker to the Nottoway County, Virginia, Civil War memorial that would honor the African Americans who served the Confederate cause. They succeeded in winning the unanimous approval of the local government, a decision reversed after the intervention of Melvin Austin, the local NAACP representative. Citing the prophet Isaiah, Austin warned, "Woe unto them that call evil good," and he asserted that any memorial honoring this "dark side" of American history was an attempt to do just that. The Confederacy cannot be separated from slavery, Austin declared. The idea that slaves were happy was an attempt to justify the institution. There was no justice in honoring those who were forced to serve their masters, and if there were any willing to fight to defend the Confederacy, this was nothing to be proud of.[54] The Civil War, Austin told me, is still being fought in Virginia.

Notwithstanding these nearby events, a number of scholars encouraged the display of the Heyward Shepherd monument, and its curators decided that the erasure of the unpalatable views the memorial expressed was no more desirable than the unvarnished views themselves. In June 1995 two years after the NAACP had defeated a proposal for the Nottoway County memorial, the Heyward Shepherd memorial was reexposed. Accompanying it, however, was a text referring to the memorial's history and displaying the response to it by W. E. B. Du Bois.[55]

Du Bois's disgust at the memorial's dedication, which he described at the time as a "pro-slavery celebration," chimed with the responses of NAACP secretary Walter White and those of some of the leading black newspapers in the United States. Indeed, their assessment of the memorial's significance was quite apt, given the content of some of the dedication speeches pronounced from a platform draped with the Confederate colors. One speaker dwelt on John Brown and slavery, portraying Brown as a crazed criminal and describing slavery as a beneficial "period of indenture" or "racial apprenticeship" preparing African Americans for freedom. The president general of the UDC spoke of how well fed and clothed slaves had been, reminisced about her "black mammy," and rejoiced in the continual progress of the black race. "We sympathize with their aims and ambitions" as directed by leaders such as Booker T. Washington, she declared.[56] (Booker T. Washington was specifically praised by the white politician at Maya Angelou's graduation ceremony.)[57]

One who felt decidedly out of sympathy with the proceedings, though, was Pearl Tatten, the music director of Storer College, whose singers rose to provide music after the UDC leader's address. Tatten had already questioned the Storer College president's decision to participate in the dedication ceremony. Now she found herself and her singers, whether fortuitously or through tactical shrewdness, in a position to have the last word. Making an unscheduled statement before the singing began, she said, "I am the daughter of a Connecticut volunteer, who wore the blue, who fought for the freedom of my people, for which John Brown struck the first blow. Today we are looking to the future, forgetting those things of the past. We are pushing forward to a larger freedom, not in the spirit of the black mammy but in the spirit of new freedom and rising youth."[58] I wish I could report what the singers performed on that day; whatever it was, I think we can trust that Tatten's choice of repertoire did not do honor to the spirit of the Confederacy.

Although Tatten's statement would mark a fitting climax to the occasion, it was not her last word in the attendant debate, nor the end of the story. The furor attending the dedication resounded for months, much of it focused on the Storer College president's decision to participate in the ceremony. As a corrective to this earlier stance, the NAACP asked that it be allowed to place a tablet on the John Brown Fort, with a text written by Du Bois and an acknowledgment of the NAACP's sponsorship and the date. College president McDonald objected to the inscription and requested a simpler statement along the lines of "John Brown 1800–1859 'His Soul Goes Marching On.'" The NAACP, though, saw the Heyward Shepherd memorial as symbolic of an increasing stridency on the part of defenders of the South. At an NAACP meeting discussing Storer College's refusal to allow the tablet, Du Bois defended McDonald's proposed inscription and, suggesting that the UDC had put pressure on the college president, expressed sympathy for his predicament. And as she had at the dedication ceremony, Pearl Tatten made another unscheduled intervention. The students at the college, she said, did not need sympathy.[59]

What can we make of this exchange? In challenging the leading African American intellectual of his day, by rejecting sympathy as an appropriate response, what was Pearl Tatten getting at? Later, this statement was interpreted as meaning that the students and teachers opposed the university administration's decision, but that's not quite what she says. Surely the more direct rebuttal to Du Bois's statement of sympathy for McDonald would be to say that the students need Du Bois's sympathy, not the college president. Instead, Tatten questions both the appropriateness of the response and the quarter to which it is directed. You offer sympathy to McDonald, but the students do not need sympathy. The unanswered, unanswerable question Tatten forces us to ask is, Why not sympathy, and if not, what?

SYMPATHY

Paul Laurence Dunbar's poem "Sympathy" has three stanzas, each of which begins with a statement of shared knowledge: the poet says that he knows what the caged bird feels, how the bird beats his wing, and why the bird sings.[60] The narrator of the poem never tells us how he knows these things. And yet every element of the poem—the stirrings of spring that the bird sees, hears, and smells; the scars on wings beating vainly on the bars; and the song that the bird sings out to heaven—helps answer the question. If the narrator knows what the bird feels, it can only be because of a felt similarity to the bird's condition that the poem describes. Sympathy is not, therefore, a passive state of observation but is an imaginative projection through which one reads one's own experience through the medium of another.

The poem doubles this state of sympathy by requiring of the reader the capacity for imaginative projection that the poem itself describes. In order to make sense of the poem, the reader has to imagine how the narrator's feelings could be akin to those of the bird. And, no matter what answer one produces, one has to perform the kind of projective imagination that the narrator practices. "Sympathy" is the poem's title and subject, but it is also the condition produced in the reader by the act of reading.

The poem also dramatizes the act of expression. Whatever else a reader knows about Dunbar, we know that he is a poet. When we see, in the third and final stanza, that the bird's song is not a carol of joy or glee but a prayer flung up to heaven, we can deduce that Dunbar's poem can be described in the same terms, that what unites the narrator and his subject is not just their common entrapment but the pained, necessitous expression of the heart's deep core—even if, and perhaps especially if, the prayer is never heard. As the bird cannot escape the cage but can send aloft his song, so the poet cannot escape his bonds but can send forth his words. None of us can guess the content of the prayer or its effect, and the poet does not know whether or how his voice will be heard. And so we come to our starting place, but with a more problematic idea of sympathy. Sympathy is the condition of possibility for, and the measure of, understanding; but the poem also sits poised before the impossibility of knowing whether sympathy has been, or can ever be, achieved.

Maya Angelou answers by calling her autobiography *I Know Why the Caged Bird Sings.* Just as she, a poet, pays homage to generations of poets and singers, some unknown, so she seems to say to Dunbar, Yes, I get it; I know that, too.[61] In this way she places her own writing within a living tradition that does not refer to but constitutes a chain of collective recollection. Readers familiar with Dunbar's poetry can gather and extend this chain of references. Thus the literary allusion replicates at a lower register the sympathetic vibrations descending from the heavens with the caged bird's song.

I am trying to set off a resonance here with the deep bass note, the elusive knowledge to which I referred before. Maya Angelou writes of the inscrutability of people who speak in enigmas and parables, but it is not just her mother or members of her race who are hard to read. If understanding another's experience while respecting the other's difference is always a paradoxical task, this task has both a special urgency and some sharp difficulties when trying to share knowledge of racial oppression in a society in which such oppression still exists. Mutual knowledge is the product and the condition of possibility for whatever we might call communication. Yet some truths may be too painful to speak lightly, too heavy to bear without the dignity of many shoulders to carry the full weight of grief and indignation; representations of slavery may be just such proprietary truths to which no right of casual witness exists.[62] The deepest, least accessible reservoir of thought and feeling may also be the largest repository of a knowledge on which all other knowledge can draw.

So far as historical representation is concerned, the choice is not between opposed absolutes—visibility versus invisibility, truth versus falsehood—but is more finely measured. Our strategies for sharing historical knowledge must therefore recognize that the truths we convey and that others glean will always depend on the premises from which we proceed, and that discovering the subfoundations of our personal and our shared ground by inches and increments may be both inescapably vexing and painfully necessary.

NOTES

1. Introduction: Home Ground

1. Dell Upton, "White and Black Landscapes in Eighteenth-Century Virginia," in *Material Life in America, 1600–1800*, ed. Robert Blair St. George (Boston: Northeastern Univ. Press, 1988), 357–69; Mechal Sobel, *The World They Made Together: Black and White Values in Eighteenth-Century Virginia* (Princeton, NJ: Princeton Univ. Press, 1987).

2. James Weldon Johnson, *The Autobiography of an Ex-Coloured Man* (New York: Knopf, 1928). My thanks to Matthew Cohen for bringing this passage to my attention.

3. See the exemplary ethnographic accounts of this process by Keith H. Basso: "Wisdom Sits in Places: Notes on a Western Apache Landscape," in *Senses of Place*, ed. Steven Feld and Keith H. Basso (Santa Fe, NM: School of American Research Press, 1996), 53–90, and "'Stalking with Stories': Names, Places, and Moral Narratives among the Western Apache," in *Text, Play, and Story: The Construction and Reconstruction of Self and Society*, ed. Edward Bruner (Washington, DC: Proceedings of the American Ethnological Society, 1983), 19–55.

4. See also Maya Angelou's recollection of her grandmother's yard in *I Know Why the Caged Bird Sings* (New York: Bantam Books, 1969), 3–39. I thank John F. Szwed and Joanne Braxton for pointing out important passages.

5. Zora Neale Hurston, "The Gilded Six Bits," *Story* 3:14 (1933): 60.

6. Minnie Hite Moody, *Death Is a Little Man* (New York: Julian Messner, 1936), 4–5. Much of this local color and dialect literature is patently exoticizing, often racist, yet, read critically, the actual descriptions can be informative given the lack of other sources. For example, Donald Gray, *Black Echo* (New York: Pegasus Publishing, 1932), 103: "How much did Peggy or Mrs. Morris really know about Callie, Clay mused one day? Or about Mammy Sukey? What did they know of the dead live oak tree he had discovered one day, standing deep in the palmetto thicket, its bare limbs covered with a foliage of rags and fluttering papers and strings of other odd objects?"

7. Ben Robertson, *Red Hills and Cotton* (New York: Knopf, 1942), 60.

8. William Mahoney, *Black Jacob* (New York: Macmillan, 1969), 108.

9. V. S. Naipaul, *A Turn in the South* (New York: Knopf, 1989), 13.

10. On grave decoration and markers, see Robert Farris Thompson, *Flash of the Spirit: African and Afro-American Art and Philosophy* (New York: Vintage, 1983), 132–42; Robert Farris Thompson and Joseph Cornet, *The Four Moments of the Sun: Kongo Art in Two Worlds* (Washington, DC: National Gallery of Art, 1981), 193–210; Newbell Niles Puckett, *Folk Beliefs of the Southern Negro* (Chapel Hill:

Univ. of North Carolina Press, 1926), 80. See also John Michael Vlach, *The Afro-American Tradition in Decorative Arts* (Cleveland: Cleveland Museum of Art, 1978); Samuel Miller Lawton, "The Religious Life of South Carolina Coastal and Sea Island Negroes" (Ph.D. diss., George Peabody College for Teachers, 1939), 194–222; Elaine Nichols, ed., *The Last Miles of the Way: African-American Homegoing Traditions, 1890–Present* (Columbia: South Carolina State Museum, 1989); M. Ruth Little, "Afro-American Gravemarkers in North Carolina," in *Markers VI: The Journal of the Association for Gravestone Studies*, ed. Theodore Chase (Lanham, MD: Univ. Press of America, 1989), 102–34. On altar areas inside the home, see Lizzetta LeFalle-Collins, *Home and Yard: Black Folk Life Expressions in Los Angeles* (Los Angeles: California Afro-American Museum, 1987), 13–14, and her paper on "Mixed Media Assemblages in the Home" (Tuskegee, AL: The National Endowment for the Arts and Tuskegee University, 1985).

11. See my "African American History, Cosmology, and the Moral Universe of Edward Houston's Yard," *Journal of Garden History* 14:3 (Autumn 1994): 179–201, for a case study.

12. Melville J. Herskovits, *The Myth of the Negro Past* (rpt. Boston: Beacon, 1958), 197–206.

13. Comments about objects often echo those about expressive and performance styles.

14. Ernest Ingersoll, "The Decoration of Negro Graves," *Journal of American Folklore* 5 (1892): 69–70.

15. See Elizabeth Fenn, "Honoring the Ancestors: Kongo-American Graves in the American South," *Southern Exposure* 13:5 (1985): 42–47; Thompson and Cornet, *Four Moments*, 193–210, Wyatt MacGaffey, *Religion and Society in Central Africa: The Bakongo of Lower Zaire* (Chicago: Univ. of Chicago Press, 1986), 57.

16. E. J. Glave, "Fetishism in Congo Land," *Century Magazine* 19 (1891): 835; H. Carrington Bolton, "Decoration of Graves of Negroes in South Carolina," *Journal of American Folklore* 4 (1891): 214.

17. See illustration in Cynthia Connor, "Archaeological Analysis of African-American Mortuary Behavior," in Nichols, *Last Miles*, 55.

18. Puckett, *Folk Beliefs*, 124.

19. Harry Middleton Hyatt, *Hoodoo—Conjuration—Witchcraft—Rootwork: Beliefs Accepted by Many Negroes and White Persons, These Being Orally Recorded among Blacks and Whites* (Hannibal, MO: Western Publishing, 1970), 1304.

20. John F. Szwed and Roger D. Abrahams, *Afro-American Folk Culture: An Annotated Bibliography of Materials from North, Central, and South America and the West Indies*, 2 vols. (Philadelphia: Institute for the Study of Human Issues, 1978).

21. Effie Graham, *The Passin' On Party* (Chicago: McClurg, 1912), 24–25.

22. Ibid., 26.

23. Wyatt MacGaffey, "The Black Loincloth and the Son of Nzambi Mpungu," in *Forms of Folklore in Africa: Narrative, Poetic, Gnomic, Dramatic*, ed. Bernth Lindfors (Austin: Univ. of Texas Press, 1977), 148. Sewing machines or stone or cement replicas also appear on Bakongo graves; see Thompson and Cornet, *Four*

Moments, 144, 146. On whiteness and kaolin, see Thompson, *Flash*, 134–35; Lawton, "Religious Life," 148–54. R. F. Thompson also pointed out to me (personal communication, July 20, 1993) that the wheeled baby buggy is a mobilized vehicle, ideal for transport to and from the other world. Also, as Mrs. Hamler said in an interview on Dec. 20, 1989, of the many wheels and tire planters in her yard: "They show we're rolling; in this house we're rolling." Black audiences sometimes call, "You're rolling now!" to show approval for a performer who has hit his or her stride. Another factor in the significance of the wheel in some African American yards in the southern United States is the fact that the pronunciation of the words *wheel* and *will* are virtually the same. Thus the wheel can serve logographically as a material sign for "will," as in *God's will* / *God's wheel*.

24. Richard Westmacott, *African-American Gardens and Yards in the Rural South* (Knoxville: Univ. of Tennessee Press), 103–4.

25. Ibid., 48.

2. Vibrational Affinities

1. The few hints given by Lusane for viewing his work are located within his automobile. A note on the decorated dashboard says, "If you don't like / my shit / please / look another way." Elsewhere, under a label that says "inspirational Words to Live By" is: "Please don't / make fun at my work / Because Everything / I do I try to do it Good if you don't believe it please / try me." And scattered throughout the car are commercial stickers such as "Samuel Johnson: 'Great works are performed not by strength but by perseverance,'" and "Thomas Edison: 'Genius is one percent inspiration and ninety-nine percent perspiration.'"

2. This line appears in later recordings as well, such as the western swing version, "Garbage Man Blues," by Milton Brown and His Musical Brownies in 1934 or the Harlem Hamfats' "The Garbage Man" in 1936.

3. John O'Brian, *Interviews with Black Writers* (New York: Liveright, 1973).

4. Greg Tate, "Silence, Exile, and Cunning," *Village Voice*, Oct. 15, 1991, 87, 90.

5. Ian Hoare, "Mighty, Mighty Spade and Whitey: Black Lyrics and Soul's Interaction with White Culture," in *The Soul Book*, ed. Ian Hoare, Tony Cummings, Clive Anderson, and Simon Firth (New York: Dell, 1975), 193.

6. Neil Strauss, "Trippping the Light Ecstatic: Psychic TV and the Acid House Experience," *Option* 25 (March–April 1989): 82.

7. Graham Lock, *Forces in Motion: Anthony Braxton and the Meta-Reality of Creative Music* (London: Quartet Books, 1988).

8. Umberto Eco, *The Open Work* (1962; rpt. Cambridge: Harvard Univ. Press, 1989), 4.

3. Big-Hearted Power: Kongo Influence on the Landscape and Art of Black America

This chapter was organized from typescripts provided by Professor Thompson which, together, summarize his research on yard shows to date. Portions of this research have also appeared in Thompson's publications *The Four Moments of the*

Sun: Kongo Art in Two Worlds (Washington, D.C.: National Gallery of Art, 1981); "The Circle and the Branch: Renascent Kongo-American Art," in *Another Face of the Diamond: Pathways through the Black Atlantic South* (New York: INTAR Latin American Gallery, 1988); "The Song That Named the Land: The Visionary Presence of African-American Art," in *Black Art: Ancestral Legacy* (Dallas: Dallas Museum of Art); and *Face of the Gods: Art and Altars of the African Americas* (New York: Museum for African Art and Munich: Prestel, 1993).

1. John Noble Wilford, "Old Pipes Offer New View of Black Life in Colonies," *New York Times*, July 12, 1988, C1.

2. Matthew Emerson, an anthropologist at the University of California, Berkeley, quoted in ibid.

3. Mechal Sobel, *The World They Made Together: Black and White Values in Eighteenth-Century Virginia* (Princeton, NJ: Princeton Univ. Press, 1987), 37.

4. The estimate of a third stems from a lecture by Philip Curtin at Calhoun College in Yale University in 1977; the estimate of one-fourth comes from James A. Rawley's *The Trans-Atlantic Slave Trade* (New York: Norton, 1981), 335.

5. For details, see my chapters in Robert Farris Thompson and Joseph Cornet, *The Four Moments of the Sun: Kongo Art in Two Worlds* (Washington, DC: National Gallery of Art, 1981).

6. Ibid.

7. Karl Edward Laman, *The Kongo III* (Upsala: Statens Humanistiska Forskningrad, 1962), 102. The term *nkisi lusoli* comes from fieldwork in Manianga, Bas-Zaire, summer 1986, and Vili country in the People's Republic of Congo, summer 1987. I thank Balu Balila of Mwanda, Bas-Zaire, and the chief of Luango in the R. P. du Congo for facilitating this research. See also Buakasa Tulu Kia Mpansu, *L'impensé du discours* (Kinshasa: Faculté de Théologie Catholique, 1980), 234.

8. Informants: Balu Balila, Mwanda, and Fu-Kiau Bunseki, from Kumba, Bas-Zaire.

9. Laman, *Kongo III*, 136.

10. Thompson and Cornet, *Four Moments*, chap. 2.

11. Ibid.

12. Yvette Grimaud and Gilbert Rouget, *Notes on the Music of the Bushmen Compared to That of the Babinga Pygmies* (Cambridge: Peabody Museum, n.d.), 3.

13. Quoted in Harold Courlander, *Negro Folk Music U.S.A.* (New York: Columbia Univ. Press, 1963), 81.

14. Albert Murray, *Train Whistle Guitar* (New York: McGraw-Hill, 1974), 8. The very title of this novel demonstrates Murray's impeccable sense of black aesthetic history.

15. Daniel G. Hoffman, "Jazz: The Survival of a Folk Art," *Perspectives USA* 15 (spring 1956): 33.

16. Earl Leaf photographed an early transformation of oil drum into percussion drum in his *Isles of Rhythm* (New York: A. S. Barnes, 1948), 191.

17. Compare also Charles Keil's chapter "Soul and Solidarity" in his *Urban Blues* (Chicago: Univ. of Chicago Press, 1966), 164–90.

18. Telephone conversation, Oct. 1, 1988, with Judith McWillie, who kindly shared this information with me.

19. Kongo cosmogrammatic phrasing is documented in the oldest known Kikongo dictionary, Latin-Spanish-Kikongo, dated 1652, Georges de Gheel, which lists:

Nza: world, universe

Nza ya yonzo: the universe

Nza yanene: macrocosm

Nza yawelo: microcosm

See *Le plus ancient dictionnaire Bantu, Vocabularium Georgii Gelensis*, ed. J. Van Wing and C. Penders, S.J. (Louvain: Imprimerie J. Kuyl-Otto, 1928), 279. See also Wyatt MacGaffey, "Bakongo Cosmology," *The World and I*, Sept. 1988, 512–21.

20. Quoted in John M. Janzen and Wyatt S. MacGaffey, *An Anthology of Kongo Religion* (Lawrence: Univ. of Kansas, 1974), 34. In this citation Fu-Kiau also remarks that "the cross was known to the Ba-Kongo before the arrival of the Europeans, and corresponds to the understanding in their minds of their relationship to the world."

21. Laman, *Kongo III*, 217

22. A. Fu-Kiau Kia Bunseki-Lumanisa, *N'Kongo Ye Nza Yakun'zugdila: Nza Kongo* (Kinshasa: Office National de la Recherché et de Développement, 1969), 9.

23. Thompson and Cornet, *Four Moments*, 28.

24. Ibid., 152.

25. Cf. Lydia Cabrera, *La regla Kimbisi del Santo Cristo del Buen Viaje* (Miami: Peninsular Printing, 1977); *Reglas de Congo* (Miami: Peninsular Printing, 1979); *Vocabulario Congo* (Miami: Daytona Press, 1984).

26. I am grateful to Andy Porrón for allowing me to document protective *palo* (Kongo-Cuban signs) at Botánica San Antonio, June 1, 1984, New York City.

27. Glossed by Fu-Kiau Bunseki, personal communication, June 1984.

28. Thompson and Cornet, *Four Moments*, 152.

29. Sterling Stuckey, *Slave Culture: Nationalist Theory and the Foundations of Black America* (New York: Oxford Univ. Press, 1987).

30. Marshall Stearns, *The Story of Jazz* (New York: Oxford Univ. Press, 1956), 13.

31. See also my *Face of the Gods: Art and Altars of Africa and the African Americas* (New York: Museum for African Art and Munich: Prestel, 1993), 85, 93, 95.

32. Personal communication, June 1984.

33. Cited under the caption "Tire Art" on a postcard dated 1976 published by the Center for Southern Folklore, Memphis. I thank William Ferris for bringing this visual document to my attention.

34. Lucas, telephone conversation, Aug. 1988.

35. Michael D. Hall, *Stereoscopic Perspective: Reflections on American Fine and Folk Art* (Ann Arbor, MI: UMI Research Press, 1988), 242 and fig. 64.

36. Brad Drach, with Maria Leonhouser, "Scene," *People*, Aug. 15, 1988, 58–60.

37. Telephone interview with Tyree Guyton, Aug. 1988.

38. Interview with Joe Light, Aug. 1988.

39. Courlander, in his *Negro Folk Music U.S.A.*, 52, talks about black religious singing focusing on the image of the gospel wheel in Ezekiel:

"And the big wheel run by faith
And the little wheel run by the Grace of God
A wheel within a wheel
Way in the middle of the air."

40. Interview, Oct. 1988.

41. Ralph Wiskiser, Carol Durieux, and John Crady, *Mardi Gras Day* (New York: Henry Holt, 1948), illustration at p. 19. See also p. 18, on "the Spasm band": "The leader gives the beat, and the washboard rhythm, from tin cans, wires, and homemade percussion instruments."

42. I am grateful to Marion Brown for allowing me to examine photographs of his shining metal disks and other percussion from the early 1970s. I also thank Leo Smith for data on his "steelophone" during conversations in New Haven, summer 1974.

43. A. B. Spellman, *Black Music* (New York: Schocken Books, 1970), 36–37.

44. Informant: John Biggers.

45. Ibid. I am enormously indebted to John Biggers for sharing the lore of his youth in Gastonia, N.C. Not only is he a major American artist, he is also a living Rosetta Stone for the decoding of the African American yard show. I could not have written this without him.

46. Informant: Lonnie Holley, Birmingham, Ala., 1988.

47. Robert Farris Thompson, *L'éclaire primordial* (Paris: Editions Caribéens, 1985), 154–55. See also Robert Farris Thompson, *Flash of the Spirit: African and Afro-American Art and Philosophy* (New York: Random House, 1983).

48. Lizzetta LeFalle-Collins, *Home and Yard: Black Folk Life Expressions in Los Angeles* (Los Angeles: California Afro-American Museum, 1988), 16.

49. John M. Janzen, *Lemba, 1650–1930: A Drum of Affliction in Africa and the New World* (New York: Garland Publishing, 1982), 52.

50. John H. Weeks, *Among the Primitive Bakongo* (London: Seeley, Service, 1914), 117.

51. Ibid., 238.

52. Informant: Fu-Kiau Bunseki, summer 1988.

53. Weeks, *Bakongo*, 239.

54. Informant: Fu-Kiau Bunseki, summer 1987.

55. L'Abbé Proyart, *Histoire de Loango, Kakongo, et autres royaumes d'Afrique* (Paris: Bruyset-Ponthus, 1776), 192–93. My translation.

56. John M. Janzen, *The Quest for Therapy: Medical Pluralism in Lower Zaire* (Berkeley: Univ. of California Press, 1982), 164–68. See especially the fascinating map of Nzoamambu's garden village with its plants and their uses.

57. Janzen and MacGaffey, *Anthology of Kongo Religion*, 35.

58. Thomas Atwood, *The History of the Island of Dominica* (London: Johnson, 1791).

59. Samuel Selvon, *Ways of Sunlight* (Bungay: Longman Drumbeat, 1957), 95–96.

60. Esteban Montejo, *The Autobiography of a Runaway Slave*, ed. Miguel Barnet (New York: Pantheon Books, 1968), 142.

61. Lyle Saxon, Edward Dreyer, and Robert Tallant, eds., *Gumbo Yaya: A Collection*

of Louisiana Folk Tales (New York: Bonanza Books, 1945), 554–55, 543, , 542.

62. Peter H. Wood and Karen C. C. Dalton, *Winslow Homer's Images of Blacks: The Civil War and Reconstruction Years* (Austin: Univ. of Texas Press, 1988), illustrated at p. 57. Wood argues a relation between gourds and the Big Dipper in the sky at night, which blacks called "The Drinking Gourd" pointing north in the direction of freedom at the end of the Underground Railroad.

63. Personal communication from Tom Crocket, Feb. 2, 1988.

64. Montejo, *Autobiography*, 142.

65. Marie Rudisill with James C. Simmon, *Truman Capote* (New York: William Morrow, 1983), 144. I have standardized Rudisill's overwrought "dialect" transcription.

66. Informant: Thornton "Buck" Dial, North Bessemer, Ala., July 1988.

67. From a conversation with Willie Collins, UCLA, Los Angeles, spring 1989.

68. James Seay, "The Bluebottle Tree," *Mississippi Folklore Register* 111:3 (fall 1969): 108.

69. Telephone conversation with Thornton Dial, Oct. 1988.

70. Informant: Fu-Kiau Bunseki, summer 1985.

71. I warmly thank Jack Maxie, of Eleuthera, for documenting on my behalf a bottle tree there in 1985 in a style not unlike the one described by Selvon on the island of Trinidad.

72. Personal communication, Dec. 11, 1986. William Eiland remembers several bottle trees in his childhood in Perry County, Ala., and notes the making process: "breaking the branches of the tree and jamming a coke bottle or some similar and readily available bottle." He also notes the recent trend toward plastic Clorox bottles, which is also occurring in Mississippi.

73. John Nunley, personal communication, May 1993.

74. Laman, *Kongo III*, 125, fig. 20.

75. Ibid., 112.

76. Wyatt MacGaffey, "Complexity, Astonishment, and Power: The Vocabulary of the Kongo Minkisi," *Journal of Southern African Studies* 14:2 (Jan. 1988): 196.

77. I thank Patricia Dwight, of Charleston, S.C., for bringing this story to my attention in a conversation on Oct. 2, 1987. Nina Langley, who played by a pool believed to be inhabited by simbi on the Pooshee plantation at some point between 1915 and 1921, is Patricia Dwight's mother.

78. For a published account of simbi worship on Pooshee plantation in Berkeley County, S.C. (the pools and the plantation were all later submerged by Lake Moultrie), see Robert Wilson, *Half Forgotten Byways of the Old South* (Columbia, SC: The State Company, 1928), 156–57: "We come suddenly upon a dozen or more little basins, the largest not over six feet by nine, which have no outlet whatever. . . . You must go fifteen miles before reaching another of these springs or fountains, and then ten more to do the last of the chain, the famous Eutaw Springs. . . . Here, then, must be a subterranean river . . . at least twenty-eight miles long. . . . The imagination of the negroes has not been idle in such a suggestion field, and they have peopled these fountains with spirits which they call 'cymbies.'"

79. Laman, *Kongo III*, 38.

80. For details, see Wyatt MacGaffey, *Religion and Society in Central Africa: The Bakongo of Lower Zaire* (Chicago: Univ. of Chicago Press, 1986), 86: "Women of a matrilineage in which twins are born are supposed to know which streams or pools are the homes of the particular bisimbi incarnated in their lines." See also ibid., 85: "Twins, as *bisimbi*, use supernatural power."

81. E. C. L. Adams, *Nigger to Nigger* (New York: Scribner's, 1928), 228, "Gullah Joe": "When I thinks er my tribe an' my friend an' my daddy an' my mammy an' de great feenda [cf. Kikongo, *mfinda*, "forest"] a feelin' rises up in my th'oat an' my eye well wid tear."

82. Conversation with Ralph Griffin, Aug. 1988.

83. Fernando Ortiz, *Los instrumentos de la música afrocubana* I (Havana: Ministerio de Educación, 1952): 196–203. According to Ortiz, the hook of the *lungówa* mystically "hauls in spirits or persons" (198).

84. See Robert Farris Thompson, "Siras Bowens of Sunbury, Georgia," in *Chant of Saints*, ed. Michael S. Harper and Robert Steptoe (Champaign: Univ. of Illinios Press, 1979), 234, pl. 4.

85. Interview, Oct. 1988.

86. See Thompson and Cornet, *Four Moments*.

87. See illustration in Thompson, *Face of the Gods*, 86, pl. 71.

4. Art, Healing, and Power in the Afro-Atlantic South

All quotes, unless otherwise indicated, are from conversations of artists with the author recorded on videotape between 1984 and 1995.

1. Marc Dachy, *The Dada Movement, 1915–1923* (Geneva: Editions d'Art Albert Skira, 1990), 74.

2. James Clifford, *The Predicament of Culture: Twentieth Century Ethnography, Literature, and Art* (Cambridge: Harvard Univ. Press, 1988), 95.

3. Robert Plant Armstrong, *The Powers of Presence: Consciousness, Myth, and Affecting Presence* (Philadelphia: Univ. of Pennsylvania Press, 1981), 71.

4. Ibid., 72.

5. Grey Gundaker, "Double Sight," *Even the Deep Things of God: A Quality of Mind in Afro Atlantic Traditional Art* (Pittsburgh: Pittsburgh Center for the Arts, 1990), 5.

6. Albert Murray, *The Blue Devils of Nada: A Contemporary American Approach to Aesthetic Statement* (New York: Pantheon Books, 1996), 94.

7. Robert Plant Armstrong, *Wellspring: On the Myth and Source of Culture* (Berkeley: Univ. of California Press, 1975), 30.

8. Photographs may be seen at the Georgia Historical Society, Savannah, Ga.

9. Gabriel M. Setiloane, *African Theology: An Introduction* (Johannesburg: Skotaville Publishers, 1986), 10.

10. Gundaker, "Double Sight," 4.

11. Arthur C. Danto, "Artifact and Art," in *Art / Artifact: African Art in Anthropology Collections* (New York: Center for African Art and Prestel Verlag, 1989), 18.

12. Armstrong, *Powers*, 10–11.

13. Harry Middleton Hyatt, *Hoodoo—Conjuration—Witchcraft— Rootwork: Beliefs Accepted by Many Negroes and White Persons, These Being Orally Recorded among Blacks and Whites* (Hannibal, MO: Western Publishing, 1970), 934, 935–36, preface.

14. Robert Farris Thompson and Joseph Cornet, *The Four Moments of the Sun: Kongo Art in Two Worlds* (Washington, DC: National Gallery of Art, 1981), 183.

15. See Gianfranco Baruchello and Henry Martin, *Why Duchamp? An Essay on Aesthetic Impact* (Kingston, NY: McPherson, 1985), 38.

16. Hesketh J. Bell, *Obeah: Witchcraft in the West Indies* (London: Sampson Low, Markston, 1893), 1–5.

17. Personal communication, 1986.

18. Armstrong, *Powers*, 7, 10–13.

19. Armstrong, *Wellspring*, 31–32.

20. Marcel Duchamp quoted in *Theories and Documents of Contemporary Art: A Sourcebook of Artist's Writings*, ed. Kristine Stiles and Peter Selz (Berkeley: Univ. of California Press, 1996), 819–20.

21. Ibid., 119.

22. Armstrong, *Powers*, 10.

23. William Rubin, *Dada, Surrealism, and Their Heritage* (1968), quoted in Thompson and Cornet, *Four Moments*, 181.

24. Hyatt, *Hoodoo* 5:4018.

25. Armstrong, *Powers*, 72, 67–69; see also chap. 3 above.

26. Adin Steinsaltz, "To Strive toward Spirit," *Parabola: Myth, Tradition, and the Search for Meaning*, fall 1996, 62.

27. Armstrong, *Powers*, 69.

28. Stephen Jay Gould, *Time's Arrow and Time's Cycle: Myth and Metaphor in the Discovery of Geological Time* (Cambridge: Harvard Univ. Press, 1987), 15–16.

29. Hyatt, *Hoodoo* 2:941.

30. Armstrong, *Powers*, 122, 68–69.

31. See Thompson and Cornet, *Four Moments*, and chap. 3 above.

32. Wyatt MacGaffey, *Religion and Society in Central Africa: The Bakongo of Lower Zaire* (Chicago: Univ. of Chicago Press, 1986), 45, 119.

33. Armstrong, *Powers*, 70.

34. Wole Soyinka, *Myth, Literature, and the African World* (Cambridge: Cambridge Univ. Press, 1976), 10, 144.

35. Ibid., 10.

36. Duchamp quoted in Stiles and Selz, *Theories*, 819.

37. Baruchello, *Why Duchamp?* 54, 36.

38. See Murray, *Blue Devils*, 137.

5. Sacred Places and Holy Ground: West African Spiritualism at Stagville Plantation

1. John S. Mbiti, *African Religions and Philosophy* (1969; rpt. London: Morrison & Gibb, 1979), 4–5.

2. Ibid., 3.

3. Ibid., 4–5.

4. Ibid., 4.

5. Ibid., 121.

6. Ibid.

7. Ibid., 121–22.

8. Ibid., 122.

9. Malidoma Patrice Somé, *Of Water and the Spirit: Ritual, Magic, and Initiation in the Life of an African Shaman* (New York: G. P. Putnam's Sons, 1994), 2–3.

10. Basil Davidson, *African Kingdoms: Great Ages of Man* (New York: Time-Life Books, 1971), 148–49.

11. Kwabena F. Ashanti, *Rootwork and Voodoo in Mental Health* (Durham, NC: Tone Books, 1990), 203.

12. Ibid.

13. Ibid., 207–9.

14. Ibid., 95–96.

15. *Encyclopedia of Magic and Superstition* (London: MacDonald, 1988), 26–27.

16. Ibid., 27.

17. Ibid., 26.

18. A. E. Jones, "Afro-American Cultural Traditions of Stagville and Fairntosh Plantations" (M.A. thesis, North Carolina Central University, 1986), 46–52.

19. A. E. Jones, "Afro-American Cultural Traditions of Stagville and Fairntosh Plantations: Part 2" (Oral History Interviews, Stagville Plantation Center, 1988), app.

6. South of the North, North of the South: Spatial Practice in David Bradley's *The Chaneysville Incident*

Thanks to Grey Gundaker and Susan Craddock for extensive feedback on the ideas presented in this chapter. I am grateful to members of the Yale Agrarian Studies Colloquia, particularly Dilip Menon, for more incisive comments than I could ever hope to respond to in a work of this length. I wish also to acknowledge Kay Williams of the Pioneer Historical Society of Bedford County and Joseph Williams and Bill Anderson who graciously opened their homes and shared their thoughts about Bedford with me. The chapter is dedicated to David Bradley, who will most likely think I've talked about John Washington too much.

1. David Bradley, *The Chaneysville Incident* (1981; rpt. New York: Avon, 1982), 143.

2. Madan Sarup, "Home and Identity," in *Travellers' Tales: Narratives of Home and Displacement*, ed. George Robertson et al. (New York: Routledge, 1994), 97–98.

3. Examples of the theoretical literature on the spatial constitution of social relations which have been key to my thinking are: Derek Gregory and John Urry, *Social Relations and Spatial Structures* (Basingstoke, UK: Macmillan, 1985); Allan R. Pred, *Making Histories and Constructing Human Geographies* (Boulder, CO: Westview, 1991); Henri Lefebvre, *The Production of Space*, trans. Donald Nicholson-Smith (Cambridge: Basil Blackwell, 1991); Doreen B. Massey, *Spatial Divisions of Labor* (New York: Methuen, 1984).

4. The uneven development of "modernization," it goes without saying, is not just spatial. It is spatial-historical. Consider this comment from the slave narrative of Isaac Williams: "Then master got me to persuade Matthew [his fellow slave] not to run away. He wouldn't tell Matthew he was afraid of his running, but would tell him he couldn't get away,—that times were so straight with the telegraph and railway, that he couldn't get away. And that's what keeps the poor fellows there" (Benjamin Drew, *A North-Side View of Slavery. The Refugee: or the Narratives of Fugitive Slaves in Canada. Related by Themselves, with an Account of the History and Condition of the Colored Population of Upper Canada* [1856; rpt. New York: Johnson Reprint Corp., 1968], 58). Thus, in Williams's wry comment, what made whites mobile, kept blacks in place.

5. See Michel de Certeau, *The Practice of Everyday Life*, trans. Steven Rendall (Berkeley: Univ. of California Press, 1984), especially the chapter "Walking in the City." Strictly speaking, spatial practice for Certeau denotes a praxis resistant to the "concept city" of planning authorities. My meaning is closer to that elaborated by Pred, *Making Histories*, and Pred and Watts, *Reworking Modernity: Capitalisms and Symbolic Discontent* (New Brunswick, NJ: Rutgers Univ. Press, 1992), in that practice must be seen as at one and the same time both enabling and constraining.

6. As there are a number of possible meanings of *signifying* (or *signifyin[g]*) in African American culture, I should specify its use here. I use the term at what I take to be its most basic level of meaning: it is, following Gates, the trope-indicative trope, the "trope of tropes." To signify is to indicate (in speech but also in other communicative acts) that one is communicating in figures, that one intends there to be multiple meanings in the utterance. See Henry Louis Gates Jr., *Figures in Black: Words, Signs, and the "Racial" Self* (New York: Oxford Univ. Press, 1987), especially the last chapter; and Gates, *The Signifying Monkey: A Theory of Afro-American Literary Criticism* (New York: Oxford Univ. Press, 1988). I am struck by something Gates says in the preface of the latter book which may shed some light on spatial practice and signifying in *Chaneysville*. "My fascination with black language stems from my father's enjoyment of absolute control over its manipulation," Gates writes on p. xi. "My father has mastered black language rituals, certainly; he also has the ability to analyze them, to tell you what he is doing, why, and how. He is a very self-conscious language user. He is not atypical." In light of this, can one not be even a little more stunned at Moses taking John on such a silent tour, whose silence seems now more bursting with content? Moses, we learn later, is the master of space. He knows every surface of the South County, from the inner sanctums of the local bourgeoisie to the caves and outcropping of the forests. It is as if rather than telling John in words what

he is doing, John must enter the language itself, must act (it) out, must apprehend signifieds before broaching signifiers.

7. Gerald Early, *Culture of Bruising: Essays on Prizefighting, Literature, and Modern American Culture* (Hopewell, NJ: Ecco Press, 1994), 161. The potential burden of preserving too much should be read against the obstacles of writing African American history at all. See Charles Blockson's thoroughgoing account of the difficulties of reconstructing genealogical histories, *Black Genealogy* (Englewood Cliffs, NJ: Prentice-Hall, 1977).

8. See James Scott, *Moral Economy of the Peasant* (New Haven: Yale Univ. Press, 1976). For a discussion similar to what I am calling moral economy of information, see Dorris Sommer, "Resisting the Heat: Menchu, Morrison, and Incompetent Readers," in *Cultures of United States Imperialism*, ed. Donald Pease and Amy Kaplan (Durham, NC: Duke Univ. Press, 1993), 407–33.

9. The conditions under which former slaves wrote their own stories is nonetheless a matter of debate. It was not unusual for the narratives to have been ghostwritten or dictated. See Charles Davis and Henry Louis Gates Jr., eds., *The Slave's Narrative* (New York: Oxford Univ. Press, 1985), introduction and especially the contribution by Robin W. Winks, "The Making of a Fugitive Slave Narrative: Josiah Henson and Uncle Tom—A Case Study," 112–46. Related to the debate over authorship is the response of nineteenth-century white northern audiences to the orations of fugitive slaves. They wondered whether the accounts were factual or not. See Larry Gara, "The Professional Fugitive in the Abolition Movement," *Wisconsin Magazine of History* 48 (1965): 196–204.

10. Frederick Douglass, *My Bondage and My Freedom*, ed. William L. Andrews (1855; rpt. Chicago: Univ. of Illinois Press, 1987), 196.

11. Ibid., 197. In his earlier autobiography Douglass made similar statements. See Douglass, *Narrative of the Life of Frederick Douglass, an American Slave* (1845), ed. Houston A. Baker Jr. (New York: Penguin, 1987), 137–38.

12. James Olney, "'I Was Born': Slave Narratives, Their Status as Autobiography and as Literature," in Davis and Gates, *The Slave's Narrative*, 152–53 and n.3. See also Gara, "The Professional Fugitive."

13. Gara quotes a New Bedford, Mass., abolitionist who regretted the withholding of details because "many and many a tale of romantic horror can the slaves tell." In this particular instance the man felt it was "a great pity, for there never was a prettier one [i.e., tale]" (Gara, "The Professional Fugitive," 197). N.B.: the subtitle to Still's *The Underground Railroad* is "narrating the hardships, hair-breadth escapes and death struggles."

14. Douglass, *My Bondage*, 4.

15. Bradley, *Chaneysville*, 49–50.

16. There is a double meaning to "what a man's dying really means" that becomes apparent later. The first, as John Washington indicates, has to do with what is lost. The second has to do with what returns, the spirit, which can in fact help to fill in the "gaps." In the case of Old Jack, his return comes in the form of a voice that John hears just before telling Judith the story of the slaves near the end of the

novel. I discuss this later in the chapter. I read these aspects of the novel in light of
Berry and Blassingame's discussion of ghosts, hants, etc. "Many features of African
cosmology regarding ghosts were retained in the Americas. The slaves believed that
a person's soul remained on earth three days after death, visiting friends and enemies, and that ghosts remained near graveyards, communicated with and could harm
or help the living, and might return to claim property which had belonged to them.
The main function of the ghost in the quarters was as in Africa, to engender respect
for the dead. The slaves universally believed, according to many nineteenth-century
observers, that if 'the living neglect in any way their duty to the dead, they may be
haunted by them'" (Mary F. Berry and John W. Blassingame, "Africa, Slavery, and
the Roots of Contemporary Black Culture," in *Chant of Saints*, ed. Michael S.
Harper and Robert B. Stepto [Chicago: Univ. of Illinois Press, 1979], 248).

17. Bradley, *Chaneysville*, 37.

18. For example, ibid., 72–73.

19. Ibid., 23–24.

20. Ibid., 1.

21. Ibid., 399.

22. Ibid., 400.

23. Slave narratives are riddled with humorous accounts of the stupidity of
whites who cannot read their signs. Two examples from Isaac Williams's narrative,
both recalling his near capture while on the run: "I said to him [Dr. ——], 'Yes, we
are willing to go with you, and will go without any trouble, —I came without any
trouble, and will go without any trouble,'—but he did not know my meaning." And,
"On our way we met two white men, who asked us, 'Where are you going?' I told
them, 'home.' 'Where?' 'In Baltimore.' 'Where have you been?' 'Chopping wood for
John Brown'" (Drew, *A North-Side View of Slavery*, 60, 66).

24. Bradley, *Chaneysville*, 408.

25. Ibid.

26. Paul Jefferson, ed., *The Travels of William Wells Brown* (New York: Markus
Wiener Publishing, 1991), 61.

27. Ibid., 66.

28. Drew, *North-Side View*, 60.

29. Bradley, *Chaneysville*, 145.

30. Two excellent examples of the literature on black migration are: W. E. B. Du
Bois, *The Black North in 1901: A Social Study* (New York: Arno Press, 1969); Daniel
M. Johnson and Rex R. Campbell, *Black Migration in America: A Social
Demographic History* (Durham, NC: Duke Univ. Press, 1981).

31. Bradley, *Chaneysville*, 69.

32. Ibid., 70–71.

33. Douglass, *My Bondage*, 291.

34. Bracha Lichtenberg-Ettinger, "The Becoming Threshold of Matrixial
Borderlines," in Robertson, *Travellers' Tales*, 38.

35. See Julius Yanuck, "The Garner Fugitive Slave Case," *Mississippi Valley
Historical Review* 40 (1953): 47–66, which recounts a similar episode in which

Margaret Garner, an escaped slave from Kentucky, took the lives of two of her children rather than let them be returned to slavery.

36. Bradley, *Chaneysville*, 449. N.B.: The figures that John names here, Crawley, Graham, and Iames, are real historical figures. Crawley and Graham are long-known "operatives" on the Underground Railroad in Bedford County. See Wilbur H. Siebert, *The Underground Railroad from Slavery to Freedom* (New York: Macmillan, 1899). Iames is the name of a Bedford County family who has long resided in the area. The unmarked stones can be seen in the old family plot on a remote hillside outside of Chaneysville.

37. See Stanley Campbell, *The Slave Catchers: Enforcement of the Fugitive Slave Law, 1850–1860* (Chapel Hill: Univ. of North Carolina Press, 1968), 112, 6.

38. The first of the national fugitive laws was in 1793. It was ineffective in that extradition was left up to slave owners and local officials. See Paul Finkelman, ed., *Fugitive Slaves* (New York: Garland Publishing Co., 1989), and Thomas D. Morris, *Free Men All: The Personal Liberty Laws of the North* (Baltimore: Johns Hopkins Univ. Press, 1974). In 1826 Pennsylvania passed a law which was supposed to make capture easier but in practice was an impediment. Not only did it require the slave owner to provide proof of ownership, but it reduced the number of officials with the authority to administer the 1793 law. See William R. Leslie, "The Pennsylvania Fugitive Slave Act of 1826," *Journal of Southern History* 13 (1952): 429–45. In fact the articulation of federal and local legislation was a perennial problem for slave-holding interests. Preventing such articulation through the passage of personal liberty laws was a fundamental strategy of the North to prevent encroachment of southern power. Abolitionists favored these laws for obvious reasons. And northerners who had no particular feeling one way or the other about the slaves favored the laws because they were perceived as stymieing southern economic expansion. In 1842 the Supreme Court found the personal liberty laws unconstitutional in *Prigg v. Pennsylvania*. Not to be stopped, Pennsylvania passed legislation five years later which prohibited state officials and judges from taking jurisdiction in fugitive slave cases and prevented the use of state or local jails and prisons for incarcerating captured slaves. Nor were slaves to be taken heedless of due process. When the next piece of national legislation on the capture of fugitives came down in 1850, it encouraged the passage of yet newer versions of personal liberty laws. See Paul Finkelman, "*Prigg v. Pennsylvania* and the Northern State Courts: Anti-Slavery Use of a Pro-Slavery Decision," *Civil War History* 25 (1979): 5–35; Campbell, *The Slave Catchers*.

39. Campbell, *The Slave Catchers*, 169. See also Larry Gara, "The Fugitive Slave Law: A Double Paradox," *Civil War History* 10 (1964): 229–40; Jane H. Pease and William H. Pease, *The Fugitive Slave Law and Anthony Burns: A Problem in Law Enforcement* (Philadelphia: J. B. Lippincott, 1975).

40. Gerald E. Eggert, "The Impact of the Fugitive Slave Law on Harrisburg: A Case Study," *Pennsylvania Magazine of History and Biography* 109 (1985): 537–69.

41. Campbell, *The Slave Catchers*: on forcible, armed resistance, see 115, 149–51, and on the law's effectiveness, see 186. R. J. M. Blackett, "'Freedom or the Martyr's Grave': Black Pittsburgh's Aid to the Fugitive Slave," *Western Pennsylvania*

Historical Magazine 61 (1978): 130, reports on the networks of information that centered on hotels where blacks worked. Hotels were key places where news and rumors of fugitives could be passed along and forms of resistance organized.

42. Campbell, *The Slave Catchers*; Siebert, *The Underground Railroad*.

43. William M. Hall, *Reminiscences and Sketches Historical and Biographical* (Harrisburg, PA: Meyers Printing House, 1890), 57–60.

44. Larry Gara, *The Liberty Line: The Legend of the Underground Railroad* (Lexington: Univ. of Kentucky Press, 1961), 185.

45. Ibid.; Charles L. Blockson, *The Underground Railroad* (New York: Prentice-Hall, 1987), 229; Siebert, *The Underground Railroad*.

46. Edward Raymond Turner, "The Underground Railroad in Pennsylvania," *Pennsylvania Magazine of History and Biography* 36 (1912): 309–18; Blockson, *The Underground Railroad*, 227.

47. See Drew, *A North-Side View of Slavery*; Gara, *The Liberty Line*; Blockson, *The Underground Railroad*; Still, *The Underground Railroad*; Siebert, *The Underground Railroad*. Berry and Blassingame, "Africa, Slavery, and the Roots," 249, makes the larger point that many signs and omens deployed in African American traditions were newly invented in the African American context because of the different environment here. The enslaved Africans learned here of the existence of flora, fauna, weather, climate, and topography that had no necessary counterpart back home. See also Michael Mullin, *Africa in America: Slave Acculturation and Resistance in the American South and the British Caribbean, 1736–1831* (Chicago: Univ. of Illinois Press, 1992), on the long history of acculturation and resistance.

48. Siebert, *The Underground Railroad*, 61–62.

49. Jean-Paul Sartre, *What Is Literature?* trans. Bernard Frechtman (New York: Harper and Row, 1956), 55.

50. Lefebvre, *Production of Space*, 53.

51. I make this point not to put limits on the field of African American literary production—that is, not to invoke the idea that it reduces to race whether it wants to or not, whereas producers of the mainstream (white) literary canon transcend all such reductions. Instead I raise the point because of what Bradley claims for the novel. *Chaneysville* is a "work of historical reconstruction."

52. Charles L. Blockson, *The Underground Railroad in Pennsylvania* (Jacksonville, NC: Flame International, c.1981), 141.

53. Bedford County Heritage Commission, *The Kernel of Greatness: An Informal Bicentennial History of Bedford County* (State College, PA: Himes Printing Co., n.d. [1976?]), 73.

7. A Search for Place: William McNorton and His Garden of the Lord

1. Loren Schweninger, "A Vanishing Breed: Black Farm Owners in the South, 1651–1982," *Agricultural History* 63 (1989): 41–60. According to Schweninger, the largest number of African American farm owners at any time in the South was 17,785.

2. James M. McPherson, *The Struggle for Equality: Abolitionists and the Negro in Civil War and Reconstruction* (Princeton, NJ: Princeton Univ. Press, 1964), 122.

3. Eric Dardel, *L'homme et la terre: Nature de la realité géographique* (Paris: Presses Universitaires de France, 1952), 56, trans. Edward Relph, from his essay on "Geographical Experiences and Being-in-the-World: The Phenomenological Origins of Geography," in *The Human Experience of Space and Place*, ed. Anne Buttimer and David Seamon (London: Croom Helm, 1980).

4. Edward Relph, "Geographical Experiences and Being-in-the-World: The Phenomenological Origins of Geography," in *Dwelling, Places, and Environment: Towards a Phenomenology of Person and World* (New York: Columbia Univ. Press, 1985), 27.

5. Ibid., 26.

6. John.Michael Vlach, "Plantation Landscapes of the Antebellum South," in *Before Freedom Came: African-American Life in the Antebellum South*, ed. Edward D. C. Campbell Jr. and Kym S. Rice (Richmond: Museum of the Confederacy and Charlottesville: Univ. Press of Virginia, 1991), 23. Vlach credits Donald W. Menig with the origin of this idea. See Donald W. Menig, ed., *The Interpretation of Ordinary Landscapes: Geographical Essays* (New York: 1979). Vlach believes that although slaves owned nothing, they created their own living spaces and that this creation of space speaks to a deeper interpretation of their values apart from those of their masters. I agree with Vlach and believe that these ideas were what sustained them after slavery in their search to define a place for themselves in this country. Although McNorton was not a slave, his mother and brothers were, and that orientation carried into his formative years because he did not go west until he was twenty years old.

7. Richard White, *"It's Your Misfortune and None of My Own": A New History of the West* (Norman: Univ. of Oklahoma Press, 1991), 199.

8. Mechal Sobel, *The World They Made Together: Black and White Values in Eighteenth-Century Virginia* (Princeton, NJ: Princeton Univ. Press, 1987), 95.

9. Neil Fullerton Papers, box 5, folder 5, Montana Historical Society Archives. See also Lorraine Dufresne, "The Legend of Nigger Bill," in *A Heritage Remembered: Early and Later Days in the History of Western Sanders County* (Thompson Falls, MT:Sanders County Ledger, 1976), 78–82.

10. Fullerton Papers.

11. Michael P. Malone, Richard B. Roeder, and William Lang, *Montana: A History of Two Centuries*, rev. ed. (Seattle: Univ. of Washington Press, 1976), 84.

12. Ibid.

13. Ibid.

14. Fullerton Papers, box 5, folder 5.

15. Malone, *Montana*, 85.

16. The Blue Slide was the name given to the sections of land that bordered Graves and Fantom Creeks in Sanders County.

17. His two brothers, one a successful physician, lived near Missoula, but they were not close.

18. Fullerton Papers, box 5, folder 5.

19. Ibid.

20. Patricia Limerick, *A Legacy of Conquest: The Unbroken Past of the American West* (New York: Norton, 1987), 27. Limerick states that three western states passed laws against miscegenation, California, Oregon, and Nevada. See Malone, *Montana*, 84–85, for the details of the laws passed prohibiting blacks and other minority ethnic groups from access to the vote, public schools, and jury duty in Montana.

21. Fullerton Papers.

22. Ibid.

23. Ibid.

24. Ibid.

25. Ibid.

26. Quintard Taylor, *In Search of the Racial Frontier: African Americans in the American West* (New York: Norton, 1998).

27. Oscar Micheaux, *The Conquest: The Story of a Negro Pioneer* (1913; rpt. Lincoln: Univ. of Nebraska Press, 1994), 53. See also Janis Herbert, "Oscar Micheaux: A Black Pioneer," *South Dakota Review* 11:4 (winter 1973–74): 63–69.

28. Daisy Anderson Leonard, ed., *From Slavery to Affluence: Memoirs of Robert Anderson, Ex-Slave* (Steamboat Springs, CO: Steamboat Pilot, 1967), 44–47, 55–57.

29. Todd Guenter, "'Y'all Call Me Nigger Jim Now, But Someday You'll Call Me Mr. James Edwards': Black Success on the Plains of the Equality State," *Annals of Wyoming* 61:2 (fall 1989): 23–27.

30. Terry Tempest Williams, *An Unspoken Hunger: Stories from the Field* (New York: Pantheon, 1994), 10.

31. Ibid.

8. Rivers Underground: Rebellious Young Men, Community Parks, and the Surfacing of Culture in Barbados

1. See also the poem by Elombe Mottley, "When Banja Play, Bajan Come," *African-American Art* 7:1 (1989): 32, in which the suppression and use and resurrection of Banja goes "underground" and survives despite a legal ban on banjo playing.

2. Edward Kamau Brathwaite, *Contradictory Omens* (Kingston, Jamaica: Savacou, 1974), 31, 62.

3. Hilary Beckles, *A History of Barbados* (Cambridge: Cambridge Univ. Press, 1990), 52.

4. Edward Kamau Brathwaite, *Mother Poem* (Oxford: Oxford Univ. Press, 1977).

5. Brathwaite, *Omens*, 31.

6. Beckles, *History*, 52; see also Sidney Mintz and Richard Price, *An Anthropological Approach to the Afro-American Past: A Caribbean Perspective* (Philadelphia: Institute for the Study of Human Issues, 1976), 6.

7. For background on yard shows, Robert Farris Thompson, "The Circle and the Branch: Renascent Kongo-American Art," *Another Face of the Diamond: Pathways*

through the Black Atlantic South (New York: INTAR Latin American Gallery, 1988),
23–59; see also Thompson, *The Face of the Gods: Art and Altars in the African
Americas* (New York: Museum for African Art and Munich: Prestel, 1993).

8. Thompson, *Face of the Gods*, 22, 28, 48, 80.

9. In numerous interviews with Barbadian artists and craftspersons conducted
between 1990 and 1992 for my doctoral dissertation, I was told that books were primary teachers for the "self-taught" artist. Barbadians are literate, and literacy is
reported at 98 percent. There is little doubt that books on African art on the book-
shelves of Rastafarian artists in Temple Yard (a Rastafarian artist area in Bridgetown)
have provided them with important source material. Books are shared, and a single
book can influence many artists.

10. A coal pot is a low-fired clay stove containing hot coals elevated on a base
for the ashes to drop below and to allow a space for fanning to increase the heat.
Today, many coal pots are made of metal.

11. "Follow Pattern, kill Cadogan" is a Barbadian expression that means that
to follow someone, to copy them, leads to trouble.

12. Of course, the idea for the use of wheels at the entrance to great houses could
just as easily have originally come from African Barbadian gardeners and
groundskeepers.

13. Grey Gundaker first pointed out some of the similarities to African American
dressed yards in a 1988 visit to Barbados as I prepared to do fieldwork on art and
craft in Barbados from 1990 to 1992. It was Grey that encouraged me to look more
closely at Barbadian yards and community parks. While community parks were not
the focus of my research, they formed a recurrent border in relation to other art forms
that are commodified for sale to visitors-outsiders.

14. Barbados *Sunday Sun*, Jan. 20, 1991, 7B.

15. *Weekend Investigator*, Friday, July 19, 1991.

16. Frank Collymore, *Barbadian Dialect* (Bridgetown: Barbados National Trust,
1970).

17. Barbados National Trust, "Community Mini Parks Project," *Our Heritage,
the Newsletter of the Barbados National Trust* 8:3 (1992): 10.

18. Graham Dann, *The Quality of Life in Barbados* (London: Macmillan,
1984), 50.

19. Errol Barrow was the first prime minister of Barbados at independence
in 1966.

20. Robert Farris Thompson, "The Song That Named the Land: The Visionary
Presence of African American Art," in *Black Art: Ancestral Legacy* (Dallas: Dallas
Museum of Art, 1989), 123–24.

21. Thompson, *Face of the Gods*, 79–80.

22. Barbadian traditional kites are three-stick kites with patterns cut with precision from brightly colored reflective material, for example, from the tin foil on the
inside of a cigarette box. Simple kites follow particular rules and combinations of
shapes such as "star-diamond," "krapeller" (propeller), diamond krapeller, etc. Is it
by chance that these patterns appear as a cosmogram-like drawing at the entrance

of the "Pride of Checkerhall" or in the paintings of African American painter John Biggers described by Robert Farris Thompson as "a living Rosetta Stone for decoding of the African American yard show" (Thompson, "Song," 140)?

23. Grey Gundaker found the use of red and white flowering plants in the American South. The red stands for "communicating" and the white for "the other world" (Thompson, *Face of the Gods*, 59).

24. According to Robert Farris Thompson (ibid., 91), this practice, used to "provide a spiritual barrier to protect houses," was found in Loango, Kongo, at least as early as the seventeenth century.

25. Special pools, as Thompson has pointed out, may be manifestations of powerful spirits called "simbi" in Kikongo (ibid., 48). Empty aquariums were found at Mango Park and Wilson Hill. Wishing wells were found at several of the parks including Checker Hall and Mango Park.

26. *Weekend Investigator*, Friday, July 19, 1991, 12.

27. Grey Gundaker, "African American Dressed Yards and Home Exteriors in the Southeastern United States" (manuscript, May 10, 1990), 46.

28. Dann, *Quality*, 142; Collymore, *Dialect*, 90. Collymore defines the rum shop as "usually a small shop where rum and some other alcoholic drinks are sold, together with such commodities as bread, cheese, sliced ham, etc., and a place where men gather to discuss the topics of the day. The rumshop, which might be classified as a modest 'pub,' is to be found not only in Barbados, but throughout the Caribbean."

29. Roger D. Abrahams, *The Man of Words in the West Indies* (Baltimore: Johns Hopkins Univ. Press, 1983), 151.

30. Ibid., 151–52.

31. *Barbados Advocate*, Sept. 16, 1991, 5.

32. Bridgetown *Daily Nation*, "St. George Gangs Set for Showdown," May 16, 1991, 12.

33. A journalist commented in the *Weekend Nation* on Friday, Nov. 29, 1991, that "one thing that has not changed in the parish of St. John over the past 25 years, is the fellowship between the residents—of both age groups" (9B). The rural parish of St. John was the site of the prizewinning Mango Park and Pride of Wilson Hill.

34. The photographing, observations, and informal interviews took place at various times, usually on Sunday or a bank holiday, on trips around the island with my husband, Ken Corsbie. Some of the enthusiasm in showing us the parks may have stemmed from the fact that the popular *Caribbean Eye* series in which Ken starred had recently appeared on television. The series details elements of Caribbean culture so Ken is often greeted by people who say, "You should do a *Caribbean Eye* on . . . ." His presence, journalistic style, and ability to walk into "male" spaces assisted in the gathering of information for this chapter.

35. See "Ogun" in *Islands* from Edward Kamau Brathwaite, *The Arrivants* (Oxford: Oxford Univ. Press, 1983), 242–43.

36. Brathwaite, *Mother Poem*, 103.

37. A reference given by Brathwaite in a 1994 lecture at the State University of

New York at Stony Brook when a student asked how one could describe and articulate the quality of spirituality available in Spiritual Baptist services.

9. Symbolic Geographies and Psychic Landscapes: Decoding the Hegemonic Discourse of Urban Renewal in the Case for Billy Weems v. the City of College Park, Maryland

1. Lyn Petzold, "Just across the Street: Urban Renewal at Lakeland," *Argus*, Jan. 1969, 7–10. The photographs and commentary in this student publication from the University of Maryland tend to falsely characterize Lakeland, a mostly middle-class community of working families, as a slum. There are, for example, few photographs of the many well-maintained Victorian and rancher-style homes that comprised the community.

2. In 1967 the Urban Renewal Field Office was set up and opened in a trailer in Lakeland. "A Lost Dream," in the *Prince Georges' County Sentinel*, Aug. 18, 1977, attests that "Lakeland was never a slum to begin with. It had substandard houses, crumbling and unpaved roads which were largely the result of city neglect, but Lakeland was a living, breathing viable community with a rich 80-year history. This rare, once-cohesive area would be shattered forever with the implementation of Mr. Weiner's current plans. There would be very little of the Lakeland community left to which uprooted residents could return."

The article cites the city's promise to "retain the community's spirit and identity." In 1970 city administrator Robert A. Edwards told a reporter that "no one (in Lakeland) will be displaced," but by 1977 sixty-seven families had already "been moved out and another 44 were expected to be." Despite an early commitment to build mostly single-family homes, such as those that comprised the community before urban renewal, most of the new housing units consist of an apartment building (filled mostly with college students), section 8 townhomes and cluster homes, and a senior citizen's complex. Among the other public buildings erected in formerly residential sections in Lakeland are a recreation center, a firehouse, and an elementary school.

3. Petzold, "Just across the Street," 9. See also *Lakeland, an Urban Design Study*, prepared by Murphy Levy Wurman, Architecture and Urban Planning, for the Mayor and City of College Park and the Department of Urban Renewal. The design criteria espoused in this early plan were never fully met, and HUD monies allocated in connection with the project were often spent to improve other parts of the city not directly affected by urban renewal. See also Mayor and Council of the City of College Park, *Urban Renewal Plan for the Lakeland Urban Renewal Area* (Aug. 1970).

The project was plagued with cost overruns and red tape, partly because white citizens from other districts objected to money being spent in Lakeland. In 1972 the field office was shut down and the project was nearly abandoned because HUD found "the city had not taken adequate action to fulfill the Housing Assistance Plan, which called for building new houses and rehabilitationg old ones." See Steven Katz and Denise Tann, "City Petitions HUD," *Prince Georges' County Sentinel*.

4. Petzold, "Just across the Street," 10.

5. Ibid., 8. Contrary to the assertion in Petzold's article, Lakeland residents understood very well that their houses would be destroyed. From the beginning, community residents organized to oppose changes to the original plans that virtually eliminated the construction of new single-family dwellings. Community residents were publicly maligned when they expressed their concerns. In "Lakeland Plan near Approval," in the *Prince Georges' Sentinel*, Mary Dawn Rigdon quoted Mrs. Mary Holloman, the community coordinator for the Lakeland residents: "I'd rather see what we wanted from the beginning. We need flood control and houses. We don't need high rises geared to teachers and students at the University of Maryland. We don't need people who are going to be moving in and out. We need people as we had—people who will stay in the community for generations. People who will pay $400 a month rent aren't going to stay." Holloman also pointed out that a large proportion of the HUD funds was spent improving parts of College Park outside of the designated urban renewal area.

Mayor St. Claire Reeves's response to these issues is revealing. He is quoted as saying: "Mary Holloman will never be satisfied with any plan. She's been opposed to any apartments period. She wanted us to spend all the community development money in Lakeland. We made a decision not to do that. The $1 million the city is spending in there is enough. We have put enough money in there."

By 1976 the city had gone back completely on its earlier promise to designate the proposed eight-story apartment building as nonstudent faculty housing. In the University of Maryland *Diamondback*, Sept. 15, 1976, Reeves was quoted in "Campus Eyes City for Housing," an article referring directly to the Lakeland project, "I'm convinced that the University would like to be out of the housing business." To a certain extent, the construction of the Berkeley Apartments in the area formerly known as Lakeland helped the university to realize that goal.

6. Petzold, "Just across the Street," 10.

7. Constance Sandidge et al., "History of Lakeland," n.d. See also Eugene L. Meyer, "Urban Renewal and Lakeland," *Washington Post*, Dec. 26, 1976.

8. Ibid. Early white residents, who inhabited Lakeland beginning in 1890, apparently burned the town hall and other buildings when blacks began moving into Lakeland in 1901. According to the "History of Lakeland" prepared by the Lakeland History Committee, "When the black families began to move into Lakeland many of the old beautiful homes were burned down in an effort to keep black families out." In 1970 white youths fired over forty rounds of .22-caliber ammunition into the home of Harry M. Braxton, a black civic leader. The youths claimed they thought that the home was unoccupied.

9. Urban renewal decreased the geographic area of Lakeland by about half. Neither of the promised bridges nor the pool or tennis courts were ever built. Few single-family dwellings were erected. Most of the displaced residents were not relocated in Lakeland in a timely fashion and settled elsewhere. The community was largely dispersed.

10. Masthead, *American Planning and Civic Association Journal* 1955.

11. Photograph of Gen. U. S. Grant III, ibid. In the 1950s this publication cov-

ered urban renewal issues in articles with titles like "Role of the Citizen in Urban Renewal," "Organized Dispersal of Urban Populations," and "Space for Our Congested Cities." Most of these articles failed to consider adequately the importance of community, pride of place and ownership, or family and kinship networks to dispersed populations.

12. Albert Bettman, "Urban Redevelopment Legislation," ibid., 51. In the case of Lakeland, flood control made alternative use of low-lying land within the beltway more feasible. Improved transportation brought service workers from farther away.

13. Morton J. Schussheim, "Urban Renewal and Local Economic Development," *Journal of the American Institute of Planning*, 118.

14. Petzold, "Just across the Street," 8. The Berkeley Apartments did, in fact, become a primary source of housing for University of Maryland students.

15. Carl Feiss, "Needs of Our Growing Population: Space for Our Congested Cities," *APCA Journal*, 1955, 157–61.

16. Ibid., 161.

17. Lady Bird Johnson, "Beauty for America," *Proceedings of the White House Conference on Natural Beauty*, May 24–25, 1965, 1.

18. John Dyckman, "National Planning for Urban Renewal: The Paper Moon in the Cardboard Sky," *Journal of the American Institute of Planning*, 49–59; Peter Marris, "The Social Implications of Urban Redevelopment," ibid., 180–86; Marc Fried and Peggy Gleigher, "Some Sources of Satisfaction in an Urban Slum," ibid., 305–6.

19. Fried and Gleigher, "Some Sources of Satisfaction in an Urban Slum," 305–6; Marris, "The Social Implications of Urban Redevelopment," 180.

10. The Slave in the Swamp: Affects of Uncultivated Regions on Plantation Life

1. William Byrd, *Histories of the Dividing Line betwixt Virginia and North Carolina*, ed. William K. Boyd (Raleigh: North Carolina Historical Commission, 1929), 56.

2. David C. Miller, *Dark Eden: The Swamp in Nineteenth-Century American Culture* (New York: Cambridge Univ. Press, 1989), 71.

3. Eugene D. Genovese, *Roll, Jordan, Roll: The World the Slaves Made* (New York: Random House, 1976), 650, 653.

4. Linda Brent [Harriet Jacobs], *Incidents in the Life of a Slave Girl* (New York: Harcourt, 1973), 116.

5. John W. Blassingame, *Slave Testimony: Two Centuries of Letters, Speeches, Interviews, and Autobiographies* (Baton Rouge: Louisiana State Univ. Press, 1977), 340.

6. Melville Herskovits, *The Myth of the Negro Past* (1941; rpt. Boston: Beacon Press, 1990), 113.

7. Norman R. Yetman, *Life under the "Peculiar Institution": Selections from the Slave Narrative Collection* (New York: Holt, Rinehart & Winston, 1970), 128.

8. George Rawick, *The American Slave: A Composite Autobiography* (Westport, CT: Greenwood Press, 1972), 6 AL-1:123–24.

9. Blassingame, *Testimony*, 395.

10. Genovese, *Roll*, 652.

11. Blassingame, *Testimony*, 395.

12. Johann David Schoepf, *Travels in the Confederation, 1783–1784*, trans. Alfred J. Morrison, 2 vols. (Philadelphia: William J. Campbell, 1911), 2:99–100.

13. Herbert Aptheker, "Maroons within the Present Limits of the United States," *Maroon Societies: Rebel Slave Communities in the Americas*, 3d ed., ed. Richard Price (Baltimore: Johns Hopkins Univ. Press, 1996), 151–67.

14. Ulrich Bonnell Phillips, *American Negro Slavery: A Survey of the Supply, Employment, and Control of Negro Labor as Determined by the Plantation Regime* (1918; rpt. Baton Rouge: Louisiana State Univ. Press, 1966), 509–10.

15. Quoted in Aptheker, "Maroons," 156.

16. Samuel Warner, "Authentic and Impartial Narrative of the Tragical Scene Which Was Witnessed in Southampton County (Virginia) on Monday the 22nd of August Last When Fifty-five of Its Inhabitants (Mostly Women and Children) Were Inhumanly Massacred by the Blacks!" (1831), in Henry Irving Tragle, *The Southampton Slave Revolt of 1831* (Amherst: Univ. of Massachusetts Press, 1971), 296, 297.

17. R. H. Taylor, "Slave Conspiracies in North Carolina," *North Carolina Historical Review* 5:1 (1928): 25.

18. Aptheker, "Maroons," 161, 154.

19. George Blow to Richard Blow, Oct. 31, 1816, Blow Family Papers, Swem Library Archives, College of William and Mary, Williamsburg, Va.

20. Yetman, *Life*, 128.

21. Taylor, "Conspiracies," 24–25.

22. Aptheker, "Maroons," 163, 160–61.

23. Robert G. MacLean, ed., "A Yankee Tutor in the Old South," *North Carolina Historical Review* 47 (1970): 56–58.

24. Frederick Law Olmsted, *A Journey in the Seaboard Slave States*, 2 vols. (1856; rpt. New York: G. P. Putnam's Sons, 1904), 2:178.

25. James Redpath, *The Roving Editor: or, Talks with Slaves in the Southern States* (New York: A. B. Burdick, 1859), 291, 292.

26. Ibid., 294.

27. Charles L. Perdue Jr., Thomas E. Barden, and Robert K. Phillips, eds., *Weevils in the Wheat: Interviews with Virginia Ex-Slaves* (rpt. Bloomington: Indiana Univ. Press, 1980), 125.

28. Warner, "Tragical Scene," 298.

29. Perdue, *Weevils*, 209–10.

30. Rawick, *American Slave*, 4 TX-1:97–98, 261.

31. Blassingame, *Testimony*, 537–38.

32. Perdue, *Weevils*, 252.

33. Blassingame, *Testimony*, 395.

34. Perdue, *Weevils*, 62.

35. MacLean, "Yankee," 62.

36. Taylor, "Conspiracies," 23.

37. Aptheker, "Maroons," 154.

38. Quoted, ibid., 161.

39. Perdue, *Weevils*, 266, 245.

40. Albert J. Raboteau, *Slave Religion: The "Invisible Institution" in the Antebellum South* (New York: Oxford Univ. Press, 1978), 22–25.

41. Herskovits, *Myth*, 233.

42. M. Charles Jedrej, "Cosmology and Symbolism on the Central Guinea Coast," *Anthropos* 81 (1986): 500.

43. Ruth Bass, "Mojo," *Mother Wit from the Laughing Barrel: Readings in the Interpretation of Afro-American Folklore*, ed. Alan Dundes (Englewood Cliffs, NJ: Prentice-Hall, 1973), 285.

44. Lawrence W. Levine, *Black Culture and Black Consciousness: Afro-American Folk Thought from Slavery to Freedom* (New York: Oxford Univ. Press, 1977), 84.

45. Yetman, *Life*, 37.

46. Redpath, *Roving*, 293.

47. Blassingame, *Testimony*, 461.

48. Zora Neale Hurston, *Mules and Men* (1935; rpt. Bloomington: Indiana Univ. Press, 1978), 23.

49. Rawick, *American Slave*, 6 AL-1:263, 264, 265.

50. J. G. Clinkscales, *On the Old Plantation: Reminiscences of His Childhood* (1916; rpt. New York: Negro Universities Press, 1969), 30–34.

51. Rawick, *American Slave*, 6 AL-1:78.

52. Ibid., 4 TX-2:28.

11. Liberty and Economy in Lowcountry South Carolina: The Case of the Freedmen's Bank

1. The Registers of Signatures, or signature cards, of the Freedmen's Savings and Trust Company record the patron's sex, complexion (among African Americans; Caucasian depositors were classified as white), birthplace and place of upbringing, residence, age, and occupation and employer. They also record names of family members and names, ages, and residences of children. Underneath this information depositors were to sign their names or affix their marks. Finally, a small space near the bottom of the cards lists a patron's "Remarks." Benjamin River's portrait has been drawn from his signature card, number 2882 in the Freedmen's Savings and Trust Company (FS&TC), Registers of Signatures, Beaufort, S.C.: 1868–74, General Records of the Department of the Treasury, Record Group 56, National Archives, Washington, D.C. Benjamin's story is based, as well, on secondary sources describing Sea Island life between Nov. 1861 and 1868. See, for example, Willie Lee Rose, *Rehearsal for Reconstruction: The Port Royal Experiment* (New York: Vintage, 1964). A comprehensive contemporary description of Sea Island life during this period is found in Rupert Sargent Holland, ed., *Letters and Diary of Laura M. Towne* (New York: Negro Universities Press, 1969).

2. Rose, *Rehearsal for Reconstruction*, 104.

3. Many slaves, aware that they were soon to be liberated, went to Beaufort to "celebrate" their impending liberation in their masters' town homes (George Rawick, ed., *The American Slave: A Composite Biography* [Westport, CT: Greenwood, 1972], 2, pt. 2: 280; Rose, *Rehearsal for Reconstruction*, 12, 106–7).

4. Claim of Josiah Jackson, no. 18002, Testimony of Joseph McWright, March 10, 1877, Beaufort County, S.C., Southern Claims Commission, Disallowed Claims, M1407, Report 9, Office 1127, Records of the United States House of Representatives, RG 233, National Archives, Washington, D.C. Allowed claims are found in the case files, Beaufort County, S.C., Southern Claims Commission, Records of the Third Auditor, Records of the U.S. General Accounting Office, RG 217, ibid.

5. Rawick *American Slave* 3, pt. 3: 275.

6. Leon F. Litwack, *Been in the Storm So Long: The Aftermath of Slavery* (New York: Knopf, 1979), 77–86. For documentary evidence relating to the formation of the First and Second South Carolina volunteers, see Berlin, *Freedom*, ser. 2, 49–55; see also Thomas Wentworth Higginson, *Army Life in a Black Regiment* (East Lansing: Michigan State Univ. Press, 1960).

7. Litwack, *Been in the Storm So Long*, 172–78.

8. Detailed descriptions of South Carolina lowcountry topography can be found in William W. Freehling, *Prelude to Civil War: The Nullification Controversy in South Carolina, 1816–1836* (New York: Harper and Row, 1966), 7–24, and Freehling, *The Road to Disunion: Seccessionists at Bay, 1776–1854* (New York: Oxford Univ. Press, 1990), 214–31, as well as Rose, *Rehearsal for Reconstruction*, and Charles Joyner, *Down by the Riverside: A South Carolina Slave Community* (Urbana: Univ. of Illinois Press, 1984), esp. 9–40.

9. Peter Coclanis, *Shadow of a Dream: Economic Life and Death in the South Carolina Lowcountry, 1670–1920* (New York: Oxford Univ. Press, 1989), 112; Lewis Gray, *History of Agriculture in the Southern United States to 1860* (rpt. Clifton, NJ: A. M. Kelley, 1973), 1:48–59, 278–84, 2:679.

10. Discussion of lowcountry African American culture in the early colonial period can be found in Peter Wood, *Black Majority: Negroes in Colonial South Carolina from 1670 through the Stono Rebellion* (New York: Knopf, 1974). Lowcountry African American life and culture is also examined in Daniel C. Littlefield, *Rice and Slaves: Ethnicity and the Slave Trade in Colonial South Carolina* (Baton Rouge: Louisiana State Univ. Press, 1981). A cogent summary of lowcountry African American cultural origins can be found in Ira Berlin, "Time, Space, and the Evolution of Afro-American Society on British Mainland North America," *American Historical Review* 85 (1980): 44–78. See also Margaret Washington Creel, *"A Peculiar People": Slave Religion and Community Culture among the Gullahs* (New York: New York Univ. Press, 1988).

11. Joyner, *Down by the Riverside*, 41–70, 127. For the origins of the task system in the lowcountry, see Ulrich B. Phillips, *American Negro Slavery: A Survey into the Supply, Employment, and Control of Negro Labor as Determined by the Plantation Regime* (1918; rpt. Baton Rouge: Louisiana State Univ. Press, 1966), 247; Ulrich B. Phillips, "The Slave Labor Problem in the Charleston District," in

Plantation, Town, and County: Essays in the Local History of American Slave Society, ed. Elinor Miller and Eugene D. Genovese (Urbana: Univ. of Illinois Press, 1974), 9; Philip D. Morgan, "Work and Culture: The Task System and the World of Lowcountry Blacks, 1700 to 1880," *William and Mary Quarterly,* 3d ser., 39 (1982): esp. 565–68, 575–80; Philip D. Morgan, "The Ownership of Property by Slaves," *Journal of Southern History* 49:3 (1983): 399–420; John Scott Strickland, "Traditional Culture and Moral Economy: Social and Economic Change in the South Carolina Lowcountry, 1865–1910," in *The Countryside in the Age of Capitalist Transformation,* ed. Steven Hahn and Jonathan Prude (Chapel Hill: Univ. of North Carolina Press, 1985), 141–78; John Scott Strickland, "No More Mud Work: The Struggle for the Control of Labor and Production in Lowcountry South Carolina, 1863–1880," in *The Southern Enigma: Essays on Race, Class, and Folk Culture,* ed. Walter J. Fraser Jr. and Winfred B. Moore Jr. (Westport, CT: Greenwood, 1983), esp. 45–47. For a contemporary description of the application of the task system in the cultivation of Sea Island cotton, see R. F. W. Allston, "Sea Coast Crops of the South," *De Bow's Review* 16:2 (1854): 591–96.

12. Joyner, *Down by the Riverside,* 128–30.

13. Morgan, "Ownership," 416–18.

14. Ibid., 399–420. For a highly speculative psychoanalysis of market relations in master-slave relations, see Lawrence T. McDonnell, "Money Knows No Master: Market Relations and the American Slave Community," in *Developing Dixie: Modernization in a Traditional Society,* ed. Winfred B. Moore Jr. et al. (Westport, CT: Greenwood, 1988); see also Loren Schweninger, "Property-Owning Free African-American Women in the South, 1800–1870," *Journal of Women's History* 1:3 (1990): 13–44.

15. Rawick, *American Slave* 3, pt. 3: 200–201.

16. Testimony found in disallowed claim of Josiah Jackson, no. 18002, March 10, 1877, Beaufort County.

17. Claim of Mooney Sinclair, no. 5764, Dec. 4, 1876, Beaufort, S.C., S.C.C.; testimony of Andrew Jackson, no. 11198, Dec. 4, 1876, Beaufort, S.C., S.C.C. The Beaufort, S.C., and Liberty, Ga., case files of the Southern Claims Commission are replete with testimony from ex-slaves regarding cultivation of gardens and raising of livestock. Though produce and animals were often exchanged, proceeds from sales were almost always put toward purchase of commodities that would supplement rations. Hogs, cattle, and foodstuffs were most commonly cited by claimants as objects raised and traded. Slaves chose to raise these commodities because they provided them with the greatest benefit. Slaves did produce cotton or other staples for exchange in a broader local market. They also chose to raise commodities for family or personal use. Every addition to their own means of support decreased the need for owners' rations.

18. One example of such a success story is William Ellison. Ellison, born a slave, rose to privileged ranks in lowcountry society and even owned slaves himself. His tale is told in Michael Johnson and James L. Roark, *Black Masters: A Free Family of Color* (New York: Norton, 1984). Slave ownership among African Americans is analyzed in Larry Koger, *Black Slaveowners* (Jefferson, NC: Mcfarland, 1985); on wealth

among free African Americans, see Loren Schweninger, *Black Property Owners in the South, 1790–1915* (Urbana: Univ. of Illinois Press, 1997).

19. Testimony found in disallowed claim of William H. Riley, Feb. 5, 1874, Beaufort County.

20. Rawick, *American Slave* 2, pt. 2: 193; for examples of property ownership among slaves in Beaufort County, see disallowed claim of Josiah Jackson, no. 18002, Beaufort County, and disallowed claim of William H. Riley, no. 8014, Beaufort, S.C.C.; see also Morgan, "Ownership," 410–18, and Morgan, "Work and Culture," 586–97.

21. Strickland, "No More Mud Work," 47.

22. Most African Americans who purchased land bought roughly ten acres. Prices ranged from $1.00 to $6.50 per acre (Carol R. Bleser, *The Promised Land: The History of the South Carolina Land Commission, 1869–1890* [Columbia: Univ. of South Carolina Press, 1969], 7; Rose, *Rehearsal for Reconstruction*, 371; see also Martin Abbott, *The Freedmen's Bureau in South Carolina, 1865–1872* [Chapel Hill: Univ. of North Carolina Press, 1967], 61–62).

23. Bleser, *Promised Land*, 9–13.

24. Abbott, *The Freedmen's Bureau in South Carolina*, 66–77. Further discussion regarding contract making can be found in Joel Williamson, *After Slavery: The Negro in South Carolina after Reconstruction, 1861–1877* (New York: Norton, 1975), 68.

25. Abbott, *The Freedmen's Bureau in South Carolina*, 73. "Sherman's Reservation" in South Carolina extended from Charleston south and from the Sea Islands inland thirty miles. This amounted to approximately 485,000 acres. For analysis of land distribution developments, see ibid., chaps. 1, 2; see also Claude F. Oubre, *Forty Acres and a Mule: The Freedmen's Bureau and Black Landownership* (Baton Rouge: Louisiana State Univ. Press, 1978), 46–71; Rose, *Rehearsal for Reconstruction*, 355–57.

26. Williamson, *After Slavery*, 135–36. Freedpeople contracted under various arrangements. Like many other African American Southerners, some lowcountry residents negotiated to work under some form of sharecropping or share-wage arrangement. These arrangements, though prevalent in much of the South, were uncommon in the lowcountry. The nature of lowcountry slavery, and the problematic land issue during emancipation, made it difficult for landowners to come to terms other than those which provided substantial autonomy to lowcountry workers. See Morgan, "Work and Culture," 594–95.

27. Bleser, *Promised Land*, xiv–vv; Williamson, *After Slavery*, 45–63, 81–86.

28. For the final address by Lt. Col. C. T. Trowbrige to Benjamin River's regiment, the Thirty-third U.S. Colored Infantry, see Berlin, *Freedom*, ser. 2, 786–87.

29. Carl Osthaus, *Freedmen, Philanthropy, and Fraud: A History of the Freedman's Savings Bank* (Urbana: Univ. of Illinois Press, 1976), 79–80.

30. Rose, *Rehearsal for Reconstruction*, 152–54.

31. Osthaus, *Freedmen, Philanthropy, and Fraud*, 1–3; Williamson, *After Slavery*, 210–12.

32. Abby L. Gilbert, "The Comptroller of the Currency and the Freedman's

Savings Bank," *Journal of Negro History* 57:2 (1972): 125. Willie Lee Rose deals extensively with attempts to inculcate Northern middle-class values among Sea Island residents in *Rehearsal for Reconstruction*. For an excellent analysis of the Northern ideological underpinnings, the inculcation of republican habits, and the relation between Northern and Southern educational ideas, see Ronald E. Butchart, *Northern Schools, Southern Blacks, and Reconstruction: Freedmen's Education, 1862–1875* (Westport, CT: Greenwood, 1980). See also Sandra E. Small, "The Yankee Schoolmarm in Freedmen's School: An Analysis of Attitudes," *Journal of Southern History* 45 (1979): 381–402.

33. Osthaus, *Freedmen, Philanthropy, and Fraud*, 3–4. 34. Rose, *Rehearsal for Reconstruction*, 23–25; Osthaus, *Freedmen, Philanthropy, and Fraud*, 49–52, 55.

35. Osthaus, *Freedmen, Philanthropy, and Fraud*, 44–78. 36. For information regarding Lavina Palmer, see signature card no. 2816, FS&TC. Her antebellum status is not recorded in the signature cards.

37. Our understanding of light-skinned patrons is somewhat sketchy since many did not list occupations.

38. Many rural depositors listed farming as their primary occupation along with carpentry, fishing, or general labor.

39. Of the ten, only eight signature cards contain information in addition to residence. Women composed only 8 percent of St. Helena's patrons. Information found in Celia Brown's signature card, no. 3934. No mention is made in Laura Towne's diary regarding Celia Brown's deposit. As one of the region's foremost teachers and missionaries, Towne no doubt encouraged the young girl to deposit her earnings in the bank. Detailed discussion of Laura Towne's effort on St. Helena is found in Rose, *Rehearsal for Reconstruction*; see also Holland, *Letters and Diary of Laura M. Towne*.

40. Computed from signature cards, FS&TC Depositors were not required to provide details regarding spouse's occupation or date of death. In some instances widows informed clerks that their husbands had been killed or were missing in action. It is, however, impossible to ascertain in these instances how long these women had been widowed as none provided details of their spouse's death.

41. In some instances the "Remarks" section of the bank cards provides information in this regard. But these women provided no information regarding objectives or purposes for their accounts.

42. Rawick, *American Slave* 2, pt. 2: 104.

43. Seventy-four percent of urban women listed siblings; however, only 27 percent listed children. The average number of children among urban women whose cards listed children was two (computed from signature cards, FS&TC).

44. On slave ownership of property, see Morgan, "Ownership" and "Work and Culture." Loren Schweniger takes a stance similar to Morgan though he focuses mainly on free African Americans. He argues familial and occupational needs led free African American women "to acquire property as a means of protection, economic independence, and self-sufficiency" (Schweninger, "Property-Owning Free African-American Women in the South," 30).

45. Although these women do not represent a statistically significant proportion

of patrons, it is curious that these few elderly widows were virtually the only women from the island to open accounts at the bank, that we know of.

46. Osthaus, *Freedmen, Philanthropy, and Fraud*, 128–31, 136; Morgan, "Ownership" and "Work and Culture." See also Strickland, "Traditional Culture and Moral Economy." For further discussion of the struggle for independence in a low-country context, see Eric Foner, *Nothing but Freedom: Emancipation and Its Legacy* (Baton Rouge: Louisiana State Univ. Press, 1983), chap. 3. For the philosophical underpinnings of independence among African Americans, especially in the short-staple cotton South, see Gerald David Jaynes, *Branches without Roots* (New York: Oxford Univ. Press, 1986), esp. chap. 14.

47. Janet Cornelius, "'We Slipped and Learned to Read': Slave Accounts of the Literacy Process, 1830–1865," *Phylon* 44:3 (1983): 174. Anyone caught teaching slaves was also subject to punishment. Whites faced $100 fines and six-month prison terms. Free blacks caught teaching their slave brethren were fined $50 and given fifty lashes (James D. Anderson, *The Education of Blacks in the South, 1860–1935* [Chapel Hill: Univ. of North Carolina Press, 1988], 16–17).

48. Eugene D. Genovese, *Roll, Jordan, Roll: The World the Slaves Made* (New York: Pantheon, 1974), 561–66; Butchart, *Northern Schools, Southern Blacks, and Reconstruction*, 17–21; Osthaus, *Freedmen, Philanthropy, and Fraud*, esp. chap. 3.

49. Berlin, *Freedom*, ser. 1, 3:148–50; Robert C. Morris, *Reading, 'Riting, and Reconstruction: Freedmen's Education in the South, 1861–1870* (Chicago: Univ. of Chicago Press, 1981), 2. Willie Lee Rose also documents education efforts in *Rehearsal for Reconstruction*.

50. Rawick, *American Slave*, 3:203.

51. Anderson, *The Education of Blacks in the South*, 12–15; Berlin, *Freedom*, ser. 1, 3:206.

52. For a broad overview of African American efforts in this regard, see Litwack, *Been in the Storm So Long*, chap. 9.

53. A similar line of reasoning is pursued in Anderson, *The Education of Blacks in the South*, 22–23, 27–28.

54. Ibid., esp. chaps. 5, 6.

12. The Praise House Tradition on St. Helena Island, South Carolina

1. Kenneth C. Doe, "The Praise House Tradition and Community Renewal at St. Joseph Baptist Church" (Ph.D. diss., Erskine Theological Seminary, 1991), 43; Margaret Washington Creel, *A Peculiar People: Slave Religion and Community Culture among the Gullahs* (New York: New York Univ. Press, 1988), 222, 228.

2. Doe, *Praise House*, 44.

3. Mikell Jenkin, *Rumbling of the Chariot Wheels* (Columbia, SC: The State Company, 1923), 134–35, quoted in Doe, *Praise House*, 45.

4. Doe, *Praise House*, 45.

5. Theodore Rosengarten, *Tombee: Portrait of a Cotton Planter* (New York: William Morrow, 1986), 37. John's Island, another well-noted Sea Island, is located

in Charleston County. John's Island is known for the work done by Guy and Candie Carawan on Mrs. Janie Hunter and the Moving Star Hall Shouters.

6. Theodore Rosengarten provides a detailed description of the division and conditions of the plantations and the geographic and environmental makeup of the area from 1795 through the mid-1840s (ibid., 54–57).

7. Ibid., 55.

8. Elizabeth Jacoway wrote *Yankee Missionaries in the South: The Penn School Experiment* (Baton Rouge: Louisiana State Univ. Press, 1980), which details the relationship between Penn School and Hampton Normal and Agricultural School, now Hampton University. When I went to work at Penn Center in 1987, I formally rekindled the relationship between Hampton and Penn.

9. Alan Lomax went into the Sea Islands and recorded spirituals in the 1940s. Lomax's works can be purchased from the Office of Folklife Programs, Smithsonian Institution, Washington, D.C. Guy and Candie Carawan also recorded many of the spirituals sung by the Moving Star Hall Shouters. Their works can be found at the Highlander Folk School in Tennessee.

10. Mechal Sobel, *Trabelin' On: The Slave Journey to an Afro-Baptist Faith* (Westport, CT: Greenwood Press, 1979), 37; Creel, *Peculiar*, 276; Rosengarten, *Tombee*, 57.

11. Creel, *Peculiar*, 233, 276.

12. Interview with Deacon Garfield Smalls, Croft Praise House, St. Helena Island, S.C., Nov. 12, 1993.

13. There are at least twenty-five Baptist churches on St. Helena Island. Brick Baptist Church is the mother church. Brick is closely aligned with Penn School because this is where the first classes were taught, and the teachers and students attended services there. Brick Baptist Church sevices are known as more conservative than the other Baptist churches located on the island.

14. Interview with Julia Reynolds, Mary Jenkins Praise House, St. Helena Island, S.C., Nov. 13, 1992.

15. Creel, *Peculiar*, 277.

16. Smalls, Nov. 23, 1993.

17. Reynolds, Nov. 13, 1993.

18. Samuel Miller Lawton, "The Religious Life of South Carolina Coastal and Sea Island Negroes" (Ph.D. diss., George Peabody College for Teachers, 1939), 71, 82.

19. Ibid.

20. Creel, *Peculiar*, 231.

21. Lawton, "Religious Life," 69.

22. Creel, *Peculiar*, 277.

23. Smalls, Nov. 12, 1993.

24. Creel, *Peculiar*, 58.

25. Albert J. Raboteau, *Slave Religion: The "Invisible Institution" in the Antebellum South* (New York: Oxford Univ. Press, 1980), 238.

26. Smalls, Nov. 12, 1993. Smalls moved to live in Eddings Point, the home of his late wife, from Dr. White's plantation.

27. Reynolds, Nov. 13, 1993; Lawton, "Religious Life," 74–75.

28. Interview with Sara Wilson, Mary Jenkins Praise House, St. Helena Island, S.C., Nov. 13, 1993.

29. Lawton, "Religious Life," 74–75.

30. Other Sea Island communities are known to have distinct multirhythmic styles of worship as well. It is interesting that the styles may vary just a little on each island, just as the Gullah language is spoken in different dialects based on region.

31. Reynolds, Nov. 13, 1993.

32. Ray Allen Billington, ed., *The Journal of Charlotte Forten: A Free Negro in the Slave Era* (New York: Norton, 1981), 206, 212. The July diary entry refers to the visit of Colonel Shaw of the Fifty-fourth Massachusetts, who was sent to St. Helena Island with his black troops. Later in the diary Forten recounts the battle at Folly Island, S.C., that was depicted in the movie *Glory.*

33. Raboteau, *Slave Religion,* 73–74.

13. "Trash" Revisited: A Comparative Approach to Historical Descriptions and Archaeological Analyses of Slave Houses and Yards

1. Igor Kopytoff, "The Cultural Biography of Things: Commodization as Process," in *The Social Life of Things: Commodities in Cultural Perspective,* ed. Arjun Appadurai (Cambridge: Cambridge Univ. Press, 1986), 64–94. The epigraphs are from *The Interpretation of Ordinary Landscapes: Geographical Essays,* ed. D. W. Meinig (New York: Oxford Univ. Press, 1979).

2. Terrence Epperson, "Race and the Disciplines of the Plantation," *Historical Archaeology* 24:4 (1990): 29–36; Dell Upton, "White and Black Landscapes in Eighteenth-Century Virginia," in *Material Life in America, 1600–1860,* ed. Robert Blair St. George (Boston: Northeastern Univ. Press, 1988), 357–69.

3. Charles E. Orser Jr., ed., "Historical Archaeology on Southern Plantations and Farms," *Historical Archaeology* 24:4 (1990); Edward D. C. Campbell Jr. and Kym S. Rice, eds., *Before Freedom Came: African-American Life in the Antebellum South* (Richmond: Museum of the Confederacy and Charlottesville: Univ. Press of Virginia, 1991).

4. Upton, "White and Black Landscapes."

5. Grey Gundaker, "Tradition and Innovation in African American Yards," *African Arts* 26:2 (1993): 58–71, 94–96.

6. Mary Douglas and Brian Isherwood, *The World of Goods* (New York: Norton, 1979), 66.

7. Roger D. Abrahams and John F. Szwed, eds., *After Africa: Extracts from British Travel Accounts and Journals of the Seventeenth, Eighteenth, and Nineteenth Centuries concerning the Slaves, Their Manners, and Customs in the British West Indies,* assisted by Leslie Baker and Adrian Stackhouse (New Haven: Yale Univ. Press, 1983), 11.

8. Douglas and Isherwood, *Goods,* 5; Meinig, *Landscape.*

9. Toni Morrison, *Song of Solomon* (1977; rpt. New York: Penguin, 1987), 125.

10. Ibid., 27, 39.

11. John Michael Vlach, *Back of the Big House: The Architecture of Plantation Slavery* (Chapel Hill: Univ. of North Carolina Press, 1993); Campbell and Rice, *Before Freedom Came*, 21–49; Herbert G. Gutman, *The Black Family in Slavery and Freedom, 1750–1925* (New York: Random House, 1976).

12. Hildred Roach, *Black American Music: Past and Present*, 2d ed. (Malabar, FL: Krieger, 1992).

13. Eric Klingelhofer, "Aspects of Early Afro-American Material Culture: Artifacts from the Slave Quarters at Garrison Plantation, Maryland," *Historical Archaeology* 21:2 (1987): 112–19.

14. Theresa A. Singleton, "The Archaeology of Slave Life," in Campbell and Rice, *Before Freedom Came*, 158; William M. Kelso, *Kingsmill Plantations, 1619–1800: Archaeology of Country Life in Colonial Virginia* (New York: Academic Press, 1984); Cheryl J. La Roche, "Beads from the African Burial Ground, New York City: A Preliminary Assessment," *Beads: Journal of the Society of Bead Researchers* 6 (1994): 3–20.

15. Charles L. Perdue Jr., Thomas E. Barden, and Robert K. Phillips, eds., *Weevils in the Wheat: Interviews with Virginia Ex-Slaves* (Charlottesville: Univ. Press of Virginia, 1976), 295.

16. Ibid., 316.

17. Abrahams and Szwed, *After Africa*, 329.

18. Paul D. Escott, *Slavery Remembered: A Record of Twentieth-Century Slave Narratives* (Chapel Hill: Univ. of North Carolina Press, 1979), 95; Robert Farris Thompson, *Face of the Gods: Art and Altars of Africa and the African Americas* (New York: Museum for African Art and Munich: Prestel, 1993); Robert Farris Thompson, *Flash of the Spirit: African and Afro-American Art and Philosophy* (New York: Random House, 1983); see also Grey Gundaker, "African American History, Cosmology, and the Moral Universe of Edward Houston's Yard," *Journal of Garden History: Special Issue on Ecology and Landscape Ethics* 3 (1994): 179–205.

19. Parker B. Potter Jr., "What Is the Use of Plantation Archaeology?" *Historical Archaeology* 25:3 (1991): 94–107.

20. Elaine Nichols, ed., *The Last Miles of the Way: African-American Homegoing Traditions, 1890–Present* (Columbia: South Carolina State Museum, 1989); see also Thompson, *Flash of the Spirit*.

21. Gundaker, "Tradition and Innovation."

22. Thompson, *Flash of the Spirit*.

23. Frederick Law Olmsted, *The Cotton Kingdom: A Traveller's Observations on Cotton and Slavery in the American Slave States*, ed. Arthur M. Schlesinger Sr., intro. Lawrence N. Powell (New York: Modern Library, 1984), 184–85.

24. Vlach, *Big House*; John Michael Vlach, "Plantation Landscapes of the Antebellum South," in *Before Freedom Came: African-American Life in the Antebellum South*, ed. Edward D. C. Campbell Jr. and Kym S. Rice (Richmond: Museum of the Confederacy and Charlottesville: Univ. Press of Virginia, 1991). For more on plantation landscape, see Larry McKee, "The Ideals and Realities behind

the Design and Use of 19th-Century Virginia Slave Cabins," in *The Art and Mystery of Historical Archaeology: Essays in Honor of James Deetz*, ed. Anne Elizabeth Yentsch and Mary C. Beaudry (Ann Arbor, MI: CRC Press, 1992), 195–213; Epperson, "Disciplines"; Upton, "White and Black Landscapes."

25. McKee, "Ideals."

26. Fraser D. Neiman, "Temporal Patterning in House Plans for the 17th-Century Chesapeake," in *The Archaeology of 17th-Century Virginia*, ed. Theodore R. Reinhart and Dennis J. Pogue (Richmond: Dietz Press, 1993): 251–83.

27. McKee, "Ideals."

28. Perdue, *Weevils*, 82.

29. Eugene Genovese, *Roll, Jordan, Roll: The World the Slaves Made* (New York: Random House, 1974), 534.

30. Mechal Sobel, *The World They Made Together: Black and White Values in Eighteenth-Century Virginia* (Princeton, NJ: Princeton Univ. Press, 1987), 100–101, 103.

31. Rpt. in Genovese, *Roll*, 527.

32. Booker T. Washington, *Up from Slavery: An Autobiography of Booker T. Washington* (Avenel, NJ: Gramercy Books, 1993), 14–15.

33. See Olmsted, *Cotton Kingdom*, 42. Archaeologists have uncovered the remains of slave houses at Kingsmill, Carter's Grove, and Rich Neck plantations in Virginia. Their designs are similar to the ones Olmsted described (Reports on file at the Colonial Williamsburg Foundation, Department of Archaeological Research, Williamsburg, Va.).

34. Olmsted, *Cotton Kingdom*, 290.

35. McKee, "Ideals"; see also Ywone D. Edwards, "Master-Slave Relationship: A Williamsburg Perspective" (M.A. thesis, Anthropology, College of William and Mary, 1990).

36. Genovese, *Roll*, 607–8.

37. Sobel, *World*, 111.

38. Leland Ferguson, *Uncommon Ground: Archaeology and Early African America, 1650–1800* (Washington, DC: Smithsonian Institution Press, 1992), xliv.

39. See Jean E. Howson, "Social Relations and Material Culture: A Critique of the Archaeology of Plantation Slavery," *Historical Archaeology* 24:4 (1990): 90.

40. Larry McKee, "The Earth Is Their Witness: Archaeology Is Shedding New Light on the Secret Lives of American Slaves," *Sciences*, March–April 1995, 36–41.

41. James Deetz, *Flowerdew Hundred: The Archaeology of a Virginia Plantation, 1619–1864* (Charlottesville: Univ. Press of Virginia, 1993).

42. Dennis J. Pogue, *King's Reach and 17th-Century Plantation Life* (Annapolis: Jefferson Patterson Park and Museum, 1990).

43. Julia King and Henry M. Miller, "A View from the Midden: An Analysis of Midden Distribution and Composition at the Van Sweringen Site, St. Mary's City, Maryland," *Historical Archaeology* 21:2 (1987): 38; Mary C. Beaudry, "The Archaeology of Historical Land Use in Massachusetts," ibid., 20:2 (1986): 39.

44. King and Miller, "View."

45. Douglas V. Armstrong, *The Old Village and the Great House: An Archaeological and Historical Examination of Drax Hall Plantation, St. Ann's Bay, Jamaica* (Urbana: Univ. of Illinois Press, 1990).

46. Stephen Mrozowski, "Historical Archaeology as Anthropology," *Historical Archaeology* 22:1 (1988): 19–24.

47. For discussion of these sites and root-cellar trash, see Kelso, *Kingsmill Plantations*; L. Daniel Mouer, "Chesapeake Creoles: The Creation of Folk Culture in Colonial Virginia," in Reinhart and Pogue, *The Archaeology of 17th-Century Virginia,* 105–66; Maria Franklin, "'Shocker and Hester Were Here': Ongoing Investigations of the Rich Neck Slave Quarter," and Ywone D. Edwards, "'Primitive' and 'Folk' in African American Archaeology," papers presented at the Society for Historical Archaeology Meeting, Washington, D.C., 1995; McKee, "Ideals"; Edward A. Chappell, *Forum: Social Responsibility and the American History Museum* (Wilmington, DE: Henry Francis du Pont Winterthur Museum, 1989).

48. Marley R. Brown III and Patricia Samford, "Current Archaeological Perspectives on the Growth and Development of Williamsburg," in *Historical Archaeology of the Chesapeake*, ed. Paul A. Shackel and Barbara J. Little (Washington, DC: Smithsonian Institution Press, 1994), 231–45; Michael Olmert, *Official Guide to Colonial Williamsburg* (Williamsburg, VA: Colonial Williamsburg Foundation, 1985).

49. McKee, "Ideals," 197.

50. Jack P. Greene, ed., *The Diary of Colonel Landon Carter of Sabine Hall, 1752–1778,* 2d ed. (Richmond: Virginia Historical Society, 1987), 843.

51. Joanne Bowen, "Slavery at Mount Vernon: A Dietary Analysis," paper presented at the Society for Historical Archaeology Meeting, Washington, D.C., Jan. 1995.

52. Ferguson, *Uncommon Ground.*

53. Douglas W. Sanford, "The Archaeology of Plantation Slavery in Piedmont Virginia: Context and Process," in Shackel and Little, *Historical Archaeology of the Chesapeake,* 115–30.

54. Singleton, "Archaeology."

55. Campbell and Rice, *Before Freedom Came.*

56. Kenneth L. Brown, "Material Culture and Community Structure: The Slave and Tenant Community at Levi Jordan's Plantation, 1848–1892," in *Working toward Freedom: Slave Society and Domestic Economy in the American South,* ed. Larry E. Hudson Jr. (Rochester, NY: Univ. of Rochester Press, 1994), 95–118.

57. Thompson, *Face of the Gods,* 57–59.

58. Deetz, *Flowerdew Hundred,* 144–46.

59. Ibid.

60. Ibid., 139.

61. Rpt. in James O. Breeden, ed., *Advice among Masters: The Ideal in Slave Management in the Old South* (Westport, CT: Greenwood Press, 1980), 120; see also McKee, "Ideals," 203.

62. McKee, "Ideals," 209.

63. Jane Busch, "Second Time Around: A Look at Bottle Reuse," *Historical Archaeology* 21:1 (1987): 67–80.

64. Gundaker, "Tradition and Innovation," 59; Lawrence W. Levine, *Black Culture and Black Consciousness: Afro-American Folk Thought from Slavery to Freedom* (Oxford: Oxford Univ. Press, 1977), 78.

65. Rpt. in Breeden, *Advice*, 132.

66. Genovese, *Roll*, 525.

67. *Virginia Gazette or Weekly Advertiser* (Nicholson and Prentis), Jan. 19, 1782, rpt. in *Runaway Slave Advertisements: A Documentary History from the 1730s to the 1790*, vol. 1, *Virginia and North Carolina*, ed. Lathan A. Windley (Westport, CT: Greenwood Press, 1983), 211–12.

68. Genovese, *Roll*, 531.

69. Rpt. in Singleton, "Archaeology," 170.

70. Sobel, *World*, 19.

71. Frederick Douglass, *Narrative of the Life of Frederick Douglass, an American Slave, Written by Himself* (1845), rpt. in *The Classic Slave Narrative*, ed. Henry Louis Gates Jr. (New York: Penguin, 1987), 245, 331, 263; W. E. B. Du Bois, *The Souls of Black Folk* (New York: Signet, 1969), 267.

72. Gundaker, "Tradition and Innovation," 59, 67.

73. Sobel, *World*, 19.

74. See Elaine Nichols, ed., *The Last Miles of the Way: African-American Homegoing Traditions, 1890–Present* (Columbia: South Carolina State Museum, 1989); Harriet Jacobs, *Incidents in the Life of a Slave Girl*, ed. Jean Fagan Yellin (Cambridge: Harvard Univ. Press, 1987).

75. Jacobs, *Incidents*, 90–91.

76. Gundaker, "History, Cosmology," 191.

77. Nichols, *Last Miles*; Thompson, *Flash of the Spirit*.

78. La Roche, "Beads."

79. Ida B. Wells, *Crusade for Justice: The Autobiography of Ida B. Wells*, ed. Alfreda M. Duster (Chicago: Univ. of Chicago Press, 1970), 9.

80. Gustavus Vassa, *The Interesting Narrative of the Life of Olaudah Equiano, or Gustavus Vassa, The African: Written by Himself* (1814), rpt. in Gates, *Slave Narrative*, 16.

81. Rpt. in Olmsted, *Cotton Kingdom*, 81–82.

82. Armstrong, *Old Village*, 293.

83. Genovese, *Roll*, 527.

84. Armstrong, *Old Village*, 292.

85. Genovese, *Roll*, 528.

86. Greene, *Diary of Colonel Landon Carter*, 357, 362.

87. Rpt. in Breeden, *Advice*, 128–29.

88. Olmsted, *Cotton Kingdom*, 290.

89. For more information on color symbolism and wallpaper as protection, see Thompson, *Flash of the Spirit*, 222.

14. Race and the Politics of Public History in the United States

1. See Clayborne Carson, "Mississippi: Is This America?" in *The Eyes on the Prize Civil Rights Reader*, ed. Clayborne Carson et al. (New York: Penguin, 1991), 166–68.

2. The brother of one of the victims described his frustration in the face of police indifference in the television documentary "Murder in Mississippi" (United Kingdom Channel 4, broadcast Jan. 13, 1997).

3. Museums sponsoring exhibitions in the last twenty years include the Museum of the Confederacy, Richmond; the Valentine Museum, Richmond; the Maryland Historical Society, Baltimore. Recent monuments include the Civil Rights Memorial, Montgomery, Ala.; the Civil Rights Monument, San Francisco; the Buffalo Soldiers Memorial, Fort Leavenworth, Kans.

4. The new label reads "Overseer's Quarters"; it describes the duties of the overseer and his wife and Washington's dependence on them for the success of his estate.

5. The label reads: "Greenhouse Slave Quarters. The sun never caught [George Washington] in bed, and he was unwilling it should find any of his people sleeping"; it also describes the slave population and lists other living spaces for slaves on the estate.

6. Interviews with Glen Porter, Hagley Museum, Nov. 1992; Charles Lyle, Maryland Historical Society, Nov. 13, 1992; Candice Metallic, SUNY Museum Studies Graduate Program, Cooperstown, N.Y., Nov. 12, 1992. Cf. American Association of Museums, *Excellence and Equity: Education and the Public Dimension of Museums* (Washington, DC: AAM, 1992). See also John Dorsey, "Museums Move Away from 'Art-Apartheid,'" *Baltimore Sun*, April 26, 1992, 1M.

7. Docents at historical museums insist on using the word *servants* (Leni Sorenson, personal communication).

8. Michael D. Shear, "Anniversary Revives a Legacy of Strength: Mount Vernon Slave Memorial to Mark 10th Year," *Washington Post*, Sept. 16, 1993, 1, 6; Philip Burham, "Eating Jim Crow," *Washington City Paper*, Feb. 2, 1996, 32.

9. See *Williamsburg Magazine*, Aug. 1995, 13.

10. Michael Wallace, "Visiting the Past: History Museums in the United States," in *Presenting the Past*, ed. Susan Porter Benson, Stephen Brier, and Roy Rozenzweig (Philadelphia: Temple Univ. Press, 1986), 154; cf. remarks in Ada Louise Huxtable, "Inventing American Reality," *New York Times Review of Books*, Dec. 3, 1992, 24, and the exchange in the *Journal of American History* 81 (June 1994): 119–36, 137–63.

11. Warren Leon and Margaret Piatt, "Living-History Museums," in *History Museums in the United States*, ed. Warren Leon and Roy Rosenzweig (Urbana: Univ. of Illinois Press, 1989), 77.

12. Wallace, "Visiting the Past," 156–57; Colonial Williamsburg *Visitor's Companion*, July 31–Aug. 6, 1995.

13. Colonial Williamsburg Foundation, *400 Years of History at Carter's Grove* (n.d.).

14. For example, interpreters use call-and-response modes of storytelling that allow the audience to shape the course of a story actively; cf. Julius Lester, "How the

Snake Got His Rattles," in *Talk That Talk: An Anthology of African-American Storytelling*, ed. Linda Goss and Marian E. Barnes (New York: Simon and Schuster, 1989), 82–87.

15. Presentation by James Horton at the American Historical Association Annual Meeting.

16. Leon and Piatt, "Living-History," 78.

17. Michelle Singletary and Spenser S. Hsu, "Disney Says Va. Park Will Be Serious Fun," *Washington Post*, Nov. 12, 1993, A1.

18. Mike L. Pacala, quoted in Michelle Singletary, "Disney Sees Challenge in Recreating Honest, Fun Past," *Washington Post*, Nov. 14, 1993, B1.

19. See, for example, Michael A. Janofsky, "Learned Opposition to Disney Park," *New York Times*, May 12, 1994, A16.

20. See, e.g., Michael Wallace, "Mickey Mouse History: Portraying the Past at Disney World," in Leon and Rosenzweig, *History Museums*.

21. Robert Weis, quoted in Bentley Boyd, "How Will CW Fare? 'Real' History Fans Fear Competition from Disney Park," *Hampton / Newport News Daily Press*, Nov. 13, 1993, C3.

22. Quoted in Bentley Boyd, "A Small, Tough World of Tourism," ibid., Feb. 4, 1994, C2.

23. See, for example, Dave Bruns, "Patriots, To Arms!" ibid., May 29, 1994, H1.

24. Bentley Boyd, "CW Black History Director Wants to Broaden Scope," ibid., Sept. 14, 1994, W1-W2.

25. Jamestown, settled in 1607, was the first enduring British colony; in 1619 it became the site of Virginia's first representative legislative assembly.

26. Bentley Boyd, "CW Auctions Slaves," ibid., Oct. 11, 1994, A2.

27. Tamara Jones, "Living History or Undying Racism? Colonial Williamsburg 'Slave Auction' Draws Protest, Support," *Washington Post*, Oct. 11, 1994, A18.

28. Bentley Boyd, "CW Plans Mock Slave Auction," *Hampton / Newport News Daily Press*, Oct. 6, 1994, C2.

29. Tina Jeffrey, "Tourism Has Changed the Face of Lifestyles in Williamsburg," *Williamsburg Magazine*, Aug. 1995, 50–57.

30. Part of the problem arose because in dramatic forms such as a reenactment the audience tends to identify with active protagonists rather than the passive objects of action. Reading and other literary forms better convey inner thoughts and feelings.

31. Maya Angelou, *I Know Why the Caged Bird Sings* (New York: Bantam, 1969), 180.

32. See the painting by John Antrobus reproduced in Charles Joyner, "The World of the Plantation Slaves," in *Before Freedom Came: African-American Life in the Antebellum South*, ed. Edward D. C. Campbell Jr. and Kym S. Rice (Richmond: Museum of the Confederacy and Charlottesville: Univ. Press of Virginia, 1991), 72, 81; Elaine Nichols, ed., *The Last Miles of the Way: African American Homegoing Traditions, 1890–Present* (Columbia: South Carolina State Museum, 1989), 51–52; Eugene D. Genovese, *Roll, Jordan, Roll: The World the Slaves Made* (New York: Vintage, 1976), 197–98.

33. Joyner, "World," 69, pl. 13; Robert Farris Thompson, *Flash of the Spirit: African and Afro-American Art and Philosophy* (New York: Vintage, 1983), 130; Peter Kolchin, *American Slavery* (London: Penguin, 1993), 146–47.

34. Nichols, *Last Miles*, 36, 38, 48; cf. Patricia R. Loughbridge and Edward D. C. Campbell Jr., *Women in Mourning* (Richmond: Museum of the Confederacy, 1986), 18.

35. Grey Gundaker, "'Without Parse of Script': The Interaction of Conventional Literacy and Vernacular Practice in African American Expressive Culture" (Ph.D. diss., Yale University, 1992), chap. 4; Robert Farris Thompson, *Face of the Gods: Art and Altars of Africa and the African Americas* (New York: Museum for African Art and Munich: Prestel, 1993), 76–78.

36. Thompson, *Face of the Gods*, 61; Joyner, "World," 87.

37. Angelou, *Bird*, 180.

38. Henry Louis Gates Jr., "The Face and Voice of Blackness," in *Facing History: The Black Image in American Art, 1710–1940*, ed. Guy C. McElroy (Washington, DC: Corcoran Gallery of Art and Bedford Arts, 1990), xxix–xxx.

39. But note the scathing reference to the word *sympathy* in Angelou, *Bird*, 201.

40. Ibid., 201, 218.

41. Lawrence Levine, *Black Culture and Black Consciousness* (Oxford: Oxford Univ. Press, 1977), 120; Peter Parish, *Slavery* (Halifax: BAAS, 1979; rpt. 1992), 34; Kolchin, *American Slavery*, 154–55.

42. Parish, *Slavery*, 189.

43. Angelou, *Bird*, 89.

44. Paul Gilroy, *The Black Atlantic* (Cambridge: Harvard Univ. Press), 37. See also Jon-Christian Suggs's letter to the editor, *PMLA* 112:1 (Jan. 1997): 116–17.

45. Donna Graves, "Representing the Race: Detroit's *Monument to Joe Louis*," in *Critical Issues in Public Art*, ed. Harriet F. Senie and Sally Webster (New York: HarperCollins, 1992), 222.

46. David Nicholson, "Confronting Our Past: We Can't Rewrite the Legacy of Slavery by Denying That It Happened," *Washington Post National Weekly Edition*, Jan. 1–7, 1996, 25.

47. Mary Johnson, "Heyward Shepherd Memorial and John Brown Fort Tablet: Special History Study" (National Park Service, third draft, July 31, 1995), 13. Bruce Noble of the National Park Service sent me this manuscript.

48. See Genovese, *Roll*, 353.

49. Gaines Foster, *Ghosts of the Confederacy: Defeat, the Lost Cause, and the Emergence of the New South, 1865 to 1913* (New York: Oxford Univ. Press, 1987), 7; Robert E. McGlone, "Rescripting a Troubled Past: John Brown's Family and the Harpers Ferry Conspiracy," *Journal of American History* 75 (March 1989): 1184.

50. Johnson, *Shepherd*, 7

51. Ibid., 19.

52. Kolchin, *American Slavery*, 205.

53. Art historian Kirk Savage drew my attention to this memorial.

54. Interviews with Edwin Carpenter, SCV, Jan. 21, 1994, and Melvin Austin, Feb. 21, 1994; Charles Edward Foiles, SCV, letter to the editor, *Richmond Times-Dispatch*, Nov. 6, 1993; Melvin Austin to the Nottoway County Board of Supervisors, Oct. 20, 1993.

55. Johnson, *Shepherd*.

56. Ibid., 14, 23, 25.

57. Angelou, *Bird*, 173.

58. Johnson, *Shepherd*, 26.

59. Ibid., 30, 31.

60. *The Complete Poems of Paul Lawrence Dunbar* (New York: Dodd, Mead, 1962). I thank Joanne Braxton for her comments on an earlier version of this chapter, presented at the Collegium for African American Research, Liverpool, UK, April 26, 1997. See *The Collected Poems of Paul Laurence Dunbar*, ed. and intro. Joanne Braxton (Charlottesville: Univ. Press of Virginia, 1993); chap. 6 of her *Black Women Writing Autobiography: A Tradition within a Tradition* (Philadelphia: Temple Univ Press, 1989).

61. Angelou, *Bird*, 201.

62. For a view contrary to that expressed here, see Nicholson, "Confronting Our Past," 25.

CONTRIBUTORS

Elizabeth Barnum has spent over five years living and working in Barbados, first in the Peace Corps and more recently as the recipient of a Fulbright grant to study the relationship between tourism and Barbadian art and craft. She received her doctorate in anthroplogy and education at Teachers College, Columbia University. Currently Assistant Dean in the Graduate School, she teaches anthropology and advises international students and scholars at the State University of New York at Stony Brook.

Joanne M. Braxton is Francis L. and Edwin L. Cummings Professor of American Studies and Professor of English at the College of William and Mary where she directs the Middle Passage Project. A poet and scholar, she is the author of *Sometimes I Think of Maryland* and *Black Women Writing Autobiography: A Tradition within a Tradition.* She has edited an anthology of Afra-American writing, *Wild Women in the Whirlwind,* and an expanded edition of the *Collected Poems of Paul Laurence Dunbar.* Having taught at the College of William and Mary for eighteen years, she has received numerous awards for excellence in teaching.

Marland E. Buckner Jr. is currently Senior Policy Adviser to Congressman Harold Ford Jr. Previously, he served as visiting research analyst at the Joint Center for Political and Economic Studies in Washington, D.C. His work has appeared in the *Washington Afro-American, Focus Magazine,* and the *Washington Post,* and he is completing a doctoral dissertation in American studies at the College of William and Mary entitled "Black Social Thought in Revolutionary America."

Tynes Cowan is currently Adjunct Instructor of English and completing his doctorate in American studies at the College of William and Mary. He grew up in Birmingham, taught high school in rural Alabama, and taught English for four years at Northeastern University in Boston. His dissertation focuses on the themes of swamps and escaped slaves in nineteenth-century America.

Ywone D. Edwards is Staff Archaeologist in the Department of Archaeological Research of the Colonial Williamsburg Foundation. She has published numerous papers on African American material culture and is currently investigating healing practices in the southeastern United States and Jamaica.

Grey Gundaker teaches American studies and anthropology at the College of William and Mary. Her research interests include the visual arts, material life, landscape, and education. She is the author of *Signs of Diaspora / Diaspora of Signs: Literacies and Vernacular Practice in African America.*

Patrick Hagopian teaches American history and American studies in the School of Humanities and Social Sciences, University of Glamorgan, Wales. He is the author of a forthcoming book on the social memory of the Vietnam War and currently is investigating the interpretation of African American history in museums and other sites.

George L. Henderson holds a Ph.D. in geography from the University of California, Berkeley. Currently, he is Assistant Professor of Geography and Cultural Studies at the University of Arizona. His research focuses on economic and political aspects of actual and fictional landscapes, and he is the author of the forthcoming book *Romancing the Sand: California and the Geographical Imagination, 1882–1924.*

Alice Eley Jones is African American History Coordinator for Historic Stagville in Durham, North Carolina, serves on the Human Sciences Department faculty at North Carolina Central University, and is researching black builders and architects for Preservation North Carolina. She also researched the social history of slave families and communities for the development of the Pleasant Company's Addie Walker African American doll and is a specialist in history programs for young people.

Frances Jones-Sneed teaches history at Massachusetts College of Liberal Arts in North Adams, Massachusetts. She received her Ph.D. at the University of Missouri, Columbia. Her specialities are American history and African American history with emphasis on the American West.

Judith McWillie teaches drawing and painting at the University of Georgia and has been documenting and curating exhibitions of Afro-Atlantic art from the southeastern United States for nearly two decades. Her numerous publications include *Another Face of the Diamond* and *The Migrations of Meaning* for INTAR Latin American Gallery.

John F. Szwed is John M. Musser Professor of Anthroplogy, Afro-American Studies, Music, and American Studies at Yale University, where he teaches courses on American film, the history of jazz, and creolized literatures. He is the author of *Space Is the Place: The Lives and Times of Sun Ra* and with Roger D. Abrahams edited *Afro-American Anthropology, Discovering Black America, After Africa,* and the annotated bibliography *Afro-American Folk Culture.*

Vanessa Thaxton is Curator of History and Coordinator of Membership and Community Programs at the Hampton Museum, Hampton University. Formerly associated with the Penn Center on St. Helena, she is especially interested in the material and expressive culture of the Sea Islands.

Robert Farris Thompson is Master of Timothy Dwight College and the Colonel John Trumbull Professor of the History of Art at Yale University. Since his earliest writing for the *Saturday Review* in the 1960s his work has set the standard for comparative study of visual art, performance, and aesthetics in the Afro-Atlantic diaspora. His most notable publications include *African Art in Motion, The Four Moments of the Sun: Kongo Art in Two Worlds, Flash of the Spirit: African and Afro-American Art and Philosophy,* and *Face of the Gods: Art and Altars of Africa and the African Americas.*

INDEX

abolition, 125, 137, 138, 148, 200, 217
Abrahams, Roger D., 19, 171, 248
acculturation, 223
adapt(ation), 146, 150, 205, 207
aesthetic, 6, 14, 15, 45, 59, 60, 71, 74, 84, 85, 90, 120, 157, 250
affirmation, 18, 44, 55, 68, 135
Africa(nization), 3, 5–8, 14–22, 32, 37–40, 42–43, 45, 54–55, 58–60, 63–64, 67–73, 84, 86, 90–96, 101–9, 114, 115, 118, 119, 121, 132, 136, 142, 143, 145–49, 155–56, 171, 175, 199, 204–7, 212–19, 221–24, 227–32, 234–37, 239–42, 245–53, 256, 258, 260–62, 264–70, 273–78, 280–82, 284–91
Alger, Horatio, 286
alienation, 73, 133, 278
Allen, W. F., 241
Alvord, John, 218, 222
ancestors, 14–16, 18, 19, 38, 40, 61, 63, 68, 69, 94, 95, 101, 107–9, 265, 267
Anderson, Robert Ball, 152–53
Angelou, Maya, 284–87, 290, 292
Angola, 37, 45, 63
antebellum, 94, 118, 119, 194, 197, 234
architecture, 64, 104, 107, 184, 186, 259
Argus, 177, 184

Armstrong, Douglas, 257–58
Armstrong, Robert Plant, 68–69, 71, 73–74, 89
Armstrong, Zebedee ("Z.B."), 89–91
Ashanti, Faheem C., 94, 102, 104
assimilation, 45, 186
audience, 116, 117, 121, 125, 130, 240, 276–78, 280–83, 286, 289
Austin, Melvin, 290
autonomy, 74, 216, 223, 224, 260, 270

Bakongo, 38, 40, 55, 56, 59, 60, 251, 252
balance, 41, 64, 93, 107, 195
bank(ing), 15, 23, 150, 152, 211, 212, 216–25
bankita, 61
Barbados, 16, 155, 157, 170–73, 175, 267
Baruchello, Gianfranco, 92
basimbi, 61
beads, 159, 261, 267
Beaudry, Mary, 257
Beckles, Hilary, 155
belief, 21, 22, 57, 61, 65, 70, 71, 88, 95, 115, 126–28, 186, 221, 227, 245, 247, 251–53, 261, 264
Bell, Hesketh J., 72
Bell, Malcolm and Muriel, 70
Biggers, John, 57–59
Black Codes, 215
blacksmith, 107, 108, 282
Blassingame, John, 94
Blockson, Charles, 142
blues, 39, 40, 42, 63, 64, 85, 284–85

Bolden, Hawkins, 62, 84
bones, 16, 45, 54, 55, 57, 73, 84, 169, 170, 250, 258, 260–62, 266, 267
border, 65, 83, 86, 114–17, 119–20, 125, 132, 133, 135–39, 143, 169, 252
bottle, 4, 5, 17, 20, 25, 26, 45, 54, 56, 57, 59, 60, 63, 65, 67, 69, 71, 72, 84, 85, 191, 249, 261–63
bottle garden, 66, 67
bottle shelf, 60
bottle tree, 42, 44, 56, 58–60, 62, 63, 71
boundary, 14, 15, 20, 25, 41, 45, 55, 61, 65, 83, 105, 116, 169, 193, 196, 205, 252, 287
Bowens, Cyrus, 62, 69–71
Bowens, Eddie, 69–70
Bowens, Eva Mae, 70
Bradley, David, 4, 113–43
Braxton, Anthony, 34–35
Braxton, Harry, 179
breakage, 15, 17, 20
broken wheels, 17
Brown, Henry Box, 118
Brown, John, 288–91
Brown, Kenneth, 261
Brown, Marion, 44
Brown, William Wells, 130
burial, 15–19, 38, 117, 121, 135, 140, 141, 250, 261, 265–67, 285
Burse, Clarence, 83–84
Byrd, William, 193, 207

cabin, 94, 106, 115, 116, 132, 151–53, 197, 201, 232, 234, 252–56, 258–59, 261–63, 265, 268–70

Campbell, Stanley, 136–37
Capote, Truman, 58
Caribbean, 6, 16, 22
Carolina yell, 39
celebration, 103, 170, 239, 290
ceramic(s) 84, 159, 251, 256, 259, 260, 263, 267
Chaney, James, 273
Chaneysville Incident, 4, 15, 113–43
Charleston, S.C., 39, 56, 61, 63, 229–31
charms, 38, 45, 54, 56, 61, 64, 87, 109, 169, 251–52, 263–64, 266
Christian, 21, 22, 101, 102, 130, 155, 205, 222, 227, 228, 235–37, 281, 289
church, 7, 69, 71, 104, 106, 149, 155, 184, 190–91, 206, 222, 227–29, 233–40, 242, 265, 266
circles, 40–45, 55, 57, 104, 128, 169, 170, 173, 174, 178, 241, 251, 260
coins, 59, 156, 261, 267
collectors/dealers, 7, 14, 17, 20, 68
Collymore, Frank, 157
Colonial Williamsburg, 259, 264, 274, 277–83, 289
colonization, 32
Colonoware, 260
color, 19, 20, 54, 55, 57, 58, 63, 83, 84, 87, 103, 104, 127, 150, 157, 159, 171, 173, 187, 251, 252, 261, 269, 270, 277, 290
Coltrane, John, 34
commercial, 17, 66, 159, 174, 175, 234, 258, 283
commode, 67, 69, 71
commodification, 14
common ground, 4
communicate(ion), 14, 21, 44, 107, 121, 139, 203, 204, 246, 248, 270, 275, 284, 287, 293
community, 14, 16, 23, 41, 54, 55, 67, 70, 72, 86, 87,

93–96, 101, 102, 107, 108, 136, 138, 145–53, 155–59, 169, 171, 172, 174, 175, 177, 179, 184–90, 194–200, 205, 215, 216, 223, 224, 228–42, 249, 256, 259, 276, 284–86, 289
conform, 108, 118, 145, 146, 148
conjunction, 14, 71, 85
conjure, 71, 108, 205, 237, 261
connoisseur(ship), 73
consumption, 69, 213, 256, 267
containers, 44, 45, 54, 57, 59, 62, 169, 174, 258, 263, 289
containment, 45, 57–8, 65, 67, 85, 91, 93, 104, 169, 196, 251, 261
control, 15, 16, 107, 114, 193, 194, 213, 214, 227, 228, 230, 235, 237, 253, 262, 267–69, 281, 287
Cooley, Rossa, 230
cosmic, 93
cosmogram, 21–2, 38, 40–43, 45, 57, 61, 169, 251, 261
court, 136, 150, 236
cowrie shells, 93, 106, 109, 261, 267
Crabtree, Ray, 67
Craft, William and Ellen, 119
creativity, 246, 247, 249
Creel, Margaret Washington, 231, 234–35
creole, 32, 41, 45, 54, 57, 155
creolization, 32, 33, 67, 247
crime, 119, 236
Criss, Ester, 43
Croft Praise House, 232–36, 242
Crossman, Ann, 279
crossmark, 6, 21, 41, 54, 57, 69, 169, 235, 251, 260
crossroads, 41, 42, 70, 171, 262

crucifix, 7, 86, 87
Cuba, 41, 57, 58, 62, 211
cultural production, 6, 8, 15, 21, 22, 92, 94, 116, 141, 214, 249
cultural resistance/retentions, 72, 156, 231, 239
culture, 8, 14, 16, 19, 21, 22, 37–45, 56, 61, 65–67, 71, 73, 105, 117, 119, 155–57, 186, 223–24, 229–31, 236, 245–49, 251–57, 260, 261, 267, 280, 286
Cunningham, Baily, 254
currency, 261

Dada, 65, 67
dancing/dance, 37, 40, 42, 43, 59, 60, 101, 104, 106, 150, 177, 241, 250, 277
Danto, Arthur C., 71
Dardel, Eric, 145–46
Davenport, Elijah, 83–84
dead, the, 15–18, 20–22, 38, 40, 41, 55, 56, 58, 62, 69, 93–96, 104, 107–8, 115, 127, 130, 251, 265, 273
death, 4, 5, 15, 21, 41, 55, 56, 88, 101, 105, 108, 121, 122, 193, 251, 265, 266
decode, 246
decorations, 7, 8, 15, 17, 18, 20, 37, 40, 43–45, 54, 57, 60, 72, 83, 86, 104, 159, 169, 170, 173, 235, 247, 250, 251, 264, 265, 267, 268
decorative, 8, 15, 156, 158
Deetz, James, 262
devil, 60, 71, 86, 88, 205, 236
Dial, Thornton, 59
diaspora, 6, 7, 16, 21, 37, 132, 156, 246, 247
discipline, 213, 228, 235, 246
discontinuity, 68
disenfranchise, 225

Disney, 278–80, 282
disruption, 68, 136
divination, 141, 285
divining rods, 93, 106, 109
doctor, 71, 72, 74, 102, 107,
    108, 205, 237
Dodd, Lamar, 85
Doe, Kenneth, 238, 242
Dominica, 56
Door, David, 173
Dorsey, Henry, 54
Douglas, Mary, 248
Douglass, Frederick, 113,
    118–21, 125, 132, 140,
    265
Doyle, Sam, 230
dreams, 4, 92, 130, 147
drums, 39, 40, 43, 44, 58,
    101, 102, 108, 212, 277
Duchamp, Marcel, 65–68,
    71, 74, 83, 91–92
Dumas, Henry, 37, 63
Dunbar, Joseph, 254
Dunbar, Paul Laurence, 286,
    291–92
Dyckman, Henry, 186

Early, Gerald, 116
Eco, Umberto, 35
economic(s), 14, 67, 147,
    184, 213–15, 217, 218,
    221, 223, 224, 232, 245,
    247, 248, 256, 259, 264,
    267, 276, 281, 282, 284
ecstatic, 39, 42, 66, 91
Eden, 146
education, 59, 96, 102, 134,
    157, 187–89, 222–24,
    229, 282
Edwards, James, 152–53
elders, 3, 4, 130, 219, 221,
    237, 239, 240
emancipation, 16, 18, 135,
    145, 213, 221, 222, 224,
    270, 275, 287, 288
Emerson, Matthew, 250
encode, 40, 156, 252, 263
encryption, 287
Equiano, Olaudah, 267
escape, 89, 96, 101, 102,
    115–20, 125, 130, 133,

135, 136, 138–43, 155,
    184, 194–204, 275, 281,
    282, 284, 292–93
Escott, Paul D., 251
ethnocentrism, 73, 284
ethnography, 16, 18, 156,
    248
Evans, Susie T., 21–22
evil, 38, 41, 45, 55, 57–60,
    63, 73, 88, 103, 105,
    195, 251, 252, 263, 269,
    290
exhibit, 18, 65, 67, 73, 234,
    250, 252, 273, 274, 276,
    281
exoduster, 146, 147
exploitation, 184, 193, 245

face jug, 60, 63
family, 3, 6, 7, 14–17, 20,
    39, 44, 58, 69, 93, 96,
    101, 102, 105–7, 117,
    120, 121, 129, 133, 134,
    136, 142, 143, 147, 149,
    153, 155, 158, 159, 172,
    178, 193, 201, 202, 206,
    212, 213, 217, 218, 232,
    238, 239, 249, 252, 255,
    257, 259, 261, 262, 268
farmers, 107, 117, 121, 145,
    147, 152, 211, 219, 220,
    261
federal, 136, 212, 215, 216,
    222, 273, 276, 288
Feiss, Carl, 184–85
fence, 5, 15, 20, 83, 84, 86,
    139, 158, 196, 229, 252,
    255, 257
Ferguson, Leland, 260
fertility, 61, 109
festival, 233
fetish, 108
field hollers, 39
figuration, 45, 169
flash, 14, 20, 40, 44, 54, 58,
    59, 69, 169
Flemming, Fox and Juanita,
    83
folk, 8, 19, 40, 127, 236,
    238
folk art, 8, 87, 230

folklore, 17, 39, 57, 115,
    141, 205, 206, 286
folklorist, 71, 253
forest, 20, 38, 39, 58, 61, 62,
    95, 116, 194, 202, 205,
    206
Forten, Charlotte, 230, 241
found objects, 68, 157
Freedmen's Bank, 15, 211,
    212, 217, 222, 224, 225
Fried, Marc, 186
Fugitive Slave Act, 115, 132,
    136
Fuller, Richard, 227–28
function, 59, 67, 71, 93,
    101, 141, 173, 184, 205,
    207, 218, 233, 236, 237,
    242, 247, 250, 257
funeral, 16–18, 70, 126, 139,
    234, 251, 267
futu, 56

Gallman, Simon, 220
garbage, 68, 158, 172, 257,
    258, 262
garden, 6–8, 21, 38, 43, 56,
    60, 62, 66, 67, 72, 83,
    145, 146, 148, 151,
    156–59, 169, 170, 174,
    177, 185, 199, 202, 213,
    221, 252, 253, 258, 259,
    267, 276
gatepost, 21
Genovese, Eugene, 195, 231,
    264, 269
geography, 4, 7, 22, 101,
    104, 114, 118, 134–35,
    139, 145, 178, 246
geography, historical, 118,
    139
geography, social, 134
gesture, 38, 43, 45, 62, 64,
    131
ghost, 105, 140
Gilmore, Ruby, 84
glass, 4, 14, 17, 20, 42, 56,
    60, 84, 86, 87, 233, 251,
    252, 255, 267, 285
Glave, E. J., 17
Gleigher, Peggy, 186
Glory, 287

Goodman, Andrew, 273
Graham, Effie, 19–20
grave, 14, 17–20, 38, 40, 54,
     56, 62, 69, 86, 90, 104,
     117, 129, 142, 143, 191,
     264–67, 273
grave dirt, 252
Gravely, Jack, 281–82
graveyard, 15, 16, 18, 20,
     22, 40, 45, 54, 55, 117,
     130, 133, 170, 251,
     265–67
Great Migration, 15
Greely, Sim, 215
Greer, Charlie, 84
Griffin, Ralph, 61
Gullah, 45, 229, 231–33,
     235–37
Gullah Jack, 45
Gundaker, Grey, 70, 84, 171,
     247, 251, 266
Guyton, Tyree, 43–44, 84

habitus, 116, 122
Haiti, 40, 57, 104, 198
Hall, Dilmus, 43, 85–88, 90,
     92
Hamler, A. J., 20–21
harmony, 107, 171, 235
Harper, Bob, 84
Harris, Trudier, 140
Harvey, Bessie, 73
haunt, 39, 118, 279
healer, 45, 54, 55, 65, 86,
     247, 265, 270
healing, 18, 45, 54, 55, 65,
     86, 247, 265, 270
hegemony/hegemonic, 121,
     177, 179, 185, 186
herbs, 38, 45, 54–55, 57, 59,
     102, 169–70, 174, 231,
     251–52, 265–66
heritage, 57, 63, 64, 90, 146,
     192, 230, 239, 240
Herskovits, Melville, 16, 205
Hill, Saul, 54
historical reconstruction, 3,
     4, 14, 18, 20–23, 113,
     118, 125–28, 142, 277
historical representation,
     274, 280, 281, 293

history, 4, 63, 66, 70, 93,
     101, 107, 118, 121,
     133–35, 139, 141, 143,
     146, 149, 153, 221, 231,
     239, 246, 256, 263, 270,
     273, 274, 276–84, 287,
     290
Hoffman, Daniel G., 39
holiday, 63, 156, 174
Holley, Lonnie, 68–70, 90–91
Holloway, Joseph, 231
Holmes, Lula, 242
holy ground, 93, 96, 104,
     107
homefolk, 238
home ground, 3, 4, 8, 14, 15
homeplace, 3, 4, 18, 148
Homer, Winslow, 57
honor, 14, 16, 18, 41, 69,
     85, 86, 95, 101, 104,
     276, 285–91
hoodoo, 18, 71, 72, 252
House, Grace, 230
hubcaps, 7, 21, 22, 39, 40,
     43–45, 65, 83
Hudson, Colin, 156
Hurston, Zora Neale, 4–5,
     94, 206
Hyatt, Harry Middleton, 41,
     71–72, 89

icon(ography), 20, 44, 45,
     54, 58, 60, 63, 84, 85,
     194
identity, 101, 117, 119, 145,
     179, 248, 251, 281, 284
ideogram, 91
ideography, 38, 56, 65
improvisation, 5, 68, 139,
     249, 251, 253
Ingersoll, Ernest, 17
initiation, 40, 93, 95, 96,
     101–4, 107, 108, 125
inkabera, 59
interaction, 26, 247, 249,
     278
interpret(ers), 3, 5, 7, 8,
     21–23, 26, 35, 39, 41,
     43, 86, 93, 101, 120,
     156, 220, 245, 250, 252,
     256, 259–61, 263, 267,

269, 273–74, 276–81,
     283, 291
inversion, 114, 136, 143,
     206, 207
invocation, 71, 73, 74, 88,
     89, 286
Isherwood, Baron, 248

Jackson, Henry, 84
Jacobs, Harriet, 195, 266
Jamaica, 7, 246, 250, 257,
     268
jars, 45, 57, 59, 63, 89, 260
Jefferson, Thomas, 260, 279
Jim Crow, 3
John, Beverly, 231
Johnson, James Weldon, 4,
     286
Johnson, John C., 178
journey, 40, 95, 139, 146,
     151, 206, 212, 232
junk, 7, 20–22, 68, 177

King, Julia, 257
kinship, 178, 186, 238
Kongo, 25, 37–45, 54–63,
     169, 251, 252, 260, 261,
     266
Kornegay, George, 84

labor, 6, 7, 15, 17, 93, 96,
     148, 158, 200, 212, 213,
     215–21, 227, 253, 254,
     269, 279
land, public/private owner-
     ship, 3, 15, 39, 65, 96,
     101, 145–49, 151–53,
     155, 157–59, 171, 174,
     175, 179, 184, 188, 193,
     194, 200, 214–20,
     228–30, 234, 236, 242,
     258
landscape, 3–6, 8, 14, 21, 22,
     37, 64, 68, 94, 106, 107,
     114, 117, 129, 131–36,
     139–41, 146, 151, 153,
     156, 158, 175, 177–79,
     184, 185, 194, 227, 245,
     248, 250, 252, 253, 256,
     262, 265, 269–71
Langley, Nina, 61

law, 15, 56, 89, 101, 120,
    136–38, 150, 157, 171,
    198, 203, 236
Lee, Cornelius, 42, 59
Lee, Robert E., 201, 288
LeFalle-Collins, Lizzetta, 84
legend, 43, 45, 74, 115, 129,
    133, 135, 140–43, 148,
    149, 153
LeGree, Prince, 240
libation, 41, 94, 190, 191
liberation, 114, 214–18, 222,
    225, 287
Lichtenberg-Ettinger,
    Bracha, 133
Light, Joe, 44
liminal, 125, 193
liming, 157, 170–74
Lincoln, Abraham, 188, 207,
    218, 222
literacy, 221–24
lowcountry, 211–18,
    221–24, 228, 229
Lusane, Bennie, 25, 35, 84

MacGaffey, Wyatt, 61, 91
magic, 18, 57–58, 94–95,
    105, 107, 155, 186, 205,
    280
Mahoney, William, 6
maroons, 155, 194–200,
    203, 204
Marris, Peter, 186
Martinique, 33, 56
Mary Jenkins Praise House,
    232–37, 242
mask, 21, 71, 84, 108
material culture, 14, 16, 22,
    43, 247, 249, 253
Matthews, Christy, 277, 280
Maum Katie, 237
McKee, Larry, 253, 263
McNorton, William, 8,
    145–53
McWright, Joseph, 212, 214
mediation, 38, 41, 262
medicine, 41, 45, 55–57, 59,
    61, 72, 93, 107, 108, 155,
    156, 169, 231, 252, 261
Meinig, D. W., 245
Melancon, Victor, 83

memorial, 20, 142, 276,
    288–91
memory, 4, 6, 63, 64, 137,
    147, 152, 192, 270, 274,
    275, 284
metaphysics, 21, 34, 58, 71,
    84, 128
Micheaux, Oscar, 152–53
Middle Passage, 16, 156
migration, 15, 18, 70, 146,
    147
Miller, David, 194
Miller, Henry, 257
Milligan, Clara, 61
mirrors, 20, 22, 25–27,
    40–42, 45, 58–60, 67,
    69, 70, 83, 169, 190
Mississippi Delta, 39, 43
Mitchell, Sam, 214, 222
monument, 69, 70, 170, 173,
    174, 273, 284–90
Moody, Minnie Hite, 5
moral economy, 116–22,
    126, 140–42
moral intimidation, 55
Morrison, Toni, 37, 248
motion, 40–45, 58, 83, 169,
    234
Mrozowski, Steve, 258
Murray, Albert, 39
Murray, Ellen, 230
Murray, J. B., 40
museum, 22, 66, 68, 70, 73,
    83, 234, 274–76, 279,
    281–82, 284, 287–88
music, 27, 33–35, 39, 40, 42,
    44, 101, 150, 231, 234,
    238–240, 249, 250, 265,
    271, 278, 284, 285, 290
myth(ologies), 88, 90, 92,
    117, 138, 194, 279, 288

nails, 54, 87, 252, 261
Naipaul, V. S., 7
narrative, 6, 115, 118–20,
    125, 127, 129, 130, 133,
    140, 141, 177, 248, 266,
    286
nationalist, 170
Native Americans, 94, 95,
    148, 250, 260

negotiate(d), 142, 250, 255
neighborhood, 3, 6–8, 43,
    65, 67, 83, 86–87, 158,
    177, 203–4, 289
nexus, 67, 71, 281
nkisi/minkisi, 38, 41, 45,
    54–56, 58–61, 169, 252

obeah, 72, 74, 155, 157, 252
object encoding, 85
objects, 5, 8, 14, 16–18,
    20–22, 25, 38, 40, 44, 54,
    57, 60–61, 65, 67–73, 83,
    86, 89, 101, 156–57, 234,
    245–52, 259–67, 270, 285
O'Brien, John, 27
Olmsted, Frederick Law, 39,
    184, 200, 252, 255,
    268–69
Olney, James, 120
Olson, Charles, 113
omen, 126, 128, 130
Opala, Joseph, 231
oppression, 38, 125, 133, 247,
    274–75, 278–79, 293
oral tradition, 249, 264, 271
outlaw, 197–98, 203–4

Packnett, Gyp, 15
Palmer, Lavina, 218–19
palo, 62
Pandi, Mayolo, 56
park(s), 16, 19, 155–59,
    169–75, 184, 278–79,
    282, 289
participation, 66, 171, 185,
    213, 223
past, 4, 18, 21, 65, 71,
    91–92, 115–16, 118,
    122, 134, 185, 237,
    245–49, 256, 265–66,
    270–71, 274–79, 283,
    287, 291
patrols, 285
Paul, William, 73
performance, 16, 35, 71,
    245, 249, 276, 281–82,
    286
Petzold, Lynn, 178
Picasso, Pablo, 58
Pierce, E. L., 222

pipes, 20–21, 25, 37–38, 40, 45, 54, 67, 69–70, 84, 86, 174, 250, 267–68
plantation, 15–16, 19, 37, 39, 94, 101, 104, 148, 193–96, 202–6, 212–15, 218–19, 227–32, 234, 236, 241, 247, 253–65, 270, 275, 285, 288; Carter's Grove, 258, 270, 277; Drax Hall, 257; Dunbar, 254; Flowerdew Hundred, 262; Garrison, 250; Hampton, 264; Kingsmill, 258–59; Ladies Island, 222; Levi Jordan, 261; Mary Jenkins, 234; Monticello, 260–61; Mount Vernon, 260, 275–77; Parker, 69; Pooshee, 61; Rich Neck, 258–59; Sea Island, 211; Stagville, 93, 102, 105; Wakefield, 174; Willcox, 262
Polite, Sam, 212
popular, 67, 114, 119, 133, 138, 156, 275
postmodern, 14, 64, 71, 92
pottery, 20, 55, 57, 67, 174, 251, 267
power(s), 19–20, 37–42, 45, 57–58, 62–63, 65–74, 83, 86, 88–89, 91, 93, 95, 101–3, 107–9, 114, 116, 127, 131–32, 140, 146, 156, 184, 202, 251, 263, 265, 274, 285–86
praise house/prayer house, 227–43
Presha, Rachel, 57–58
priest, 40–41, 71, 94, 102–8
property, 3, 14–15, 22, 42, 45, 84, 107, 149–51, 213–15, 217, 221, 225, 227, 239, 257, 263, 282, 283
proprietary, 275, 293
protection, 14, 38, 41, 45, 86, 104–5, 107, 109,

130, 196, 247, 252, 268, 270, 285
Puckett, N. N., 17
pun, 38, 83, 85, 251
Pygmy, 39

quarter, 3, 15, 105, 205, 232, 250, 252, 254–55, 258–70, 276–77

race, 7, 88, 114, 116, 125, 132, 135, 140, 143, 145, 147, 149, 153, 219, 222–23, 263, 273–74, 281, 290, 293
rags, 54–55, 57, 269
readymades, 65, 68, 74
Reagon, Bernice Johnson, 242
Reconstruction, 15, 132, 212, 230, 288
refuge, 15, 149, 153, 193, 288
reification, 134
reiteration, 5
religion, 16, 21, 40–42, 54, 56, 62–63, 72, 85–86, 88, 90, 94–96, 101, 105–7, 151–52, 155–56, 159, 175, 205, 227–28, 231, 233, 235–37, 239–42, 251–52, 260–61, 278, 285
repetition, 45, 115
resistance, 72, 136–39, 155, 186, 194, 204–5, 228, 265, 284
response, 42, 84, 101, 126, 185, 240, 246, 248, 252–53, 284, 290–91
Reynolds, Julia, 233–42
Riley, William, 214
ring shout, 38, 40, 42–43, 234, 241
rite(s), 71, 95–96, 105, 205, 251, 285
ritual, 41–42, 55, 59, 62, 92, 95, 101, 103, 105, 108, 228, 247–50, 252, 260–61, 267, 269
Rivers, Benjamin, 211–21

Roach, Hildred, 249
Robertson, Ben, 6
Robinson, Solon, 254
Rockefeller, John D., Jr., 277
rod(s), 67, 70, 93, 106, 109
Rogers, Henry, 263
root cellar, 255, 258–60, 263
roots, 4, 6, 15, 18, 38, 45, 54, 57, 60–62, 68, 71, 73, 102, 156, 169–70
root spirit, 60
Rose, Willie Lee, 230
Rosengarten, Theodore, 229–30, 232
Rubin, William, 83
runaways, 115, 129, 136–37, 139, 143, 193–207, 256, 264, 270

sacred (places), 21–22, 84, 93, 96, 101–7, 175, 205–7, 249–50, 266, 280
safekeeping, 14
sanctuary, 8, 14, 104
Sartre, Jean Paul, 141
Sarup, Madan, 114
Saxton, Rufus, 217
scarecrow, 62, 83–85
Schussheim, Morton J., 184–85
Schwerner, Michael, 273
Scott, James, 116
sculpture, 40, 45, 58–59, 61, 68, 70, 84, 86, 88, 101, 108, 169–70
Sea Islands, 39, 211–16, 219–24, 227–32, 235, 242
Seay, James, 58
secret society, 71, 96, 102, 107, 236
secular, 22, 40, 249–50, 363–64
self-consciousness, 91, 217, 223–24
semiotic, 285–86
Setiloane, Gabriel, 70
shaman, 261
shells, 17, 21, 38, 43, 45, 54, 67, 69–70, 93, 106,

shells *(cont.)*
109, 170, 173, 251–52,
260–70
Shepherd, Heyward,
289–91
Sherman Reservation, 215
shouts, 38–43, 106, 231,
234, 239–42
Showers, Susan, 16
signifying, 38, 108, 114–20,
128, 139–43, 193,
195–96
simbi, 61
slave, fugitive, 115, 117–21,
129–30, 134, 136–42,
193–207
slave auction, 274, 278,
280–81, 283, 289
slave houses, 3, 15, 245–70
slave narrative, 118–20,
130, 140, 266
slavery, 38, 56, 96, 118–20,
125, 138, 143, 145,
147–48, 195, 204, 212,
215–16, 218–24, 228,
230, 236, 245–49,
255–56, 264–67, 270,
274–75, 277, 279, 281,
284, 286–87, 290, 293
slave-time, 7, 22
Smith, Leo, 34, 44
Smith, Theophus, 231
snake, 57, 94, 102–6, 109,
195, 207
Sobel, Mechal, 3, 232, 254,
265–66
soul, 39–41, 56, 61–64, 105,
127–28, 206, 228, 251,
266
Soyinka, Wole, 91
space, 3, 5, 14, 38, 40,
43–44, 89, 91, 105,
113–16, 132, 138–43,
146, 151, 156–57, 159,
172, 175, 184–85, 190,
193, 201, 205, 207, 234,
242, 246–47, 249, 253,
257–59, 262, 264,
269–70, 275, 287
spatial practice, 113–19,
122, 130–36, 140–41;

situated practice, 114,
120
spectacle, 281–82
spells, 18, 57, 126, 128
spiral, 38, 40, 86, 106
spirit, 16, 18–20, 38,
40–45, 54–65, 72, 74,
83, 90, 93, 96, 101, 103,
105–8, 126, 128, 169,
205, 217, 228, 240–41,
251–52, 264–66, 277,
285, 291
spiritual, 16, 21, 40–43, 55,
58, 61, 63, 65, 68–72,
74, 83, 88–89, 92–96,
102–8, 146–48, 175,
194, 205–6, 236–37,
249, 251–52, 263–65,
277
spiritual music, 43, 64, 231,
236–41
St. Helena, 211–12, 215,
218–19, 221–22,
227–35, 239–43
Steinsaltz, Adin, 88–89
sticks, 56, 58, 62, 88,
93–94, 105–9, 202, 250,
253–54, 268
stones/rocks, 14, 21, 42, 45,
54–56, 61, 63, 68, 84,
90, 126, 134, 142, 157,
169–74, 261, 266,
285–86, 288–89
Storer College, 288, 290–91
storytelling, 115–18,
121–22, 286
Stuckey, Sterling, 42, 234
Sturghill, Annie, 84–85, 89
Sun Ra, 34
superstition, 72
surveillance, 139
swamps, 39, 187, 193–207,
213, 273
symbol, 3, 21, 39, 41–43,
55, 63, 93–96, 101–8,
111, 156–57, 171, 175,
177–78, 251, 256, 261,
266, 288, 291
sympathy, 150, 202–3,
290–92
"Sympathy," 286, 291–92

syncretism, 65, 67, 71, 266
syndesis, 91
Szwed, John, 19, 248

task system, 213–14, 216,
219–21
Tate, Greg, 32
Tatten, Pearl, 290–91
Taylor, Cecil, 44
Taylor, Clyde, 37
Taylor, Quintard, 152
Taylor, R. H., 199
Temple, Paula, 72
testimony, 43, 194,
199–206, 212, 285
Thompson, Robert Farris,
8, 18, 25, 67, 72, 84,
159, 169, 251
threshold, 18, 55, 105
tomb, 38, 41, 54–55, 63,
170
Tomkins, Ivan, 69
Toomer, Jean, 37
Towne, Laura, 219, 230, 237
tradition, 21, 37–45, 54–63,
70, 72, 84–85, 93–95,
101–8, 115–17, 145,
155, 159, 169–71, 207,
224, 227, 231, 235,
237–51, 257, 264–71,
278, 285–86, 292
trains, 39–40, 114, 128,
187, 234, 288
transcendent, 39, 63, 89
transformation, 5, 14–15,
27, 41, 44, 68–69, 141
transubstantiation, 74
trash, 20, 84, 202, 245–71
trees, 6–7, 15, 21, 38, 42,
44–45, 54–63, 69–73,
83, 87, 94, 106, 108,
139, 152–53, 156,
169–74, 196, 200,
205–6, 232, 242, 249,
254, 258, 263, 266, 285
Trinidad, 7, 39, 56–57, 60
trophies, 268, 270
Turner, Lorenzo Dow, 231
Turner, Nat, 198, 203, 207,
266
twins, 61

Underground Railroad, 119, 134, 138–39, 142
Upton, Dell, 3
urban, 18, 116, 149, 185, 214, 218–20, 258, 263
urbanization, 132
Urban Renewal, 3, 177–79, 184–87, 189–90

value, 6, 73, 179, 214, 217, 224, 256, 263, 265, 288
values, 45, 63, 65, 67, 72, 150, 175, 186, 215, 218, 222–23, 247–48, 263–64, 270
veranda, 158–59
vernacular art, 38, 43, 61, 68–69, 74, 92
vessels, 15, 38, 40, 45, 60, 62, 68
violence, 133, 150, 197, 273, 277
virtuosity, 14, 74, 84
visionary, 40, 58, 64, 66, 68
visions, 4, 8, 40–43, 62–63, 68, 103, 127, 141, 151, 270
visual pleasure, 54
visual propulsion, 40
Vlach, John, 253

voodoo, 62, 73, 102–4, 107, 231, 252

Walker, George, 83
walking sticks, 93–94, 105–6
Wallace, Annie, 250
Washington, Booker T., 255, 290
Washington, George, 193, 260, 275–76
water, 5, 7, 17, 20, 38, 41–42, 44, 57, 59, 61–63, 72, 83, 85–86, 90, 106, 126, 130, 151, 155, 158, 175, 195, 198, 201, 204–5, 227, 229, 242, 251, 265, 273
Watson, Robert D. ("Lightnin"), 84
Weeks, John H., 54–55
Weems, Billy, 177–92
Wells, Ida B., 267
Welty, Eudora, 58, 60
West African spiritualism, 93–96, 104–7
Westmacott, Richard, 21–22
wheels, 21–22, 38, 40, 42–45, 63–64, 67, 83,

89–90, 92, 157, 169–70, 172, 174
White, Richard, 147
White, Walter, 290
white flight, 185
Wightman, Orrin Sage, 70
wilderness, 178, 194–95, 198, 201, 204–6, 248, 252, 265–66
Williams, Elizabeth, 62
Williams, Louise, 43
Williams, Nancy, 250
Williamson, Eddie, 65–70
Wilson, Sara, 238–39, 242
witchcraft, 71, 73, 109
witches, 6
Wolf, Corrie, 58
Woodson, Carter G., 231
worship, 4, 16

yard art, 8, 22, 45, 60; swept earth, 170
yard shows, 8, 14, 18, 44–45, 54, 57, 59, 63–64, 67–68, 156, 159, 169; dressed yard, 84, 156
yodel, 38–39

zinga, 38